D1116172

Protest and Resistance in Angola and Brazil

Published Under the Auspices of the
African Studies Center and the
Latin American Studies Center,
University of California, Los Angeles

Protest and Resistance in Angola and Brazil

Comparative Studies

Edited by
Ronald H. Chilcote

University of California Press
Berkeley, Los Angeles, London 1972

LIBRARY
EISENHOWER COLLEGE

University of California Press
Berkeley and Los Angeles, California

University of California Press, Ltd.
London, England

Copyright © 1972 by The Regents of the University of California
ISBN: 0–520–01878–8
Library of Congress Catalog Card Number: 73–142054
Printed in the United States of America

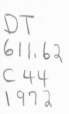
DT
611.62
C 44
1972

In memory of

Eduardo Mondlane

and

Fernando Monteiro de Castro Soromenho

Preface

There have been few scholarly comparisons of geographical areas of the Third World. As a contribution to such comparative study, the project from which the present volume evolved attemped to examine links between Brazil and Portuguese Africa. The objectives were to overlap the traditional area boundaries that separate specialists of Latin America and Africa, to focus on common themes from the perspective of varying social science disciplines, and to reassess and evaluate a variety of cases of protest and resistance. The specialized essays were to be analytical and exploratory, raising questions for possible future research.

The essays in this collection are substantially revised from the original form in which they were presented over an eight-week period from January to March 1968 to seminars of faculty and students at the Los Angeles and Riverside campuses of the University of California. The papers were distributed in advance to the seminars, and the intent was to include at least one African and one Brazilian paper at each session to provoke dialogue, debate, and discussion among Africanists and Latin Americanists alike. Of the original twenty-four contributors, ten were from the United States, seven from Brazil, three from Portugal, two from Moçambique, and one each from England and France. They represented the following disciplines: history (six contributors), political science (six), sociology (five), anthropology (four), anthropology-psychiatry (one), history-geography (one), and education (one). Ten contributors were Brazilianists, nine were Africanists, and five had undertaken research and study in both areas.*

My introduction describes the conceptualization that unifies the diverse essays. A conclusion attempts to synthesize a multitude of examples drawn from the historical experience of Brazil and Portuguese Africa. A classification is offered, and extensive reference to the literature is attempted in order to provide the reader with leads to some of the major primary and secon-

* A full report of the colloquium is in Ronald H. Chilcote, "Brazil and Portuguese Africa in Comparative Perspective," *Latin American Research Review*, IV (Winter 1969), 125–136.

dary source material. The body of this volume consists of individual essays representing varying views and perspectives focused on Angola and Brazil. The brief abstract preceding each essay attempts to synthesize content and ideas, as well as to tie the collection into an integrated and balanced whole. The rigorous criticism and dialogue of the colloquium contributed substantially to clarification and improvement of each essay. Nevertheless, some imbalance in scholarship and writing is inevitable. Further, these essays do not in any way signify consensus on the subject matter presented, and each author is solely responsible for his own essay.

Acknowledgment is due to many institutions and individuals for their contributions and assistance. I am grateful to the African Sudies Center and the Latin American Center of the Los Angeles campus, and the Latin American Research Program of the Riverside campus of the University of California who jointly sponsored the colloquium and provided the bulk of the research funds; additionally, I wish to thank the UCLA Chancellor's Committee on International and Comparative Studies and the UCR Department of Political Science for financial support. Professors Leo Kuper and Paul Proehl, respecively director and former director of the African Studies Center, and Professor Johannes Wilbert, director of the Latin American Center, were all instrumental in shaping the project.

Among the many individuals who contributed, I am deeply grateful to Castro Soromenho, Gladwyn Childs, Helio Jaguaribe, Robert Levine, John Marcum, Cândido Mendes de Almeida, Eduardo Mondlane, Adriano Moreira, Alberto Guerreiro Ramos, A. da Silva Rêgo, Nelson Werneck de Sodré, and William Zartman for their essays which were not included herein. Most of their essays are being published elsewhere. Also I wish to thank Professors Carlos Cortés, Alan Green, Ludwig Lauerhass, Martin Orans, and Gunnar P. Nielsson of the University of California, Riverside; Professors Rupert Emerson, Peter Nehemkis, Edward González, Kenneth Karst, and Charles R. Nixon of the University of California, Los Angeles; Professors Russell Chase and Francis Dutra of the University of California, Santa Barbara; Professors Timothy Harding and Donald Bray of California State College, Los Angeles; Professor Roger Cuniff of San Diego State College; and Professor Richard Kornweible of California State College, Sacramento, for their critical assessment of papers presented at the colloquium. Among the many graduate students who significantly evaluated the papers, I thank Bolivar Lamounier, Joel Edelstein, Aram Sogomoniun, Nancy Garson, Brian Nelson, Richard Stevens, Harry Meader, and George Zaharopoulos.

I am especially grateful to several researchers associated with the Latin American Research Program, Riverside: Amaury de Souza for ideas that helped in formulation of the colloquium; William Culver for critical comments and assistance on planning; Caesar Sereseres for assistance on the preface and introductions to the essays and Paul Mason for editing and proof-reading the manuscript. Additionally, the colloquium would not have been so efficiently organized without the careful planning of Hildaliza Arias Walkeapaa. Sarah Myers of the University of Chicago made substantial revisions and copy edited the essays into final draft form; her efforts have given balance and integration to the collection. I wish to thank also Diane Radke and Jessie Scott for typing the final draft. On the Los Angeles campus I would like to thank Pat Lunquist and Virginia Coulon of the African Studies Center who respectively typed and translated many of the essays, and Ana Bartos and Sandra Díaz of the Latin American Center for translating and typing other essays. Thanks are due also to Marcus Leh who meticulously prepared the index that accompanies this volume. Finally, I am especially grateful for the constructive criticism and useful suggestions of Professor Edward A. Alpers of the University of California, Los Angeles, who patiently examined the entire manuscript and contributed substantially to its present narrowed focus, cohesiveness, and balance.

Ronald H. Chilcote
Universiy of California, Riverside

Contributors

MANUEL CORREIA DE OLIVEIRA ANDRADE, born in 1922 in Nazaré, Pernambuco in Brazil, has a Ph.D. in economics and holds professorial positions in geography at the Universidade Federal de Pernambuco and the Universidade Católica de Pernambuco. Among his numerous publications on Brazil are *A terra e o homem no nordeste* (Rio de Janeiro, 1963); *A guerra dos Cabanos* (Rio de Janeiro, 1965); *Espaço, polarização e desenvolvimento* (Recife, 1967); and *A economia pernambucana no século XVI* (Recife, 1962).

ROGER BASTIDE, born in Nimes, France, in 1898, is Professeur de Ethnologie Sociale et Religieuse, Faculté des Lettres et Science Humaines, Sorbonne and Directeur d'Etudes de Psychiatrie Sociale, Ecole Pratique des Hautes Etudes in Paris. He was the recipient of an honorary doctorate from the University of São Paulo. A long-time student of African influences in Brazil, Professor Bastide has published many books and scholarly articles, including *Brésil, terre des contrastes* (Paris, 1957); *Le Candomblé de Bahia* (The Hague, 1958); *Sociologia do folclore brasileiro* (São Paulo, 1959); and with Florestán Fernandes, *Brancos e Negros em São Paulo* (São Paulo, 1959). His most recent work, published in 1967, is *Les Ameriques Noires*.

DAVID BIRMINGHAM, born in England in 1938, is Senior Lecturer in History at the University of Dar es Salaam. He was Visiting Associate Professor of History in 1968 at the University of California, Los Angeles. He has written *The Portuguese Conquest of Angola* (London, 1965), and *Trade and Conflict in Angola: The Mbundu and their Neighbours under the Influence of the Portuguese 1483–1790* (Oxford, 1966) and has edited (with Richard Gray), *Pre-Colonial African Trade* (London, 1970).

RONALD H. CHILCOTE, born in Cleveland, Ohio, in 1935 is Associate Professor of Political Science at the University of California, Riverside. His research on Brazil and Portuguese Africa has been supported by post-doctoral grants from the Social Science Research Council, the Organization of American

States, and the Haynes Foundation. His publications include *Portuguese Africa* (Englewood Cliffs, N. J., 1967), *Emerging Portuguese African Nationalism*, 2 vols (Stanford, 1969 and 1972), and *Party Conflict and Consensus: The Brazilian Communist Party, 1922–1970* (forthcoming Oxford University Press). He has published articles dealing with comparative aspects of Brazil and Portuguese Africa in *Comparative Political Studies* and *Latin American Research Review*. His present work is concerned with power structure in relation to underdevelopment and dependency in two backland communities of Northeast Brazil.

RALPH DELLA CAVA, born in 1934, is a native of New York City. He has taught history at Columbia College and presently is an Assistant Professor of history at Queens College, City University of New York. He has held a National Defense Foreign Language Award and a Foreign Area Fellowship to do field research in Brazil. He published "The Northeast," in Robert Levine's *Brazil: Field Research Guide* (New York, 1966) and *Miracle at Joaseiro* (New York, 1970).

SHEPARD FORMAN, born in Boston, Massachusetts, in 1938, is Assistant Professor of Anthropology at the University of Chicago. He has held a Fulbright Study Grant, a National Defense Foreign Language Award, a Fulbright-Hays Research Grant, and a National Institute of Mental Health Pre-Doctoral Award and in 1969–70 was a Social Science Research Council Post-Doctoral Fellow at the University of Sussex. He has published articles in *Comparative Studies in Society and History, Journal of Economic History, Journal of Latin American Studies*, among others. His book *The Raft Fishermen: Tradition and Change in the Brazilian Peasant Economy* was published by Indiana University Press in 1970. His recent work has focused on the marketing system and peasant economy of Northeast Brazil, and he is writing a book on the peasantry in Northeast Brazil, to be published by Columbia University Press.

MARVIN HARRIS, born in 1927, is a native of New York City. He is Professor of Anthropology and former Chairman (1962–1966) of the Department of Anthropology at Columbia University. He has held Ford Foundation, African Studies Program, and Social Science Research Council post-doctoral fellowships. His research has focused on race relations in Bahia (early 1950s and 1962) and in Moçambique (1956–1957). His research in Latin America also includes a study of highland Ecuador during 1960. His extensive publications include *Town and Country in Brazil* (New York, 1956); *Patterns of Race in the Americas* (New York, 1964); *The Nature of Cultural Things* (New York, 1964); *The Rise of Anthropological Theory* (New York, 1968); and his most recent work, *Culture, Man and Nature* (1971).

ALFREDO MARGARIDO, a native of Vinhais, Portugal, is Assistant de Recherches in the Ecole des Hautes Etudes, Paris. His awards include the poetry and essay prizes of the Sociedade Cultural de Angola and a grant from the Fundação Calouste Gulbenkian (1964–1967). He is the author of *Introduction à l'histoire Lunda* (a thesis for the EPHE); collaborated, under the direction of Marc Ferro, in compiling the *Dictionnaire d'Histoire* (Paris, 1971); of articles on anthropology, history, sociology of literature in *L'Afrique Littéraire et Artistique, Annales, Economies, Sociétés, Civilisations, Diogène, L'Homme et la Société, Le Mois en Afrique, Revue d'Esthétique, Revue Française des Affaires Politiques Africaines, Rivista Storica Italiana*, etc. He was also editor of the literary supplement of *Diário Illustrado*, and literary editor for Guimarães Editores. His present research is focused on "Political and Economic Structures of the Lunda Empire."

RENÉ RIBEIRO, born in Recife, Brazil in 1914, is Professor of Brazilian Ethnography at the Universidade Federal de Pernambuco, Recife, as well as Medical Director of the Sanatório Recife. He received his M.D. from the Universidade Federal de Pernambuco, and his M.A. in anthropology from Northwestern University. Among his published works are *Cultos afrobrasileiros do Recife: um estudo de adjustamento social* (Recife, 1952); "Brazilian messianic movements," in Syvia L. Thrupp, ed., *Millennial Dreams in Action* (The Hague, 1962); and "Análisis socio-psicológico de la posesión en los cultos afro-brasileños," in *Acta Neuropsiquiátrica Argentina* (1959).

MICHAEL A. SAMUELS, born in Youngstown, Ohio, in 1939, was researcher at the Center for African Education, Teachers College, Columbia University. He has held an Afro-Anglo-American Fellowship, as well as a fellowship from Columbia's Institute for International Studies. He was Senior Staff Member at Georgetown University's Center for Strategic and International Studies and currently is with the U.S. Department of State. His research has examined education within the Portuguese territory of Angola where he undertook field research in 1967; his publications include "Methodist Education in Angola, 1897–1915," in *Stúdia* (1967); "The New Look in Angolan Education," in *Africa Report* (November, 1967); *Portuguese Africa: A Handbook* (New York, 1969) and *Education in Angola, 1878–1914* (New York, 1970).

AMAURY GUIMARÃES DE SOUZA was born in Uberlândia, Brazil, in 1942. He holds degrees in sociology, political science, and public administration from the Universidade Federal de Minas Gerais. His most recent positions in Brazil have been Associate Professor of Sociology at the Escola de Sociologia da Pontifícia Universidade Católica do Rio de Janeiro and, concurrently, Research Associate, Instituto Universitário de Pesquisas do Rio de Janeiro. In 1966 he edited *Sociologia política*.

DOUGLAS LANPHIER WHEELER, born in St. Louis, Missouri, in 1937, is Associate Professor of History and Chairman of the History Department, University of New Hampshire. He has been a recipient of a National Defense Education Act Fellowship in African Studies, a Fulbright Grant for study at the University of Lisbon, a Fulbright-Hays Research grant, and in 1966 a grant from the University of New Hampshire for research in Angola. While in Africa he was a temporary Lecturer at the University College of Rhodesia, Salisbury. He has published articles about Portugal and Portuguese Africa in the *Journal of African History, Race, Foreign Affairs,* and other journals, and has contributed an essay, "The Portuguese and Mozambique," in John Davis, ed., *Southern Africa in Transition* (New York, 1966). With René Pelissier, he wrote *Angola* (New York, 1971).

Contents

Introduction

Ronald H. Chilcote

An understanding of social and political cleavages and resultant conflict and opposition in Brazil and Africa and knowledge of the historical experience of those areas immediately makes evident a pattern of protest and resistance among a variety of social and political movements. For an overview of these movements it is necessary first to identify a typology, then to analyze in depth.[1] Eric Hobsbawm has identified a variety of cases of primitive or archaic forms of social agitation in Europe, including social banditry of the Robin Hood type; the rural secret society (such as the Mafia); various peasant revolutionary movements of the millenarian sort; preindustrial "mobs" and their riots; and labor religious sects and the use of ritual in early labor and revolutionary organizations.[2] Hobsbawm's classification and, more important, his analysis of specific cases in large measure inspired my attempt to develop a classification for Brazil (especially the Northeast) and Portuguese Africa (especially Angola), although the territories in the latter are less known, and historical cases of crisis and the movements that contributed to those crises are less studied, owing to the dominant colonial presence of the Portuguese for the past five centuries. Therefore, my classification of protest and resistance movements in Brazil and Portuguese Africa (see chapter 12) is an attempt to provide a general framework for the cases included in the present volume and to spur scholars to study more carefully the much-overlooked historical details that constitute the heritage of African peoples in the Portuguese territories. It is clear that individually our studies deal with small segments of total population in the areas under investigation and that they rarely concern or have any particular impact on national politics. When synthesized into a whole, however, trends and patterns become discernible, and these are significant in comprehending past as well as current developments.

[1] See chapter 12 for an elaboration of such a typology or classification.
[2] Eric J. Hobsbawm, *Primitive Rebels: Studies in Archaic Forms of Social Movements in the 19th and 20th Centuries* (Manchester, England: University of Manchester Press, 1959).

A comparative examination of the impact of protest and resistance on social and political change in Brazil and Portuguese Africa necessitates the
clarification of these concepts through definition and the elaboration of
generalizations. While these concepts are interrelated, they also have many
distinguishing characteristics.

Protest may be manifested as a complaint, objection, disapproval, or dis-
play of unwillingness to an idea, course of action, or social condition. Protest, it may be argued, stems from an active desire for change, while the
process of developmental change frequently originates from the impact of
protest. Protest relates to the forces that cause man to reconsider his present
environmental situation. Protest may be the outcome of exposure to the
materialistic and other benefits that an anticipated "better" life can produce.
When rising expectations are not satisfied or demands for change are met
by suppression, rejection, and nonintegration, protest is likely to follow the
path of increasingly unstable and irrational means to accomplish goals. Protest activity may also be the direct result of institutional failure to accom-
modate immediate and local demands,[3] as in the situation described by
Michael Samuels.

Resistance, in the context of this volume, is the reaction of a given seg-
ment of population to certain environmental or political, economic, cultural, or social conditions which is accompanied by organizational mobilization
directed toward the amelioration of adverse conditions.[4] Amaury de Souza's
analysis of social banditry and Ralph della Cava's and René Ribeiro's focus
on messianism relate to such conditions. Eduardo Mondlane maintains that,
throughout Portuguese colonial rule in Moçambique, cultural rejection was
always combined with political resistance.[5] This resistance differed considerably from the protest of the Europeanized African *assimilado*, emphasized by Douglas Wheeler in his essay in this volume. While the former
was characterized by unification and mobilization, the latter was marked by
sporadic appeals manifested through the colonial press.

Resistance is frequently manifested through voluntary organizations,
especially of a religious nature. Syncretist movements often fused native
and colonial religions into a faith with political overtones. Protestant and
Catholic missionaries sought local reforms, resulting frequently in suppres-

[3] A theoretical discussion of protest is in Michael Lipsky, "Protest as a Political
Resource," *The American Political Science Review*, LXII (December 1968), 1144–1158.

[4] Resistance, as evident in the following discussion, is defined here as resistance to
authority rather than as resistance to social change which may ensure the persistance of
authority. On the latter, see Centro Latino-Americano de Pesquisas em Ciências Sociais,
Resistências à mudança. Fatôres que impedem ou dificultam o desenvolvimento (Rio
de Janeiro, 1960).

[5] See Eduardo C. Mondlane, *The Struggle for Moçambique* (Baltimore: Penguin
Books, 1969).

sion by the Portuguese authorities; it was through these overtly religious organizations that there occurred the politization and mobilization of many Africans[6] Alfredo Margarido describes in his essay.

Thus resistance within the indigenous populations of our areas of concern can be viewed as an embryonic stage of nationalism. Resistance functions to restructure the society in that new leaders emerge, traditional authority patterns are challenged, and anticolonialism provides for integration and cohesion among diverse ethnic and religious groupings. The Bissau dockworkers' strike in 1958, for example, illustrated urban economic resistance which had widespread influence and ultimately led to the mobilization of the rural peasantry into a nationalist movement which struggled for the independence of Guiné.[7]

Protest and resistance may lead to *crisis*, an unstable state of affairs in which a decisive change may be impending. Crisis relates to physical and human problems. In Northeast Brazil, for instance, crisis may be the result of droughts or floods.[8] It may also be caused by structural changes in the regional economy or by the successes and failures of attempts to find solutions to problems through welfare policies, the migration of people from area to area, and so forth. Crisis might be the result of class conflict and differences between oligarchical rulers and the mass of followers in a particular society. Crisis may well be related to the tensions and alienation of people who see themselves as nonparticipants in the decisions that shape a community. Crisis may also have something to do with the latent or manifest cultural patterns that persist in society over periods of time; violence, for example, is not an uncommon pattern among peasant populations in Northeast Brazil nor among tribal groups in Portuguese Africa.

The concepts protest and resistance relate also to opposition and conflict. *Opposition* is a manifestation of protest or resistance against the control and use of power in society and occurs when those subject to it experience shared feelings of exploitation and oppression. According to Blau, exploitation is dependent on social expectations, "those of the group or groups subject to the power, which determine how they react to given demands for obedience, and those of the group in power which determine the extent of

---

[6] Syncretic and messianistic movements are the focus of Sylvia L. Thrupp, ed., *Millenial Dreams in Action—Essays in Comparative Study* (The Hague: Comparative Studies in Society and History, Mouton and Company, 1962).

[7] On the relationship of resistance to nationalism, see T. O. Ranger, "Connections Between 'Primary Resistance' Movements and Modern Mass Nationalism in East and Central Africa," *Journal of African History*, IX, no. 3 (1968), 437–453, and IX, no. 4 (1969), 631–641.

[8] In his essay on Northeast Brazil, Albert O. Hirschman in *Journeys Toward Progress* (New York: Twentieth Century Fund, 1963), traces the relationship of major droughts to crisis and governmental decision making and assesses the results of those decisions as generally ineffective.

their demands for submission." [9] *Conflict* may be the result of such expectations. Conflict basically means the incidence of disagreement over fundamental values in society. Such conflict may relate to major cleavages that have historically affected society, among which might be identified cleavages emanating from differences in social and economic class, religious sects, ethnic groups, ideological divisions, and geographical regions. From this we might generalize that the more issues defined in cleavage terms the greater the likelihood of political conflict. Also, the larger the number of cleavage-related issues that must be resolved simultaneously, the more unstable the political system.[10]

There are many reasons for our focus on protest and resistance and the specific examples identified and studied in this volume. First, such examples have been treated by others largely as a series of episodes unrelated in the historical process. The various interpretations offered have generally minimized the importance of such episodes in that process. Second, the movements we have identified have often been considered as marginal or unimportant phenomena, probably because the political allegiance or character of such movements is often undetermined and ambiguous, and because such movements are unlike more commonly known and understood social movements. For instance, these movements are often cast in a world of people who neither read nor write because they are illiterate; the people comprising the movements may be known only to their friends, often only by nickname; they are inarticulate, rarely understood when expressing themselves, and prepolitical—they have only begun to find a vocabulary in which to express their aspirations about the world; they have known a world long-dominated by a system of soldiers, policemen, tax collectors, and the like, all of whom they tend to distrust and despise; and they are confronted with the task of how to adapt themselves to modern society, its life and struggles, as well as how to influence that society to provide for their needs.

This collection of essays is divided into several parts. The first part concerns examples of protest and resistance. Contributors have developed case studies drawn from the historical experience of Angola and Brazil. Each contributor was to identify the principal issues or problems as related to

[9] Peter M. Blau, *Exchange and Power in Social Life* (New York: John Wiley and Sons, 1964), pp. 227–228. Robert Dahl and colleagues have focused their attention recently on patterns of opposition; see particularly Dahl's *Political Opposition in Western Democracies* (New Haven: Yale University Press, 1966), especially chapter 11, pp. 332–386.

[10] Theoretical discussions of conflict are in Charles P. Loomis, "In Praise of Conflict and its Resolution," *American Sociological Review*, XXXII (December 1967), 875–890; Norman A. Bailey, "Toward a Praxeological Theory of Conflict," *Orbis*, XI (Winter 1968), 1081–1112; and Douglas Bwy, "Dimensions of Social Conflict in Latin America," *The American Behavioral Scientist*, II (March-April 1968), pp. 39–49.

his case study and to consider such questions as: Why had there been a crisis situation or popular resistance? Was this related to societal conditions? What were the political, social, economic, and psychocultural manifestations? Were natural barriers such as climate, terrain, and resources of significance? A second task was to examine wherever possible such theoretical aspects of protest and resistance in less developed areas of the world and to relate these to the particular case. Third, contributors were invited to evaluate the impact of the protest or resistance upon the society under study and, where possible, to comment on the relationship of conflict, tension, and alienation to issues and problem solving; the impact on recruitment, mobilization, and participation; the effect upon prevailing authority patterns and traditional and newly emerging leadership; the developmental perceptions of both elites and masses; and the restructuring of society at local, regional, and national levels.

In assessing the collection as a whole, I note that many of the authors have been concerned with at least one, if not all, of the following themes: human alienation from the sociopolitical system, violence, and nationalism. In examining alienation, many of the papers are asking the question: For whom and why is the existing sociopolitical system so unrewarding as to evoke collective protest, resistance, and violence? If it is true that almost any societal environment provokes protest and violence, then it is important to identify the social conditions that lead to protest and violence and to relate such conditions to the psychological orientations—be they real or imagined —of the actors involved. This is in fact what many of the papers have attempted, for the description and analysis is concerned with the incongruities between the values of certain individuals and groups and those of the existing political authority, the manner in which individuals believe themselves to be ineffective in reforming the sociopolitical system, and the type of behavior, such as protest and violence, that develops as a means to articulate the belief that the political system is unchangeable through peaceful alternatives.

The contributors have focused much attention on violence. Throughout the essays there is a fundamental consensus that violence is a significant topic for inquiry. Through the use of historical cases, efforts are made to explain violence in theoretical and comparative terms. There is a concern with the socialization patterns that sanction violence, with traditions of conflict, and with ideologies that justify violence and conflict.

The bulk of the essays in this volume are grouped according to geographical area. David Birmingham provides a framework linking the four Angolan essays. His concern is with the relationships of Africans and Europeans in the trade and commerce that shaped response and resistance during the seventeenth century. Alfredo Margarido views Tokoism as a socioreligious outgrowth of early protest and resistance to Portuguese occupation and as one of several early messianic and syncretic movements which have provided a forum for criticism of existing traditional institutions and opposition to white colonial rulers. With a narrowed focus, Michael Samuels examines one example of African protest directed without success at achieving educational reforms and local autonomy within an oppressive colonial system. Douglas Wheeler concerns himself with four examples of early protest writings in an attempt to document ideas and activities that later became the foundation for *assimilado* nationalism. Thus these essays on Angola emphasize protest as the African response to colonial rule. A thread of sporadic and sometimes organized African resistance, which runs throughout Angolan history, is attributable, as Birmingham makes clear, to the trade and commerce which brought changes including exploitation, to the traditional economic system, and also to Portuguese attempts at cultural domination and military conquest.

The theme of African response to international trade, which runs through Birmingham's essay, links, however crudely, with the theme of the impact of international capitalism in Brazil which runs through the five essays on the Brazilian Northeast. Ralph della Cava's analysis, in particular, stresses the impact of international capitalism on the internal politics and economy of a small backlands community. Shepard Forman analyzes the impact of capitalism on the commercialization of agriculture and the resultant peasant response which allowed protest to be channeled through organizations. International conditions also shaped the military struggle described by Manuel Correia de Andrade. Even such an isolated instance of messianism as that reported by René Ribeiro becomes wrapped up in the events of the modern world and the space age.

The major difference between the two sets of essays relates to the two areas under study. Brazil is a fully established and, despite its diversity, more or less integrated society. Angola is a colony of the Portuguese overseas "empire," underdeveloped, exploited, and fully dependent politically on Portugal and economically on Portugal, South Africa, Western Europe, and the United States. Thus, the Brazilian studies quite naturally focus on problems of political, economic, and social integration and on power struggles within both a local and national context. In contrast, the Angolan essays inevitably deal with how people avoid becoming integrated into a Portuguese-dominated society and how they persist in seeking an Angolan society. Yet, despite these differences, we do find that the participants in the Brazilian struggles described in this volume seem to be part of a system appropriately described as "internal colonialism," that their life styles and dependence on the outside world are not much different from those of their

African counterparts.[11] Thus, in Portuguese Africa it can be argued that Portugal exercises a monopoly in exploiting natural resources, labor, and import-export trade. Portugal, as the dominant power, prevents other countries from exploiting the natural and human resources of the colony, or permits them to do so at will. This monopolization extends to mass culture, and all contact with the outside and with other cultures is funneled through the colonial power. Likewise in Brazil, especially the Northeast, internal colonialism persists as a structural phenomenon bound to the policies of the national government but ultimately tied to the pressures of international capitalism, in the trade, investment, and other forms. It is not strange then that a parallel set of conditions is found in the underdeveloped and exploited parts of Angola and Brazil described in many of our essays. In both areas local communities often remain isolated from a dominant center or metropolis which maintains a monopoly of commerce and trade, credit, and monoculture, as well as discrimination in labor, landholdings, income distribution, credit, and social life. The results are often deformation and dependence, decapitalization, migration, and exodus.[12]

The five Brazilian essays are linked by several other considerations. All relate to the messianic, often fanatical and charismatic, behavior of lower-class elements in the rural Northeast. Andrade's attention to black and mulatto elements in the cabanos movement allows for an interesting comparison of black movements not only in Angola but elsewhere as well.[13] The attention of Amaury de Souza and Shepard Forman to the mobilization of alienated peasants in a highly patriarchal order exemplifies a theme of class conflict which runs through many of our studies of Brazil and Africa. Della Cava deals with such conflict, but also with internal disputes within the ruling oligarchies of backlands Northeast Brazil, while Ribeiro's study of a contemporary movement of rural lower-class elements illustrates the common social and economic conditions from which messianic movements of past and present have evolved.

As an overview, Marvin Harris and Roger Bastide offer comparative perspectives on Africa and Brazil. Their analysis applies to the territories

[11] See Pablo González-Casanova, "Internal Colonialism and National Development," in Irving Louis Horowitz, Josué de Castro, and John Gerassi, eds., *Latin American Radicalism* (New York: Vintage Books, 1969), pp. 118–139.

[12] For the Brazilian case, see the important analysis of capitalist development of underdevelopment by André Gunder Frank, *Capitalism and Underdevelopment in Latin America: Historical Studies of Chile and Brazil* (New York: Monthly Review Press, 1967), especially pp. 143–218.

[13] The revolt of Nat Turner, for example. See Herbert Aptheker, *Nat Turner's Slave Rebellion* (New York: Humanities Press, 1966), and William Styron, *The Confessions of Nat Turner* (New York: Random House, 1967).

of Guiné and Moçambique, as well as to Angola. Harris focuses on contrasting styles of colonialism and imperialism in the two areas. Both Harris and Bastide analyze patterns of underdevelopment in the two areas. They refute the Portuguese rhetoric of "civilizing" mission. While Harris examines the roots of Portuguese underdevelopment, Bastide assesses lower-class response to colonialism and domination.

Finally, as a conclusion to this volume, a classification of prenationalist movements in Brazil and Portuguese Africa is offered in an effort to reveal the wide range of examples of protest and resistance found in the experience of the two areas. As such, our conclusion extends well beyond the scope of the present volume. Our objectives are twofold. First, we hope scholars will begin to investigate in systematic fashion the many points of protest and resistance which shaped the history of Brazil and Portuguese Africa. An emphasis on such protest and resistance may lead scholars to reassess many generally accepted assumptions, theories, and myths. Second, we support our synthesis with extensive bibliographic reference to the available and generally sparse literature in the hope that the reader will read beyond the confines of this volume.

Part I Protest and Resistance in Angola and Brazil

Chapter 1 The African Response to Early Portuguese Activities in Angola

David Birmingham

[The trading relationships of Africans with Europeans shaped both their positive response and their resistance during the seventeenth century. In some regions it may have been the intense African demand for foreign consumer goods which was the dominant economic force in the slave trade. Once trade had begun, African peoples adapted themselves and their institutions with great skill to the shifting pattern of overseas trade. The Portuguese failure to achieve economic gains by cultural colonization led them to seek military domination, but this was effectively resisted by the military systems of the African kingdoms. Attention is drawn to the surprisingly effective military tactics of the Africans and to the role of weapon technology. Military conquest was attempted because Portugal was economically too weak to maintain efficient trade. African traders, however, successfully sought new outlets and new trading partners which allowed for greater profits.]

Because Angola's role in history has predominantly been that of a supplier of labor (mão-de-obra) to other parts of the world, including São Tomé, the Costa de Mina, Pôrto Bello, Brazil, Potosí, and the River Plate, the problems involved in being a large-scale supplier of involuntary migrants should be examined. Since this is not at present feasible for the nineteenth-

*This essay, written in the early part of 1968, aimed to point out the sparsity of Central African historical studies, and to illustrate some of the interesting themes. Since then the situation has been revolutionized, as four major historians have begun to publish in the field. Joseph C. Miller has worked on Cokwe and Kasanje, Jean-Luc Vellut on Angola and the Kwango states, Phyllis Martin on the Loango coast and its hinter-

century context, this essay will attempt to look at them within the framework of earlier Portuguese activities in Angola.[1] In so doing care will be taken not to overemphasize the importance of the slave trade in the overall economic picture of Angola, and time will be devoted to examining the significance of other commercial attractions.

Any study connected with the slave trade and its related activities faces a number of unsolved general questions. The field of slave trade studies has not attracted either European or African scholars. Much more has been written about the effects of African arrivals in the New World than on the effects of their departure from the old one. Historians have tended to make the tacit assumption that the driving force behind the trade was the economic strength and expanding force of Europe and its colonies. Africa is cast in the role of a passive milch cow, and the European slaving entrepreneurs, as rapacious wolves capable of extorting the manpower they required by means other than an equable exchange. This image of the slave trade as a relationship between grossly unequal partners is now undergoing reassessment. How far the pendulum will swing is not yet clear. Certainly African states now have to be studied in great detail to understand their motives, politics, structures, and attitudes; the reassessment may even go so far as to suggest that they played not only an active role in the Afro-European relationship, but a dominant role. It may come to be argued that at least in some regions, at some periods, it was the intense African demand for foreign consumer goods that was the dominant economic force in the slave trade. This is a very different proposition from the stereotype of Europeans buying slaves for handfuls of worthless trinkets.

---

land, and W. G. L. Randles on the Kongo kingdom. Their work, together with my ongoing research, the studies of several students, and the general slave-trade analyses of Rodney, Curtin, Fage, and others have led to substantial modifications of the ideas that were thrown out here. Some, such as the possible significance of pre-Portuguese trade networks, still need to be worked on. Others, such as the treatment of relationships between Lunda, Imbangala, Luba, and the long-distance trading patterns, no longer ring true. Also one must be much more skeptical than heretofore about pre-fifteenth-century "empires" in Katanga, and about the early, unstructured explosion of Lunda influences. The emphasis that the paper put on the role of the Portuguese as cabotage traders remains valid, though it now lacks originality, having been extensively illustrated in other works. Finally, the question of resistance has undergone total reassessment, and this author, at least, would like to interpret the Imbangala movement as a largely indigenous Mbundu resistance movement, with only minimal outside stimulation.

[1] Within the framework of this collection it would have been desirable to include a paper on the slave trade and other forms of labor migration in nineteenth-century Angola. Unfortunately, the basic research on this field has not, to my knowledge, been published. The external and internatonal aspects of the Angolan export of labor in this period have been portrayed recently by James Duffy, in *A Question of Slavery* (London: Oxford University Press, 1967), and by Richard Hammond, in *Portugal and Africa* (Stanford: Stanford University Press, 1967).

The prelude to a study of African response and resistance to the Portuguese in Angola occurs in the old kingdom of Kongo. Superficially, the story of the Kongo kingdom and of the first hundred years of Portuguese presence in Central Africa is well known, but as yet there has been no serious study of the massive documentation that covers the history of Kongo-Portuguese relations.[2] Fundamental questions about the aspirations of either side, about their relative political, technological, and economic strengths and weaknesses, about the nature of their associations and conflicts, have still to be more clearly examined. Occasional reference to Kongo will be brought into this paper for the purpose of comparison and discussion, but it will not form the center of focus.

The development of a more military confrontation between Portugal and Africa than that which occurred in Kongo might profitably be considered to begin in 1575, in the region of the lower Kwanza River. Both the date and the place of this development are significant. The date marks the successful completion of the first large-scale Portuguese military campaign in tropical Africa. This was the war in which a Portuguese army of six hundred men checked and eventually drove back the Jaga hordes who had driven them out of the Kongo kingdom. In the short run the Portuguese had been the winners; their use of firearms had apparently been decisive, although it was probably the psychological impact created by the noise and smoke of the matchlocks, rather than their speed or accuracy of fire, that had been decisive. Moreover, in this victory the Portuguese had been assisted by a substantial Kongo army led by the king and deeply committed to regaining its lost lands. With these two advantages the Portuguese won their first military exploit in West Central Africa between 1571 and 1574.[3] Despite their victory, the Portuguese had learned from the Jaga that armed African resistance to foreign enterprise could be sudden and devastating. The confidence and security of the early colonial pioneers melted. After 1575 a new generation of men, who had grown up under the quixotic rule of King Sebastião, took charge of Portuguese affairs in Central Africa and determined that they would hold their land by right of conquest and not

[2] See the five volumes of texts and commentary published by L. Jadin in the *Bulletin de l'Institut Historique Belge de Rome* (1961–1968) and Jean Cuvelier and L. Jadin, *L'Ancien Congo d'après les archives Romaines* (Bruxelles, 1954). The best popular account of Kongo is perhaps G. Balandier, *Daily Life in the Kongo* (London, 1968). A short analysis is found in Jan Vansina, *Kingdoms of the Savanna* (Madison, 1966). The most detailed documentation in Portuguese is in A. Brásio, *Monumenta missionária africana* (Lisbon, 1952–1968), a ten-volume collection of documents relating to Portuguese enterprise on the west coast of Central Africa from the fifteenth to the mid-seventeenth century. [This was written before Dr. Randles' thesis appeared.]

[3] See D. Lopes and F. Pigafetta, *Description du Royaume de Congo*, ed. by W. Bal (Louvain, 1963); R. Delgado, *História de Angola* (Lobito, 1953), Vol. I; and David Birmingham, *Trade and Conflict in Angola* (London, 1966).

in hazardous cooperation with any Lusophile prince such as the king of Kongo.

If the date at which the Portuguese began their military enterprise seems significant, their choice of a site is probably even more so. It seems likely that, before the Portuguese attempted to make the Kwanza their high road into Africa, it was already an important trading artery. On the south side of the river, not far from its mouth, there are important deposits of rock salt.[4] These were exploited in pre-Portuguese times and may have formed the basis of an important commercial system. The salt was quarried in slabs two feet long and used as a currency unit at least in the Angolan kingdom of Ndongo if not further afield. The Jesuit Gouveia, writing in about 1563, said that rock salt was the main richness of Angola and that traders came from many nations in the interior to buy it. He referred to one people in particular, the Dambia Songe, who came from seventeen days' journey beyond Angola to buy salt, and who were very familiar with the far interior.[5] A century later Cadornega described Lunda traders who came to the fringes of Angola to buy salt, suggesting that the trade continued to be important.[6]

In addition to rock salt there were pans of marine salt along the coast north of the Kwanza which were evidently exploited by the end of the fifteenth century. One African historical version of the opening struggle with the Portuguese sees it in terms of a struggle to control these salt supplies. The Pende tradition says that "the white men spat fire and took away the king's salt pans." It is important to note, however, that only the coastal pans and not the mines further inland were captured.[7] It seems likely that the Portuguese chose the site for their new-style colonial venture of 1575 with an experienced eye on possible trade opportunities; certainly elsewhere on the African coast they were very skilled in siting their trading posts at the terminals of pre-European trade routes, such as Elmina and Sofala. In the colonization charter of 1571, King Sebastião awarded the donatário, Paulo Dias de Novais, a monopoly of the trade both in marine salt and in rock salt.[8]

In the light of the probable importance of the Kisama salt mines, the

---

[4] Salt appears to be among the very first commodities which a community requires when its economic activity grows beyond the point of local subsistence. Its vital role in the early development of long-distance trade in Africa (or indeed in Europe) is well documented. So far all too little is known about the main salt suppliers and salt routes of Central Africa.

[5] Gouveia's correspondence in Brásio, op. cit., II, 518–521.

[6] See Cadornega, História geral das guerras angolanas (3 vols.; Lisbon, 1940–1942), a contemporary chronicle.

[7] G. L. Haveaux, La tradition historique des Bapende Orientaux (Brussels, 1954), p. 47.

[8] The charter is reprinted in Brásio, op. cit., III, 36–51.

Portuguese attempts to conquer them should perhaps be regarded as a major rather than as a subsidiary part of their attempts to control the economy of Angola. This endeavor eventually failed. In 1593 an abortive attempt was made to erect a fort near the mines; it was quickly abandoned, and in the following year the Portuguese army was resoundingly defeated by Kafushe, an important Kisama ruler. In 1602 a further setback occurred when Governor Coutinho died while campaigning in the same area.[9] Throughout the seventeenth century Portuguese governors at Luanda planned new attempts to conquer the south bank of the Kwanza, but always in vain. They tended to explain this failure in terms of the arid climate and the "barbarity" of the Kisama peoples. It now seems that perhaps their failure should be looked at more in terms of sophisticated African resistance and the protection of a vital economic lifeline from foreign take-over.

Previous studies of early Portuguese conquests in Angola have emphasized the drive towards the silver mines of Cambambe. These mines did not exist, of course, but the Portuguese apparently fought a wearisome and costly war for thirty years to reach them. It may now be more realistic to suggest that the emphasis on silver should take a secondary place to that on salt. The glamor of silver mines was certainly used by those who appealed for funds to support the Angolan venture, but perhaps they knew that in reality the profits would come from better-established commercial lines. In the sixteenth century it was comparatively easy to sell stories about fabulous silver mines to the colonial powers who had heard of the fantastic discoveries in Peru. It is still difficult to accept the idea that anything so ephemeral as the reports on Cambambe silver, especially in view of the authoritative contrary reports which were on record,[10] should have played a decisive role in any enterprise as costly as the early wars of conquest in Angola.

Another genuine economic factor, in addition to the salt trade, may have been a trade in copper which Portuguese sources frequently discuss but of which Portuguese entrepreneurs never seem to have gained control. From 1617 on, considerable efforts were made to establish a new colony at Benguela in the belief that the region yielded copper; it seems, however, that the copper ornaments the local people wore must have been acquired by trade and not locally produced. In any event, no local copper was found in Benguela, and only much later did the Portuguese find small quantities of copper in the southern part of the Kongo kingdom.[11]

---

[9] Birmingham, *op. cit.*, pp. 59–62.

[10] See, for instance, Balthasar de Castro's report of 1526 on Angola (in Brásio, *op. cit.*, I, 485–487), stating that no silver mines existed.

[11] A. A. Felner, *Angola* (Coimbra, 1933) contains the best documentation on the founding of Benguela.

The second major reason why the Portuguese chose the Kwanza Valley as the starting point of their colonial expansion into Angola may have been the presence there of the Imbangala. Although the story of the Imbangala and of their intrusion into Angola is by no means told as yet, by dint of hypotheses and counterhypotheses some progress is being made toward an understanding of this movement and its momentous significance and ramifications. At present it seems possible that by 1575 the Imbangala had opened a route from the very heart of Central Africa to the Kwanza mouth.[12] The existence of such an opening may have been a factor in the Portuguese decision to put so many men and resources into the establishment of the Luanda colony. Their awareness of the link with the far interior may have been tenuous, but potentially it was a sound basis for establishing a commercial colony.

In looking at the problem of the Imbangala, the first question to be considered is that of the interrelationship, or lack of it, between the opening of sea trade on the Atlantic coast and the turbulent political changes in Katanga that resulted in the establishment of the Lunda Empire. The opening of trade took place in the last years of the fifteenth century; by 1500, slave traders from the plantation island of São Tomé were active at the Kwanza mouth.[13] Thus the opening of the Atlantic slave trade on the coast is well documented and dated. What is much less well established is the speed with which the effects of this new and potent form of commercial activity penetrated the interior.

The interior of Central Africa is a region that appears to have a long tradition of state building. Trading states and even empires may have flourished in Katanga for the last thousand years. There is clear evidence that the region's copper resources were being exploited by the eighth century, and it seems possible that the area was connected from an early period with a long-distance trading network which reached down to the Zambezi River and hence to the international trade routes of the East African coast. Little or nothing is yet known of the earlier Katanga states; but we do know that, about the time the Portuguese began to open overseas trading routes to the west coast of Central Africa, some major changes were taking

[12] David Birmingham, "The Date and Significance of the Imbangala Invasion of Angola," *Journal of African History*, VI, No. 2 (1965), 143–152. [Although the "date" arrived at in this article seems sound, the "significance" alleged is much more dubious in retrospect.]

[13] It is interesting to note that the best slaves arriving in São Tomé at this period were not kept for local use but resold on the Gold Coast to Akan merchants in exchange for gold dust. Only slaves who would have been rejected as unfit by the Akan were retained on sugar plantations or sent to Lisbon. David Birmingham, "The Regimento da Mina," *Transactions of the Historical Society of Ghana*, XI. [A useful starting point for research on the Imbangala will be a recent article by Beatrix Heirtze on Kisama.]

place in the political alignments of the region. The key question is whether or not these events were related.[14]

The most important of the political upheavals in Central Africa was the one that led to the founding of the Lunda Empire. Before this, there had been a series of greater or smaller Luba states which ruled over Katanga with varying measures of success and continuity. One of these Luba states was responsible for spreading the idea of centralized political administration westward to the home of the Lunda and for establishing in Lunda a new dynasty which began to impose new, more severe forms of domination on the loosely united Lunda clans. Some of the indigenous Lunda leaders attempted to resist the new regime and, on failing to do so, fled westward accumulating supporters until eventually they made contact with the Portuguese. This movement probably consisted of a number of groups traveling along different routes at different times; the earliest seems to have reached the coast by the third quarter of the sixteenth century.

In his recent discussions of these movements, Jan Vansina has expressed the view that the Lunda did not arrive in Angola until the seventeenth century. He suggests that the migrant hordes in Angola in the sixteenth century were Jaga escaping from Kongo. To confuse matters further, he suggests that both the Jaga and the Lunda were locally known as Imbangala.[15] Vansina's arguments for rejecting the earlier dating of the Lunda migrations is weakest where it deals with the Lunda-Imbangala tradition. This describes their journey to the coast, not to some point in the interior which the Portuguese had reached some thirty years after the beginning of their conquest. This evidence, together with the references to the Imbangala leader Kasanje found in the Portuguese documents of the 1570s, continues to suggest that the migration was a mid-sixteenth century phenomenon rather than an early seventeenth-century one.

Vansina does, however, raise two important questions. First, if the Imbangala arrived by the 1570s, then their progress through Central Africa is exactly contemporary with that of the Jaga. There is no obvious and inherent reason they should not have been contemporary and parallel movements; in fact, so little is known of the Jaga that they could conceivably be an offshoot of the Lunda-Imbangala migration. More probably,

[14] Another whole field of speculation concerns the possibility of seaborne trade on the west coast before the Portuguese arrival. So far there is no evidence to show that this existed to any large extent or was an influential factor, but more needs to be known about the early economic history of, for instance, the Kongo kingdom.

[15] Vansina, "The Founding of the Kingdom of Kasanje," *Journal of African History*, IV, No. 3 (1963), 355–374; and "More on the Invasions of Kongo and Angola by the Jaga and the Imbangala," *Journal of African History*, VII, No. 3 (1966), 421–429; Birmingham, "The Date and Significance of the Imbangala Invasion of Angola."

the Jaga may have erupted directly from the turbulent area of the Luba states and traveled to the Atlantic coast of Kongo, while the Imbangala were indirectly set in motion by the same turbulent change when it hit Lunda. There would be no cause for surprise in the closely parallel dating of the two movements if this were true.[16] Second, Vansina fits the Imbangala dating into the chronology of the Lunda dynasty established at the same time. If a really reliable king list could be established, it might be difficult to reconcile with the earlier date. At present, however, the earliest phase of the Lunda dynasty looks a little less than reliable, and perhaps some of the early rulers' names cover a whole period of Lunda evolution rather than a single reign or generation. Even if one took a later date of around 1600 for the founding of the dynasty, some early rulers would have to have been remarkably long-lived to give an acceptable reign-length average up to the mid-nineteenth century. This, however, is a subject where one must tread warily until more thorough research has been carried out on the surviving oral traditions.

In looking at the Lunda-Imbangala migration to the coast of Angola, Africanists have tended to assume that the driving force of the movement came from behind, from the inland savanna. One has looked for population explosions, for violent invasions, for the kind of disruptions that might drive peoples out of their traditional homeland. It does seem more logical, however, to attempt to relate the changes in the central grasslands with the changes on the coast. Knowledge of the trading opportunities and particularly of the novel weapons offered by the Portuguese may have penetrated slowly into the interior, but there is no reason to believe that in fifty years, from 1500 to 1550, it had not created some echoes as far afield as Katanga. This does not for a moment presuppose that any regular two-way traffic with caravans, supplies of carriers, and all the paraphernalia of organized long-distance trade was set up in so short a time. It does, however, seem possible—and even likely—that, by a slow process of exchange from neighbor to neighbor, foreign material goods and rumors of foreign firearms filtered through the savanna and reached the Lunda and the Luba. The Luba then began to spread their influence over their western neighbors, and some Lunda groups set out to reach the source of these new trade goods.

If this picture is correct, the relationship between Africans and Portuguese in the lower Kwanza Valley would have been very much a two-way interaction. The earliest Portuguese trade was attracted by the existence of an old salt track into the interior. The growth of Portuguese trade then

[16] This interpretation has not stood the test of time, as mentioned earlier in this chapter. See my recent unpublished paper on the subject, Dar es Salaam, 1971.

had repercussions back along this route to beyond the Kwango and Kasai rivers. This influence led in turn to the establishment of tenuous links between Angola and Katanga and caused the Lunda-Imbangala migrations. Such an opening may have encouraged the Portuguese to choose the lower Kwanza for further commercial activity and as the site for a major endeavor to conquer a highway into the African interior. At the same time they had largely failed to penetrate Central Africa from the east, up the Zambezi, and so new energy was put into the search for an opening from the west.

The Angolan Wars, which began on the Kwanza River in 1575, are remarkable in the annals of African history for a number of reasons. In the precolonial period they constitute the only serious attempt by a foreign nation to acquire by conquest a piece of territory in tropical Africa. The closest parallel was probably the Dutch penetration of South Africa from the Cape. But whereas the Dutch advanced into a comparatively poor, underpopulated country and faced the resistance of mainly pre-Iron Age nomadic peoples, the Portuguese in Angola faced the full weight of an organized Iron Age society—and what is more, did so nearly a century earlier, when European firearm technology was still in its infancy.[17] Another parallel was the Portuguese penetration of the lower Zambezi; but this was very different in character from the conquest of Angola, consisting almost from the outset of a more gradual settler advance which was partly absorbed by the African host community and retained only minimal distinguishing features, and few outside links, to differentiate its chiefs from the neighboring African rulers.[18]

One of the questions that should be asked about the Angolan Wars is, of course, why did not the Portuguese, or any other foreign power, attempt this kind of military penetration elsewhere in Africa. One rather facile answer has tended to attribute this reticence to the inhospitality of the climate and to the virulence of tropical diseases. This, however, does not seem an adequate explanation. No part of Africa can have been worse than Angola for European mortality. Pero Rodrigues estimated that of the 2,000 European troops sent to Angola in the first twenty years of the war, 1,200 either died of fever or left the country hastily lest they do so.[19] This problem did not decrease with time, and for the next three centuries new arrivals

[17] For details of the wars and descriptions of the weapons and tactics used, see Cadornega, *op. cit.*

[18] For a recent study of the Portuguese on the Zambezi and their relationships with the adjacent African communities see M. D. D. Newitt, "The Zambezi Prazos in the Eighteenth Century," Ph.D. thesis, University of London, 1967.

[19] Pero Rodrigues, *História da residência dos padres da Companhia de Jesus em Angola, 1954,* cited in Brásio, *op. cit.,* IV, 546–581.

from Europe faced a very high risk of sudden death from tropical disease.

If the deterrent value of disease cannot adequately explain why a conquest colony was established in Angola and nowhere else in tropical Africa, other explanations must be sought. One argument might be that Portugal was able to find trading partners capable of responding to her commercial needs in West Africa but not in Central Africa. The Wolof states of Senegambia, the Akan kingdoms of the Gold Coast, and the empire of Benin were all states accustomed to interstate trading. They all had the machinery for accumulating commodity surpluses for external sale. They all had experience of long-distance trade with the empires of the western Sudan and through them, indirectly, with the Mediterranean world. They had evolved the state mechanisms needed to control marketing, transport, and road clearance, and to afford protection to caravans. They had worked out taxation systems to pay for the many services foreign trade required. In contrast, the western part of Central Africa was not even on the fringe of world commerce before the arrival of the Portuguese. It seems to have been one of the continent's most isolated backwaters. This is not to suggest that West Central Africa did not have an internal system of regional trade. Salt, ironware, copper ornaments, and numerous kinds of plain and decorated palm cloth were undoubtedly exchanged throughout the region. But apparently the region itself was not linked to trade outside Africa in the way that much of West Africa was and possibly that even the copper-producing states of Katanga were. West Central Africa had probably not, therefore, evolved the political means of fostering and controlling long-distance trade to the extent that other parts of Africa had.

If the conquest was indeed determined by the failure of Portugal to find stately trading partners who matched up to her needs, it was not for want of seeking them. For nearly one hundred years the Portuguese built up their relations first with the kingdom of Kongo and later with the kingdom of Ndongo. The relationship between Portugal and Kongo has usually been analyzed in religious and diplomatic terms, in other words, in the terms of the most literate Portuguese participants, the ambassadors and the priests. In analyzing what Portugal and Kongo expected from each other, one must surely look for the commercial interests of each party rather than presume another instance of "uneconomic imperialism."[20] Although much stress has been laid on the religious, diplomatic, and strategic aspects of Portuguese expansion traditionally associated with Prince Henry, these make less sense than the hardheaded commercial interests led by the merchants of Lisbon in the early fifteenth century and taken over

[20] The phrase is from Hammond, *Portugal and Africa*, and describes his interpretation of Portuguese colonial expansion in the nineteenth century.

by the crown when the Eldorado of Mina had been reached.[21] Kongo may have looked to some like the key to an encirclement of the Muslim world, but it is doubtful how important this concept was for a power as commercially motivated as was Portugal.

The eighty years of close contact between Kongo and Portugal from 1490 to 1570 should be looked at essentially in terms of a search for economic returns. This can be seen at two levels. First, at the intergovernment level there appears to have been an overall plan for large-scale Westernization and economic development on a European model. Portugal sent to Kongo a number of teachers, craftsmen, builders, and other skilled men and women in what Jan Vansina describes as an attempt at "massive acculturation." [22] It might also be described as a neocolonial search to achieve economic takeoff. It was a long-term project calling initially for a high investment of men and materials in the hope of later returns. The second level at which the Portuguese were seeking economic return from Kongo was at the level of individual traders who wished to extract what profit they could in the minimum time with the minimum investment. This ambition was often in direct conflict with the overt government aim. Instead of using the local labor supply for economic growth, the traders carried it away to invest in the new development of São Tomé and Brazil. This process rapidly undermined the Portuguese royal plans for the economic evolution of Kongo, and very soon King Manuel and his successors began to lose faith in their grandiose vision and to encourage tacitly, and even openly, the movement of labor supplies from Kongo to other Portuguese spheres of interest.

The question of why the Portuguese (and subsequently all the other European powers) found it more expedient to foster the development of American colonies with African labor rather than to encourage direct production in Africa is one that still requires much thought. Perhaps the first reason is that America had much greater resources of unused and fertile land. Although Africa may not have been very densely populated, most of the regions adjacent to the Atlantic coast probably contained as great a population as they could readily support given the agricultural methods available. Hence, land shortage may have been one reason European enterprises did not flourish in Africa. Another reason, probably a more serious one, was undoubtedly the ability of Africans and African kingdoms to resist outside encroachments on their sovereignty.

21 For a detailed study of the relative importance of Prince Henry's landowning aristocracy and the Lisbon merchants in the Portuguese expansion, see V. Magalhães Godinho, *A economia dos descobrimentos henriquinas* (Lisbon, 1962).

22 Vansina, *Kingdoms of the Savanna*, p. 37.

The question of resistance to foreign enterprise on African soil brings one back to the question of why, in the whole of Africa, was it in Angola that the one major attempt at European conquest took place. It was suggested above that West Central Africa may have been so much a backwater in African development that it had not evolved the commercial facilities European traders had become accustomed to finding in West Africa. It may be, moreover, that this same remoteness meant that the states of West Central Africa had not evolved military systems that were as effective as those of western, northern,[23] or eastern Africa in resisting outside encroachment. This argument, however, needs careful handling since the Portuguese found, once they were committed to a policy of military conquest, that their progress was exceedingly slow. Although it may have been true in the early sixteenth century that a state such as Ndongo was less well equipped to meet aggression than, say, Benin, by the later sixteenth century the situation had evidently changed. When war broke out between the Ngola of Ndongo and the Governor of Luanda in 1578, the two sides were found to be fairly evenly matched. Thus the military advantage which Portugal may have had vis-à-vis the states of Central Africa and which may have stimulated thoughts of conquest had been substantially lost by the later sixteenth century. The activities of the Portuguese themselves may have had much to do with this change in the situation. In their search for trading partners and commercial exchanges on the West African pattern, they had been in contact with Ndongo at least since 1520. The subsequent sixty years must have seen a growth in the stature, organization, and power of Ndongo which severely hampered the Portuguese when they switched policy from trade to conquest. Ndongo had developed from a small state to a substantial kingdom with considerable knowledge of European trade. It even had several dozen Portuguese resident at the court and willing to advise the king on how best to resist encroachment by rival Portuguese who had founded the new Luanda colony.[24]

Another field of discussion related to the attempt by Portugal to strengthen its position through conquest is the question of Portugal's own economic aptitude to become a major colonial trading power. The success of the later trading powers in Africa, Holland, Britain, and France was based on the sale of manufactured goods which they could produce more cheaply, if not always more skillfully, than most African nations. In exchange they

23 It must be remembered that much early Portuguese experience of colonial warfare was gained in Morocco.

24 The opening of the Angolan Wars in 1579 and the attendant inter-Portuguese factionalism are documented in papers in the British Museum manuscript collection and reprinted in Brásio, *op. cit.*, IV, 308–309.

received ivory, dyewoods, minerals, gum, and, above all, slave labor. Portugal began trading in Africa before the success of large-scale manufacturing had taken place in Europe, and even at a later date Portugal never ranked as an important industrial power. The basis of her trade was somewhat different from, and decidedly more complex than, the straight exchange of manufactures for raw materials and labor. In Kongo, Portugal was paying for the slaves it acquired with less tangible returns such as teachers, missionaries, technical assistance, and a few rich cloths and other exotic material goods for the aristocracy. The payments made by Kongo might be partially regarded as a sort of tribute to a dominant superpower. In some instances the Portuguese apparently supplied limited military aid and in return received prisoners of war. Where Portugal did not have this favorable position (in West Africa, for instance), the terms of trade often involved a multiple series of exchanges. For example, on the Gold Coast gold was sold to the Portuguese in return for slaves, cloth, and beads, all of which had been previously bought from other African trading partners, especially Benin. In Upper Guinea the development of Portuguese trade was even more complex. The main African demand was for cloth, but since Portugal either could not supply the cloth at all or could not supply it of the right quality, the Portuguese evolved a multi-tier trading system: slaves were bought for Portuguese raw materials such as iron and then taken to the Cape Verde Islands to plant cotton and indigo; at the next stage skilled African weavers and dyers were brought over to the islands to start a textile industry which produced cloth of a type acceptable to African customers; this, in turn, could be used to buy more slaves on the mainland until a surplus of slave labor had been accumulated over and above the requirements of Cape Verde. This surplus could then be exported to the Americas and exchanged for sugar and tobacco. In this way Portugal gained entry to the Atlantic slave trade with a minimum capital investment and without the need for a large and continuous flow of cheaply produced goods from a home industry. The ingredients it supplied were mainly enterprise and sea transport.[25]

In Angola something of a similar sort took place. The Portuguese used palm cloth manufactured in Loango as one of their staple means of purchasing slaves; this palm cloth even became the normal currency among both Portuguese and Africans in Angola. But palm cloth still had to be bought. The Portuguese therefore hit on the even more profitable idea of imposing sovereignty and expecting tribute in a tradable commodity.

[25] Walter Rodney, *A History of the Upper Guinea Coast* (London: Oxford University Press, 1970). In connection with the Upper Guinea trade, it may be noted that at the beginning of the European expansion the Iberian Peninsula had a comparatively advanced metallurgical industry, and iron could be efficiently produced and exported.

This latter concept, which probably grew out of the deteriorating Portuguese position in Kongo, was probably at the base of the conquest of Angola. The conquest may be thought of not as a means of encouraging trade but as a means of acquiring wealth by methods other than trade, since Portugal was not in a position to offer satisfactory exchanges. The constant emphasis placed by the participants of the conquest on the benefits they were bringing to the country—"civilization," Christianity, the suzerainty of a great Catholic prince—might be interpreted as an admission that the material goods brought were not to be considered the total exchange for those extracted.

The idea that Portugal undertook military conquests because she was economically too weak to trade efficiently may have appeared tenuous at first but probably gained strength when rival European powers began to take an interest in Angola. There is little doubt that the Dutch could offer better trade than the Portuguese and that if there had been completely free economic competition in Angola, Portugal would have lost more of her trade more rapidly to the Dutch than she actually did. As it was, the Portuguese were able to defend their position until gradually it shifted from one where slaves were acquired in return for the intangible benfits of "Lusitanianization" to one in which slaves were obtained by trade, albeit a trade in which constant military attempts were made to impose monopoly conditions and forcibly exclude foreign competition rather than economically outbid it. The gradual shift that did occur was largely due to the economic growth of Brazil in the seventeenth century that strengthened the competitiveness of Portuguese traders. Brazilian tobacco, in particular, became an essential item of any commercial exchange on the Angolan coast, and a rumlike drink called *gerebita* was also in heavy demand. These greatly added to Portuguese purchasing power, previously dependent either on coarse cloth and wines from Europe or on very expensive luxuries from India. By the eighteenth century the situation had so developed that the Portuguese and English traders sometimes furtively cooperated in order to overcome the English deficiency in Brazilian tobaccos and the Portuguese shortage of metal goods, especially brassware; clandestine exchanges took place along the Kongo coast, thus enabling both the Portuguese from Luanda and the English from Loango to offer a better range of wares to their customers. Portuguese competiveness was also temporarily increased by the introduction of direct sea communication with India, until it was found that the popularity of Indian materials virtually destroyed the market for inferior European stuffs.

A further question about the acquisition of slaves related neither to the imposition of suzerainty in order to extract tribute nor to negotiated commercial exchanges, but to the straight military capture of Africans by

Portuguese-led troops for purposes of enslavement. The capture of slaves was probably quite common and lucrative during the early campaigns of conquest. A horde of traders seems to have followed in the wake of the army in order to buy captives from the soldiers in return for cloth. This probably constituted the major form of remuneration that the soldiers received. By the early seventeenth century, however, the capture of slaves was being discouraged both by the metropolitan government, as being detrimental to the orderly raising of tribute, and by the commercial interests, for whom war was destructive of regular trade. Military campaigns were nevertheless still initiated for slave-raiding purposes, particularly by governors who found this the quickest way to supplement their lean official salaries. But, as a proportion of the total exports, the number of slaves captured directly by Portuguese soldiers must have declined rapidly from the early years as the area of involvement in the slave trade spread into the interior beyond the reach of the Portuguese forces.

It was suggested above that the Portuguese may have chosen the Kwanza as the site for the colony because it had an old established salt-trading route into the interior and because it was in this area that they met Imbangala peoples who had come from the far interior and might therefore furnish them a link with rich territories yet unknown. Any hope that the Portuguese may have had of gaining quick access to Katanga and even Moçambique was rapidly quenched by the development first of effective military resistance and secondly of powerful trading barriers. Behind these barriers, however, the economic effects of Portuguese trading spread widely and rapidly, though entirely under African control and with African organization. The growth of African institutions designed to gain benefit from the new situation created by the opening of trade on the Atlantic seaboard is perhaps the most striking facet of the African response to the early Portuguese activities. The development of military resistance, even very effective military resistance, is not so surprising, since the Mbundu people of Ndongo were fighting for their survival and for their most precious possession—land. But the evolution of a complex trading network, which by the late eighteenth century tapped the resources of much of Central Africa and at the same time prevented any entry by outsiders, was an astonishing phenomenon in an area most of which apparently had had little previous experience of organized long-distance trade.

The period of Portuguese conquest from 1575 to about 1640 and the corresponding Mbundu military resistance is a well-known story and needs no elaboration here.[26] What does still need asking, however, is how and why the military phase of Portuguese activity and of African response gave

26 Birmingham, *Trade and Conflict in Angola*, chaps. iii and iv.

way to one in which armed force played a relatively slight role. The normal explanation that, after nearly a century of fighting, Portugal had become "exhausted" is hardly enlightening. Various other explanations come to mind. The first may be that Portugal was able, by the late seventeenth century, to offer an increasing range and volume of goods from Brazil in exchange for the Angolan labor it required. This meant that the costly use of armies to participate in the process of slave acquisition could be reduced. Another possible reason for the declining use of military force in Angola may have been a decline in the Brazilian demand for slaves, the result of economic depression in plantation areas due largely to British, Dutch, and French competition in the Caribbean. Certainly the declared number of slaves leaving Luanda dropped in the late seventeenth century to one-half or even one-third of the mid-century figure. At this time the sugar plantations were becoming self-sufficient in labor, and the early eighteenth-century boom in mining, which caused a tremendous new demand for slave labor in Brazil, was yet to come.

A more important reason for the decline of military activity, however, should probably be seen in the growth of effective resistance or evasion by Portugal's opponents. In the second half of the seventeenth century, the kingdoms of Matamba and Kasanje grew to fill the places of Kongo and Ndongo. They established themselves on the line of the Kwango River and maintained armies which ensured them protection from Portuguese attack. These states not only formed an effective military barrier to further Portuguese penetration, but they also gained a strong hold on the flow of trade in the opposite direction, from the interior to the Portuguese territories. Until the nineteenth century no Portuguese is known to have crossed the Kwango, and few traders from the interior were able to reach Luanda. After nearly a hundred years of war, two states had evolved in Angola capable of matching if not exceeding the military and commercial power of the Portuguese colony. These states then began to impose their own conditions on the trade and to exact payments in their terms rather than in those of the Portuguese. The Portuguese attempted to maintain their position of commercial superiority and for long periods had a resident at the Kasanje court. But the position of the resident seems to have been as much one of the servant to the Kasanje crown as servant to the crown of Portugal; whenever his actions appeared deterimental to Kasanje, he was expelled.

The rise of the great commercial states of Matamba and Kasanje was only one of the ways by which African interests attempted to circumvent the overexacting power of Portuguese Angola. The other major development, concentrated more especially in the eighteenth century, was a sweeping reorientation of the trade routes of Central Africa. Our knowledge of these changes, and of the overall growth in trade that took place in the eighteenth century, is still so limited as to consist largely of conjectures, but these conjectures can be assembled into an outline which might be useful in stimulating further research.

It was suggested above that the opening of the west coast trade may have sparked the founding of the Lunda Empire. This foundation in turn led to the emigration of many Lunda groups who escaped from the control of the new dynasty. Gradually, however, the dynasty asserted itself; by the late seventeenth century, some hundred years after its establishment, a new type of Lunda expansion was being launched. Instead of refugees who wished to break their ties with the center, this second Lunda expansion consisted of centrally controlled expeditions establishing satellite states among surrounding peoples and bringing them into the Lunda sphere of influence. This controlled and structured expansion of Lunda was probably associated with the growth of and change in trading patterns. The most important area of expansion may have been toward the northwest, where Lunda dynasties were established on the middle Kasai and even as far west as the lower Kwango. It seems likely that this growth was associated with the growth of Dutch, English, and French trade on the Loango coast north of the Congo River.[27] The growth of non-Portuguese trade in Loango is hard to account for in terms of the immediate hinterland of the coast. By the late eighteenth century the trade may have reached 20,000 slaves a year, a fantastic number which could hardly be coming from the sparsely populated immediate vicinity. It seems more likely that the growth was linked to a supply far into the interior, beyond the lower Congo. Together these two movements—the expansion of Lunda and the growth of Loango trade—provided an effective stop to the growth of Portuguese trade; the Portuguese were very conscious of this and unsuccessfully attempted by various means to either block the trade as it crossed Kongo or else oust their competitors from the Loango coast. Incidentally, the shifting of Lunda trade away from Portuguese Angola also undercut the position of the Kwango middlemen at Kasanje and Matamba whose power had been just as effective in limiting Lunda commercial freedom as in limiting the Portuguese.

The opening of new, more profitable, and less restricted trading opportunities for Lunda also opened the way for expansion into new areas of supply for the slave trade. Parallel with the northwest expansion was an

[27] A study of the Loango kingdom in the seventeenth and eighteenth centuries is being prepared by Phyllis Martin at the School of Oriental and African Studies, University of London. [This study was completed for a Ph.D. in 1970 and will be published by the Clarendon Press, Oxford. It does not, however, shed much light on this hypothesis.]

eastern expansion which may partly be explained as an attempt to gain domination of the Central African trade toward the east but which was probably also an attempt to increase the supply of slaves that could be sent to the west coast. Such an interpretation, however, places an extreme emphasis on the role of the slave trade in the development of Lunda. Perhaps this situation should be looked at with caution.

Finally, the third major factor concerning the development of the trade network of eighteenth-century Central Africa is the development of the Ovimbundu states. When were they founded? What stimulated their founding? How different was their relationship with Benguela from that of the older states with Luanda? At what stage, if at all, did they start siphoning trade out of the Lunda Empire? What influence did they have on such important neighbors as the Cokwe and the Lozi? Let it not be forgotten that Central African history still consists of far more questions than it does answers.[28]

The picture shown here is one of several African peoples adapting themselves and their institutions to the shifting pattern of overseas trade. It began with Kongo, and to a lesser extent Ndongo, attempts to benefit from friendly contact with the Portuguese. When neither side appeared to be achieving the desired rate of economic growth the method shifted to military confrontation. Portugal sought to achieve by military domination a profit she had failed to gain by cultural colonization. But Ndongo, and more especially Matamba and Kasanje, were able to evolve military systems capable of stalemating the Portuguese in all but a one-hundred-mile stretch of the lower Kwanza Valley. The emphasis shifted again, this time from conquest to trade, and once again the African partners in the overseas trade were able to adapt their pattern of operations to gain the greatest profit. As the sources of supply spread further and further into the heart of the continent, new outlets were sought to parts of the coast not under Portuguese control; thus a major choice of options was opened to the African suppliers. Finally, in the later eighteenth century, the pattern seems to have changed again; Portugal once more became the major trader. The key to this revival probably lay in the developments taking place among the Ovimbundu south of the Kwanza River, but these developments still await detailed study.[29]

[28] For more detail and source material on this final section of the paper, consult Vansina, *Kingdoms of the Savannas*, a comprehensive but condensed account of the material so far available for the study of Central African history, highlighted with valuable and imaginative insights into the major problems and theories; and Birmingham, *Trade and Conflict in Angola*, a short, preliminary evaluation of the role of Portugal in the pre-nineteenth century history of West Central Africa.

[29] Since this was written, much new work has been done on this area, notably by Joseph C. Miller of Wisconsin, Diane Christensen of Columbia, Benjamin Hanson of London, and others.

Chapter 2 The Tokoist Church and Portuguese Colonialism in Angola

Alfredo Margarido

[The author notes the ambiguous nature of Tokoism as a black African religion portraying the white colonialists as evil, yet preaching a doctrine of passivity
and submission to white authority while remaining apolitical. This socioreligious
movement is viewed as professing puritanical values while creating a literate
African leadership that may someday "abandon its passivity and join in open
protest." Tokoism is viewed as an outgrowth of early protest to Portuguese occupation. The early messianic and syncretic movements provided a forum for
often radical, far-reaching criticism against traditional institutions as well as for
opposition to the contributions of the white rulers. Under Simon Kimbangu after
1921 the African prophetic movements grew rapidly. Most were controlled by
the Portuguese authorities, including Tokoism which was able, however, to
mobilize large masses of people. The movement's organization and ideology are
examined sympathetically and in detail. The movement's religion is discovered
to be related closely to politics. The rigid discipline of the movement's followers
is associated with a social awareness, consciousness of alienation, and an awakening of strong resistance to exploitative working conditions. Thus ambiguity
characterizes Tokoism: while the church preaches subordination to the Portuguese authorities, it also cultivates a spirit of protest and permits its followers to
be aware of the reality of colonialism.]

Since the 1870s, opposition to colonialism has taken two forms in Angola.
The first was carefully planned in the cities by intellectuals who built
around the idea of nationalism and supported the original Angolan cultural
structures as they began to discover what constitutes the uniqueness of
the color black and the African man.[1] The second is the story of the ethnic

[1] The greatest figure of the period was the poet and linguist Joaquim Dias Cordeiro
da Matta.

groups battling against colonial domination but with little or no unity among themselves. The former group gradually constructed a thesis on the peculiarities of the "Angolan nation," which are different from and opposed to Portuguese values; the latter groups continued to be active until 1918. The collapse of this last traditional movement of protest initiated a "Portuguese peace" which reigned over Angola until 1920 or 1922, when it was taken over by government and military occupation.[2]

Not until 1940 did the intellectual opposition again protest colonial oppression and attempt to reunite the opposition of the people. For the first time the intellectual opposition studied fundamental structures before planning. They attempted to organize both ideological support protesting colonialism and theoretical fundamentals for the mobilization of the proletariat. However, they committed a grave theoretical error (on the heels of errors by the Portuguese Communist party and the international Communist movement in general): they mobilized the proletariat and the industrial lumpen-proletariat in the cities and all but ignored the mobilization of the peasants.[3]

On February 4, 1961, militants of the Movimento Popular de Libertação de Angola (MPLA) attacked the prisons of Luanda to free the resisting Angolans held by the Portuguese authorities. The attempt resulted in deaths on both sides. On the battleground the attack failed, but politically it put an end to all Portuguese attempts to justify colonial domination with its sugar-coated doctrines exalting "Lusotropicalism." Portuguese retaliation was brutal: hundreds of Africans were arrested—and some were executed on the spot. The colonials, however, still hoped that the traditional *modus vivendi* could be maintained.[4] Soon afterward, on March 15, the militants launched widespread terrorism. At first the colonists were shocked because they believed in the Portuguese colonial political philosophy, but soon they retaliated.

One of the most disturbing questions arising out of the liberation strife, which has been reinforced by systematic guerrilla activity, is that of finding out if the Tokoists, the faithful of the Ebundo dia Mfumueto Yeso

[2] M. A. Morais Martins, *Contactos de cultura no Congo português* (Lisbon, 1958), p. 156.

[3] Ideological emulation led Africans of Portuguese persuasion to attempt solutions that have not been able to withstand the test of reality: "The workers of Portuguese African colonies constitute most of the revolutionary social class. The role of mobilizing and organizing the masses, and of directing the battle against colonialism, falls upon the proletariat" (*Conference of Dar-es-Salaam*, [Algiers: CONCP, 1967], p. 37).

[4] "There is absolute calm throughout the land. The Cassange, district of Malange, incidents and even the February riots of Luanda are practically forgotten and do not shake the existing trust and optimism" (H. E. Felgas, *Guerra em Angola* [Lisbon, 1962], p. 43).

Clisto ("The Church of Our Lord Jesus Christ") participated in the war or remained neutral. A former governor of the Congo district defined the position of the Tokoists as follows: "The collaboration of the Tokoists with the terrorist movement is very doubtful. They do, however, admit that some dissident groups in the North are perhaps involved." [5] This position offsets that of the Angolan political leaders, which is different from the position of the Church (an institution opposed to all political involvement) and from that of the faithful, who do not hesitate to take part in the action.

How can Tokoism be defined within the context of a prophetic movement? Is it simply a matter of sociopolitical elements opposing colonial power, or do religious aims take priority? Roger Bastide shows that one usually hesitates in judging movements caught between these two concepts:

1. *The Justification*—Messianism has been the only possible form of resistance in an agricultural society, and it has made the exploited aware of their exploiters.

2. *The Condemnation*—Messianism diverts the resistance of the exploited groups from material struggle to the field of religious myths. This has retarded the struggle between the classes and engulfed them in a morass of theology.[6]

According to Bastide, these concepts are not exactly contradictory but could be called complementary. H. Turner, however, sees these movements as being primarily religious and spiritual in nature, seeking only to obtain individual religious and spiritual autonomy. They are a creative response to the perishing customs of the traditional African society. The new groups are formed to foster friendship, security, and some rules of practical orientation. By the same token, says Turner, the movements of the independent churches may have the character of, or be identified with, movements of political and economic protest, the principal cause, however, being a religious one.[7]

The explications of Bastide and Turner follow more or less the same lines, but they are neither analogous nor homologous. They are even opposed, in the sense that in giving preference to socioeconomic data or religious significance, one is faced with movements that are almost in opposition to each other. The importance given by Turner to the religious element is essential in studying the messianic and prophetic movements of the Congo Basin, because its societies suffer from the influence of myths

---

[5] *Ibid.*, p. 47.

[6] Roger Bastide, "Messianisme et developpement economique et social," *Cahiers Internationaux de Sociologie*, XXXI (July-December 1961), 3–4.

[7] H. Turner, "African Prophet Movements," *Hibbert Journal*, LXI, no. 242 (April 1963), 112–116.

which explain the creation of the world and man, as well as the origin of power. Religious data must, therefore, be given careful consideration because all Congolese movements started with Ngunzist practices.

If, however, the religious elements are vital to an understanding of the prophetic-messianic phenomenon, they are subject to the intervention of sociopolitical elements. The sociopolitical elements are often hidden under religious structures, but they are, nonetheless, responsible for the most important changes in Congolese societies. These societies have not retained the spiritual values of colonial religious organizations, but they have retained many material values and practices.[8] The outcome is that traditional structures have not changed but have lost their original meaning; religious affirmations no longer refer to the same values. Turner's position must be tempered by this awareness: the religious elements, which remain fundamental, keep their form although in practice they change their content.

In order to reconcile traditional religious practices with the necessities of a colonial society, African societies adopted the "principle of separation" which Roger Bastide studied in Brazil.[9] This was an attempt to keep intact the traditional values of the African societies. Isolation was their answer to the threat of corruption. As the colonial order weighed more heavily upon them, however, the societies found it impossible to maintain their autonomy. The Portuguese used the kingdom of Kongo (as well as those of Ngola, Benguela, Cassange, and all the others) as supply houses for slaves. In doing so they altered the Kongolese monetary system and intro-

---

[8] Morais Martins, *op. cit.*, p. 78.

[9] Bastide presents the principle of separation as an action permitting the African societies that have migrated to America to maintain their structure. Work regulations are set by the whites, but by attempting to survive in their new locale as they had existed in Africa, the exiled organizations are able to retain their homogeneity and their fundamental values. In Africa, this principle could be understood as separating the colonial order (and its economic, religious, and political manifestations) from the traditional African order. On a very general level we find the following variants: (1) the two communities only confront one another in the market place, the principle of separation being implicitly accepted by both groups; (2) the Africans succumb to the pressure of the white society on the administrative level but refuse any intervention into African structures; (3) the African society adopts foreign religious and material elements but does not substantially modify its structures; (4) the African society accepts white values and proceeds to reorganize in order to integrate itself into the colonial system, its material structures being those of the white man; and (5) it would be almost impossible to find African societies based solely on Occidental elements; while adopting the white man's structures, the African society tempers them with its own values which guarantee the passage from one African structure to another. This process is dialectical and is aimed at opposing the power of the colonials. Tokoism may be classified in this last subcategory. It adopts the religious organization of the white men only in order to assure more adequately the continuity of the African values and to deepen the cleavage between the two communities.

duced a considerable number of agricultural products which upset not only the systems of production but the patterns of diet and work as well. The resulting instability that was imposed upon the whole of the Angolan population required unique solutions.

The principle of autonomy did not block all contact with the colonial invader, however, and religions were transformed in the process. The Kongolese sought an explanation for the unequal sharing of material benefits which characterized the colonial society. They did not find the answer in the real world, so they sought it elsewhere, in religion and myth. The principle of separation must acquire a heightened sensitivity if it is to resist adequately the pressures of technical innovations, and religion must be organized so as to reject the white man and allow the construction of an African society unable to feel the burden of the colonial order. Thus, the various material techniques brought by the white man prompted the Angolans to question their society and to search for an efficient and successful means of defense.

It can, therefore, be seen that in examining Tokoism, a movement born in the Portuguese Congo, one must seek out the presence of religious elements that change radically only when sociopolitical structures are seriously threatened. Research oriented to defining religious changes will uncover social and political changes that have modified group relations. Colonial occupation, which disrupts family societies and clans, dissolves authority and demands the formation of organizations better adapted to circumstances.

The Kongo are a matrilineal people, whose sociopolitical structure is segmented. The large political organizations are, therefore, always suffering from crises, because the action of the groups comes principally from the *kanda* ("clan") and the *ngundi* ("lineage"). There is no doubt that linguistic unity, as well as a considerable amount of cultural identity, exists among them. There are also idiosyncracies which form a network of oppositions hindering the organization of a homogenous central political power. As a result of its segmented nature, the Kongo society is subject to a permanent state of tension, explicit or implicit, which cannot be resolved by fluid institutions. One of the reasons Dona Beatrice's attempts to reunite the Kongo people in the eighteenth century failed was the impossibility of reinforcing the political power shared by several royal lineages.

Membership in a clan or lineage, as well as all authority, derives from a mythical ancestor and an assemblage of fetishes which are the outward signs of the Kongo cosmogony. These are the myths that give value to the land—patrimony of the groups which cannot be taken away from them because it can never become the property of one person. The land is the property of the *kanda,* or better still, the property of the segmented groups, and not of their living members alone. Real possession cannot be disassociated from the ancestors who first occupied the land.

The arrival of the white man disturbed all aspects of the Kongolese society as control of the slave trade gradually became more pressing. The loss in numbers to family-based social structures undermined the stability of a social organization whose economic, religious, and political independence had been total. The second attack on this traditional structure was launched when the clans and the lineage societies were forced to abandon the lands by which they were bound to their ancestors. This catastrophe could only be attributed to sorcery—the magic of the whites as compared to that of the Africans, which appeared to be stronger at the moment.

The first messianic movement the Kongo experienced was composed of numerous syncretic elements: it utilized the strong central power of Catholicism to organize a Kongolese kingdom which would have a strong hierarchy. It started during the first years of the eighteenth century, following the displacement of the Kongolese political power after the War of Ambuilá (October 25, 1665), when King António I was killed and beheaded by Portuguese troops. Dona Beatrice was a prophetess who tried to discover in the land of the Kongo places and symbols homologous to those of Christianity. She transformed the natural and cultural elements of the Kongo into Christian elements, for only Christianity could make possible the restoration of a united political power of which the Kongolese dreamed—a dream and myth that persists today in messianic and prophetic Kongolese movements.

In 1872 a protest movement against Portuguese colonialism was launched under the so-called "Concelho" dos Dembos. It extended to the division of the Caxito and to the south of the river Dande; from Zenza do Golungo to the north of Bengo and to the seventh division of the Golungo Alto; to the tenth division of the Ambaca north of Zenza. It was a movement directed against the authorities placed there by the Portuguese, who were often colored people, ideal agents for enslaving and exploiting the African population. These authorities practiced injustices and used extortion in the collection of taxes.[10]

This attack on the Portuguese authorities was preceded by a movement that sought to convert traditional practices. Established for the mass destruction of fetishes, it remained known as Kyoka (from the word *yoka,* meaning "burn"). It clearly asserted that religious beliefs were incapable of supporting the group in its resistance to the Portuguese authorities whose demands oppressed the people. This assertion was made not

[10] João d'Almeida, *Operações militares nos Dembos em 1907* (Lisbon, 1909), p. 102.

with the idea of throwing out traditional doctrines, but with the intention of doing away with religious images, which did not have sufficient magic power to oppose the intervention of the whites.[11] The movement was, nevertheless, exemplary. It gave proof of the tight association between a movement involving religious elements and the sociopolitical conditions imposed upon the people.

The process of land spoliation began after the creation of the great administrative divisions and reached its peak after World War II. However, the pattern of opposition was already established, certainly by the turn of the twentieth century, and succeeding groups were to adhere to it. Having learned through experience, and deprived of the right to carry and purchase arms by the Portuguese, the people would not engage in armed riots until 1961, when the Portuguese lost control of nearly all the Portuguese Congo.

The Portuguese used police raid tactics to subdue the people, and effective administrative occupation of the Congo began around 1887 with the creation of the Congo District on May 31 of that same year. It was not until 1892 that the occupation of Maquela do Zombo began, under provincial decree No. 30 of January 30. In 1899 and 1900 the stations of Cuilo and Cuago were created. The region of Damba could not be occupied until 1911 (October 5), and from this center the occupation of Sosso and Pombo took place. The Bembe station was established in 1912 after the suppression of the insurrectional movements organized at the village level and even quite often by a lineage alone.

Only in 1906 was a military colony organized under the command of João d'Almeida. It operated in the regions of Dembos during the year 1907. According to its commander, the colony was to:

1) Open the vast region along the rivers Zenza, Dande, Lifune, and Loge to commercial, agricultural, and mining use;
2) Study possible routes along which products from this region could be transported to other areas;
3) Punish severely all insubordinates and rebels against Portuguese authority;
4) Occupy this territory to assure the free circulation of goods without paying taxes and without being subject to the vexation of African authorities;
5) Have more effective authority over the *Dembos* and *sobas* ("rebel

---

[11] Perhaps the full technique should be explained in relation to the religious and material makeup of those images; but it is sufficient to know that it is possible to create them from certain trees and the manipulation of clay from rivers or marshes, as well as by contact with other old figures, according to a system of reproduction almost biological. Among the Yaka this produces a veritable genealogy of "muquishe."

chiefs") who would only give attention to their authority if paid.

The story of the Portuguese military expedition is long and filled with details which give a clear picture of the desperate resistance of the people and the slow but inevitable disintegration of the army, constantly harassed by the population. No convincing victory seems to have been obtained. The army that returned to Luanda was a group in flight, for all seemed to conspire against the Portuguese: "fatigue, thirst, hunger, enemy fire and ambushes."[12]

It is therefore apparent that protest against the Portuguese occupation in this area did not cease. The action was carried out not in some homogenous manner but through combat of segmented units formed by the clans and members of the lineage. This meant that a decisive victory was never won by the Portuguese, and that they had to fight the same battle a thousand times. The lives of the people were much disturbed. On the one hand, the administrative order gave authority to strangers who had no connection with traditional authority, least of all with mythical ancestors. On the other hand, fiscal demands obliged them to abandon a family-based or lineage-based economy and to accept a market economy. And to all this difficulty was added the white colonist occupation of some of the lands.

This series of movements stems from the same cultural traditions and from identical reactions to colonial occupation. They came to an end in 1918 with the overthrow of the last Mafulo movement. These movements combined two aims and two approaches. They provided a forum for often-radical, far-reaching criticism against traditional institutions, and at the same time they opposed the contributions of the white people, which were beginning to multiply.

And thus the destruction of religious images was brought about, as was the disappearance of elements introduced by the whites (hospitals, schools, dispensaries, homes, clothes—even culture, since this is related to transactions with white people.)

The movements lost their continuity and their fervor when their methods were found to be incapable of conquering white magic, for myths formed a very intimate network with the manifestations of sorcery,[13] which controlled the whole of Congolese society. At all levels was found the presence and the control of the kindoki ("sorcerer"). Doutreloux goes

[12] Another characteristic to bear in mind regarding combats is the rapid mobilization of the people. João d'Almeida affirms that "the natives were always numerous" and did not leave the brush where they continued to fight "in unfair and cowardly fashion" (d'Almeida, op. cit., p. 58).

[13] Sorcery mentioned here is not distinguished from "black magic" and sorcery per se, so often studied by specialists, which only confuses the characteristics of the phenomena and institutions.

even further by stating that "society is sapped by sorcery."[14] It is perhaps inexact to admit that sorcery played only a minor role in influencing people; but it cannot be denied that, if it often provided a release for the community,[15] it was more of a castration process in that it created a climate of instability which suppressed the free action of the people by creating fixed, inviolable situations. It is certain that a duel between a fetish and a sorcerer will give rise to dynamic conflicts, which go around in a circle with no outlet guaranteed. The society imitates the dialectic process but it is not a true dialectic process in that it has no outcome and cannot guarantee the solution of conflict. The duel is only a sedative—not a cure—and tension begins again almost immediately and almost always at the same level. Thus there is a long chain of conflicts, one brought on by another, which do not reveal any positive elements.

Ngunzism was established within this process as a positive element, a verbal response that inevitably led to action.[16] Prophets engaged in dialogue in a complex society in which the process of segmentation rendered all social advances unstable, where *ndoki* ("sorcery") created considerable psychic instability. Thus the prophet, the *ngunza*, was often led to engage in a battle against all the elements of sorcery in order to end instability. Often the *ngunza* was a prophet who, unable to put an end to the practice of sorcery, would condemn a series of magic elements without condemning the principle behind these practices. He placed them in a different context, a useful context.[17]

It was in March 1921, that prophetic practice received decisive encouragement. Simon Kimbangu stands out among all existing or preceding prophets, for he was the first person since Dona Beatrice to possess strong charismatic command over the people. They were mobilized with lightning speed, and the movement was implemented in a new way. Moral resurrection was the keyword: polygamy, religious dances, and alcohol were forbidden. A puritan program was set up to oppose white enterprise through a new rationalization of the Congolese societies. In addition, even if Simon Kimbangu never preached Congolese nationalism, members soon identified the new church with the ancient Kongo kingdom, the greatest myth in the history of the Bakongo population.

[14] A. Doutreloux, "Prophétisme et culture," in *African Systems of Thought* (London, 1965), pp. 214–239.

[15] "Release" or subduing in the psychoanalytic sense of the word.

[16] Bentley's definition cited by Andersson: "The ngunza is he who talks through the intermediary of a chief, a herald, a preacher, or a prophet." See Ephraim Andersson, *Messianic Popular Movements in the Lower Congo* (Stockholm: Almquist and Wiksells, 1958).

[17] This explains that some techniques of sorcery may be used by the prophetic churches or by the messianic movements.

Other movements came to the former Belgian Congo and added to the strength of Kimbanguism. In 1926 André Matswa founded the "Friendship Society" in Paris; in 1936 the Salvation Army was established in the Congo; and in that same year Simon Mpaudi's Mission of the Blacks came into being. In Angola there were signs of prophetic movements in 1930 in the area of Teixeira de Sousa (Lunda). In 1934 a prophetess led the people in the region of the Pombo. In 1936 a Mayangi ("Joy") movement or Nlenvo ("Obedience to the Prophet") forbade all fraternizing with whites; in 1940 the Tawa movement (also known by the names of Tonsi, Tonse, or Ntonche) spread across the northern areas. Between 1950 and 1952 prophetic movements appeared in the east (Lunda). In 1953 "Lassysme" spread very rapidly among the peoples of Vili, a province in Cabinda. In 1955 the movement of the "Saints" spread throughout the central plateau of Angola (Nova Lisboa).

But the results were not encouraging. Colonists and Portuguese authorities hindered the development of the movements, except when the original clan organizations sought support from secret societies, such as when "Lassysme" appeared. But Tokoism, the most important Angolan messianic movement since Dona Beatrice, continued to mobilize the people, despite Portuguese attempts to halt its development and keep it under rigid control. Tokoism is an Angolan movement, although it was conceived in a foreign land. Thus it was able to have a completely different approach from the one existing in Angola. When Simão Toko returned to Angola in 1950 with one hundred comrades, his church was still in an embryonic stage. Portuguese authorities had expected to see it dissolve under the violence of the control they imposed. This included the punishment by exile of Simão Toko as well as other very influential people.

An examination of the conditions in which this church was founded, as well as a study of the biography of its founder and an analysis of the characteristics of the organization, will aid in better understanding the way in which this movement became an integral part of Angolan life. What part has it played in contesting traditional authorities and what has its position been in contesting the colonial authorities? The two activities are intimately related, and as Simão Toko points out, they often group both whites and the elders in the same camp. Both do nothing but exploit the young whom they see as tools for their own purposes. The white church which defends both is an institution that should be destroyed or avoided. New institutions must be created to answer the needs of the Angolans.

Simão Gonçalves Toko was born in the village of Sadi Kiloango, in the circle of Maquela do Zombo that forms a frontier with the Congo-Kinshasa. His birthdate is not known. He began school in the Baptist Kibokolo Mission in 1926, at which time he could not have been more than eight years old. In 1933, after having finished grammar school, he entered school in Luanda, where he completed two years of secondary studies.

Very little is known about his qualifications as a student (rumored to be bad). In any event, he did not continue school but returned to his native village. In 1937 he was named to a temporary position as teacher at the Kibokolo Mission. Some time later he was promoted to a permanent position as a teacher at the mission in Bembe.

Nothing outstanding is known about him during these first years at Bembe, except that he was a young teacher working for a Protestant non-Portuguese mission. Probably about 1943 he became engaged to a young girl and found himself faced with the problem of a dowry. The elders had raised the amounts of dowries as a control over the young who would go off to work in the cities and earn enough money to threaten the domination of the elders over the traditional society. Toko requested an increase in salary, which was denied, and he decided to go to the Congo-Kinshasa to work for six months and save up for the dowry.

Simão Toko went to Léopoldville, where he found work and decided to stay. At the same time, he broke his engagement to the young girl. In Léopoldville he belonged to the Baptist Mission, where he directed the Angolan choir. The anonymous correspondent who first presented the group to Jehovah's Witnesses[18] furnished us with very important information: This first choir was probably formed by a dozen Angolans, which

[18] The precise date of the formation of this small group from which was born the Tokoist church is not known. The anonymous correspondent of Jehovah's Witnesses (*Year Book of 1955*, p. 249) gives the date as 1943. Silva Cunha, according to information given by Simão Toko, states that Toko went to Léopoldville in 1948 (see Silva Cunha, *Aspectos dos movimentos associativos na Africa Negra* [Lisbon, 1958]. Neither one of these dates should be accepted as correct; however, the first seems more feasible, as the second telescopes Tokoist evolution as follows: Toko went to the Congo in 1948; a church was founded the following year; he was exiled in 1949 and returned to Angola in 1950. A slower pace for these events seems more realistic; this is suggested in the letters written to the Jehovah Witnesses in New York from Baia dos Tigres, by the dissidents of the church sent there by the government.

For further details concerning the formation of the congregation at Léopoldville, the year books of the Witnesses give contradictory information. The *Year Book of 1955* states that the head of the congregation wrote to New York about 1949 asking for literature. And he would have been sent the *Watch Tower, Children, Joy of All People,* and *Be Glad, Ye Nations.* However, the *Year Book of 1956* (p. 262), based on the testimony of one of the members of the dissident community of Baia dos Tigres, states that Simão Toko found, in the room of one of the Baptist missionaries of the mission where he was a teacher, two small books in Portuguese, translations from *The Kingdom of Hope of the World,* that he stole them in order to translate them into Kikongo and circulate them despite the opposition of authorities and missionaries. These findings would have signified discovery of the truth for Simão Toko. The contradiction between the two books is certainly evident; and if the Jehovah's Witnesses retained the second explanation they overestimated the role of miraculous change in setting Simão Toko on the road to truth. Let us above all, not attempt against all evidence to simplify Tokoism to a reelaboration of the Witnesses' doctrines.

would mean that its formation was well planned to lead to the creation of a new religion. Following the pattern of the first twelve apostles who surrounded Christ, Simão Toko assembled twelve Angolan prophets who would form the base of the new Angolan church. It was an organization of religious format masking an as yet crudely developed national conscience but searching for a way to assert itself.

This activity came to have great importance, since Simão Toko is a Bakongo-speaking Kikongo and could very easily have joined one of the Bakongo groups or organizations which were scattered throughout Léopoldville, more or less tolerated by the Belgian authorities. Toko rejected not only the Bakongo political parties but also the Kibanguist church, where the greater part of the Congo basin population, especially the Bakongo, congregated. He considered himself first an Angolan and therefore had to create a very special kind of church which could not be confused with any of the existing African churches. This nationalist trait became stronger during the first period of the evangelization and was to serve as an element of cohesion when the group was run out of the former Belgian Congo and was forced to return to Angola.

At this point an important event in the history of Tokoism occurred: While in exile both Simão Toko and his comrades became aware of the fact that Toko was a stranger in the midst of the complex Léopoldville society. First of all, he was a black man among the whites; and not only was he black, but he was an Angolan Bakongo—a member of a people not accepted by the Congolese Bakongo. And language posed a problem in that French, the second language of the Congolese Bakongo, is the third language of the Portuguese Bakongo. In the formation of the messianic movements there was the idea of migration toward the interior of the country. However, Tokoism was certainly the first movement where national character played a decisive role in the formation of a national church by one particular ethnic group which, in spite of the fact that its members had the same origins, the same family-based social structures, the same type of authority, and the same religious and mythical organizations, was definitely broken up by the political boundaries resulting from the Berlin Conference. It is true that, in matters of myth, differences of opinion arose, but the clans around which traditional structures were built were not questioned. Thus, the Tokoist church is a unique phenomenon in the sense that it is a Bakongo project of Angolan origin. The Bakongo give more importance to their Angolan identity than to the fact that they belong to the Bakongo. The Belgian authorities were very perceptive when they ordered the expulsion of the Angolans who formed this church, even if the reasons given for the expulsion were not true.

On July 25, 1949, the second phase of the development of the church began. Toko was praying at the mission when he and his companions felt a draft. Some began to tremble and talk in foreign languages, quoting passages from the Bible, especially from Acts, chapters 2 ("The Coming of the Holy Spirit") and 4 ("Persecution of the Apostles"). Frightened, the twelve followers of Toko asked him the significance of what was happening. Toko recommended that they read Joel 2:28: "And it shall come to pass afterward, that I shall pour out my spirit upon all flesh, and your sons and your daughters shall prophesy, your old men shall dream dreams, and your young men shall see visions."

It is not impossible that these explanations were given later. Whatever the date, their intent was to establish a biblical basis for actions and events to take place and to predict what would happen to those who formed the church and the faithful ones who would follow them. The manifestation of the Holy Ghost assured the group of the Lord's favors (Acts, 2:4: "And they were all filled with the Holy Ghost, and began to speak with other tongues, as the Spirit gave them utterance"). Secondly, the theme of persecution made them conscious of the suffering they would have to endure. From such suffering would stem positive results which would bring in more faithful to confirm the faith and develop the church.

The missionaries who were dissatisfied with the activity of Simão Toko feared that the new church would expand. After reproaching Toko, they expelled him from the mission. From then on meetings were held at the home of Simão Toko; it was here that the Holy Ghost manifested itself to the group a second time. The missionaries got wind of this new heresy and denounced Toko and his comrades to the Belgian colonial authorities, accusing them of political activities. This "catchall" accusation produced the desired results. On November 22, 1949, some months after the first "visit" of the Holy Ghost, the group was arrested. That the proselytic activity among the Angolans was fruitful is evidenced by the fact that 100 comrades were arrested with Simão Toko.[19]

On December 8, 1949, a decree from the governor of the province of Léopoldville ordered that Simão Toko and his group be exiled. They were accused of practicing "the rites of a mystical-religious doctrine of hierarchic nature, which preached the arrival of a new order under the reign of a new Christ and would put an end to all present authorities and power. They would then take over and restore justice." The expulsion order was

[19] There is a contradiction in these figures and those furnished to Jehovah's Witnesses by the informer from Baia dos Tigres, who mentions a group of 500 persons. It is quite possible that both figures are correct: the 100 comrades represented the men closest to Toko; the others were followers not as yet compltely converted to the religious practice of Tokoism. But it does serve to indicate the rapid progress of a doctrine which continued to manifest itself in Angola.

quickly executed, and on January 10, 1950, Simão Toko and his group were delivered to the Portuguese authorities of Noqui at the border. The Angolans returned to their country but not to their homes.

The Jehovah's Witnesses' *Year Book of 1955* states that the Portuguese authorities did not permit the Tokoists to return to their homes. They were all sent to different places, since the authorities believed that the simple act of separation would put an end to the organization and would prevent the spreading of the doctrine among the Angolan population. Some were sent to Bembe, others to Luanda, and a small group was sent to the cocoa plantations of São Tomé as indentured workers. The largest group was placed in the camps of Loge Valley, where they were kept isolated and not allowed to have contact with the population. Another large group was sent to the Baia dos Tigres, a small fishing port far to the south on the Angolan coast which was a real concentration camp where the authorities sent all the political undesirables and "antisocial" figures of all kinds.[20]

Simão Toko found himself installed at Bembe, the village where he had once taught school. He lost no time in starting his conversion activity, which manifested itself against the interests of the colonists. He remained there two years. He was then sent to Caconda, where he also remained for two years before being transferred to Jau. Two years later he was sent to Cassinga. Wherever he was, he continued his evangelist work, which disturbed the authorities and colonists. Finally, a clever civil servant found a good way to isolate Simão Toko without having to imprison him. He was appointed lighthouse keeper at Pointe Albina in the area of Port Alexandre. Thus the government of Angola succeeded in isolating him almost completely from his church. Simão Toko only came out of his seclusion to tell the faithful not to participate in the war of the national liberation and to beg those who had gone off to seek refuge in the frontier areas to return. It was his last public intervention in the life of the church. Today he lives in the Archipelago of the Açores, far from Angolan life.

Once the difficulties of doctrine and organization were conquered, Tokoism spread like wildfire. First of all, the relationships with African religious systems had to be established. Simão Toko found himself up against the immense prestige of the Kimbanguist Church, also a Bakongo church. He depended upon special Angolan Bakongo characteristics to found and develop his church. His exile made him conscious of the differences that prevented him from totally accepting the Kimbanguist Church,

---

[20] At Baia dos Tigres the differences between Simão Toko and João Macoka became more intense and caused the establishment of a dissident group seeking protection from Jehovah's Witnesses—the protection rejected by Simão Toko. It was from this dissident community that Jehovah's Witnesses received the information published in their year books.

but the task of differentiation was certainly facilitated by the power of myth in Angola, as well as by the segmented nature of the Bakongo social organization.

The church is organized around a central council which controls the congregations set up in each village in which there is a Tokoist community. Its members are the prophet (who gradually comes to be identified with Christ) and the apostles. These congregations are directed by teachers (or catechists) who are responsible for indoctrination, for leading ritual, and for discipline. Each congregation has a council consisting of the older members (and here again we find the concept of a gerontocracy, which confirms the existence of a conflict between generations within the Congolese society) who have the last word concerning discipline. This council differs from the traditional councils in that it allows women to take an active part.

A number of symbols identify the church to the people and identify the members to each other—and distinguish members from nonbelievers or from those who have not been initiated. The main symbol is a white star with five or eight points on a red background.[21] Simão Toko rejected the cross, the one great symbol of Christianity, to adopt the star, which meant that Africa also had received enlightenment from God. According to a director of the Luanda congregation, it is the star mentioned in the Apocalypse 8:1 and following. Two signs identified the Tokoists: the white star on red background (by this they were known as the movement of the red star); and the wearing of short hair parted in the middle by both men and women.

The rules established by the church are both simple and practical and could be applied to all Angolan groups. Simplicity is an agent of proselytism, for rules established along its lines are general enough not to reject any particular group. Because of this Tokoism has been easily accepted, even though it leaves many problems bearing on traditional concepts unsolved.[22]

[21] The two colors are found in the Congolese myths. The first (white) stands for water; the second (red) for earth and fire. On a more general level of symbolism, white also stands for authority, for it is worn by the administrative authorities, as well as by the missionaries. Red is the major symbol of religion, because it is worn by the hierarchy of the white religions.

[22] Thus the people of south-central Angola who adhered to Tokoism were able to apply their own traditional concepts without departing from the general rules of the church. Among these concepts were: rejection of baptism (it is not practiced on the central coast of Angola); rejection of the color red, which traditionally appeared only in exterior symbols; and the practice of *kuxingila*, which Estermann describes as an "excitation of the spirit" (Carlos Estermann, "O tokoismo como fenómeno religioso," *Garcia de Orta*, XIII, no. 3 [1965], 327–342). There is no rule that bears upon the problems of dowry and circumcision. The church neither protests nor does anything about them.

The rules of behavior have to do with manner of dressing and personal hygiene, family life, and the relationship with authorities and superiors. Rules are categorized basically into rules for women and rules for men. Women must wear their hair short and parted in the middle; they are to wear no beads or ornaments and must cover their heads with a white or red scarf and wear white clothing. The men also must wear white clothing and part their hair in the middle. There is to be no polygamy. Before participating in any rituals of the cult, all are supposed to clean their mouths and bathe. They are to eat no pork and drink no alcohol. They are to attend services barefoot (this rule has not always been followed in the cities). There are two major rules relative to family organization: Tokoists are to take care of the women and children and send them to school so they may learn Portuguese. They must always show respect to authority in general and have an attitude of obedience toward them, and to try to do their duty to the best of their ability. These rules are to be found in the Bible, especially in Leviticus and Deuteronomy.

The rules are quite simple, and the organization itself is not too complex since it must quickly adapt to the needs of traditional societies which today are in a critical state. Thus the organization can be embraced by people both in the cities and in the villages. It is a church that finds its converts among people who have moved to the big cities, those who live in areas where they have salaried work. In fact, Tokoism finds the majority of its followers among displaced populations, or among those who have liberated themselves from traditional rules whether economic or political. Moreover, the greatest percentage of the followers is literate, which reinforces the unique character of this church.

Guilt is rejected by the group. It is something that belongs to the whites and to the traditional authorities whose desire it was to subordinate the young people. The fusion of the two groups of elders and whites acts like a monolith to block the progression of the young inside both societies (white stands for the modern society; the old society is African). It forces the young people to reject all authority and create a new organization, even if it cannot materialize in the immediate present.[23] The elders may have only a somewhat frazzled authority, but the whites have full sway of authority in Angola; it is the whites who are responsible for the unmentionable injustices that reign over all the nation of Angola.

The complicity of the elders and the whites is manifest at the political level. People confronting the two types of existing authorities have concluded that the traditional authority has been left in place because it serves as an intermediary in the domination of the whites. The latter gain in two

[23] A letter of 1956 from Simão Toko states that "the whites are like the old ones who cannot stand to see the young people with parted hair."

respects: they do not have to add to their administrative staff, and they acquire agents who have direct contact with the people. In this manner they reduce protests, since the people are not directly subject to orders from the whites. Orders come through the mediation of the elders who have entered into a pact with the whites. A certain amount of liberty is allowed to the agents and the trap is set: they can send anyone away under contract labor. Thus, each chief or agent has a coercive hold over a particular group in the interior without diminishing the number of laborers available. However, when the group is forced to leave the interior and install itself in the city, because of fiscal pressures on the men, the people then realize the complicity of the traditional leaders. Colonial exploitation is no longer disguised, and both the workers under contract and those who choose freely to work in the cities feel white domination directly. Labor regulations place all Angolans under the pressures of the whites; no one can escape them. All physically fit natives who cannot prove that they are earning their own living are forced to work. This category includes:

1) Those who cannot pay taxes due to the government;
2) Those who seem to be incapable of finding the means of feeding, clothing, and providing shelter for themselves and their families; and
3) Those who live in unhealthy conditions.

The blatant impreciseness of the regulations exposes all Angolans to the threat of compulsory work contracts in agricultural or mining enterprises or for the government.

To escape long-term labor contracts, the people must either seek work voluntarily in agriculture or with some merchant or any white, go to the big cities, or leave the country. The solution of voluntary work, as well as migration to the big cities, leaves the worker with an extremely low salary at the mercy of the Portuguese labor system. It is possible to find better working conditions in neighboring countries, especially in the former Belgian Congo. The preferred alternative is to secure work in large foreign cities. It is in the ex-Belgian Congo that sizable Angolan colonies have been organized, and these have played an important role in elaborating Angolan politics.[24]

The demand for laborers increased as the lands of the Congo were progressively taken away from the people in order to set up coffee plantations, under a capitalistic system which served to reinforce the colonial economy.

[24] When the new king of the Congo was elected in the mid-fifties, there arose a controversy between the Protestants residing in the ex-Belgian Congo and the Catholics. There was already open opposition between the Congolese and the Portuguese, the former supported a Protestant and the latter imposed a Catholic king, King Dom António III, who died in 1957.

The colonial economy was dependent for many years upon the diamond mines in Luanda. The rapid soaring of Angolan economy after World War II increased the need for labor; and the traditional African power structure, which survived up to then relatively untouched by the white occupation, was upset and its rate of disintegration increased. The rich lands of the Congo and the Malange districts were disputed by the colonists, and resistance to the massive occupation by large numbers of farmers and merchants was weak. A document from King António III attests to his anxiety regarding these exacting circumstances and sensitizes the resistance movements which sprung up among the people as a result of the occupation by the whites of the fertile lands.[25]

At the same time the farmers who continued to work their lands were subjected to the demands of the market which was entirely controlled by the Europeans. This is another form of oppression which uses any means, from faulty sales to illegal tricks, to dispossess the farmer of his land.[26] The difference between international prices and those in the Congo is often enormous. Local prices are entirely subject to the practices of the white merchants, who do not hesitate to abandon current prices often stemming from agreements set up between interested business groups. Groups of businessmen travel through the villages to buy coffee on the spot at prices lower than those in the big commercial centers. When the African farmers refuse to sell their coffee to them, they often burn the villages, forcing the people into the bush; the buying price for the coffee is then very low.

This situation is what brought about the messianic and prophetic Congolese movements, and it is in this region that the armed protest against colonialism was launched. A critical situation has evolved, brought about by the creation of a massive proletarian population and the loss of lands traditionally belonging to the people, their link to the traditional religions. Emigration appears to be the only solution to colonial oppression. This situation is a very propitious one for the appearance of religious solutions. Religions provide a way out, for they allow a glimpse of a distant solution although they hesitate to incite the people to participate in activities of which the outcome is doubtful.

In this context, the Tokoist emphasis on obedience to all authority is

---

25 A bulletin from this king, dated January 2, 1956, advised the Congolese that they ran the risk of losing their lands if they did not cultivate them at all times; the whites might consider them abandoned and occupy them. See Felgas, *op. cit.*, p. 107.

26 The coffee was weighed in the stores and a very low price was offered for it. It was known that the price would be refused. The African farmer would then walk away, but several handfuls of coffee would be taken away from the bulk—and then on and on until the final sale.

comprehensible; authority is the hypostasis of the white man. The duality of the situation is evident, for white authority is the source of all suffering in African societies. In accusing the evil brought on by the whites, Tokoism only strengthens the potentiality for good with which the Africans are endowed but which they cannot exploit because of white domination. If society functions badly, it is not because it is congenitally bad, but because the whites have imposed foreign regulations upon it. Thus they have become accomplices in the destruction of African societies. It must be recognized, however, that white society has organizational qualities that enable it to dominate. The church must therefore have a dual function. It must not only find its Angolan identity, but also seek to appropriate the logic and organizational ability of the whites.

When the Angolan political leaders tried to contact the Tokoists upon their forced return to Angola, they thought they would find an efficient organization which could give them the pattern for the opposition against Portuguese authorities. They found a group which would not discuss political issues, but which gave recognition to the logic of white behavior and based its movements on this knowledge. As the political leaders soon discovered, the Tokoists saw the situation strictly as one in which two possible types of action were opposed. One of those forces momentarily had more power than the other. This power must be overthrown in order to obtain for the Angolans their rightful position in Africa.[27]

Tokoists certainly do not dare oppose the white man politically, because they are aware of the strength of the whites in this respect and the weakness of their own position. Recognition of this African weakness, however, as well as of African behavior, does not prevent their becoming aware of the situation and studying it to discover the solution. The whites are evil—their contributions may be worthwhile, but they demand submission which crushes the Africans. The whites may set up efficient patterns for technical matters and may have a rational form of organization, but they are an established evil which must be destroyed. Their contributions must be appropriated, not blindly imitated.

This dictum explains what is apparently a contradictory attitude on the part of the Tokoists, that is, acceptance of white patterns but rejection of all unnecessary contact with them, acceptance of their technical contribu-

[27] Viriato da Cruz, of the MPLA, who had been responsible for contacting the Tokoists at that period, defined the Tokoist opinion for me, that is, the religious influence of the whites sought to destroy the personality of the blacks. Therefore, they had to be fought with an African Africa, with a church that was black, African, and Angolan. The white man is always guided by good sense, while the African seeks irrational explanations; that is, the white profits by the opportunities life gives him. Viriato believes that the Tokoists only mimicked the whites and remained complete slaves of the white cultural system.

tion but rejection of their "human" contribution. The whites are technicians and engineers, and in this domain they can be accepted. But as administrators, as bosses, as police, as foremen they constitute an alien force which threatens the stability of the groups and could bring total destruction to them. To flee the white man is to flee evil and to return to the basic goodness of the Africans. Thus Tokoism does not encourage antifetish or antisorcery activities. Intellectual belief in the traditions of their groups enable Tokoists to go directly to the core of the main problem: adapting the logic of the white industrial society to the African tradition.

This is a dialectic movement which requires a thorough comprehension of the social order because the whites must be opposed through possibilities within African societies. The whites set up revenue regulations, police regulations, work systems, and laws for everything. The Tokoist church believes that Angola is divided into two parts: the profane part which belongs entirely to the whites; and the religious part which is wholly African and which enables them to envisage a new organization to counter the action of the colonists. The regulations imposed upon the faithful make this reasoning logical, that is, the Tokoist must always obey the white authorities. In this manner, Tokoists keep white authority out of their church. By satisfying all the legal demands of the whites, by paying their taxes, by seeking work, by maintaining good relations with the administration, the Tokoists safeguard themselves against repression and thus guarantee independence for their church in its relationships with the colonial society.

This manner of comprehending social factors led the Tokoists to draw two conclusions: first, that one must work in the society of the whites and find trades which might guarantee them independence (businessmen, artisans, etc.) or find trades among those which the Africans may practice, such as would give them a high social status and high salaries. At the same time, one must accept without protest all regulations of the activity, for only in this manner will he be able to find work easily. And, in effect, it is the Tokoists, or rather the faithful of the church of the Red Star, (the m'paps)—the people with the hair parted in the middle—who are preferred by the whites, since they are considered as very good workers, well disciplined and capable.[28]

How does this attitude affect comprehension of the Angolan political situation, and what contributions does Tokoism make to movements of

[28] In protesting the attitude of white employers, a Portuguese missionary denounced the difference between the treatment given to Tokoists and that given to Catholics: "I know that in a native colony [Caconda] hundreds of Tokoists are coddled, while the few who have remained faithful to Christianity are despised" (F. Valente, "Confiança e interrogação," *Portugal em Africa*, 2d ser. XXI, no. 125 [September-October 1964], 262-274). Despite the exaggerations of the Portuguese missionaries, this information confirms the success of the Tokoist church in mobilizing the people.

colonial opposition? First of all, Tokoism rejects all political activity, because this field belongs entirely to the whites. Tokoism could then, according to the dichotomy defined by Roger Bastide, take its place among the "demobilization" movements because, by refusing to consider political questions, it invites the faithful not to concern themselves with the particular political situation in Angola.

Actually, one of the rules of Tokoism is the total separation from civic activities (in the Hegelian sense of the word) and abstention from all political activity or all forms of social demands (such as belonging to a trade union, for example). This rule causes considerable ambiguity, for no Angolan can consider himself as separated from the political affairs that control all facets of life. If the Tokoists reject voluntarily all political demands, they cannot escape the demands imposed by the laws of the whites which control the work system and revenue regulations. Thus, it is a fallacy to sever Tokoism from any kind of political action, for politics reign everywhere.

To be sure, Tokoist regulations are extremely severe. They claim above all to avoid a confrontation between the two worlds, which are on a parallel plane but entirely independent of each other, and thus in opposition. The world of the Africans is that of religion, and the world of the whites is one of politics. The Portuguese believed in this total separation of the two worlds for a long while because they felt that the Tokoist's own regulations limited their followers and that they could be trusted to operate freely. But soon the Portuguese realized that the instructions of the church could not isolate followers from the realities of a biracial society, where the Africans are always at a disadvantage. This problem was common to all Africans, Tokoists or non-Tokoists. It led the Portuguese to class all Africans in the same category and by extension to mistrust the Tokoists.

There are therefore two ways of looking at the Tokoist activity as related to Angolan nationalism: as a national church wishing to have nothing to do either with society as a civic body or with politics; and as an organization capable of mobilizing the Africans and making them conscious of their alienation. The Tokoist church must be analyzed on the basis of this dualism. It has never escaped this ambiguous but inevitable position. Mário de Andrade has skillfully singled out the fundamental role played by the social awareness which gradually seizes all Tokoists: "Unlike Kimbanguism, which found its largest audience among the detribalized peasants of the Congo, Tokoism provoked the awaking of a strong resistance to the system of forced labor among workers in the plantations of Angola." Andrade confirms this by quoting from documents of the white colonists: "Witness the circular that 24 'representatives of the economy' from the Uige district (Carmona) addressed to the governor-general of the colony on March 7,

1957, informing him of the influence of Simão Toko's disciples and complaining that they had found among the people systematic refusal to register 'voluntarily' for work in the plantations."[29]

This is one of the greatest ambiguities of Tokoism, for in preaching subordination to the authorities, by accepting the work regulations imposed by the colonists, and by meeting all fiscal demands of Portuguese authorities, the Tokoists managed to find the strength to demand that the Portuguese administrators adhere strictly to rules established by colonialism itself. Thus it is that a number of those whom the Portuguese call the *advogados de senzala* ("village lawyers") are recruited among protestant laymen or among Tokoists who then leave the church so that they may be free to practice law. Tokoism is a school of apprenticeship, and if its Ghandian peaceful resistance, as Viriato da Cruz remarked,[30] is part of a system set up to hinder the intervention of the colonial political machine into the life of the church, the teachings often force the faithful to leave the church to look elsewhere for groups and movements whose action is more immediate and more radical.

The great interest of Portuguese authorities in controlling the movement is understandable. Simão Toko was freed from his forced residence at Pointe Albina, but after a brief appearance to tell the faithful not to participate in the war against the Portuguese, he was exiled to the Açores where, although he enjoys great freedom of movement, he is completely isolated from his church as well as from Angolan life. In the same way the Portuguese government has stopped the most important Tokoist leaders from intervening in Angolan affairs by setting them up as small property owners on the farm of São Nicolau (near Moçâmedes).

Going a step further, the Portuguese authorities granted freedom of religious activity to the Tokoists whose churches were located in the center of the suburbs in Luanda and elsewhere. Also, the Information and Tourist Center of Angola (CITA) commenced to print books and other publications to be sent to the Tokoist church. These concessions have their compensations in that the leaders of the church only admit members who swear they will not participate in any freedom party or participate directly or indirectly in protest organizations. The Portuguese government counts on the magnetism of Tokoism to hinder, even prevent, the mobilization of the people which continues to occur through the União das Populações de Angola (UPA) and the MPLA.[31]

29 Mário de Andrade, "Agonie de l'empire et crise du nationalisme," *Remarques Congolaises*, XIV (July 17, 1964), 328.

30 This remark has not yet been investigated in detail but must be taken into consideration, since the passive resistance of Ghandi determined the change in English colonial policies in India.

31 Information from Joaquim de Castro Lopo suggests that Simão Toko, although

This does not stop Tokoists from playing an important role in throwing the proper light on colonialism for its followers and the population in general. Their motivations and rules of conduct compel them to do so. Tokoism is forced to analyze the political orientation of the white society in order to know what separates the profane (politics) from the religious. For this reason the split between the white society and African society which becomes crystallized in the Tokoist church neither disguises nor clarifies problems because misinformation and ignorance create situations the church cannot disregard. If Tokoism is to be classified among the movements of demobilization—movements that seek to escape into a more promising future—it cannot escape the practical reality that confronts all of its followers. Isolation of the church is ideal, never real. We must therefore accept the insidious penetration of the world of reality into the "isolated" life of congregations.

Portuguese authorities would have to study the position of each member in order to determine the attitude of the church in relation to the movement of liberation. As a worker, a taxpayer, an inhabitant of a city or village, a draftee, or a church member, the Tokoist cannot avoid being identified with the African groups who are subject to the oppression of colonialism. He cannot forget the dead, nor can he ignore the combats that continue to ravage the areas in northern Angola, where the Bakongo continue to fight colonialism and to die. The isolation of the church from white society can never be absolute; therefore, separation from civic life, such as Tokoism dictates, is absolutely impossible.

Tokoism is forced to participate in the development of an Angolan national conscience for two reasons. The first involves those who have become aware of colonial practices but who limit themselves to legal forms of protest—which nevertheless can go very far (refusing to work voluntarily, refusing working conditions in certain activities, sending letters of complaint to provincial and international authorities protesting abuses, etc.). This legal form of protest, in which Tokoists are joined by former Protestants, offers a real means of control over the activities of the colonists and administrators and can take on the appearance of a vast operation to disrupt the rural superstructures. This kind of activity is especially effective in the bush but occurs less often in urban areas, for the complexity of the situation renders strict Tokoist control there impossible. The second kind of Tokoist participation must be nuanced. It is "Tokoist" only in that it assembles all those who were once connected with the church,

---

making loud declarations against the movements of liberation, takes no definite stand on the side of the Portuguese, and tries to secure political advantage from a situation that is quite ambiguous. This information seems to confirm the exile to which the church leader was condemned.

where they learned the realities of colonialism and the practices it engenders. These people could not find in religious activity a valid means of protest. These are the future members of the resistance movements. It can be ascertained that since 1961 nationalist movements recruited numerous militants from among former Tokoists.[32]

Control of the church has become more or less impossible, despite the attempts of the Portuguese authorities. David Barrett states that after the beginning of the war of the liberation, "the movement developed more rapidly during the revolt of 1961 because of the uncontrolled moving about of the population, which made a strict control impossible." [33] It is Barrett again who states that the movement was comprised of 10,000 followers in 1963.[34] This figure has never been verified and therefore can only act as a rough estimate, but it does indicate that the group continues to be active. This mobilization must, however, be considered from two angles: the church functions as a shelter, protecting its members from the combat, and the church takes in the victims of the situation of anomie brought about by the war, who become involved in politics when they become conscious of the real situation created by colonialism.

Ambiguity is the keynote of Tokoism, an ambiguity which nonetheless contains positive elements. Amid the perturbations created when the colonial order is questioned, the church seems to possess all the elements necessary for taking a firmer and more open stand against white occupation. The official position of the church alienates it from the support of the most dynamic elements among the population. They cannot stand by any longer and refuse to admit the impossibility of coming to terms with colonialism and turn toward organizations having more radical aims. The church does, however, continue to play an important role, in that it cultivates an implicit spirit of protest. This permits its followers to be aware of the reality of colonialism and often leads them to increase their efforts of opposition. The fact that the government exiled Simão Toko in the Archipelago of the Açores (which had already been the land of exile of the notorious comrades of the great Moçambican chief, Gungunyana) shows how fearful the Portuguese are of the mobilizing power of the church. This fact also explains why the Portuguese endeavor to keep the movement in hand. The ambiguity of the followers of the red star may some day allow them to abandon their passivity and align themselves with movements of open protest.

[32] Information given by Viriato da Cruz and confirmed some years later by Joaquim de Castro Lopo.
[33] David B. Barrett, "Schism and Renewal in Africa," manuscript, p. 89.
[34] *Ibid.*, p. 378.

Chapter 3   A Failure of Hope: Education and Changing Opportunities in Angola Under the Portuguese Republic

Michael A. Samuels

[This case study examines an early twentieth-century protest movement in Angola led by António Joaquim de Miranda, who attempted to bring about educational reforms for Africans but failed. Primary focus is on protest manifested through a voluntary association, with the central issue being whether education would lead to "civilization" and social reform for the Angolan. Special attention is directed to Miranda, an educated African of antimonarchical and antielitist sentiments, who demanded local autonomy from Portugal and greater educational opportunities. His failure is attributed to a hardening of Portuguese attitudes under the Republic, and to policies limiting opportunities for native-born Angolans—a pattern that has prevailed into the 1970s.]

INTRODUCTION[1]

The history of Portuguese expansion and contact with foreign peoples, especially in Africa, reveals one constant theme: the importance of equality for non-European peoples. An understanding of this theme is confused by recurring emphases on extremes: either the Portuguese accepted non-

[1] This study was made possible by a grant from the Institute for International Studies and the Center for Education in Africa of Teachers College, Columbia University. Education in this period is thoroughly examined in Michael A. Samuels, *Education in Angola, 1878–1914: A History of Culture Transfer and Administration* (New York: Teachers College Press, 1970).

Europeans fully, as "assimilated," or they were ruthless in their exclusion of anything that stood as a barrier to their desires.

This paper shows an important vignette in Angolan history by highlighting a change in the position of African equality. Soon after the advent of the Portuguese Republic in 1910, previously existing opportunities for equality were curtailed as a result of three different developments:

1) a growing emphasis on "protecting" Africans rather than "civilizing" them;

2) increased educational requirements for previously available administrative employment; and

3) a growing emphasis on vocational education and labor, and a refusal to provide secondary-level instruction in Angola.

These developments had historical roots in the earlier Monarchy, in the colonial thinking that began to develop in the late nineteenth century, when a hardened view toward Africans and their place in colonial society evolved. As awareness of the hardening spread among Angolans, the form of protest against Portuguese rule changed. Journalistic argumentation[2] and peaceful demonstrations replaced traditional resistance through armed rebellion. In Luanda, March 12, 1911, hundreds of people, peacefully acting as petitioners to the government, marched directly to the residence of Governor-General Manuel Maria Coêlho.[3] What was unusual about the group was that all of the marchers were Africans. This was the first time that Africans had peacefully demonstrated to elicit reforms from the provincial government. Though spurred by a growing sense of unequal treatment and lack of opportunity, the participants marched with hope in their hearts. The hope was stirred by the advent of the Republic and faith in Portuguese good will. The result of the protest is the subject of this paper.

THE LEADER AND THE ISSUE

António Joaquim de Miranda was born in 1864. Nothing is known of his life before he was sixteen, when his father died. At that time, Miranda came under the care of Nicolau Rogeiro, who had been considered the best African primary school teacher of the time, a person who, educated completely within Angola, influenced "through good example and patriotism" many Africans who later had careers in commerce, the military, and public life.[4] Rogeiro may have influenced young António in this way. By the time

[2] Douglas L. Wheeler, "Nineteenth Century African Protest in Angola," *African Historical Studies*, I, no. 1 (1968), 40.

[3] The exact size of the group is unclear. Estimates range from "few in number" (*A Voz de Angola* [Luanda], March 23, 1911) to "2,000 natives" (*O Eco d'Africa* [Lisbon], October 1, 1914).

[4] *A Polícia Africana* (Luanda), November 15, 1890.

he was twenty-one Miranda had acquired a job as scribe for a plantation at Barra do Bengo, a village that had developed as a trading terminus near Luanda.[5] Thus far the pattern of his life was not abnormal.

For more than twenty years Miranda continued with the same employer. In the course of numerous journeys in the interior, he was greatly disturbed by barbarities and cruelties practiced against African workers both in the recruitment process and on the plantations themselves. Quitting his job in 1908, he wrote letters to the owner of his plantation and to Governor-General Paiva Couceiro protesting the abuses he had observed. The reaction to these letters cannot be determined; it is clear, however, that the government could not have been highly offended by Miranda's criticism, for he soon became a public employee in Luanda.[6]

Miranda had been interested in political affairs for some time. As early as 1899 he was publishing a local newspaper, *A Folha de Luanda*; later he published *O Angolense* (1907) and *O Apostolado do Bem* (1910). As a newspaper publisher and editor, Miranda was one of a number of indigenous and immigrant literati active in Luanda after 1870, most of whom were self-educated after primary school, who found journalism a useful form of protest. Furthermore, "that journalism," Mário António has stated, "was the first open door to literary callings." [7] It appealed to new literates in a society frustrated, in a sense, by the few available opportunities to practice the skills and learning that accompany literacy.

A high degree of freedom of the press often led to acrimonious, vituperative debates. Political rather than social or racial arguments were the most frequent; the need for local autonomy received the most common support. Governors-general were typically (and strongly) criticized. A reading of Angolan newspapers during the last thirty years of the Portuguese Monarchy (1880-1910) shows that a deep division existed between monarchists and republicans. "Educated and privileged African society in Luanda was divided in its political opinions—some were pro-monarchist and completely loyal to the Portuguese; others were not." [8] Miranda clearly was not.

Antimonarchic and antielitist, Miranda opposed the total Portuguese political and social system in which he saw a small number of citizens forming an elite to dominate an entire nation. To what nation did he refer? Not to a broadly defined, racially determined African one. The nation being dom-

[5] A partial biography of Miranda appeared in *O Eco d'Africa*, October 1, 1914, to March 15, 1915.

[6] The Portuguese were facing serious labor accusations from other international sources at this time. See, for example, William A. Cadbury, *Labour in Portuguese Africa* (London: George Routledge, 1910).

[7] Mário António, *A sociedade angolana do fim do século XIX e um seu escritor* (Luanda: Editorial Nós, 1961), p. 10.

[8] Wheeler, *op. cit.*, p. 52.

inated was Portugal, to which he, an African, belonged. His antimonarchic views were spurred by the growing strength of the republican movement in Angola, a movement related to the one in Portugal which succeeded in toppling the Monarchy in October 1910.

The most important issue for republicans in Angola was their desire to be autonomous, free from the tutelage of metropolitan Portugal. Such men saw autonomy as the stimulus for the everfailing development. Decentralization leading to local control over essential services was the desired first step toward economic progress. Related, and important in republican thinking, was the need for the expansion of an educational system which had developed little in spite of constant requests for a third of a century. The advent of the Republic led many to hope that their long-held desires would be satisfied.

For many years Angolans of all races and political persuasions had longed for educational revision and expansion. Newspaper editorials urged advanced teaching methods for schools, decried low teachers' salaries, and even championed compulsory education. As early as 1882 one editorial had explained that "if the province had self-government, it could resolve the problem of instituting public education itself." [9] Increased educational opportunity was a theme repeated frequently by such well-known writers as José de Fontes Pereira and J. D. Cordeiro da Matta. Perhaps the Republic would at last do something specifically to satisfy these longings.

Indeed in Portugal itself the Republic had immediately begun to attack the inadequate educational system: some 266 new schools opened in the first five months of the Republic; science had been introduced in primary schools; and religious instruction had been changed to civics in all schools.[10] The Republic began to wage a battle against both illiteracy and meaningless literacy. In the early months of the new government, the people, long ignored and illiterate, seemed to benefit.

Such were the precedents of the 1911 march. Miranda obviously felt that a new type of protest, peacefully yet demonstrably working within the system, would be effective at that time. What he advocated was a complete social reform, a reform *through* education. Under Miranda's leadership there formed in Luanda a voluntary association named Educação do Povo— Socorros Mútuos ("Education for the People—Mutual Assistance"). To Miranda such a group was necessary not only because Portugal had belied its "honest intentions as a civilizing nation," but more important because the native elites themselves had shirked their responsibility, being content to accept their absorption through assimilation.[11] Assimilation was not con-

---

[9] *A União Africo-Portugueza* (Luanda), August 4, 1882.
[10] *A Reforma* (Luanda), February 4, 1911, and March 25, 1911.
[11] *A Voz de Angola*, March 23, 1911.

demnable per se, but those who became a part of the elite group frequently ignored the rest of the community. What was also unique about this association was its emphasis on "the people," those normally ignored both by those with power and by the government. The progress of Angola would rest on raising the level of the masses, and the best way to accomplish this was through greatly expanded educational opportunities. Only then could the people and their government combine interests for the good of Angola.[12]

Thus the association drew up statutes outlining very specific policies. The march of 1911 tried to present these desires to the Governor-General. His acceptance of the policy outlined in the many statutes would have meant a reversal of the practice of educational stagnation; they would have required more active government involvement in education. Other than giving moral support, the Governor-General would oblige all government workmen and other employees to become members of the association. The government would provide facilities for deductions to be made from the salaries of all employees who desired to pay dues but who customarily spent more than they earned.[13] The government would further provide a building as headquarters and central school for the association,[14] smaller houses which could be used for preparatory schools, a monetary grant of 100 reis daily for each boarding student,[15] block grants for schools, special grants for rural schools of practical agriculture, and free water for the central school. The Luanda local government would provide furniture, light, books, and other supplies. Finally, a public subscription within both Angola and Portugal of money and books would lead to the establishment of a public library in the association headquarters.

Governor-General Coêlho received the marchers and their requests warmly; however, his official reaction and that of Lisbon, if any, remain

[12] *Ibid.*

[13] Such deductions are already being made for a government-inspired welfare system, the *Monte pio oficial.*

[14] It was suggested that such a building was already being constructed. Though intended for the teaching sisters of the São José de Cluny Order, the building presumably already appeared destined to be without an occupant. The Portuguese Republic was deeply anti-Catholic and placed certain restrictions in the way of the Church. One of these, that nuns were forbidden to appear on the streets in their habits, eventually succeeded in forcing the abandonment of Angola by all members of the order. See Dr. O. E. Higgins to Sir Earl Grey, 6/6/11. 22016, Public Records Office (London), FO 367/235.

[15] If one were to assume 250 school days in a year and 150 pupils, the government grant would have been 3,750 milreis (slightly more than $3,900 U.S., figured from West Central Africa Mission Conference, *Minutes*, 1908, p. 12), or more than the 3,616 milreis which had been budgeted for all government primary schools in the Luanda District in 1910 (*A Reforma*, December 31, 1910). To give such a large grant to a private school system would have been, to say the least, unprecedented.

unknown.[16] It is clear that the statutes were never approved, and there was no government action on any of the items requested.[17]

To Miranda, the failure of the government to assist in his scheme for educating a wide range of the population was evidence of a desire to keep Angola backward, because of a fear that an educated Angola would result in an independence movement such as had led Brazil to declare its independence a century earlier.[18] Failure to educate the Angolan masses meant that no great collective movement could develop.[19] It may be that his desire for such a movement became known to an unsympathetic government. Within a year, Miranda was transferred 250 miles into the interior to Malange, as a tax collector.[20] From all indications, the Educação do Povo did not outlast its initiator in Luanda. The government had peacefully succeeded in resisting this request for change.

A HARDENING OF ATTITUDE

Miranda's voluntary association was a product of hope at a time when new liberal ideas might have been expected. But the era of liberal ideas about educating Africans had passed with Andrade Corvo and Luciano Cordeiro, leading members of the generation that had founded the Sociedade de Geographia de Lisboa or Lisbon Geographical Society in 1875. In the years immediately surrounding the Berlin Conference and the "scramble" for Africa, there had developed a government-controlled education system which served most of the administrative centers, while education in rural areas was left exclusively to missions. The extent of the government system was limited by the slow rate of Portuguese penetration and pacification, the lack of any heritage of wide educational opportunity, and a shortage of funds exacerbated by the minimal priority given to formal education. Nevertheless, though few children were able to attend state schools, over 70 percent of those who did were Africans. Thus, of a total of 1,802 boys in primary school in 1901, 1,290 were Africans.[21]

[16] Unfortunately no official documents concerning this incident are in the collection presently open to the public in the Lisbon Arquivo Histórico Ultramarino. The present work of organizing the Arquivo Histórico de Angola in Luanda may reveal information about official reaction.

[17] *O Eco d'Africa*, October 1, 1914.

[18] *O Eco d'Africa*, February 1, 1915.

[19] *Ibid.*

[20] In Malange, Miranda remained neither passive nor quiet. He became director of a newspaper, *Era Nova*, in which he urged people not to pay the hut tax that he, as a tax official, was meant to collect until their district received some compensating benefits. This and charges that he had formed a society that met at night and aimed at killing whites led Governor-General Norton de Matos to fire him and exile him to Cabinda. See *O Eco d'Africa*, April 20, 1914, and November 1, 1914.

[21] Govêrno Geral, *Annuário Estatístico da Província de Angola*, 1901 (Luanda: Imprensa Nacional, 1905), p. 36.

The relatively large African attendance reflects both the small number of Portuguese settlers at this time [22] and the desire of Africans to attend school. Furthermore, more by practice than by policy, there was little racial discrimination in the provision of racial opportunity. Toward the end of the nineteenth century, as boundaries became fixed, Portugal prepared to give serious attention to her colonial policy. As she was doing so, the attitude toward Africans hardened. Awareness of this changing attitude may have been an important factor in the abortive formation of the Educação do Povo.

The first signs of the hardening took place in Moçambique rather than Angola. In the last decade of the nineteenth century, first António Enes and then Mousinho de Albuquerque viewed the state of their colony in East Africa and set forth the methods for bringing about necessary changes. To both, the superior civilization represented by the Portuguese nation could only be attained by Africans through manual labor, the practice of which was necessary for a full understanding of the dignity of work.[23] The previous generation of liberal colonial thinkers had seen Portuguese culture as embodying more than just physical exertion and had seen a need for schools and instruction within the Portuguese civilizing responsibility. Though mostly concerned with problems of administrative efficiency, Enes and Mousinho belittled schools as "a fiction" for the Africans whom they considered naturally inferior and childlike.

Neither Enes nor Mousinho had direct influence on Angola. Both, however, influenced men who were in the vanguard of the changing policy following the 1901 Colonial Congress in Lisbon. In the decade immediately preceding the advent of the Republic, two important governors of Angola, Eduardo da Costa and Henrique de Paiva Couceiro, had served in Moçambique under Enes and Mousinho. At the time of their leadership, the complexion of educational thinking was undergoing a change.

When da Costa moved from the district governorship of Benguela to the provincial governorship in 1906, he was faced with instructions from the Overseas Ministry in Lisbon to organize a vocational school in the province. The year before the overseas minister in Lisbon, Manuel Rafael Gorjão, had decreed a vocational school for Luanda to be named after Crown Prince Dom Carlos. Gorjão had devised a plan and arranged for the construction of a building for a similar school when he had headed a public works mission to the province between 1876 and 1880. At that time, Gorjão had attempted to solve the problems of a shortage of skilled workmen

---

[22] The white population has been estimated as 9,177 in 1900 and 12,000 in 1913. See José Mendes R. Norton de Matos, *Memórias e trabalhos da minha vida,* (Lisbon: Editôra Marítima Colonial, 1944), vol. 3, pp. 58–61.

[23] For brief but thorough accounts of each man and his views, see James Duffy, *Portuguese Africa* (Cambridge: Harvard University Press, 1959), pp. 236–242, 258.

in efficient and economical terms. His solution was to train Africans in a new school run by the public works department.[24] By the time he became minister almost thirty years later, the building he had constructed for the school remained standing, but no vocational school had ever trained a single student. Vocational education had been ignored.

Faced with the directive from Lisbon, Governor da Costa arranged for the vocational school to begin. That he did so, contrary to his own wishes,[25] is a tribute to him as an administrator. It was mainly, in fact, in the field of administration that da Costa made his most significant contribution. For da Costa the Portuguese hold over Africa depended upon a tight-fisted administrative control exercised on a local level through a powerful administrator, usually a military man. To da Costa there was need to emphasize the prestige of Portuguese juridical and administrative authority "in the eyes of the inferior races."[26] It was the effects of administrative rigidity, rather than any instructive education, that would bring Africans to civilization. Meanwhile, however, the established schools would continue with Africans being admitted as before. The apparent anomaly of giving free access to more than half the places in government schools to those same "inferior races" did not deter da Costa. The novelty came through the civilizing and educating role of the direct system of administration.

Whereas Eduardo da Costa applied his attitudes in administration, Paiva Couceiro, who became governor-general a year later, directly concerned himself with schools. Like many before him, he was willing that Africans be admitted, or "assimilated" into Portuguese life. For these people, normal Portuguese education would be available. But for the masses, the only education was work, with literacy only eventually connected, for those who could go further. The workshop and the fields were "the true school of education, and therefore of Progress and Happiness." [27]

In theory, this practical approach to educational development might have been a positive approach to Angolan needs. After all, such ideas would not normally derive from an educational system like the literary, church-derived Portuguese one. And there was no question about the lack of prac-

24 Relatórios das direcções das obras públicas das províncias ultramarinas—Angola 1877–80 (Lisbon: Imprensa Nacional, 1886), pp. 21, 40–44.

25 Da Costa explained in his inaugural speech that he felt the capital of the province deserved a higher school (A defeza de Angola [Luanda], June 7, 1906). Though many administrators felt similarly, restrictions from Lisbon delayed meaningful secondary education until 1919, although after 1908 the Catholic seminary did offer secondary courses to its boarding pupils.

26 Eduardo da Costa, "Decentralisação da acção administrativa nas colónias," in Congresso Colonial Nacional, Actas das sessões (Lisbon: Sociedade de Geografia, 1902), p. 89.

27 Henrique de Paiva Couceiro, Angola, dois annos de governo (Lisbon: Editôra Nacional, 1910), p. 206.

tical applicaton of the education offered at that time, except, as in much of Africa, to the few jobs requiring clerical skills and to trade. There was an obvious shortage of skilled laborers.

On the other hand, it was not so much the emphasis on practical education that signified a developing restrictive new policy as it was the selective nature with which such instruction was viewed. Whereas official primary schools were attended by all children, it seems clear that Paiva Couceiro envisioned only "indigenous" students in his practical schools. That he, like so many of his predecessors, failed to evoke any meaningful change in the educational system is only partly important, for he succeeded in giving official representation to what many Africans were able to observe or sense as the general attitude of whites toward them. Soon after he arrived in Angola in 1912, Norton de Matos noted the mentality that influenced white-black relations: "Respect and affection for the man of color rapidly disappeared, we began to have reluctance in considering him our equal, we were left with the belief that a black could never fully attain our civilization, to be intellectually, morally, politically, and socially equal to us." [28] That there should have been an African reaction to this attitude is not surprising; that it should have come so peacefully and that its failure to evoke change should have been so easily accepted may, however, be surprising.

NEW LIMITS ON OPPORTUNITY

The change of attitude coupled with the slowly growing Portuguese emigration to Angola gave intensified meaning to the desires of Miranda, the members of his voluntary association, and many more in both Luanda and the interior whom the association claimed to represent. But a change in African status was to come from another direction too. For years most vocal members of the Luanda elite had been government employees in the colonial bureaucracy. In the absence of any legal restrictions about minimum literary qualifications, judged through formal schooling, a modicum of literacy, frequently gained in a government primary school,[29] was adequate for entry into the local administration as a clerk. Few restrictions, either official or unofficial, impeded the progress of any dedicated, hard-working young man who, as in organizations anywhere, understood the nature of his employers. As in much of colonial Africa, monetary rewards and social prestige came to those in colonial administration.

The growth of Enes- and Mousinho-inspired ideas, however, threatened

[28] Norton de Matos, *op. cit.*, p. 24.

[29] No tradition had developed for students of mission schools, educated at a rudimentary level and almost always away from administrative centers, to search for government employment.

to block this long-accepted channel of progress. As early as 1906, José de Macêdo, though an early republican championing the cause of autonomy and other matters associated with the thinking of masonic societies, warned against an African "propensity for little bureaucracy" and the threat of growing competition for official employment.[30] Would obstacles now develop along the familiar road of advancement?

Furthermore, though government service had provided an outlet for local advancement, it had done so to the detriment of professionalization. After the beginning of the Republic, Angolan administration followed the example of Moçambique by replacing military with civilian administration. With the development of civilian control, strongly advocated by republicans and symbolized by a professional Colonial School begun in Lisbon in 1907, care was taken to raise the standards of employment, that is, legally to exclude those who lacked what was considered the necessary educational qualifications.

The Educação do Povo thus represented a reaction to two different kinds of change. On the one hand, Miranda and his collaborators felt the growing threat to their customary employment and social opportunities. On the other hand, they felt that the changed government, embued by the world current of enlightened republican ideas, standing as it did for a new order of things, could not only end this threat but provide the educational development for which some Angolans had been clamoring for more than a quarter of a century. The official reaction could only have left them sorely disappointed.

The professionalization of the administration led to the raising of standards of entry. A decree of October 1911 limited entry into the lower professional ranks to those with qualifications of the fifth year of *lyceu* (the academic secondary school.) This was five years beyond the highest level of government educational provision in Angola. Four years before, a new bishop had requested that the Luanda seminary be allowed to offer the five-year *lyceu* course, but his request had been refused by the Overseas Ministry. In spite of this, *lyceu*-equivalent courses were available to a handful of boarding students at the seminary each year.[31] Nevertheless, neither the provincial nor the metropolitan government made any attempt to provide facilities in Angola for anyone to be educated to a level that would allow him to enter government service. While not spelling it out, Portugal was telling Angola that it was to be administered rather than to help administer. As the effects of this increasing reliance on educational qualifications

---

[30] *A Defeza de Angola*, May 10, 1906.

[31] As a result, in later years the only Angola-born men to rise in the colonial administrative bureaucracy were those who either had been educated at the seminary with the ostensible goal of the priesthood or had been fortunate enough to have been sent to metropolitan Portugal by parents or friends.

for advancement became clear, one newspaper fruitlessly urged a "disequality of job entrance" as long as there was "disequality of job opportunity."[32]

It was too late. By the middle of 1913 administrators, secretaries, and clerks of local government in Angola were appointed in Lisbon.[33] Demands were heard for a double standard in pay, since "in the majority of cases the black employee *cannot* in good justice, working alongside whites, receive the same salary," since the needs of colored civil servants were not so many as those of Europeans.[34] More than had been true for the previous two centuries, Angola under the Republic had begun to develop a true colonial situation.

From another direction came other new limits. Earlier concerns with civilizing the African easily gave way to desires to protect him. The 1913 creation in Angola of a special Department of Native Affairs was the final straw that broke the back of African opportunity.

Although Portugal had lagged behind most of Europe in creating a geographical society, since 1875 the Lisbon Society had been in the vanguard of Portuguese concern for Africa. However, whereas matters of geography and exploration had received due attention, anthropological ones were overlooked. Though Portugal had been in Angola for more than four centuries, little was known about the inhabitants there. After becoming convinced that Lisbon would choose to continue in the dark, Norton de Matos issued a provincial order in April 1913, for the creation of the Department of Native Affairs.[35] As head of this department, José de Oliveira Ferreira Dinis became the third most important man in the provincial hierarchy, behind the governor and the secretary general.

The Native Affairs department was to codify indigenous customs, study and improve African institutions, create an indigenous penal code, organize justice, conduct a census, regulate the supply of laborers, begin a child assistance program, and more. As if these tasks were not enough, Norton de Matos relied upon his friend Ferreira Dinis for help in outlining a plan for educational revision sent to Lisbon later in 1913. Key to the plan was that future African schools were to be "more workshops than schools."[36] With the lack of any other competent governmental niche into which to fit the African side of educational thinking, the Native Affairs department

---

[32] *O Eco d'Africa*, July 1, 1914.

[33] *Revista Colonial* (Lisbon), no. 11 (November 1913), p. 31.

[34] *Ibid.*, no. 18 (June 1914), p. 185.

[35] Norton de Matos had requested such a department from the Overseas Ministry more than half a year earlier, but there had been no reply. He thus acted on his own in creating the new department. A year later the overseas minister authorized the department.

[36] José de O. Ferreira Dinis, *Negócios indígenas* (Luanda: Imprensa Nacional, 1914), p. 103.

became an easy repository. As such, Ferreira Dinis might have become Angola's first *de facto* director of education.

Such, however, was not the case. Lack of funds and personnel limited departmental activity. Pressing needs in other areas, specifically in the description and cataloging of tribal customs, captured the attention of the department. Furthermore, Ferreira Dinis himself had only limited interest in formal education. In his view Portugal had a "civilizing mission" in Angola in which major importance rested on collective, rather than on individual, education. It was through such large-scale activities as commercial, agricultural, and industrial contact, gradually improved political and juridical institutions, and improved health conditions that the Portuguese would succeed in their age-old mission.[37] In the process Africans would be passive receivers, patiently awaiting advancement to be provided for them.

Within such an educational philosophy, schools were bound to suffer. Directly instructional individual education was valuable only as a component to more broadly social activities. To Ferreira Dinis, Africans derived from a background of such deep cultural inferiority that there was no reason to provide them with higher culture because it could not be understood, nor could the teaching of the traditional Portuguese primary school be "well assimilated by people without the least trace of literary culture."[38] The only education that was fit for the great mass of Angolan inhabitants was vocational, and that only through the slow and progressive improvements of traditional techniques.

With Ferreira Dinis's thoughts, educational ideas reached a natural conclusion from the impetus of the ideas of Enes and Mousinho. What gave these ideas increased importance was that they were practical. They surely provided the easiest educational policy that an understaffed and underfinanced administration could advocate. Unable and unwilling to extend schooling widely or to draw on any vocational tradition from metropolitan Portugal, Ferreira Dinis could use the existing levels of technology as one needing improvement. Because little was known about this level, however, no plan of improvement could have meaning. To his general desire for a program, he added few actual plans.

The Department of Native Affairs is vital to an understanding of education in Angola under the Republic. By being charged with a concern for all native affairs, this department had *de facto* control of African education. It was not, however, intended to regulate existing government education. Thus, as early as 1913 there existed an administrative division in education —for Europeans and assimilated Africans under the secretary-general of

[37] José de O. Ferreira Dinis, *A missão civilisadora do estado em Angola* (Lisbon: Tipografia Colonial, 1926), pp. 7–8.
[38] *Ibid.*, p. 70.

government, and for the mass of Africans under the secretary for Native Affairs. It was precisely this type of division which António Joaquim de Miranda had attempted to forestall. His vision of a unitary, rather than a bifurcated, system derived from his view of an undivided Angolan society with equality of opportunity. It was a society that fellow Angolans would continue to exhort even in the face of a growing racial backlash, a society with "peace, harmony, and concord among people, without distinction of race, nationality, or religion."[39] Educação do Povo had been an attempt to avoid the oncoming crisis of secondary citizenship by inducing change before a new pattern became established. Events imply that this movement affected few people—neither government, nor African elites, nor even those who became associated with the movement. The protest of António Joaquim de Miranda had been conducted peacefully within a system little responsive to stirrings from below. His waves remained mere ripples on the ocean of Portuguese colonial policy. Though his protest accurately reflected the evolving crises in African opportunity, an unsympathetic government resisted the changes he had desired. His movement was ignored, and he was transferred. The subsequent gradual changes of the Republic followed directions toward which Angola had been headed since the influence of the ideas of Enes and Mousinho. Instead of positive republican ideals, therefore, the new government brought negative changes. In only a few short years, the Republic had made long strides in establishing a colonial foundation in practice which more than a decade later a new government the *Estado Novo*, more in an ex post facto manner than has traditionally been regarded, would codify as a system of *Indigenato*.

Within the context of colonial Africa, Angola was not alone in experiencing a situation such as the Miranda protest. Areas under other European powers also witnessed African movements requesting more or different educational opportunities, but they differed in several ways from the Miranda movement. Elsewhere, the leaders had been educated by Christian missions, they frequently developed their own local schools, they usually put pressure on the missions rather than on the government, and they invariably met with some success. These differences deserve further study. Why was the Angolan protest different? Were missions weaker there? Was the government stronger? Perhaps Angola already had a higher degree of assimilation than elsewhere in Africa. In any event, it is interesting that one observer has noted, "Just at the moment when Africans were beginning to demand better education and more opportunities of sharing in the white man's world, Europeans were becoming less and less ready to give active and confident help in this transition."[40]

39 *O Eco d'Africa*, April 20, 1914.
40 Richard Gray, quoted in T. O. Ranger, "African Attempts to Control Education in East and Central Africa," *Past and Present*, no. 32 (December 1965), p. 67.

Chapter 4 Origins of African Nationalism in Angola: Assimilado Protest Writings, 1859-1929

Douglas L. Wheeler

[This case study concerns a facet of early Angolan resistance as manifested in *assimilado* protest writings. While in the past African resistance had been manifested through armed conflict, late nineteenth-century protest also was embodied in journalistic argumentation. The author notes that from the frustration of the *assimilado* grew the sociopolitical alienation that would transform into an Angolan nationalism. The content of *assimilado* nationalism is examined through four examples of protest over two generations: the journalism of José de Fontes Pereira (1823–1891); a book, *Voz d'Angola clamando no deserto*, published in Lisbon in 1901; the protest volumes of António de Assís Júnior, 1917–1918; and articles from the colonial and national press in the 1920s. A major conclusion is that many of the fundamental assumptions of Angolan *assimilado* nationalism were Portuguese, not African, in character, and that loyalty to Portugal was an aspect of Angolan self-assertion and nationalism. This tradition of protest was carried on by a rebellious, post-1948 elite which absorbed outside ideological influences not present in previous generations, and this led to the eventual break of *assimilado* intellectuals with Portugal.]

THE PROBLEM OF NATIONALISM IN ANGOLA

While there were a number of European autonomy and independence movements in Angola before the middle of the nineteenth century,[1] there

[1] There were several European movements and conspiracies in Luanda and Benguela in the 1820s and 1830s, including the Confederação Brazilica of 1822–1823, which proposed that Angola join newly independent Brazil in a union, or that Angola break with Portugal over the issue of the abolition of slave trade. See Carlos Selvagem and Henrique Galvão, *O império ultramarino português* (3 vols.; Lisbon, 1953), III, 95.

was not true "nationalism" among native-born Angolans until that period. In the context of local conditions in Angola, "nationalism" can be defined as a *modern* expression (using European techniques) of a "collective griev-ance against foreigners."[2] The traditional form of African resistance and protest against Portuguese rule in Angola was armed violence, repeated on countless occasions over a period of three hundred or more years. This pat-tern of "traditional resistance," or "primary resistance," [3] was not "nation-alism" as such but tribal reaction to conditions in one locality. In line with Minogue's thesis regarding Angolan nationalism, it should not be assumed that "any form of political group-consciousness which takes an aggressive form" is nationalism.[4] The form such expressions take must be *both* aggres-sive and *modern*. In Angola, therefore, nationalism begins to develop when Angolans express their protests and resistance by using European tech-niques and by believing that "Angolans" or "sons of the country" have col-lective problems, grievances, and a "nationality" which transcend local identities.

It is true that a kind of "micronationalism" existed in the Kongo king-dom before the beginning of Angolan nationalism. Letters of protest against the Portuguese slavers of São Tomé written by several kings of Kongo be-ginning in the seventeenth century may well represent a kind of "national" expression. But in the mid-nineteenth century we find better examples of Kongo micronationalism in the activities of two Westernized Kongo princes, Aleixo (Alexus) and Nicolau (Nicolas) of Agua Rosada e Sardó-nia.[5]

Prince Alexus was a brother of King Henry II of Kongo (1842–1857) and was in fact an *assimilado*. He became a "rebel" not in the Kongo king-dom itself but in Dembos territory, when, in 1841, he stirred a major chief there to refuse to pay a new Portuguese tax. Alexus was captured and im-prisoned by the Portuguese authorities between 1842 and 1856. The Ger-man traveler, Georg Tams, visited Alexus in prison about 1845 and was told in good Portuguese, in Tams's words:

the Queen of Portugal [Maria II, 1834–1853] was not his rightful Queen . . . ; that she had no direct right to rule his country, . . . because this prerogative be-longed only to him and to his brother, the King of Congo.[6]

[2] K. R. Minogue, *Nationalism* (New York: Basic Books, 1967), p. 29.

[3] The term of Terence Ranger, used in his "Dr. Rotberg's Africa," *Journal of African History*, VIII, no. 1 (1967), 170. (Ed. note: The reader should see Ranger's "Connections between 'Primary Resistance' Movements and Modern Mass Nationalism in East and Central Africa," *Journal of African History*, Part I in IX, no. 3 [1968], 437–453 and Part II in IX, no. 4 [1968], 631–641).

[4] Minogue, *op. cit.*, p. 153.

[5] See my article, "A Nineteenth Century African Protest in Angola: Prince Nicolas of Kongo," *African Historical Studies*, I, no. 1 (1968), 40–59.

[6] Georg Tams, *Visita ás possessões portuguezas na costa occidental d'Africa* (2 vols.; Oporto, 1850), II, 17–19.

A younger relative and fellow "rebel" was Prince Nicolas, a son of King Henry II. Nicolas was an *assimilado* who had been educated in Lisbon and Luanda and who joined the civil service in Angola. Reacting against Portuguese attempts to subjugate the Kongo kingdom, Nicolas wrote three protest letters, including letters to the King of Portugal and to the Emperor of Brazil. In one letter, published in a Portuguese daily newspaper in 1859, Nicolas asserted that the Kongo kingdom had a fully independent status vis-à-vis Portuguese Angola and that he, as an educated member of royalty, was responsible for protecting the kingdom against Portuguese abuses.[7]

To some extent, therefore, both Alexus and Nicolas deviated from earlier forms of protest by native-born Angolans. Yet they were essentially traditional leaders who simply happened to be *assimilados*, for they applied their learning to help only the Kongo kingdom, as yet not integrated or absorbed into Angola. Resistance by Bakongo leaders continued along traditional lines but the activities of the "rebel" Princes seem to have had little impact upon the minds of the budding Angolan nationalists in Luanda. Although Nicolas was to some extent influenced by a movement for independence about 1860, his example was not directly connected to later protest activities in Angola.[8]

If Alexus and Nicolas were only precursors to the later nationalists, excepting perhaps Nicolas's remarkable protest letter published in 1859, their circumstances were similar to those of their successors among the *assimilado* population. The *assimilado* was the first nationalist in Angola, for he was the first native-born Angolan to conceive of Angola as a "nation" and to call for reform using the ideologies and techniques of Western civilization.

THE FIRST PHASE OF ANGOLAN NATIONALISM, 1860–1930

A study of Angolan history suggests that so far there have been three major phases of Angolan nationalism: "stirrings," 1860–1930; "struggle in Angola," 1930–1961; "struggle from exile and insurgency," 1961 to the present. Angolan nationalism has not yet reached what might be called the "consolidation" phase of its course.[9] There follows a brief survey of the first phase of Angolan nationalism, 1860–1930, as background for a study of only one of the activities of this phase: protest writings.

Several misconceptions about the first phase of Angolan nationalism should be discussed at the outset. Material that has recently been found in unpublished documents and in pre–1930 Angolan newspapers and gaz-

---

[7] The letter was published on December 1, 1859, in the Lisbon daily, *Jornal do Commercio.*

[8] Alfredo de Sarmento, *Os sertões d'Africa* (Lisbon, 1880), pp. 66–68.

[9] See Minogue, *Nationalism*, pp. 29, 153.

ettes reveals nationalist activity well before 1923, the first date usually mentioned in connection with the Pan-African Congress in Lisbon and with the Liga Africana.[10] Furthermore, it is too often assumed that Angolan nationalism was united and homogeneous in its early phases and became fragmented only after the 1950s. New materials also suggest some revision of the concept that "emergent nationalism [is] an extension of earlier tribal resistance to Portuguese rule." [11] There is increasing evidence, moreover, to suggest that Angolan nationalism began more as an *assimilado* movement than as an African movement.

Although there was an obscure and abortive movement of liberal Portuguese, expatriate Brazilians, and *assimilados* in several Angolan towns about 1859–1860 which proposed that Angola be declared an independent republic under Brazil or the United States,[12] the most serious part of the first phase of the period of "stirrings" was the protest by a number of educated *mestiço* and African *assimilados* in the Luanda press beginning in the 1870s. A Portuguese scholar claims that the "intellectual movement" in Angola originated with Luanda journalism in the nineteenth century; [13] the same might be said of Angolan nationalism. In this same expert's words, the era of the "free press," 1867–1922, was marked by a Portuguese official policy of only ephemeral censorship and by a more flexible approach to protest.[14] Yet under the so-called liberal monarchy during the reigns of King Luís I and King Carlos I and under the first Republic (1910–1926), authorities did occasionally silence the Angolan press, jail editors, and deport journalists. Compared with the post–1926 policy, however, the era of 1867–1922 was indeed a "free press" phase, when the beginning protests of Angolan *assimilados* were published and read by the public.

Who were the men in the first phase of Angolan nationalism, and what were their origins? Some were African, with no Portuguese ancestry, but the majority of them in the early phase were probably *mestiços*, many with Portuguese fathers and African mothers. Most were born in Luanda or its hinterland or in towns like Ambaca, Massangano, Iccolo e Bengo, and

[10] See James Duffy, *Portuguese Africa* (Cambridge, Mass.: Harvard University Press, 1959), pp. 305 and 374 n; and Patricia M. Pinheiro, "Politics of a Revolt," in *Angola: A Symposium; Views of a Revolt*, ed. by Philip Mason (New York: Oxford University Press, 1962), pp. 106–107.

[11] Ronald H. Chilcote, *Portuguese Africa* (Englewood Cliffs, N. J.: Prentice-Hall, 1967), p. 127; see also pp. 74–76 and 125.

[12] See Sarmento, *op. cit.*, p. 67, and Governor-General Coêlho do Amaral document to Lisbon, March 9, 1860, Codice A-15-3 (Angola), Arquivo Histórico de Angola (Luanda).

[13] Júlio de Castro Lopo, "Subsídios para a história do jornalismo de Angola," reprint from *Arquivos de Angola* (Luanda: Edições do Museu do Angola, 1952).

[14] Júlio de Castro Lopo, *Jornalismo de Angola: subsídios para a sua história* (Luanda, 1964), p. 19.

Malange. It is clear that although European stimuli aided the beginnings of the movement, the ideas of Angolan-born *assimilados* formed the crucial part of the movement.

The occupations of the early nationalists were varied. Most of them were probably employed at one time or another in the Portuguese colonial civil service as clerks, aides, assistants, and lawyers. Most of them completed at least several years of primary schooling in Angola, and a few were able to continue their education in Lisbon. The majority of them, however, were largely self-educated men who mastered the techniques of reading and writing Portuguese and learned a great deal from resident Europeans, some of whom were political exiles from Portugal. Luanda (and to a lesser extent Benguela) was the crucible of Angolan nationalism, for there were located the major schools, churches, and social groupings that produced political activities. Until communications improved and the foreign missionaries established themselves in the hinterland after 1880, Luanda monopolized such activities.[15]

There was a certain interdependence between European movements for Angolan autonomy and independence from Portugal and early African naationalism. Europeans initiated the Angolan press in a private capacity in the late 1860s, thus providing a ready forum for African grievances. European cries for reform and autonomy certainly inspired Angolan nationalists in their cause, but it is not yet clear just how dependent on European agitation the *assimilados* were. Nevertheless, the *assimilado* protest was, to a great extent, beholden to European benefactors, who financed its presses and newspapers and who paved the way in fighting for Angolan autonomy. The European ideology of republicanism lent a useful vehicle to discontented Angolans who sought reform from a decaying monarchy. Many *assimilados* and their European friends were ecstatic when the Republic was declared in Lisbon in 1910; Luanda celebrated the news because it was thought that a Republic would mean autonomy for the territory.[16] A logical consequence seemed to be more rights for the native-born Angolans.

In the early phase, reform and autonomy were more common demands of Angolan *assimilados* than was complete independence from Portugal. The idea of independence was much discussed at various times, but only rarely did it gain the support of more than a handful of European and radi-

[15] Rivalry has long existed between the capital, Luanda, and the town of Benguela to the south. Like the rivalry and enmity felt between Lisbon and Oporto in Portugal, this Angolan version fed on the disparity of resources between the two towns and on the feeling of citizens of the smaller town that Luanda neglected the interests of Benguela. Separatist feelings developed as a result.

[16] See the Luanda weekly newspaper, *Voz de Angola*, for October 8, 1910. The headline announcing this news was probably the largest yet seen in the Angolan press, one inch high and at least thirteen inches across.

cal *assimilados*. Redress of grievances was a more common form of protest at first. Indeed, a broad humanitarianism characterized the leaders of the various protest movements.

The humanitarianism behind the reform ideas was in part inspired by religion. A number of the early Angolan nationalists were liberal priests and canons, trained in Portugal or in Luanda. Some were African priests trained in the Catholic Seminary of Luanda, founded in 1861.[17] One distinguishing mark of the early phase of Angolan nationalism was that it was more Catholic in character than were the later phases. The coming of Protestant foreign missions, therefore, did not mean the beginning of a religiously inspired humanitarian feeling among Angolans: such a feeling existed before the founding of the first Protestant mission in 1878. But the arrival of the Protestant missions in Angola did signify an increase of humanitarian protest and political conflict which would soon play their roles in Angolan nationalism. Several Angolan protesters immediately published their feelings of admiration for the new foreign Protestant work. For their part, the Portuguese were fully aware of the potentially "subversive" nature of the new missionaries, and they expressed their doubts from the beginning.[18]

There were three general means of modern protest and resistance in the first phase of nationalism: journalism, associations, and government. The journalism was confined at first to the Luanda press, but after 1880 newspapers were established in other towns. The first anti–*status quo* paper was the pro-republican weekly, *O Cruzeiro do Sul* of Luanda, which began publication in 1873. It initiated a radical, dissenting tradition in the free press era and combatted the more conservative, more Europe-oriented papers supported by European settlers. The *Cruzeiro* was succeeded by a host of short-lived, controversial sheets, some of them employing African writers. Although the European-owned and -edited press dominated the free press era, a small and persistent African, or native, press began publication in 1881 with *O Echo d'Angola* and continued into the 1920s.[19]

Another forum for Angolan grievances was the associations. Here again, European precursors were important catalysts. The earliest associations of a private nature were commercial groups such as the Associação Commercial de Loanda, founded in 1863,[20] or the commercially and scientifically inspired Luanda branch of the Sociedade de Geographia de Lisboa (1881). Although at first these groups were almost exclusively Portuguese, some Africans joined them later. Other associations of signficance were the Euro-

---

17 Manuel Alves da Cunha, *Missões católicas de Angola* (Luanda, 1935), pp. 7–10.
18 See the article on missionaries by J. Fontes Pereira in *O Futuro d'Angola* (Luanda), May 13, 1882; and the *Gazeta de Angola*, October 25, 1881.
19 Castro Lopo, *op. cit.*, p. 75.
20 For the founding of the Associação Commercial de Loanda, see *O Commercio de Loanda* (Luanda), September 18, 1867.

pean, and later *mestiço* and African, social clubs established in Luanda beginning in the early 1870s.[21] An early organization with African membership was the Filharmônica Africana, a music society with African voices and European instruments, founded in 1889 in Luanda.[22]

No organization or association of native-born Angolans with political interest was established in Angola until the twentieth century. The lawyer and writer Fontes Pereira proposed the formation of an association of the "sons of the country" to discuss Angolan "nationality" and grievances in 1882.[23] A colleague, Carlos da Silva, another *mestiço*, proposed a similar association or league in 1889 to protect Angolans' interests.[24] But no such association materialized until the earliest African association, the Liga Ultramarina, was founded in Lisbon in 1910.[25] The following year the Liga Colonial came into being,[26] and in 1912 the first Angolan association, the Liga Angolana, was founded in Luanda by *mestiço assimilados*.[27] The Lisbon associations of Africans resident in Portugal were essentially moderate, pan-Portuguese African groups fighting for greater colonial autonomy and an end to racial strife. They established branches of their organizations in Angola and several other territories.

Perhaps a dozen parties and political groupings with Angolan membership were established between 1910 and 1922, the year various Angolan associations, including the original Liga Angolana, were proscribed by High Commissioner Norton de Matos. These groups, along with their European counterparts in Lisbon and Luanda, were able to function in comparative freedom under the first Republic up to 1926, although their freedom was dependent also on the policy of the respective governors-general and upon Portuguese law.[28]

One of the more important early African parties was the Partido Nacional Africano (PNA), founded in Lisbon in 1921 and active until 1931. Influenced by the League of Nations as well as by pan-Africanism, the group issued petitions on key issues, such as the question of labor for São Tomé.[29]

---

21 For the early social clubs see Oscar Ribas, *Izomba* (Luanda, 1965), pp. 27–39; and Manuel da Costa Lobo, *Subsídios para a história de Luanda* (Lisbon, Edition of the Author, 1967), pp. 198–199.

22 *O Mercantil* (Luanda), September 1, 1889.

23 *O Futuro d'Angola*, May 13, 1882.

24 *O Arauto Africano* (Luanda), March 17, 1889.

25 *A Reforma* (Luanda), June 10, 1911.

26 *A Reforma*, March 25, 1911.

27 *Boletim Official* (Luanda), March 8, 1913; *Independente* (Luanda), June 30, 1919; and information obtained from interviews with several members of the *assimilado* associations in November 1966, by the author.

28 A law of 1895 ordered that all associations register with the government of Angola.

29 "A nossa orientaçao," *A Voz d'Africa* (Lisbon issue), July 8, 1929, declared that the PNA sent delegates to the League of Nations' International Labor Organization.

Like many other groups in this period, the PNA was moderate, reformist, and *assimilado* in outlook. Not working for independence for Portuguese African territories, it instead sought racial and cultural accomodation with Portugal. Along with the Angolan-based associations founded after 1910, the PNA criticized the abuses of slavery, continuing forced labor, poor economic conditions, and a lack of educational opportunities in the territory. While these issues were common focuses for complaint and agitation through petition, the deeper issues continued to be racial discrimination in the civil service and jobs, racial hatred, and the character of Portuguese colonization. While the Liga Angolana proclaimed itself to be "representative of the native peoples" of Angola, the PNA was representative of Africans all over Portuguese Africa.[30]

Associations as a forum for nationalism became less effective as the government came to restrict their activities and leaders. The years 1922 to 1930 form a watershed in the history of these fledgling associations: the government banned them, closed down the African press, and arrested and deported many *assimilado* leaders. First High Commissioner Norton de Matos in 1922 and then the *Estado Novo* regime of 1926 reacted to what they considered a threat from the "nativist movement" in Angola,[31] and the tradition of two generations of Angolan dissent was emasculated. Several groups emerged from their banning, renamed their organizations, and continued functioning but under greater governmental control and scrutiny. The Liga Angolana, refounded as the Liga Nacional Africana in 1929 but officially approved by the Governor-General only in 1930,[32] endured as a less militant group of moderate *mestiços* and Africans with social and educational goals. The identification of these groups with the interests of Angola and Angolans in political terms had been effectively limited by official pressures.[33]

The third forum for early Angolan nationalism was the government. A number of prominent *assimilados* played important roles in the judicial branch of the government in Angola and tried cases involving political and racial issues.[34] Others became candidates for deputy from Angola to the Portuguese Cortes and participated in elections. Some *mestiço* Angolans were nominated and elected to important secondary positions, including

---

[30] *A Voz d'Africa* (Oporto issue), October 18, 1928.

[31] *Ibid.* See the partially censored article, "Instrução! Instrução!"

[32] *Boletim Official* (Luanda), series 2, no. 29, July 19, 1930.

[33] It is true, however, that in some ways the LNA continued to pressure Portugal for reforms.

[34] In addition to Fontes Pereira and Assís Júnior, both lawyers, there was Eusébio de Lemos Pinheiro Falcão (1818–1851), the Luanda-born lawyer and *mestiço* abolitionist. See the anonymous book, *Voz d'Angola clamando no deserto: offerecida aos amigos da verdade pelos naturaes* (Lisbon, 1901), p. 191.

the office of the secretary-general, in the provincial government. A few became army officers and others were elected as presidents of the Camara Municipal.[35] In general, however, this forum was much less effective than journalism or even associations, since the highest positions were invariably held by Europeans. Moreover, elections to the Cortes were often rigged, and representative government retained an odious reputation. In general, Angolan nationalists preferred the press as a reforming instrument and tended to exaggerate its powers as a "civilizing" element in society.

Although a few African associations and newspapers limped along after 1930—and the Liga Nacional Africana did achieve certain minor reforms through lobbying in Angola[36]—Angolan nationalism underwent a change in personnel, techniques, and goals. Official government suppression had effectively influenced the course of nationalism. An opportunity for significant free expression by Westernized Africans was lost after 1922. Legitimate political activity was much more difficult, and as a consequence underground organization became more common. (Clandestine organizations with secret presses became the rule after World War II.) A final blow was the wave of deportations that occurred between 1928 and 1930. It was in these years that Angolans lost most of their political leaders through deportation to other Portuguese territories, including faraway Timor.

Perhaps the closest Angolan society came to revolution in terms of political and social change was between 1900 and 1922, when "autonomy" was in the air, when an African press operated, and when *assimilados* constituted a much larger percentage of the urban population of Angola than they would in the later years. After 1880, Portuguese emigration to Angola began to increase significantly, and the *assimilado* felt the impact more than any other native-born group. A regeneration of Portuguese expansion and colonization, especially in the towns, brought new pressures to what was still an Africanized society.[37] Part of the impetus behind the first phase of Angolan nationalism, therefore, was the resentment and fear produced by the new European competition and usurpation of positions in the towns. Indeed, some of the ferment of the 1920s came from *assimilado* resistance to the destruction of what rights and autonomy they had already achieved.

SELECTED PROTEST WRITINGS, 1873–1929

Four examples of Angolan protest writings have been selected and will

[35] For an account of the names and positions of Africans in the Angolan administration between 1880 and 1900, see *ibid.*, pp. 55–56.

[36] The Liga Nacional Africana claims to have improved the position of the African in the civil service and army and education in Angola. In the LNA organ, see "Figuras Angolanas: Francisco Alves Fernandes," *Angola*, no. 166 (January-June 1963), p. 6.

[37] For complaints that Africans held more skilled jobs in the early nineteenth century in Angola, see *O Futuro d'Angola*, May 13, 1882.

be presented in chronological order. Though the styles vary, the grievances and themes presented in two generations of written protest are remarkably alike.

THE JOURNALISM OF JOSÉ DE FONTES PEREIRA (1823–1891)

Fontes Pereira was a lawyer by profession, a *mestiço assimilado* who made his mark as a radical journalist between 1873 and 1890. A devout Roman Catholic and a republican, Fontes Pereira began his writing career in 1873 with *O Cruzeiro do Sul* in Luanda and soon gained a reputation as the *enfant terrible* of the press. During his career he wrote articles for at least eight weekly papers in Luanda and perhaps four metropolitan journals in Lisbon as well.[38] For his spirited attacks on governors-general and on Portuguese character and policies, he suffered social ostracism, attacks in the local press, the loss of his position in the civil service on two occasions, and threats against his life.[39] His articles covered many subjects, including the political history of Angola, social humanitarian criticism, political reformism, and the assertion of African rights. He attacked the widespread practices of forced labor, slavery, the shipment of coerced African workers to the island of São Tomé, the low status of Angolan citizens of all colors in competition with the more privileged metropolitan Portuguese, lack of schools, the wretched conditions of local prisons, and many other problems.

All of the major themes of Fontes Pereira's writings were repeated and elaborated upon in later Angolan publications. One major theme was that a lack of education in Angola was contrived, not simply the result of Portuguese poverty and weakness. This was a case of "false civilization," a concept developed further by African writers in a 1901 publication discussed below. The Portuguese, Fontes Pereira wrote in 1886, did not encourage education because "they understand that the son of Angola who learns his brutal customs will be able to proclaim the independence of his country."[40]

Commanding the techniques of sarcasm and innuendo, this *mestiço* writer attacked the corruption, inefficiency, and chicanery he observed in Angola. Despite his outrage at a society afflicted by what one governor-general aptly termed "the moral deficit," Fontes Pereira was a Portuguese in culture. In some of his political activities, especially in the early phase of his career, he advocated Portuguese expansion and pacification of Angolan territory. In the same article he could praise the efficiency of Henry

[38] See *O Futuro d'Angola*, May 16, 1891, for his obituary. Other obituaries appeared in *O Mercantil*, May 7, 1891, and *O Desastre*, May 30, 1891.
[39] *O Cruzeiro do Sul*, August 27, September 27, December 30, 1875; February 26, 1876.
[40] *O Futuro d'Angola*, November 10, 1886.

Morton Stanley and French missionaries and also deplore the fact that Portugal had failed to extend her rule over the Congo coast or to pacify the unruly Dembos territory.[41] Although he attacked Portuguese rule in the 1870s and early 1880s, he remained essentially loyal as an *assimilado* until about 1882 or 1883, when he became discouraged with Portugal as a likely means of "civilizing" reform and eventual independence for native Angolans. At this time he began to advocate Angolan independence from Portugal. By 1890 he was so bitter and desperate that he was willing to exchange colonial masters and replace Portugal with Great Britain.

Fontes Pereira was convinced that Angolans had lost their "nationality" through the pressures of Portuguese rule. On one occasion he wondered why Angolans had to celebrate an anniversary of Portugal's freedom from Spain in 1640 while Angolans had lost their own lands and independence one hundred years before.[42]

Frustrated as an office-seeker, snubbed by better-educated and prejudiced Europeans, and persecuted as a radical, he stepped up his personal campaign against Portuguese rule. In articles written early in 1890, he openly advocated Angolan support for Britain in the colonial dispute over African territory and suggested that Britain take over Angola. These controversial articles stirred up a hornet's nest in Luanda. Fontes Pereira was prosecuted by the government, lost his job, and probably wrote no more after this incident. He died within sixteen months of the publication of these unusual articles. His most fiery editorial—considered treasonous by the Portuguese—is worth quoting at some length:

One does not wonder that foreigners, understanding all this [Portuguese weaknesses] would try to take over Portuguese lands which are still preserved in a state of nature, or that they would take advantage of them as potential wealth in order to exploit them and to civilize the natives, making them useful citizens for them and for the rest of humanity. For our part, we would advise these foreigners not to waste time discussing in Europe matters which would benefit them in Africa; it is necessary for them only to address themselves to Africa's inhabitants, the natural lords that they are of their own lands, and make with them all the necessary treaties of commerce and reciprocal protection. If they do this, they will be received with open arms for it has been proven that we have nothing to expect from Portugal except the swindles and shackles of slavery, the only means she has in order better to brutalize and subjugate the natives! And with this conclusion, we declare that we trust neither in the good faith nor in the sincerity of the Portuguese Colonial Party, whose members are only crocodiles crying in order to lure their victims. We know them only too well. Out with them!![43]

---

[41] *O Futuro d'Angola*, April 15, 1882. See also *O Ultramar*, August 1, 1882.
[42] *O Arauto Africano*, January 6, 1890.
[43] From *O Arauto Africano*, January 20, 1890.

Fontes Pereira was the most radical of the early Angolan nationalists. In his spirit and criticism he was ahead of his time. Among his own circle of *assimilados*, he was in a minority as one who finally rejected Portuguese rule, but he inspired more moderate *assimilados* in his championship of the rights of Angola and Angolans. His name and reputation lived on.[44]

Voz D'Angola Clamando No Deserto

In a book published in Lisbon eleven years after the final editorial blast of Fontes Pereira, another bitter *assimilado* reaction to racial problems in Angola emerged. The book (*Voz d'Angola clamando no deserto* [Lisbon, 1901]) was composed of many articles published in the Luanda press between 1889 and 1901. The authors were mainly *assimilados* (such as the *mestiço* writer A. J. do Nascimento) but also included the liberal European editor, Francisco Pinheiro Bayão.[45] The articles reflected the authors' concern with increasing racism in Angola; they attacked particularly the verbal assaults on African character and rights that appeared in the European-run newspaper, *Gazeta de Loanda*.

This bitter tract developed the concept of the "false civilizers," especially those Portuguese settlers with little education and economic motives. "Social progress," the authors agreed, had been stopped by racial hatreds and discriminations in the last decade. While the government, at least in theory, proclaimed equality for all races, "something else" took place in the social clubs of Luanda, where *assimilados* were rejected and forbidden.[46] This racial discrimination, the authors stated, thwarted all the "Christian maxims and the fundamental law of the state."[47]

The very provocative title, *The Voice of Angola Crying in the Wilderness*, suggests the isolation of the *assimilado*, as well as the courage of Angolans' dissent in a sensitive community. The authors sought reforms in education as a key to progress, reflecting a pattern in *assimilado* writings: education meant "civilization," and "civilization" was a value they identified with. However, as the *assimilado* authors observed in Angola, Portuguese "civilization" did not meet the much-heralded standards claimed by

[44] There is a reference to the memory of Fontes Pereira as a defender of Angolans' rights in *Voz d'Angola*, and he was commemorated in the name of a *mestiço* social club in Luanda in the 1920s, *Voz d'Angola clamando no deserto*, p. 77. See Ribas, *op. cit.*, pp. 38–39.

[45] Angolan nationalist leader Mário de Andrade recalled one "Nascimento" as "polemicist and distinguished collaborator" in the *Voz d'Angola*, when he submitted a list of biographical subjects to the *Encyclopaedia Africana* (Accra, Ghana). See *Information Report No. 12*, September 1965, p. 5.

[46] *Voz d'Angola*, p. 23.

[47] *Ibid.*, pp. 24–25.

the Portuguese to be typical of their work in Africa. *Voz d'Angola* describes not civilization but a society of "exploitation"—perhaps the first Angolan writing to employ this word so frequently.[48]

The following passage gives an economic interpretation of Portuguese rule in Angola:

Who does not know that the black, even the most uncivilized, is an indispensable element and is irreplaceable in certain localities where European settlement is impossible? Who can ignore the fact that without the work of the black no ship could leave port here with its cargo? . . . If the black is as yet uneducated . . . it is because he is an instrument acquired for barbarous labor.[49]

The general tone of defensive outrage only occasionally turned to counterattack. When it did, the authors expressed the feeling that Angola was a collective unit. Angola, they wrote, was "the land of the black man," not of the Portuguese, and the "emancipation" of Angola was "inevitable" despite Portuguese policy.[50]

Carrying on the tradition of writers like Fontes Pereira, the authors of *Voz d'Angola* showed how discouraged they were with the possibility of improvement in Portuguese rule. Portuguese control was unfortunate, not because the Portuguese were spreading civilization but precisely because they were not practicing what they preached:

Portugal having conquered this colony over 400 years ago, has done nothing for the progress of the country, neither in matters material, literary, or moral. The people are brutalized, as in their former primitive state. . . . This is a crime of outrage against civilization, leaving this very rich colony stagnant. . . . Only the negligence of its rulers explains this state of affairs . . .[51]

This passage, which illustrates a theme commonly found in Fontes Pereira's writings, demonstrates how the bitter feelings of the authors caused them to exaggerate conditions and to oversimplify causes. This exaggeration, however, is rather typical of the Angolan press of the tropics: *assimilado* writers exhibited the same weaknesses as their European teachers. Although these *assimilados* tended to accept European assumptions about Angola (such as the fabled wealth of the country), they produced an African definition of what "civilization" meant. Indeed, one writer defined civilization as being synonomous with "sacking, devastating, selling, torturing, killing . . . ." [52] This same writer continued to criticize what Africans had

[48] *Ibid.*, pp. 5–6, 90, 197, 174–175, *et passim.*
[49] *Ibid.*, p. 29.
[50] *Ibid.*, p. 68.
[51] *Ibid.*, p. 88.
[52] *Ibid.*, p. 90.

learned from Portuguese civilization and pointed out that the African was brought up "in an authoritarian and violent way of life."[53]

In this bitter polemic, this classic in Angolan protest literature, there is a definite tendency for the *assimilado* writer to sympathize with and identify with the tribal Africans in Angola. More than in the writings of Fontes Pereira, the *preto boçal* is praised as a kind of "noble savage." While the Portuguese is "vicious, criminal, and bloody," the black is the incarnation of "simplicity, submission, and tranquility."[54] This idealized portrait, however, does not fit the description by one author, who claimed that some Africans preferred prison to forced labor in Angola, "for the preservation of their personality."[55]

All in all, *Voz d'Angola* is a remarkable testament to Angolan self-assertion. The *assimilado* bold enough to write protest quite naturally called forth the memory of the dissenting *assimilados* of the previous decades; even the Portuguese liberal statesman and defender of Africans' rights, the Marquis of Sá da Bandeira, was cited in this book for his defense of Negro character. According to one author, the Marquis would "emerge from his grave"[56] to attack the "whites of the lowest type" who had so angered Angolan *assimilados* that they produced this cooperative protest book, surely one of the most desperate pieces of anti-European and pro-African literature in nationalist achives.

THE PROTEST VOLUMES OF ANTÓNIO DE ASSÍS JÚNIOR, 1917–1918

Assís Júnior's two-volume tract, *Relato dos acontecimentos de Dala, Tande, e Lucala*,[57] is more than one *assimilado's* reaction to a government suppression of a rumored "nativist conspiracy" in 1917. It is also a defensive, bitter assertion of African dignity and rights. The background of this suppression was continued traditional, tribal resistance by peoples in various regions of Angola. For Portuguese rulers, the years of World War I were particularly fear-ridden and turbulent. There were notable revolts in Kongo, 1913–1915; Cuanhama (in the extreme south of Angola), 1914–1916; Dembos, 1916–1917; in Amboim and Seles in 1917; and in other areas. Besides dispatching reinforcements from Europe and expeditions to the hinterlands to pacify the tribes, the Portuguese arrested and imprisoned a group of *assimilados* rumored to have been plotting a general uprising to end Portuguese rule. Various pieces of information, some of them rumors,

[53] *Ibid.*, pp. 97–98.
[54] *Ibid.*, p. 40.
[55] *Ibid.*, p. 20.
[56] *Ibid.*, pp. 41–42. During his public career as a statesman, Sá da Bandeira was instrumental in introducing antislave trade and antislavery laws into the Portuguese Cortes, especially between 1836 and 1858.
[57] António de Assís Júnior, *Relato dos acontecimentos de Dala, Tande, e Lucala* (2 vols.; Luanda: Typografia Mamã Tita, 1917–1918).

were received by authorities in Luanda: the march of some forty repat-
riated *serviçães* from São Tomé, armed with *catanas*, threatened a European farmer in Dala-Tando (presently named Salazar, Cuanza Norte
district); the murder of a European clerk by Africans; the discovery of
hidden arms and dynamite; and the rumored activities of the Liga Angolana
(dubbed "Associação de Mata-branco" in local settlement parlance).[58] In
what Assís Júnior aptly described as an "ignoble tragi-comedy," the Portuguese authorities mistook rumor for fact, and in July and August 1917
they arrested dozens of *assimilados* and threw them into Luanda prisons
without trial. Some were imprisoned for five months and longer. Rumors
along these same lines ran riot in Malanje, Benguela, and Lucala, as fear
pervaded the small settler communities. In retaliation, some African villages
were burned. The official wave of arrests involved Assís Júnior, who, as
he himself wrote, composed his works while in prison.[59]

António de Assís Júnior (1878–1960) was an African, perhaps with some
European ancestry. At an early age he entered the competitive civil service
in Luanda and moved to higher positions. Trained in law, he was also a
journalist and novelist. His most important contribution to the dissenting
tradition of Angolan nationalism was not his novel on Angolan life but his
two short volumes published in 1917 and 1918 in Luanda by an obscure
press.[60] His analysis of the "strictly repugnant" affair of 1917–1918 is
shrewd and cogent. Like the *assimilado* writers of the selections quoted
above, Assís Júnior noted a "bloodlust" among Portuguese settlers which
was vented periodically on *assimilados* and on Africans with the discovery
of every "plot." The rumored conspiracy of 1917 was only one of a series
of such incidents which suggested to Assís Júnior an analysis of the nature
of European society, composed as it was of time-servers, army deserters,
degredados ("convicts"), and exiles.

Still composed mainly of men who do not know from whence they came nor
where they are going, men motivated simply by the desire to get all they can, to
acquire and grab, our society is extremely sick. . . . In his own land, the native
is no more than a jew [sic] and at that, a jew [sic] as he was treated in the time of
religious fanaticism.[61]

The volumes of this astute *assimilado* are especially valuable to the historian, for they portray the stresses and strains of being an *assimilado*, a
"marginal man," as it were. Like other *assimilados*, Assís Júnior aspired to
a higher position in Portuguese society in Angola, but he found his way

[58] *Ibid.*, II, 29n.
[59] *Ibid.*, I, 1–2.
[60] Assís Júnior published a novel depicting life in Angola, *O segredo da morta*
(Luanda, 1934).
[61] Assís Júnior, *Relato*, II, 55.

blocked. And below him, the uneducated African hindered racial unity, rejecting the "civilized" African, who "thus sees himself caught between two fires." [62]

Despite these obstacles to racial unity and harmony in Angola, Assís Júnior had hopes of future understanding. He believed, at least at this time, that the African could be both "Angolan and Portuguese," [63] a concept that attracted a great deal of debate when he wrote it and afterward. He hoped to be able to work for unity and for the end of what he observed around him in Angola: "petty persecutions and cowardly violences of the strong against the weak." [64] His criticism of the nature of Portuguese repression of African self-assertion—a repression pictured in Portuguese African colonial literature as the true function of celebrated pantheons of "Heroes of Africa"—gives an African perspective on European pacification in much of tropical Africa. His two volumes are sprinkled with biting aphorisms, such as "The black never can be right," [65] or "In order to have heroes, one must have victims . . . ." [66]

This remarkable writer ended his days far from his native Angola. Sometime after 1920, he went to Lisbon, where he taught the Kimbundu language in several schools.[67] His days of active protest were over. Whether or not he went completely over to the enemy in his later years, at least he played the role of a professional *assimilado* nominally loyal to Portugal at a time when systematic repression of Angolan nationalism was well entrenched. He died in 1960.

ARTICLES FROM THE COLONIAL AND NATIONALIST PRESS, 1920s

In 1921 a number of *assimilados* from several parts of the Portuguese African empire formed the Partido Nacional Africano (PNA). This party's precursor was the better-known Liga Africana, founded in 1919 as a federation of Portuguese African parties.[68] The PNA was formed in part as a rival organization; while the Liga Africana supported the pan-Africanism of Dr. W. E. B. DuBois, the PNA tended to support the ideas of Marcus Garvey. The conflict between the two organizations ended only in 1931, when an umbrella organization, the Movimento Nacionalista Africano, was founded. The Liga Africana played a key role in hosting the Lisbon session of the Pan-African Congress of 1923, and it is clear that in general its goals

[62] *Ibid.,* pp. 55–56.
[63] *Ibid.,* p. 65.
[64] *Ibid.,* p. 57.
[65] *Ibid.,* I, 36.
[66] *Ibid.*
[67] Assís Júnior published a Kimbundu-Portuguese dictionary in Luanda in the 1940s.
[68] For material on the rivalry between these organizations, see Eduardo Dos Santos, *Ideologias políticas africanas* (Lisbon, 1967), pp. 61–70.

were similar to those of the PNA. Both organizations were dominated by an elite of *assimilados* who tended to be moderate and reformist.[69]

In 1925 the PNA started an African newspaper (which had been founded and refounded in 1911 and 1913 under other sponsorship). Very early the PNA began to discuss identification with the African masses and the idea of a classless, raceless society in which Africans could play a vital role. It also acted as a pressure group, petitioning the League of Nations beginning in 1925. The issue around which all these early nationalist parties could rally and could temporarily unify with European liberal groups was the controversial question of forced labor and the export of Angolan labor to the islands of São Tomé and Príncipe.[70] A great deal of the debate in the Angolan press in the 1900–1920 era centered on this issue, since it represented continuing grievances in Angola and since the debate with settlers and authorities involved a disagreement over the nature of the African character. A constant theme in the 1920s, therefore, was the PNA defense of the African as a hardworking, exploited individual.[71]

Like Assís Júnior and the others of the *Voz d'Angola* before him, the PNA leaders hoped to achieve compromise and accommodation with Portugal. Though the fringe members of this party may have had revolutionary aims, the majority of the leadership was for peaceful change and evolution. They deplored violence in Portugal as well as in Angola, since they believed that all anarchy and violence would work against accommodation with the Republic and its representatives in Angola. Demanding "justice within democracy,"[72] these writers struggled for racial harmony, at the same time defending a special identity as Africans:

We are not simply Portuguese. Before being Portuguese we are Africans. We are Portuguese of the negro [sic] race. We have pride in our double quality. But we possess above all, the racial pride. . . . We are proud of being negroes. . . . We must cooperate with the whites.[73]

The reformist, accommodating course of the first phase of Angolan nationalism is further illustrated by an interview published in 1924 in *Província de Angola*, a major Luanda newspaper, European-settler in outlook. The African spokesman interviewed, one Afonso Baptista Franque, an *assimilado*, was described by a reporter as "an evangelist of the Negro race"[74] and was said to be a member of the Supreme Council of the PNA. Franque

[69] "A nossa orientação," *A Voz d'Africa* (Lisbon), July 8, 1929. This was the newspaper of the Partido Nacional Africano.
[70] *A Voz d'Africa*, July 8, 1929; and *A Reforma*, March 25, 1911.
[71] *A Voz d'Africa*, October 18, 1928.
[72] *A Voz d'Africa*, July 8, 1929.
[73] *Ibid*.
[74] "Aspirações africanas," in *Província de Angola* (Luanda), October 25, 1924.

stated that Africans in Angola were in a bad position for future responsibilities because, he claimed, "the Portuguese government has always attempted to keep Africans out of the higher government posts and away from the managing of the interests of their own land." [75] Franque went on to say:

What we want is that our rights be respected, that is, that our newspapers, now suppressed, be allowed to continue publication; that our persecuted journalists be allowed, with all guarantees, to exercise their noble mission; that our associations, such as the Liga Africana, which were closed arbitrarily, be reopened and their leaders respected in their rights; that the African public functionaries now compromised or deprived of their positions unjustly be allowed to reoccupy them. . . .[76]

Behind most of these writings was the hope that arguments by educated Africans might bring the Portuguese authorities to understand the African position, the possibility that the past repressions might be reversed in favor of African self-assertion and interracial understanding. There was also the tendency to believe that the government in Lisbon could act as a mediator between the *assimilado* and the European settler community in Africa. The protest writers of the 1920s observed increasing racial conflicts in Angola and deplored new laws and practices that tended to repress African freedom.

Despite the tradition of African hopes for the first Republic (1910–1926), *assimilado* writers commented upon disturbing changes in Portuguese policy during the first decade of the Republic. They claimed that the policy had been altered from old traditions of multiracialism to a new policy which could be "disastrous." In 1920 a lead editorial in an African newspaper in Luanda thus suggested that the racial question was becoming predominant and that racial separation was increasing in Angola.[77] The author hoped that the assimilated African would be a useful middleman in achieving harmonious relations between races. The persistence of this *assimilado* hope is a major feature of the first phase of Angolan nationalism; even into the era of the *Estado Novo*, the *assimilado* continued to hope that he could lead a movement toward multiracialism in spite of the growing evidence of increased official repression and settler intransigence and fears.

CONCLUSIONS

Protest writings by educated *mestiços* and Africans were more than just a single episode in the first modern expression of Angolan nationalism: they

[75] *Ibid.*
[76] *Ibid.*
[77] "Brancos e pretos," *Independente* (Luanda), April 29, 1920.

proved the continuity of that movement. Their publication in the Portuguese language—however much patriotic Portuguese grammarians might ridicule it—was the earliest instance of Angolans using the techniques of nineteenth-century European civilization to achieve political and social goals. The protest writings, more than the perennial secret conspiracies for independence and autonomy, left readable proof for later generations that there was a basic unity to circumstances surrounding Angolan nationalism past and present. They left a legacy of evidence that the grievances of 1890 were largely the grievances of 1930 and not unlike those of 1961; that the programs and goals of the African associations and parties founded after 1910 were foreshadowed in the dreams of *assimilados* like Fontes Pereira and Assís Júnior; and that, indeed, some of the fundamental ideas about race, repression, economic exploitation, and Portuguese culture involved in the 1961 debate were long ago argued by educated Angolans. Once again the basic unity of the history of colonial Angola emerges.[78]

In its first phase, Angolan nationalism was especially Portuguese in character. Many of the fundamental assumptions behind the protest writings were in fact quoted chapter and verse from Portuguese writings. Angolan *assimilados* applied Portuguese concepts of racial and political democracy current at the time, some of which were early forms of the "lustotropicology mystique," [79] and found that the practice did not fit the theories in Angola. Although the *assimilado* was willing to be a racial middleman in Angolan society and to urge assimilation of uneducated non-African and African elements into society, he was not willing to remain silent after repeated instances of repression.[80]

Assimilados realized that they were more than simply Portuguese. In the words of Assís Júnior, they were men "caught between two fires," the fire of Portuguese nationalism and the fire of traditional African hostility.[81] The surveyed protest writings indicate the basically insecure and frustrated nature of the *assimilado* lawyer, civil servant, journalist, or writer who seemed to be foreigners in the land of the black man. In the early period of this phase of nationalism, there was more opportunity for social and political mobility for the educated African. Even this slight opportunity, however, won some African patriots for Portugal: the idea that only in Por-

---

[78] See Douglas L. Wheeler, "Towards a Histroy of Angola," in *Boston University Studies in African History*, Vol. III, ed. by Daniel F. Mc Call (New York: Praeger, 1969), pp. 45–68.

[79] See the discussion of lusotropicology in Chilcote, *Portuguese Africa*, pp. 47–49, 51.

[80] For two instances of *assimilado* thoughts of the "assimilation" of other groups, see *União Africa-Portugueza* (Luanda), December 2, 1882, regarding the Cabinda community in Luanda, and the editorial by Carlos da Silva, editor, in *O Arauto Africano*, March 17, 1889, regarding the tiny Goanese (Indian) community in the capital.

[81] Assís Júnior, *Relato*, II, 55.

tuguese Africa could "a black raise himself to such a position" (as an *assimilado* in the colonial civil service in Angola) was trumpeted by a black African writer, a post office official, who attacked the radical protest writing of Fontes Pereira in 1890.[82] Fontes Pereira's published disloyalty to Portugal, therefore, was met with a counterprotest by *assimilados* who felt dependent upon Portuguese patronage.

The question of loyalty to Portugal remained an important aspect of Angolan self-assertion and nationalism. Any protest writings were likely to be deemed treasonous by all but the most liberal Portuguese officials. But even liberalism did not always dampen the fires of patriotism. Indeed, a study of the history of nationalism in the *assimilado* population of Angola suggests that this elite community was divided on the question of loyalty to Portugal at a very early stage and that this loyalty issue tended to separate the Luanda *mestiço* from the hinterland African. The Liga Angolana, for example, desperately tried to show its loyalty to Portuguese authority during the uproar over frequent African revolts between 1914 and 1917. In doing so, the association, like the *assimilado*, was caught between the two forces of Portuguese nationalism and African traditionalism. Thus the early nationalist, as much as he sympathized with African insurgents, found to his dismay that there could be no middle ground on the question of loyalty to Portugal in a public crisis.[83] If the Liga Angolana and various other associations and their polemic press desired "progress" in political rights for the *assimilado*, they would have to cooperate with the authorities by criticizing African rebellions.

The years from 1928 through 1930 formed an important watershed in Angolan self-assertion. At this time, political repression increased, built upon the patterns of two previous decades. There was a lapse in Angolan literature, in terms of both protest and intellectual creativity.[84] The impressive if ephemeral sum of protest literature—including over twenty African newspapers and journals and several books produced between 1881 and 1930—retreated into the past, only to be rediscovered by a new generation. Better educated, perhaps, but with greater inclination to rebel, the post-1948 elite absorbed outside ideological influences not present in the

---

[82] "Partido Colonial," *O Mercantil*, January 30, 1890.

[83] For the consternation of moderate *assimilados* in the Liga Angolana over the political repercussions of tribal rebellion between 1914 and 1917, see Assís Júnior, *Relato*, II, 29n. See *A Província* (Luanda), October 30, 1914, for the adverse reaction of the Liga Angolana leaders to the "revolutionary agitation" reported in the Kongo rebellion, 1913–1914.

[84] Angolan literature suffered a retrogression in the 1930s; only two native-born Angolans managed to attain literary stature in this interim era Francisco Castelbranco and Alberto de Lemos, both *mestiço* historians. See Mário António, "Literatura angolana," *Ultramar* (Lisbon), no. 15, (1964), p. 88.

previous generations. These influences built upon Angolan grievances, accumulated over centuries and articulated especially after 1860. After 1948, therefore, the issue of loyalty to Portugal was clouded by new, more radical means of achieving change and reform. These new means invariably included a final break with Portugal, thus severing a final link between the hopes of eager republican *assimilados* of Liga Angolana vintage and the new generation's hopes for an essentially non-Portuguese solution to the problem of Angolan nationalism.[85] The attempt of the moderate *assimilado* to bring change through reasoned, pro-Portuguese protest seemed to be finally bankrupt,

[85] For evidence that the *assimilado* was again singled out for persecution in 1961, see R. Davezies, *Les Angolais* (Paris 1965), pp. 33–35; Thomas M. Okuma, *Angola in Ferment* (Boston, 1962), pp. 25, 82–92; James Duffy, *Portugal in Africa* (Cambridge, 1962), pp. 215–221; and Chilcote, *Portuguese Africa*, pp. 74–81.

Brazil

Chapter 5 The Social and Ethnic Significance of the War of the Cabanos

Manuel Correia de Andrade

[This nineteenth-century Afro-Brazilian guerrilla movement was rooted in the political crisis that developed after the abdication of the Crown by Dom Pedro I. The guerrilla violence, described as a style of political articulation, is analyzed in relation to the existing socioeconomic structure and by examining the indicators of alienation. Also described are the guerrilla and counterguerrilla tactics, and there is a characterization of the movement's leader, mulatto Vicente de Paula. Conclusions reached acknowledge that there existed no definite ideological direction and the war was an attempt on the part of lower classes to obtain power in a rigidly structured society. The War of the Cabanos represents one of several examples identified as a nationalistic-oriented local rebellion and was similar to other nineteenth-century revolts, including the Cabanagem in Pará, the Balaiada in Maranhão, the Sabinada in Bahia, and the War of Farrapos in Rio Grande do Sul. The War of the Cabanos differs in that it occurred primarily in the countryside with the participation of the rural population. Andrade's case study offers insight into the fanatical, messianic behavior, of lower-class elements in the Brazilian Northeast. The reverence of the illiterate masses for Pedro I, the hero who returned to Portugal to save the monarchy, was similar to their belief that the famous sixteenth-century King Sebastião would one day return from the dead.]

SOCIAL AND ETHNIC STRATIFICATION
IN NORTHEASTERN SOCIETY IN THE FIRST HALF
OF THE NINETEENTH CENTURY

Northeastern society in general, and that of Pernambuco in particular, during the struggle for political independence (1817–1822) and during the Regency period (1831–1840), was highly stratified into a hierarchy of rigid classes. Urban life was of little importance: the urban population was small, and the main cities and towns of the provinces, which were burned in the War of the Cabanos—Goiana, Olinda, Recife, Maceió, in the state of Alagôas, and Penedo—had only administrative and commercial functions. They were ports through which passed agricultural exports, especially sugar and cotton, as well as manufactured products imported from Portugal, England, and France.

The mill owners, possessing great tracts of land, many slaves, and usually large herds of cattle and goats, composed the most important class of the society, economically and politically. They almost always owned property in the coastal humid portion of the country, where they cultivated sugarcane and made sugar, and in the rural areas of the semiarid backlands, where cotton was planted and cattle were raised, or where the cattle were sent during the rainy season. They generally resided in the humid region, in woody areas, where they built large adobe dwellings in which the patriarchal family lived, along with dependents and guests. The economic conditions of the rural owners varied quite a bit from one area to another or from one sugar mill to another, and political influence varied along with economic conditions.

In the cities, only merchants and public officials did not depend on the mills; at times, as in 1710 and in 1821, these two groups opposed with force and dominated the rural landowners. The merchants and public officials were generally foreigners—Portuguese and, less often, French and English —or descendants of the sugar mill operators who did not have a vocation or the opportunity of establishing themselves as landowners and sugar makers. They dedicated themselves to commerce or to a military or ecclesiastical career, or they became public officials. Many times the foreign merchant or official came from another province, married the daughter of the sugar mill owner, and tied his interests to those of his father-in-law.[1]

If these predominantly white groups were located at the top of the social scale, the slaves were found at the bottom, generally descendants of Africans of pure Negro stock or *mestiços* with Negro blood predominating. Most of the slaves, destined for heavy labor in sugarcane agriculture and in the cultivation of foods, were treated very harshly, for they were considered the property of the *senhor* and were subject to his caprices and abuses of power. Through subservience and servility, however, some slaves who were used in domestic service gained their master's confidence and friendship and thus received better treatment. It was these relationships that made possible the influence of African beliefs, of African words, of African foods, and even of African blood upon the formation of Brazilian

[1] Gilberto Freyre, *Inglêses no Brasil: aspectos da influência britânica sôbre a vida, a paisagem e a cultura do Brasil* (Rio de Janeiro: Livrariá José Olympio Editôra, 1948).

culture. The mixture of blood was due to sexual relations between masters and Negro or mulatto girls, which resulted in an enormous number of mulattos. Mulattos who were born free or who were freed by their parents had an opportunity to rise economically and socially, as occurred with the Bahian poet Luís Gama, with the Carioca romanticist Machado de Assís, and with the essayist Antônio Pedro de Figueiredo, from Pernambuco.[2]

Between these two social classes, however, an enormous number of individuals—servants or free workers—were forced to remain dependent on those who had power. As the industrial capacity of the sugar mills was small and the territorial area was large, the marginal lands farthest away from the mill or the least fertile were given to the inhabitants, tenant farmers, who cultivated subsistence products on them, paying the owner an annual rent in kind or in money.[3] These tenant farmers did not submit easily to the authority of the rural landowners; [4] they could be led into battle by those who wanted to stand up to the landowners of the province. In addition, in each sugar mill there were many free employees (such as machinists, carpenters, stewards, body guards), and in the cities there were many employees in commerce (almost always Portuguese), and artisans. These groups were the germ of a middle class, already gestating in the first half of the nineteenth century, almost always composed of *mestiços* in which the quantity of white and Negro blood varied considerably, of whites who had fallen into bad economic circumstances, and of Negroes who had obtained their freedom.

A political hierarchy was also present. Only a "good man," who had a certain annual income, had the right to vote. Only these could hold the office of municipal counselor, justice of the peace, or alderman. It became common for those who were influential or rich to escape punishment by remaining under the protection of the authorities who were generally friendly. There were also, among the humble persons, criminals who put themselves under the protection of a powerful rural *senhor* and were able to escape justice; the crimes they committed against poor people remained unpunished.[5] The situation was further aggravated by the quality of the

[2] Manuel Correia de Andrade, *A terra e o homem no nordeste* (2d ed.; São Paulo: Editôra Brasiliense, 1965), pp. 49–143.

[3] *Ibid.*, p. 78.

[4] Tollenare, *Notas dominicais* (Salvador: Livraria Progresso Editôra, 1956), p. 94.

[5] The situation was such that the *Harmonizador*, a newspaper belonging to the "Harmonizador Patriotic Society," which contained the moderate element of Pernambuco society, affirmed in its issue of March 31, 1832, that "one of the evils of the province was the impunity of the criminals, the important fact being that the landowners were used to protecting criminals" and that "the authorities themselves freed them or didn't bother them on request of someone or for money." It concluded by exclaiming, "How many poor people are persecuted because they won't allow children or friends of the Justice of the Peace to take their wife or daughter."

magistracy, which was highly politicized and subservient to the powers of the day. The press of the day violently criticized the magistracy.[6]

Under these conditions, without lands to work, without capital and means to develop commercial skills, without facilities and guarantees for employment, it was natural for the great majority of the poor population to react against the caprices and abuses of power of the landowners by forming their own "groups for protection," or by means of banditry. They even waited for the moment when a leader would appear to lead them into revolution. Revolution, depending on the moment and the circumstances by which it was determined, had the most diverse aims. The people would only follow a leader in whom they had trust, whether he was a liberal or an absolutist, a republican or a moderate.

Thus, the absence of justice provoked the generalized use of revenge by the offended against the offender. This led to the formation of veritable armies, particularly on the sugar mill lands, armies that were as big as the economic possibilities allowed or as large as the number of enemies of the rural *senhor*.

The public power, unprepared to exercise its authority directly in an area so large and so badly organized with respect to transportation, organized the rural population into militias in which the officers were the large landowners. They recruited their troops from their dependents on occasions when political agitations caused the captain general and the president of the province to call them. After Independence, and during the period of the Regency, the organization of the militia was replaced by the national guard. This measure was taken by Padre Feijó, a moderate politician who sought to strengthen the dominant classes in the face of popular revolts which arose from north to south in all corners of the empire.

THE ABDICATION OF DOM PEDRO I AND THE PROBLEMATIC POLITICS OF THE NORTHEAST

The proclamation of the independence of Brazil by the Portuguese heir to the throne, who was crowned as the first emperor, represented a great

---

[6] The *Diário de Pernambuco,* a newspaper that had a moderate line with respect to the political struggles of the Regency, editorialized on May 17, 1833, that, "Such is the general clamor against the Magistracy and so scandalous and habitual are their injurious actions, misconduct, and veniality, despite honorable exceptions, that a resignation or dismissal produces public rejoicing to which all deliver themselves even without examining if it is deserved or not. And who will say that the people are not right? Isn't it fair and extremely necessary to punish men who so frankly traffic with the most sacred of obligations, those of justice? Whoever auctions and bids the most gets the decisions he wants. . . . Many skip over all the regular procedures and only consider those who are able to pay the most, and only the miserable are declared guilty, those who have nothing to give . . . ."

victory for the dominant social groups and was carried out without struggle, without the necessity of the participation of the less favored classes. Because the great rural senhores feared a social transformation which would put an end to slavery and bring serious economic problems and a civil war which would threaten their possessions and disturb the economic life of the country, they agreed to an independence which would only sever Brazil's ties with Portugal but would keep the institutions, the form of government and even the dynasty. Portuguese businessmen, officials, and military men stayed on.

The liberal groups active in the Northeast and the groups of free men without economic opportunities and participation in political life felt restless under the Monarchy and the centralization which it entailed. The penetration of the native revolutionary ideas of the intellectuals who fed the French Revolution and the mark left by the executions resulting from the 1817 and 1824 uprisings in the Northeast remained latent in the spirit of numerous groups of elites—above all priests and officials of the armed forces —and of the northeastern people who awaited the opportunity for revenge. On the other hand, conservative groups led by landowners and slaves, which had great support among the military, not only defended the imperial government and the restless and often discussed person of the emperor, but they advocated the abolition of the constitutional regime through annulment granted in 1824 and through the granting of absolute power to the Emperor Dom Pedro I. Thus, at the end of 1826, when the repressive measures against the Confederação do Equador (1824) were reduced, the population was sharply divided into two groups: absolutists and liberals. The former vindicated absolutism and the maintenance of a centralizing regime; the second was composed of constitutional monarchists who were at times partisans of a federation and at times of a republic.

Suffering pressures of all types in an almost uninhabited country of continental dimensions, the emperor gave way to his adventurous spirit and on the night of April 7 abdicated the throne and departed for Europe. His romantic gesture, delivering the throne of Brazil to a five-year-old prince, gave the abdicating emperor an aura which evoked sympathy, even among those opposed to his government, such as General Abreu e Lima and the Andrade brothers.

For the great majority of Brazilians, however, the gesture of abdication signified the nationalization of the government, the expulsion of the Portuguese and of the absolutists from key posts and from political offices. The political instability and the difficult economic situation led the people to desperation; eager to free themselves from the tutelage of the leading groups, the people rose up spontaneously under the direction of leaders who were against the imperial government and the provincial governments which were dependent on them. Revolts occurred, among the more lasting of which were those of the Cabanagem in Pará, the Balaiada in Maranhão, the War of the Cabanos in Pernambuco and Alagôas, the Malés Negroes in 1835 and the Sabinada in 1837 in Bahia, and the War of the Farrapos in Rio Grande do Sul.

In Pernambuco a series of mutinies followed the abdication in 1831.[7] In November, rebels in Recife occupied the Fort of the Five Points and demanded a series of measures from the president of the province which were directed against the Portuguese and the absolutists.[8] Not receiving overwhelming popular support nor support from the federal society, the rebels resolved to abandon the fort and to disperse. The situation of the provincial government was difficult; seized by the government of the Regency, and being moderate, it could not take measures that would take heed of popular aspirations. Pressed hard, it had to seize and collect the rebel soldiers on anchored ships in the port or send them to the fortress of Fernando de Noronha. The interior continued to be at the mercy of the large landowners through the authorities elected by them. Government by these authorities was characterized by the greatest absurdities and irregularities.

The jeopardized economic situation worsened, the issuance of false copper money made the life of the most humble, who received their salaries in money of this type, more difficult. Those punished as a consequence of their participation in the revolutions of 1817 and of 1824 returned from exile and pleaded for reemployment in the jobs they had lost. Absolutist officials and functionaries who had enriched themselves with public money during the First Empire refused to loan money to them. During this animated atmosphere, the absolutists worked for the return of the ex-emperor as the best solution for the reorganization of the country and for the restoration of order and discipline in national life. Eminent politicians of the southern part of the country organized a political scheme which favored the restoration of some of their members and went to Europe to advise Dom Pedro of the situation in Brazil.[9]

---

[7] On May 6, when the news of the abdication was received, there was a mutiny headed by Francisco Roma which demanded the overthrow of the authorities, who were confirmed absolutists. In September, the tropa de linha, which became dissatisfied with the delay in the payment of its soldiers and with the strictness of the officials, rose up and dominated Recife for three days without obeying anyone, its personnel drinking and sacking the commercial establishments. See Manuel Correia de Andrade, "As sedições de 1831 em Pernambuco," *Revista de História* (São Paulo), no. 28 (1956), pp. 374–391.

[8] *Ibid.*, pp. 397–404.

[9] Some absolutists were more radical and more restless, such as General Pinto Madeira in the Cearense Cariri, who rebelled in 1831 against the government and was beaten in a few months (*Pernambuco e a revolta de Pinto Madeira* [Recife: Edições Nordeste, 1953]). His defeat, however, did not quiet his coreligionists, who went on to

After several short-lived uprisings, rebels came under the leadership of Torres Galindo. A farmer from Bonito, in the south of Santo Antão, Galindo knew the region and the men well. He went to the town of Panelas and convinced António Timóteo, a small landowner, of the opportunity to begin the struggle there. Calling on the poor people in the south of Pernambuco and in the northern part of Alagôas, they revolted against the lack of effort by the Regency government to help them. They rose for the reinstatement of Dom Pedro I, who, free from the constitution, could resolve their problems. Torres Galindo and António Timóteo convinced many that they could understand the poor and the ignorant, who were ready to participate in any movement against the government because they believed they would get an opportunity to better their standard of living, even by sacking the towns and lands.

Thus began a four-year struggle. The first contingent was increased by large numbers of slaves, who saw in the revolt the possibility of freedom, and of Indians from Jacuípe, who were tired of being humiliated and exploited by the large landowners of the region. Without fear of the consequences of his actions, the rich landowner and cattle raiser Torres Galindo began a popular rebellion which soon slipped away from his control into the hands of more men, such as António Timóteo, Vicente de Paula, and Captain Caetano Gomes. The revolution succeeded in dominating a large area for a long time, not only because of the weakness of the Regency government and the indecision of the provincial president and officials, but also because of its geographical position, away from roads, which made it difficult to provide troops during the rainy season, and among large forests where the rebels took shelter.

THE WAR

The war began in Panelas in the month of May 1832 and then spread to the east through the valley of Una as far as São Miguel de Barreiros and

---

conspire in Pernambuco and in Alagôas. They planned a revolt which reverberated throughout the province, making action on the part of the president difficult. It was led in Recife by Colonel Francisco José Martins and Top Sergeant José Gabriel de Morães Meyer; in Santa Antão da Vitória by Captain Domingos Lourenzo Torres Galindo; in Barra Grande by João Batista de Araújo; in the region of Una by millowner Alfonso de Milo; in Panelas do Miranda by small landowner António Timóteo; and in Jacuípe by Director of Indians Alexandre Gomes de Oliveira. The uprising in Recife began on April 14, 1832, thanks to the total support of the population. The fighting was suffocated after some days, and the rebels took refuge on ships anchored in the harbor. A similar uprising occurred in Santo Antão but the government acted rapidly and sent forces under the command of Captain Carapeba, provoking the retreat and dispersion of the forces that had gathered and also causing restoration under the orders of Torres Galindo.

to the south through Alagôas to Pôrto Calvo. The rebels used guerrilla tactics. They knew the region well and ate from forest fruits, honey, and abundant animals; they also made small gardens of manioc, corn and potatoes with which they supplemented their diet. Humble and rustic men, accustomed to the life of the interior, they rapidly adapted themselves to the conditions of life. The government troops, in contrast, were men from the city or from other rural areas of a less inhospitable climate, who needed a long period for adaptation.

In order to understand the significance of the War of the Cabanos, it is necessary to analyze the manner in which the government, rebels, and the ecclesiastical authorities proceeded. Government leadership was concentrated in the hands of two men, the president of the province and the commander of arms, both of whom were named by the central government. The first was always or almost always a civilian, at times from the province and generally a businessman or landowner, at other times a high civil functionary designated to administer one or another province. When the president was deposed, authority passed to the president of the legislative council, a man from the province. The commander of arms was always a military man who was responsible to the president but who represented the supreme authority for the armed forces in the province. He was generally a man from another area who was not identified with his troops or with the problems they faced. Moreover, ideological and political divergences were frequent among the officials and soldiers. This created disciplinary problems, which made the conduct of the war more difficult.

Various factors diminished the efficiency of the governmental forces: the soldiers and officers, for the most part, were not professionals but civilians, militia, or national guard who had been mobilized for the fight. They generally came from other areas and were isolated from their families, possessions, and interests; as a consequence, they had difficulty in adapting to the new environment. There was no unity of command during certain phases of the struggle. This created serious misunderstandings between the military leaders of the different theaters of operation or between the commanders of the forces of Pernambuco and of Alagôas, the two provinces involved in the war. Only after several years of fighting was the general command unified in the hands of Major Luís de Souza.

In addition to being poorly trained and neither motivated nor psychologically prepared for the war, the troops were not fed well and did not receive their daily wages in good money; this created serious problems for the commanders, who were constantly demanding provisions, as well as payment, for the troops. Many times, the soldiers deserted in large numbers because they lacked food or had gone several months without pay.

The economic life of the province was completely disorganized as a consquence of the war. Men were lacking for labor in the fields and for other phases of production. Moreover, during the rainy season the roads were blocked, making it difficult and many times impossible to transport supplies—manioc flour above all—to the theater of operations.

All vestiges of efficiency were eliminated from the governing forces, which were still being undermined by political discord. Thus, during the military campaign, officers were arrested on suspicion of being absolutists, of being partisans of the restoration of Emperor Pedro I, and of furnishing arms and weapons to the cabanos.[10]

The rebels were rustic men who lived on sugar mill plantations, or were small landowners, runaway slaves, or poor people who lived in the ravaged area. Being humble, they were used to going through the large forests of the region and to crossing the rivers in search of animals and fruits. They experienced few difficulties in such a precarious venture, even when attacked by enemies who were stronger and better armed. They retreated to the forests where they built cottages and made small gardens of manioc, the *roçados*, which furnished them with the flour necessary for their sustenance. Game and fish were abundant, as were honey and wild bees. Some landowners of the region and inhabitants of the towns were at times in sympathy with the rebels' political ideas and so collaborated with them. Others collaborated out of fear of having their lands destroyed. In reality, many sugar mill owners stimulated and aided the popular revolt hoping to gain political advantage and thereby to rise to higher positions.[11]

The cabano chiefs were popular leaders, simple men who were poor and who participated along with their men in the discomforts and needs of the moment. The men of economic and social position who inflamed the war were held in the city or fled to other areas, not being able to withstand the life in the forest. Among these leaders, António Timóteo was the most outstanding. He was a small landowner in Panelas do Miranda who, because he was poor and humble, was looked upon with displeasure by the author-

[10] Such implications became very serious after the apprehension of the letters of General Abreu e Lima, the hero of the revolution of 1817 and a friend of Simón Bolívar in the War of Independence of Colombia and Venezuela. He had advised his brother, Luís Roma, "to go to Panelas and direct the cabanos to await the arrival of the 'General of the Masses' (see Manuel Correia de Andrade, *A guerra dos cabanos* [Rio de Janeiro: Edições Conquista, 1965], p. 10). This fact provoked the opening of inquiry and the punishing of the Roma brothers, who were accused of connivance with the enemy, thus preventing a joining of the warriors of Agua Preta and Panelas do Miranada with the restoration party of the court.

[11] Diegues Júnior affirmed, "Of the cabanada, which had no relation with movements of the same name occurring in other parts of the empire—mainly in Pará—of the cabanada it can be said that it was a movement stimulated by the sugar mill owners, owners from the North, mainly the Mendoça who were allied with Vicente de Paula" (*O bangue nas Alagôas*, p. 170). In truth, however, many sugar mill owners complied out of fear. If they resisted, they feared murder or the burning of their mills.

ities. They affirmed on July 13, 1832, that "at the head of a band of robbers he stole and murdered throughout the area and made a show of pursuing patriots." [12] Then the president of the province, referring to the rebels, called them a "band of thieves and criminals."

After the death of António Timóteo, however, the true leader arose, the supreme chief of the cabanos, the guerrilla fighter Vicente Ferreira de Paula. A mulatto, the son of a Catholic priest of Goiana, Vicente Ferreira de Paula served in the army and attained the position of sergeant, thus gaining knowledge of the military art. He afterward deserted and applied this knowledge in the conduct of the war that made him famous. Valiant, clever, cruel, and courageous, he knew how to unify all the cabanos under his command and organized the struggle in a manner extremely unfavorable to the government forces. He entrenched himself in the center of the forest, in areas of difficult access, where he placed his compatriots and their families. He divided the cabanos into various groups situated at diverse points and led by commanders as rude as himself. From there, they went out on sorties and attacked government forces in the woods, in the mills, and in villages, almost always by surprise. If the reaction was strong and the result seemed favorable to the enemy, they quickly retreated to the forest, hiding from their pursuers. If the result was favorable, they occupied the enemy position, freed their supporters, sacked the enemy, and only then returned to the forest. This system of fighting, employing guerrilla tactics, confounded the governmental forces, who were accustomed to more conventional types of warfare.

The government, after a few months, realized its disadvantageous position and the need to organize a system of suppression of the guerrillas—a term that was already used by the press in 1832.[13] Perceiving the differences between the classic wars and guerrilla wars, by May of 1833 President Manuel Zeferino dos Santos had recommended to Major Felipe Duarte Pereira that the means of combatting the cabanos would not consist only of providing fortified points and of guaranteeing the security of the towns and roads but also of penetrating the forests, seeking the rebel fields in order to destroy them, and not giving the rebels any rest, obliging them to lead a nomadic existence and impeding thus their ability to provide themselves with food. He also recommended an increasing strictness with those who were found armed and with those who were suspected of being rebels. These people were to be imprisoned and taken to other places in the province.[14]

[12] Manuscript of the Biblioteca Pública do Estado (Oficios do Govêrno).

[13] *O Equinoxial*, nos. 18 and 24, October 26 to December 8, 1832.

[14] Andrade, *A guerra dos cabanos*, p. 75.

Such measures were really only put into practice at the end of 1834, when Manuel de Carvalho Paes de Andrade, the leader of the Confederação do Equador, came into power. He formed an understanding with the president of Alagôas, resolving that they would both leave their capitals and enter the theater of operations, the first in the Limeiras sugar mill and the second in the town of Pôrto de Pedras. Before leaving, however, he suspended constitutional guarantees, arresting, in the process, those declared suspects and enemies by the government. Once at the battle front, he organized the *corpos de batedores*, who combed the forests, arresting and killing the cabanos and destroying everything that the rebels could utilize or possess. He beseiged an extensive area from the littoral to the interior, bounded in the north by the Una and Jacuípe rivers and in the south by the Manguaba River. Within this extensive area, the town of Abreu and the mill at Pracinha were separated off as an "island" of shelter. The inhabitants of the area at large were given eight days to evacuate or to gather at the shelter mentioned. At the end of this period the area would be attacked by the *corpos de batedores* and all those who had disobeyed the order would be considered as enemies, arrested, and deported. Although this measure was efficient from the military point of view, it was arbitrary from a sociopolitical point of view because, disrespecting individual rights, it obliged the inhabitants to abandon their possessions, homes, and property to the mercy of the cabanos and government troops and to gather in a place where there would be no opportunities for work.

The siege planned and the soldiers trained, the government forces began to make raids into the forests. At first they fearfully followed the "trails" and roads bordering the forests of the cabanos. When they found houses that could be utilized by the enemy, they destroyed them and laid waste any nearby fields. After a while the government began to see favorable results from these tactics and from the removal of the population from the area. This deprived the rebels of their arms supply, of the ammunition which had always come from the city, and of the indispensable support of the rural population. The cabano territory came more and more under surveillance, and cabano encampments, some formed of hundreds of huts, were burned. The death of Dom Pedro I in Portugal and the consolidation of the Regency government under the priest Diogo Feijó ended a large part of the support that the cabanos received from the cities. They became more and more isolated.

Those in hiding were attacked constantly by the enemy and were deprived of food and deficient in munitions. The lack of food drove them to eat fruit and roots of all types, causing them to become seriously ill. The government, in an attempt to stimulate desertion among the rebels, began to give good treatment and food to those who gave themselves up, per-

LIBRARY
EISENHOWER COLLEGE

mitting some prisoners to return to the forests to convince the others to give themselves and their arms up. Hunger and constant defeats prepared the spirit of the cabanos for surrender, and only the strongest, or those who had much to lose from the cessation of the struggle, were willing to continue the war; among these were the runaway slaves who were afraid to go back to captivity and the punishments to which they would be subjected. They became the most audacious and fearless followers of the tireless Vicente Ferreira de Paula. When the fate of the cabanos arms was decided and only the most recalcitrant groups remained in the forests, the president of the province of Recife returned with the Bishop of Olinda, Dom João Perdigão, and passed through the war-torn area. That which had not been entirely gained by force of arms was to be gained through the spiritual force of religious persuasion. Military victory would be complemented by the pacific action of the Church.

Bishop Dom João Marquês da Purificação Perdigão was, in reality, a conservative, as was the entire structure of the Catholic Church at that time. In February of 1835 he arrived to fulfill his mission in the war area. In Pôrto Calvo, he set down an agreement with the commander in chief, a proclamation in which he entreated all the rebels to deliver themselves up because they were living in sin and that they would only obtain pardon from God if they lay down their arms. He promised those who gave themselves up that they would be treated well and remain free and not be put in jail. To impress these points on the rebels he journeyed with a strong escort from Pôrto Calvo to Agua Preta, confirming, baptizing, and marrying those who sought him out. He complemented spiritual action by distributing advice, food, and clothing. The action of the Bishop was well taken and after a while the cabanos went to him.

Vicente Ferreira de Paula, seeing that his situation was becoming critical, gathered together some of his followers, most being runaway slaves who were his most loyal men, to attempt a sortie, but the events of May convinced him of the impossibility of continuing the fight. Supplies and arms were becoming scarcer and scarcer; the men hidden in the forests were becoming more and more vulnerable and weaker in fighting spirit, and their numbers were steadily decreasing. In May the priest, José António, who had lived with him in the forest for more than two years, and one of his principal first lieutenants, Captain Caetano Gomes, with his company, abandoned him. This stimulated the desertion of other cabanos and even led him to the point of fighting with his own companions. Since March, the government had been furnishing agricultural tools to those who had given themselves up, seeking to cause them to return to rural life and to organize the economic life of the area which had been in turmoil for more than three years. Recognizing defeat and not wanting to give himself up, Vicente de

Paula gathered together a group of fifty to sixty loyal Negroes who feared return to captivity and abandoned the region, heading east toward the almost inpenetrable forest zone. There, deep in the forest, more than sixty kilometers from the nearest towns of Capoeiras, Panelas, and Jacuípe, he founded his town, Riacho do Mato, where he lived with his followers without being bothered by or bothering anyone. Contact with him was not reestablished until 1841, when the missionary friar José Plácido de Messina sought him out on request of the president of the province, the Baron of Boa Vista. The friar met him in Panalas and accompanied him to Riacho do Mato, where he erected his missions in an attempt to establish friendly relations with the cabano chief and the authorities of the neighboring towns.

Having great influence over those he led, harboring runaway slaves, and participating in political struggles in Alagôas and in Pernambuco, Vicente de Paula was an influential man in the area from 1841 to 1850. Courted by politicians who wanted his support, he participated in Alagôas in the battles between the *lisos* and *cabeludos*, and he triumphantly visited Maceió during the government of President Caetano Maria Lopes Gama, the future Viscount of Maranguape.

His continued protection of runaway slaves, however, provoked the hatred of the landowners and of slaveowners after the Praieira Revolution (1848–1849). President Honório Hermeto Carneiro Leno arrested him, in spite of the fact that he had supported the government during the revolution, and sent him to the fortress of Fernando de Noronha. There he remained for ten years, only regaining his freedom at the age of seventy, when he was incapable of leading men and of threatening the powerful sugar mill owners of the Una and Jacuípe river valleys.

THE PERSONALITY AND THE POLITICS
OF VICENTE FERREIRA DE PAULA

The personality of Vicente de Paula deserves fuller consideration because he was an authentic leader of the masses. He was born in Goiana in 1791, and he served in the armed forces. He led a humble, uneventful life until 1833, when he appeared as one of the cabano leaders. His rise was rapid, and he obscured the rest of his companions, coming to lead all of them. Having served in the armed forces, he sought to organize his men militarily.[15]

[15] His military organization can be seen in some of his orders of the day. On November 26, 1833, he issued the following: "All my men who wish to complain or to change companies, or to be discharged, can only request this of me in written form, on any day in the morning and can expect a reply by noon. . . . In this encampment all money is good, the only money not being accepted is that which is deemed to be entirely

Vicente de Paula's authority over his men was supreme: he nominated and promoted the officers in the cabano army. He exercised such authority in the hope that the organization would be of a future government which he would set up upon the return of the old emperor. He put forth proclamations, was courted and looked upon with confidence by those who favored restoration and who held high positions. Such men not only helped him from Recife to Rio de Janeiro but even thought of transferring themselves to the theater of operations.

The restoration and absolutist desire of the cabanos led them to maintain contact with the high restoration leaders, and they hoped for help from them. In Rio de Janeiro, however, the most prominent Pernambucan restorationists, Abreu e Lima, Lamenha Lins, and Moraes Meyer, disputed the overall leadership of the party, became hostile to each other, and endangered their cause through accusation of each other. Nevertheless, we know that Abreu e Lima, the famous "General of the Masses" and a friend of Bolívar in the Wars for Independence of the Spanish colonies, not only looked sympathetically on the cause of the cabanos, but sought to introduce his brothers and himself into the struggle. Thanks to the capture and publication by the government of his letters to his brother, Luís Roma, we know that his plan failed and we know of the series of disagreements existing in Rio de Janeiro among the various "column" leaders. In several of the letters, Abreu e Lima urged his brother to transfer to Jacuípe and assume the leadership of the rebels; the famous "General of the Masses" clearly did not know either the means by which the operations were developed or the strong personality of the caudillo Vicente de Paula.

Despairing of his conspiratorial friends in Rio, Abreu e Lima announced that he would transfer to the rebel territory. However, his plans were frustrated by the seizure of his letters and the detention in Fernando de Noronha of his brothers. The forceful energy of Manuel de Carvalho caused the abortion of the conspiracy being urged by the tireless Abreu e Lima. The death of Dom Pedro I in Portugal, after his victory over Dom Miguel, caused the party that desired his return to Brazil to disappear in 1834. Thus, in 1835 the cabanos were the only partisans of Dom Pedro who continued to keep their arms not so much because they doubted his death but because they had not found a satisfactory solution to a conflict that had already lasted for more than two years.

---

worthless or of a small amount." On November 24, 1833, he determined certain security measures, such as: "In this encampment, after praying the Santa Terço, silence will be kept . . . ."

THE SOCIAL SIGNIFICANCE OF THE WAR OF THE CABANOS

The War of the Cabanos undeniably constituted, along with the Cabanada do Pará, the Balaiada do Maranhão, and the War of the Farrapos of Rio Grande do Sul, one of the most important Brazilian revolutions considering the extent of the area that the rebels came to dominate, the duration of the struggle, the peoples mobilized by the revolutionaries to attain their goals, and the provincial governments mobilized to subdue them. In these aspects the War of the Cabanos differs from other Brazilian revolutions, which were planned and carried out almost entirely in the cities and which were realized almost entirely without any participation of the population of the countryside. Also, many of the citizens' revolutions were not carried out but were aborted while still in the conspiratorial phase, or came to dominate the urban center but had no expression in the interior. Considering the military organization, the goals, and the support or sympathy cultivated in distant provinces in turmoil, none of the four revolutions mentioned could be compared with the innumerable slave revolts which occurred in the country. The latter were normally carried out by a group of Africans fleeing captivity who took refuge in the forest desiring to attain liberty through flight and violence. From among all the slave revolts, only the Guerra dos Palmares was able to break the curtain of silence of the official historians; only recently has interest in the others begun to increase.[16]

Among the four large revolutions mentioned, the War of the Farrapos stands out as having been led by men coming from the dominant classes, by officers coming from the army, and even by the high provincial public administration. Although the Cabanada or Cabanagem, the Balaiada, and the War of the Cabanos might initially have had the support of influential politicians, they were led for years by leaders coming from the people who were tied to them by common interests, customs, and convictions. These leaders were loved and respected by their followers who considered them one of themselves; they were considered by their enemies to be simple robbers and bandits and therefore did not rate the attention of the historians for more than a century. Today three revolutions, those of Pará, of Maranhão, and of Pernambuco and Alagôas, are considered revolutions, popular revolutions with respect to the composition of their followers.

There is, however, a great difference between the Cabanada and the Balaiada on one hand and the War of the Cabanos on the other. The first two revolutions were popular in their objectives, initially having republican tendencies and combatting the monarchial form of government then dom-

[16] See Aderbal Jurema, *Insurreições negras no Brasil* (Recife: Livraria Mozart, 1932); and Clóvis Moura, *Rebeliões de senzala* (São Paulo: Editôra Zumbi, Limitada, 1959).

inant in the country,[17] whereas the War of the Cabanos was profoundly regressive and reactionary. It was closely involved with the sympathizers of the restoration party and even with the most reactionary elements of the clergy. Thus absolutist character and influence, which reached a fanatical point, dominated the cabanos until the end of the struggle. This influence led Vicente de Paula to revere priests and bishops and to attend to their requests, while at the same time sacking plantations and punishing violently his disobedient subordinates.

This contradiction of being a revolution of the masses which was absolutist with respect to its goals and which sought to be more popular in the composition of its followers can be explained by several facts: (1) the socioeconomic structure of the province; (2) the political circumstances dominant in Pernambuco and Alagôas during the First Empire and the Regency; and (3) the ideological formation and strong personality of Vicente de Paula, who became the absolute leader of the revolution after the death of António Timóteo. He so identified himself with the movement that one can hardly be separated from the other. The war represented an explosion of popular sentiments in a moment of crisis. The dominant classes, however, provoked and seeing themselves in danger, united, organized and, using the same military techniques as their enemies, conquered the cabanos, thereby maintaining the socioeconomic structure favorable to their interests.

SUMMARY

The War of the Cabanos was one of the popular armed movements in Brazil during the Regency period (1831–1840). Since the government was weak, a power crisis occurred: dissatisfied politicians, liberals, and partisans of a federal regime for Brazil, or absolutists who desired the restoration of Dom Pedro I, led the masses in a struggle for control and power. The masses, for the most part, were composed of Negro slaves, Indians who were marginal to the Portuguese colonization, and poor whites and mulattos. Although they had no definite ideological formation, they rebelled and occupied large areas in the interior of the country where the presence of forests guaranteed food and allowed the organization of guerrilla units.

In Pernambuco and Alagôas in Northeast Brazil, the rebels were able to gather under an authentic popular leader, the mulatto Vicente Fer-

[17] The cabanos, after hesitating, proclaimed the separation of the Province of Pará, adopting the Republic as the form of government. The Balaios, in spite of their ties with the liberal party, did not formulate, as far as we know, a public definition of republican ideas. Divided into autonomous groups, led by caudillos who were hostile to each other at times, they did not have their political objectives clearly defined. On the whole, they had no absolutist or restoration character, for Dom Pedro had already died by the outbreak of the revolution.

reira de Paula. In spite of the composition of his followers, which was over-whelmingly popular, and because of his authoritarian spirit and religious training, Vicente de Paula declared himself in favor of absolutism and of the restoration of Dom Pedro I. The war took place in the forests and was at first favorable to the cabanos, but after 1834, when the government forces adopted the antiguerrilla system of fighting, the rebels were gradually defeated and destroyed. After the military defeat, the Bishop of Olinda went to the war-torn area and called the last remaining rebels to order in the name of God and religion. Vicente de Paula, defeated, fled to an inaccessible place with fifty or sixty runaway slaves who remained loyal to him.

Thus movement of the cabanos represents an attempt of the lower classes to obtain power in a context in which social stratification was superimposed upon ethnic stratification.

Chapter 6 The Cangaço and the Politic of Violence in Northeast Brazil

Amaury de Souza

[Illustrating another type of social protest movement, this case study focuses on a historical synthesis and types of social banditry. The use of organized violence is related to the local patriarchal social and political order and to a realignment of the patterns of power and a system itself distinct from the patriarchal order. Violence is interpreted as an institutionalized and secularized phenomenon. The analysis below includes a detailed historical study of several "bandit" movements and their leadership. Conclusions include: that an alienated peasant can become an entrepreneur of violence, that violence is a catalyst for the decay of the patriarchal order, and that violence is a mode of access to socioconomic achievement.]

For more than two centuries Northeast Brazil was a synonym for banditry and endemic violence. Interfamilial struggles were reported as early as the seventeenth century and the existence of quasi-professional private militias was a tradition in the backlands dating from colonial times. As described by Oliveira Vianna, "there was a sort of widespread and permanent state of war among the [rural] dominions which was expressed in a regime of mutual pillage of cattle and animals, of fire and destruction of buildings, and of recruitment and protection of escaped slaves and criminals pursued by the police and the law."[1]

This state of war was basically a function of the isolation of the backlands, a society devoid of and hostile to the public law enforcement agencies, where the extended family was at the same time the government, the police, and the courts. The maintenance of order in the isolated feuds—even if to the benefit of the dominant families—was not solely a matter of

[1] *Instituições políticas brasileiras* (Rio de Janeiro: Livraria José Olympio Editôra, 1949), p. 223.

sheer force: a complex set of patrimonial and paternalistic relationships and values, topped by the unquestionable authority of the patriarch and his kindred, also assured the compliance of the rural populations. Notwithstanding, violence—the infliction of physical harm to the enemy—was a common denominator in the disputes between the dominant families or clans.

These blood feuds frequently resulted in the formation of short-lived bands of kins or families, especially when one of the clans found itself in the good graces of the provincial government and was thus able to mobilize additional support or immunity from the states. Under these circumstances, life in highly mobile armed bands was the only alternative to death or imprisonment; but it was far from a permanent situation. In fact, these *condottièri* did not become outcasts and could resume their normal activities once the fight was over. As opposed to rural professional banditry—the *cangaço* of the late nineteenth century—these early warriors were in the eyes of the dominant social order, not outlaws but rightful defenders of their clans and their personal honor.[2]

The patriarchal authority of the landlords rested ultimately on their capacity to enforce decisions by violent means, that is to say, on the number of armed men they were capable of mobilizing. Their private militias were, for that reason, their most visible power resource. The militias were formed of two major elements: first, the *jagunço*, the landlord's bodyguard and military strategist (often a rural worker with a criminal record, or even a hired gunman, who found in the chieftains' dominions a perfect sanctuary); second, the *cabra*, or *cangaceiro manso*, the rural tenant worker whose work contract implied the unconditional defense of the landlord. Those militias were the accurate expression of the relations of dependence that cemented the patriarchal order: the *jagunço* or the *cabra*'s commitment to the landlord's violence was indeed reciprocated with protection from his enemies and from the public authorities. As a matter of fact, the use of violence in interpersonal disputes was a prescribed response among rural workers, but it was drastically limited to disputes *inter pares*. When directed toward other aims, "a pool of this violent potential [had to] be sponsored and channeled by the patriarchal authority of the landlord." [3] There were scattered manifestations of unsponsored violence among rural workers, usually in the form of recurrent bands of road assailants; but these were to be subdued by the police and the landlords.

Toward the end of the nineteenth century the social controls of the pat-

---

[2] The terms *cangaço* and *cangaceiros* denote the ancient bandits' habit of carrying the blunderbuss across their shoulders in the manner of a yoke or *canga*. See Gustavo Barroso, *Heróis e bandidos: os cangaceiros do Nordeste* (Rio de Janeiro: Livraria Francisco Alves, 1931), p. 31.

[3] Bolivar Lamounier, "Consensus and Dissensus in Brazilian Politics: An Interpretation," University of California, Los Angeles, 1968 (mimeographed).

riarchal order were loosened, and its virtual monopoly of the use of violence was broken apart and scattered to the lower strata of the population. The *cangaço* then emerged as the expression of the collective use of violence independent from, unsponsored by, and quite frequently directed against the patriarchal landlords. The organizational forms and the warfare experiences of the early bands of *condottieri* proved to be a priceless asset for the newborn *cangaço*. As a matter of fact, both existed for some decades until the former faded away, making room for the full development of professional banditry. Professionalization and autonomy were indeed the essential characteristics that differentiated the bands of *condottieri* and *cangaceiros*. As accurately described by Rui Facó, "the bands of *cangaceiros* were formed of men who had achieved autonomy, if only relative, vis-à-vis the rural power structure. The *cangaceiro* was not a hired criminal. He perpetrated crimes on his own risk and interests. But what made him a distinctive character was the fact that he was a rebel against the dominant order." [4]

At this point, it is worthwhile recalling that the patriarchal order was based mainly on the set of dependency relations between the landlords and the rural masses. Of utmost importance were those relations that prescribed mutual defense: either the peasant's commitment to the landlord's violent actions, or the landlord's sponsorship of his tenants' and subjects' violence. If such a situation was taken for granted, then why did autonomous groups of *cangaceiros* appear at all? It is suggested in the present paper that neither the patriarchal order nor the public agencies were capable at a given time— a relatively short but nevertheless crucial period of time in terms of its consequences—of providing protection for the rural populations. This period of time expressed the historical moment when two lines of development— the decay of the private power of the landlords and the expansion of the regulative capabilities of the states—intersected, creating a point of indifference where neither of them was strong enough to offset the other.

At that moment the rural masses, caught between landlords and public authorities, principally the state police, had to resort to self-help against the excesses of both. As one would expect, the *cangaço* was modeled in the likeness of the patriarchal order, protecting and sponsoring the violent actions of its own clientele. Notwithstanding, adherence to a band of *cangaceiros* was not motivated solely by desire for revenge or self-defense. Once these bands became independent, they provided the rural masses with a

---

[4] Rui Facó, *Cangaceiros e fanáticos: gênese e lutas* (Rio de Janeiro: Editôra Civilização Brasileira, 1963), p. 63. (Ed. note: while Souza correctly generalizes on the connection between the decline of the power of the rural landowner-patriarch and the rise of the *cangaço*, it should be made clear that there were large areas such as the Chapada Diamantina in Bahia where the patriarchal power survived and cangaceiros did not thrive.)

means of access to hitherto denied areas of achievement—and not only economic achievement. Whereas the distribution of power and prestige within the patriarchal communities was a function of ascribed statuses: age, sex, lineage, and the like, in the *cangaço* it was rather a function of prowess, a personal attribute. For that reason, recruitment to the bands was open not only to the avengers, but also to the most dynamic, daring elements within the lower stratum.[5]

The *cangaço* was both a symptom and an accelerating factor in the decay of the patriarchal order. It emerged when the economic, social, and political integration of Northeast Brazil opened deep fissures in the backlands' society. Mass emigration to other areas was a first result. The flourishing rubber enterprise in the Amazon attracted hundreds of thousands of workers, many of whom later returned to the backlands bearing new experiences, aspirations, and discontent. A second migratory flow was caused by the catastrophic droughts of the 1870s which ousted the rural populations from the backlands to the coastal cities and, from there, to other parts of the country. These migrations created a labor shortage that almost brought the agricultural and cattle-raising economy of the backlands to collapse, badly undermining the economic foundations of the patriarchal order. The end of the drought was immediately followed by the proclamation of the Republic and the creation of a more cohesive national political system. During the first three decades of republican history, the integration of the isolated feuds into a broader political framework was largely achieved at the expenses of the rural chieftains' power resources, relentlessly mobilized for the overthrow of old and new oligarchies.

Therefore, local governments found themselves unable to cope successfully with the emerging *cangaço*. Banditry had grown into an enterprise, independent enough to turn the landlords' commands into sterile words. The state governments were in no better situation. The political instability of the first republican decades, for one thing, prevented any significant commitment of resources for the repression of banditry. During the bands' crucial period of consolidation they had to rely on semimercenary mobile police forces, the *volantes*. These police units, far from exterminating banditry, encouraged it; formed by police officers, ex-criminals, and people seeking personal revenge, the *volantes*, with few exceptions, acted as violently as the *cangaceiros*. Some thirty years of unsuccessful repression, however, only strengthened the state governments' commitment to

---

[5] The fact that regional literature has been centered around the dyad migration-banditry as alternatives to dependence on the landlords, seems to be more than a coincidence. The romance, *Cangaciros*, by José Lins do Rêgo, is the most well-known example of this approach.

the annihilation of the *cangaço*, not so much because of the damages it inflicted on farms and villages, even though these were not negligible but because the *cangaço*, as a living model of independence susceptible to emulation by the rural masses, posed a permanent threat to the established order. The *cangaço* survived for a few years after the disarmament of the local chieftains—accomplished by the Revolution of 1930—but was annihilated in 1940. That is to say, it witnessed the results of the very process it had hastened in Northeast Brazil: the monopolization of the use of violence by the state apparatus.

The demonstration of hypotheses about historical phenomena of the kind analyzed here only too frequently smack of *post factum* interpretations. The aim of this paper is to minimize the risk of advancing such explanations by spelling out the theoretical orientations of this as well as of other studies on the genesis and the consequences of the *cangaço*.

THE PATRIARCHAL ORDER AND THE *CANGACEIRO-HERÓI*

The patriarchal order in Brazil was a social community maintained by a complex set of relations of dependence and centered around the familial organization and the regime of large landed estates. The conditions of the agricultural enterprise in the colonial times—the relatively high degree of isolation of the rural dominions and the virtual absence of public law enforcement institutions—reinvigorated the then-decadent type of Portuguese patriarchal family, a pyramidal system topped by a paterfamilias which was the main source of order and discipline and the final arbiter for all disputes and decisions. The patriarchal family had at its center the married couple, their offspring, and relatives, and at its periphery the small multitude of rural tenants, godsons, and slaves, constituting a "powerful system for political and economic domination and for acquisition and maintenance of prestige and status." [6]

The familial clans' ambitions for increased power and prestige—in terms of political hegemony or the expansion of their common land patrimony—resulted in a series of blood feuds throughout colonial and imperial Brazil. Incorporation of new lands to the *sesmarias*, the enormous landed estates donated by the Portuguese Crown, was a prime motive for these struggles. The war between the clans of the Montes and the Feitosas is one notorious example. Set off by a dispute over land, it mobilized a broad network of

---

[6] See Maria Isaura Pereira de Queiróz," O mandonismo local na vida política brasileira," *Anhêmbi*, XXIV-XXVI (1956–1957), pp. 263 ff. The patriarchal family in Northeast Brazil was exhaustively studied by Gilberto Freyre, especially in his *Casa grande e senzala* (Rio de Janeiro: Livraria José Olympio Editôra, 1934).

allied clans in the backlands of Ceará and its consequences were still felt in the early nineteenth century.[7] During the imperial period these conflicts were displaced to the villages as the clans fought to gain control of the municipal councils and to enjoy the prestige of being in a governmental capacity. The search for a dominant power position in the local government would split the community into two irreconcilable factions clustered around the major clans and would frequently end in the annihilation or removal of one of the parties or the dismemberment of the municipality. Whichever their motivations, however, these struggles quite often transcended the immediate political or economic stake into a deep-seated and self-perpetuating hate between the clans. The war between the Carvalhos and the Pereiras, for example, began in 1849 when the former lost the local elections but prevented the latter from assuming office. A series of blood feuds, which were to last until the late 1920s, followed that action, and the clans soon replaced the aims of electoral victory with the aims of mutual extermination. In 1917, Leonardo Mota interviewed one *coronel*, Antônio Pereira, then imprisoned in the penitentiary of Fortaleza: "Do you want to know something?" asked Pereira. "There, in my Pageú, before a Pereira's child is hardly grown he's already saying: 'I wish to become a man soon to kill a Carvalho!' Their children say the same thing. That's the way it is: it's a matter of blood." [8]

The central government did not have a consistent policy toward such wars, whether in the villages or in the countryside. Once in a while it performed the role of the arbitrator, trying to reconcile the clans by means of a treaty of peace, as it did, for example, in the war between the Mourões and the Moreiras.[9] Most frequently, the provincial governments would openly support one clan against the other. But "if the party damned by the government happened to defeat the one it first supported, it would immediately join with and support the winner." [10] In fact, the very indecision of the governmental intervention was a built-in condition of the stability of the political system. By adopting a highly flexible strategy toward these

---

[7] See L. A. da Costa Pinto, *Lutas de famílias no Brasil* (São Paulo: Companhia Editôra Nacional, 1949), pp. 146 ff. The mobilization of allied clans—in that case, the Inhamuns—is described in Nertan Macêdo's *O Clã dos Inhamuns: uma família de guerreiros e pastores das cabeceiras do Jaguaribe* (Fortaleza: Editôra Comédia Cearense, 1965),

[8] Interview transcribed in Leonardo Mota's *Violeiros do norte* (Rio de Janeiro: Editôra A Noite, 1955), p. 184.

[9] See Nertan Macêdo, *O bacamarte dos Mourões*, (Fortaleza: Editôra Instituto do Ceará, 1966), and Gerardo Melo Mourão, *O país dos Mourões* (Rio de Janeiro: Edições GRD, 1963.

[10] Pereira de Queiróz, *op. cit.*, p. 265. (Ed. note: The average tenure of provincial presidents in the nineteenth century was eighteen months or less, with a six- to twelve-month hiatus between presidents.)

struggles, the central government and its surrogates, the presidents of provinces, were able to endorse the doctrine of the *fait accompli*, accepting any winner as the legitimate representative of the community. By doing so they also maintained violence at the lower levels of the system, reducing the struggles for power to a purely local affair, the outcome of which was to be decided by the clans.

The local chieftains' absolute authority was the counterpart of the governmental strategy. In their communities, "the governmental action was limited to the collection of taxes and it did not intervene in the decisions of the chief of the clan. There were no written laws or codes. The chief was the law." [11] The multifunctionality of the municipal councils was, in fact, an expression of the prevalence of private power; policing of the community, for example, was in the hands of a locally elected judge, the *juiz de paz*. The creation of the police in 1841 did not alter this situation substantially. As described by Pereira de Queiróz, "those unfortunate marshals, lost in the middle of the backlands, lacking troops with which to effectuate captures and isolated from the provincial centers, could only survive under the shadow of the local chieftains." [12]

Given the limitations and fragilities of the states' regulative apparatus, reliance on the dictatorial rule of the local chieftains proved to be the only solution for maintenance of order in the more isolated communities. This situation found its institutional expression in the creation of the National Guard in 1832. The higher ranks of the guard—colonel, major, and captain—were comprised of the most powerful chieftain and his subordinates, in that order, thus legitimizing their *de facto* political leadership. Political power in the backlands was a function of the patriarchal authority of the landlord and the scope of his economic enterprise: in a word, it was a function of the number of laborers who depended on him for employment and protection. The capacity to mobilize a considerable number of armed men was indeed the ultimate test of the landlord's authority. In such emergencies he could certainly count on his relatives and bodyguards. The diffuse character of the patriarchal relationships assured him as well of his tenant workers' support: in fact, wrote Rui Facó, "When a rural chieftain admitted a new worker in his farm he did not need to contract his services as a member of his private militia, whether to defend his possessions or to attack his enemies. [The obligation to render these services] was implicit in the very fact of his admission to the farm." [13]

[11] M. Rodrigues de Melo, *Patriarcas e carreiros* (Rio de Janeiro: Pongetti Editôres, 1954), pp. 30 ff. The patriarchal rule is also described by Wilson Lins, *O médio São Francisco: uma sociedade de guerreiros e pastôres* (Salvador: Livraria Progresso, 1952).
[12] Pereira de Queiróz, *op. cit.*, p. 493.
[13] *Ibid.*, p. 147.

Again, the tenant workers' commitment to the landlord's violence was not unreciprocated. Survival in a hostile environment and in communities devoid of public institutions had to be based on mutual defense and on severe sanctions against "improper" behavior. It is safe to assume that, at least in colonial and imperial Brazil, violence was a cultural norm shared by all members of the patriarchal communes; landlords and peasants alike resorted to violent actions as a prescribed response to a wide range of social situations, especially those involving one's character as a man, his family, and sexual honor. Notwithstanding, this value system was also structured along another dimension, namely, subordination and deference to the upper stratum. If and when a tenant worker was compelled to respond violently to people in a superordinate position, quite often public officers, his action had to be sponsored by the chieftain. Through the practice of "receiving deliveries" (peasants pursued by the police), the landlords were able to assure protection to their subjects across regional or state boundaries. By doing so, they also made sure that those of the rural lower stratum would not undertake independent actions. Limited acceptance of tenant workers into higher statuses had similar functions: the *jagunço* himself was an example. He was, quite frequently, a member of the farm, a tenant worker experienced in the use of firearms. Nevertheless, "he had a slightly higher status and higher aspirations; he often initiated the defense planning; he was allowed to keep a rifle in his hut, contrary to most others in the private army who would not be given weapons until the time was ripe for action; and he inevitably had the *coronel* baptize his children, becoming his *compadre*. This was as much social mobility as he could hope for, probably; but as Costa Pinto points out, it was sufficient to channel—and neutralize—a large potential for violence, by recruiting into the structure the most active among the lowest stratum."[14]

To sum up: internally, the patriarchal order was sustained by the absolute authority of the landlord and the subordination of his tenant workers; externally, by the fragility of the states' regulative powers and their consequent acceptance of any dominant faction as the legitimate representative of the municipality. The survival and expansion of a particular patriarchal community was, therefore, a function of its success in achieving—and maintaining—control of these internal and external resources. That is to say, it was a function of its success in suppressing competitors.

Ancient banditry expressed, directly or indirectly, the clans' competition for a dominant power position at the local level. As members of the rural upper stratum, these men were, from the viewpoint of the dominant order, neither criminals nor *cangaceiros*. As suggested by Graciliano Ramos, they are better defined as the *cangaceiros-herói*, avengers of their

[14] Lamounier, *op. cit.*, p. 56.

families and their personal honor, and models of heroism and unselfishness for the peasantry.

A biographical survey of the most famous chiefs of bands in nineteenth-century Northeast Brazil shows that they were indeed men of "respectable origins," driven into a nomadic life by the interfamilial struggles. The fight between the Brilhantes and the Limões produced Jesuíno Brilhante and the bands of the Limões and Viriatos. Luiz Padre, Sinhô Pereira, and Antônio Quelé came from the hundred-year war of the Pereiras against the Carvalhos. Silvino Ayres, Liberato Nóbrega, and, later on, Antônio Silvino, the undisputed "governor of the backlands," were a result of the war between the Dantas-Cavalcanti Ayres and the Carvalho Nóbregas.[15] Their social origins had much to do with their mores, the acts of *noblesse oblige* immortalized by the blind singers. During the drought of the 1870s, Jesuíno Brilhante, for example, assaulted rich convoys in the deserted roads and distributed the cargoes among the migrant peasants, boasting the fact that he never robbed for himself. These *cangaceiros-herói* were remarkably selective in their use of violence, always hitting the inimical clan and no other target. The hate for the enemy was, nevertheless, overwhelming, and the strategy of mutual annihilation often proceeded to the point where little was left to fight for. But the subtle line between vengeance and rebellion was never crossed. After all,

Casimiro Honório, the Moraes, Jesuíno Brilhante, and Antônio Silvino had something to lose: lands, farms, or even a family name that had a traditional value. They could not all of the sudden show themselves as demolishers of respectable institutions. On the contrary, they upheld [these institutions] for—if reprobates—they were somehow elements of Order, fond of Property, of all the attributes of Property. They did not fight against Property *per se* but rather their enemies' properties.[16]

At mid-century, however, external forces set in motion an irreversible process of change. The rapid integration of Northeast Brazil into the national society carved deep fissures in the hitherto monolithic structure of the patriarchal order, and the use of violence began trickling down to the rural lower stratum.

---

[15] The relations between interfamilial wars and the rise of ancient banditry are excellently described in Maria Isaura Pereira de Querióz, *Os cangaceiros: les bandits d'honneur brésiliens* (Paris: Julliard, 1968).

[16] Graciliano Ramos, "Dois cangaços," in *Viventes das Alagôas* (São Paulo: Livraria Martins Editôra, 1962), p. 150.

MIGRATIONS AND INTERMITTENT BANDITRY

Any attempt to explain the rise of professional banditry in such a society has to reckon with some basic questions, all of which were implicit
in the description of the patriarchal order. First, it is hardly conceivable
that tenant workers would resort to independent banditry without previous
subversion of the patriarchal value imperatives of dependence and deference. The social isolation of the patriarchal communities did not provide
their subjects with alternative modes of life; experience—actual or vicar-
ious—of different social situations, was thus necessary in order to raise their
aspirations. That is to say, the adoption of independence as a paradigm of
social behavior implied the perception of his situation in terms of relative,
not absolute, deprivation. Second, it is also difficult to envisage any significant changes in power distributions had the mechanisms of paternalist protection and repression remained intact. As long as the patriarch's capabilities could match the workers' expectations, including the expectation of
violent repression of nonsponsored actions, higher aspirations were more
likely to induce resignation than rebellion. Therefore, a relative decrease
of the patriarchs' capabilities was a necessary condition for the translation
of aspirations into action. Third, banditry could hardly succeed as a collective response if there were no normative and group supports that facilitated
its institutionalization. This question is further discussed below.[17]

Experiences of relative deprivation on a broad scale were intimately tied
to the economic integration of Northeast Brazil. The economy of the backlands did indeed offer very slender channels of social mobility, notwithstanding the fact that slavery was almost nonexistent. The cattle-raising
enterprise was a system of work on shares; the cowboy was not a serf but
a partner, with rights to a fourth of the calves produced by the herd under
his supervision and, eventually, to a narrow strip of land on which to grow
crops. These activities, of course, barely sufficed to keep him and his family at a subsistence level; but the system provided few other occupational
alternatives. He could become a *jagunço* or perhaps a *cantador*, a singer in
the marketplaces, moving one notch up the social ladder. That hardly
meant a substantial betterment of his situation; yet, in his eyes, such accom-
plishments must have loomed large. In any event, that much social mobility was enough to gain his commitment to the patriarchal landlords.

The rubber enterprises in the Amazon changed this situation quite drastically. A new frontier, it rapidly attracted the most dynamic men from
the lower stratum, dazzling them with the prospects of enrichment on a
personal merit basis. It is estimated that, from Ceará alone, some 300,000

---

[17] For a more systematic discussion of these propositions, see Ted Gurr, "Psychological Factors in Civil Violence," *World Politics* (January 1968), pp. 243–278.

people moved to the rubber fields between 1869 and 1900, a third of whom returned to the province during the same period.[18] The results were far from surprising, as Rui Facó observed:

The simple act of migrating pulled the rural worker out of his centennial social immobility and represented a first step toward a way of life other than subordination to the landlords. The experience of migration made him aware of his original situation and those who returned were not the same. Contact with different people, with different forms of social life, the unrestrained competition among the rubber trees' owners, and the hard struggle for livelihood had changed his mentality.[19]

Governor Benjamin Barroso was not altogether incorrect when he associated the surge of banditry with the return of the migrants, men who brought to the state "new habits acquired in the North, where they lived isolated from the local authorities and where they became accustomed to the daily use of guns." [20] Four decades sooner, however, such an assertion would have underestimated the patriarchal order's capabilities for dealing with the new rebels. As a matter of fact, the first migrants found out that the practices of sponsored violence left little room for the development of independent banditry. Beyond recruitment to the bands of *cangaceiros-herói* or to the private militias, there were no alternatives. The patriarchal chieftains rested assured that this potential for violence was under control; for, if banditry had to exist at all, then it would better be kept under the control of the *condottieri*, of those who at least respected the rules of the game of violence. Yet it was a provisional solution. It was doubtful whether these men would conform in the long run, to the strategy of leaders who prided themselves on the fact that "neither they, nor their men ever robbed for their own sake." The death of Jesuíno Brilhante when his men, embittered by the fierce discipline he imposed on the band, abandoned him exemplified the artificiality of these solutions.

But until the drought of 1877–1879 the patriarchal landlords and their militias were an insurmountable barrier to the proliferation of independent bands. The drought came after a period of more than thirty years of regular rainfall, during which the economic activities of Northeast Brazil had expanded significantly. Three years of dry seasons, however, sufficed to shatter the economic life of large areas, forcing hundreds of thousands of people to flee the backlands. The annual report of 1879 by the president of Ceará summarized the consequences of the catastrophe:

[18] Joaquim Alves, "Notas para uma introdução à história das sêcas," in Raimundo Girão and A. Martins Filho, *O Ceará* (Fortaleza: Editôra Fortaleza, 1945), p. 342.

[19] Facó, *op. cit.*, p. 32.

[20] Address to the State Legislature of Ceará in 1914. Quoted in Abelardo F. Montenegro *História do cangaceirismo no Ceará* (Fortaleza: A. Batista Fontenele, 1955), p. 77.

The two industries that support the Province, agriculture and cattle raising were almost annihilated. . . . There were no cereals, and water, impure and brackish, was only obtainable at deep drilling. Commerce was dead. The public service tended toward complete disorganization. The Municipal Councils, the jury, and the various administrative agencies of the government could not function, given the insufficient number of qualified persons. Teachers abandoned the schools and some curates, the parishes. Policemen were beginning to desert.[21]

A series of ensuing dry seasons magnified the catastrophe of 1877: the droughts of 1888 and 1900 left more than a hundred thousand victims, and similar figures were added to the credit of the disaster by the droughts of 1915 and 1919.

Dead crops and cattle and labor migration brought the economy of the backlands to the brink of collapse. The patriarchal landlords, many of whom sought refuge in the coastal cities, were almost impotent to provide the rural population with jobs, protection, or even a meaning to their lives. Haunted by the threat of starvation, thousands of the migrants from the drought areas thus resorted to pillage and robbery, creating a surge of intermittent banditry throughout the backlands. "These bandits loot properties in the most unrestrained fashion," panicked the newspaper O Cearense in 1878, "as if communism had already been proclaimed among us." [22] Predictably enough, the cangaceiros-herói, in the absence of the patriarchal landlords, became the champions of law and order. The new bands of the Carirí Valley, for example, were rapidly ousted from Ceará by João Calangro. Furthermore, they resumed the landlords' paternalist functions, distributing booty among the poor, protecting villages, and arbitrating disputes.

Following the end of the drought, these bands decreased in number and boldness. Notwithstanding, the power resources of the local chieftains were badly affected by the catastrophe: labor was now concentrated in a few areas spared by the drought, and the backlands were faced with the problems of economic reconstruction, practically without governmental assistance. A decade later, however, before these tasks were accomplished, the landlords were forced to commit their meager resources to the tasks of integrating the region into the republican political structure.

[21] Quoted in Raimundo Girão, História econômica do Ceará (Fortaleza: Editôra Instituto do Ceará, 1947), p. 395. Refer also to Rodolpho Theophilo, História da sêca do Ceará: 1877 a 1880 (Rio de Janeiro: Imprensa Ingleza, 1922).
[22] Quoted in Montenegro, op. cit., p. 52.

THE CORONELISTA STRUCTURE AND THE POLITICS OF VIOLENCE

The term *coronelismo* refers, in a general sense, to a political arrangement resulting from the decay of the private power of the landlords and the simultaneous increase of the regulative powers of the federal and state governments.[23] Following the extension of franchise in 1889, a bargain was established between the local chieftains and the state governments: the chieftains, by virtue of their domination of the communities, delivered their votes; the states, in turn, gave them virtually unlimited control of the governmental apparatus at the local level. A similar bargain, formalized under the name of *política dos governadores*, existed between the federal and state governments. The government of each state was entrusted to an oligarchy, a complex of extended families and their allies, organized into the Republican party. They elected congressmen unconditionally favorable to the president's actions and in return were given complete freedom of action within their states, especially to suppress opposition groups. The presidency itself was definitely out of the reach of most states, for it was occupied, alternately, by the two leading states of the federation, Minas Gerais and São Paulo.

If anything, this structure implied a much tighter integration among all levels of political leadership. The coronelista bargain generally sufficed to assure the local chieftains' commitment to the state obligarchy. Notwithstanding, the increased importance of local domination could quite easily lead the political factions into a struggle for mutual extermination: in fact, to be deprived of local power positions meant to be threatened with suppression by those in control of the governmental apparatus. As Juarez R. Brandão observed:

At any given moment all power positions of the community were controlled entirely by one of the political factions. The ascent to political dominance of the other faction, when it occurred, meant in a short time a complete change and the occupation of all focal power-statuses by the new group. The dominant group of a given time had, locally, a virtual power monopoly and was backed by the state oligarchy.[24]

This strategy was, to be sure, a remnant of imperial Brazil; the difference was that the Empire controlled these local transfers of power, for they reflected the institutionalized rotation of Liberal and Conservative in the cabi-

---

[23] This is the now-classical definition proposed by Victor Nunes Leal in his *Coronelismo, enxada e voto: O município e o regime representativo no Brasil* (Rio de Janeiro: Livraria Forense, 1949).

[24] "Some Basic Developments in Brazilian Politics and Society," in *New Perspectives of Brazil*, ed. by Eric N. Baklanoff (Nashville: Vanderbilt University Press, 1966), p. 70.

net. Under the Republican regime, however, no such mechanism was available and the contest for power was fiercer than ever. Sometimes the rapid intervention of the state oligarchy was required to mediate a struggle that might otherwise degenerate into a broad civil strife. In the Carirí Valley, for example, nine local chieftains were violently deposed between 1900 and 1910, and the repeated mobilization of armed militias kept the area in a state of war. The governor had the valley's chieftains agree to a pact of mutual support, the *Pacto dos Coronéis*, which stated that henceforth no attempts to depose a copartisan would be made and that, in case of dispute, the chief of the party—the governor himself—would decide the matter.[25]

A high degree of political integration also implied a high degree of responsiveness to changes in national politics. Unexpected shifts within the national power structure, or the need to bring a reluctant oligarchy into alignment with the presidency, required the local chieftains' active participation in statewide political mobilizations. Ceará's Revolt of 1914 is an example. Shortly after his inauguration as president of the Republic, Marshal Hermes da Fonseca, in order to strengthen his position, sponsored the deposition of the governors who opposed his candidacy, notably the northern and northeastern oligarchies. To do so, he supported military candidates in the next gubernatorial election and charged the oligarchies with electoral corruption when his candidates were defeated. Federal intervention followed this action, toppling the Rosa e Silva's oligarchy in Pernambuco and the Accioly's oligarchy in Ceará. The time was ripe for the countercoup, sponsored by the national chief of the Republican party, Senator Pinheiro Machado. In order to depose the governor of Ceará, Army Colonel Franco Rebelo, he resorted to the Carirí Valley chieftains, organized by Padre Cícero, a charismatic leader.[26] Under his guidance, they created another state assembly, establishing an illegal legislative power and thereby legitimating the federal intervention. Shortly before the intervention was decreed, however, an army of some 5,000 people—private militias, bandits, and religious fanatics—invaded the capital of the state and toppled the government.

Under the coronelista structure, a heavy commitment was thus required of the northeastern chieftains. A series of political mobilizations took place throughout the First Republic's forty years of existence: the overthrow of

[25] See Irineu Pinheiro, *O Joaseiro do Padre Cícero e a revolução de 1914* (Rio de Janeiro: Irmãos Pongetti Editôres, 1938), pp. 174–180.
[26] The relationship between messianism and the political structure is excellently discussed by Ralph della Cava, "Brazilian Messianism and National Institutions: A Comparison of Canudos and Joàzeiro," paper read at the annual convention of the American Historical Association, Columbia University, New York, January 1967; published in *Hispanic American Historical Review*, XLVIII, 3 (August 1968), 402–420.

the Bahian government in 1920 and the revolt of Princesa, in Paraíba, in 1927, are other well-known examples of mobilization involving thousands of armed men.[27] These struggles finally undermined the power resources of the local chieftains: for one thing, the commitment of their followings to large-scale political operations deprived their economic enterprises of a substantial number of laborers. In fact, the politics of violence soon came to rely upon gunmen made available in some strategically located villages, such as Pageú das Flôres, in Pernambuco; Juàzeiro, in Ceará; Princesa, in Paraíba; and Piranhas, in Bahia. Those men were, so to speak, the remnants of the chieftains' military campaigns, who found agricultural work to be far less exciting as a means of earning a living than the pillaging of properties.

The chieftains' political struggles also rendered them less capable of providing their followings with protection and sponsorship of violent actions. In addition, the chieftains had to bargain with what was now a more powerful government for the sake of maintaining their local domination. Therefore, by its own dynamics *coronelismo* led to a stalemate in which neither the chieftains nor the government could completely capture one another's functions, but both could interfere, if only partially, with one another's actions. That was true in communities long shaken by violent struggles; the marshals were a bit bolder than one would expect; the judges, less willing to yield to the chieftains' will. In these communities, the practices of traditional violence by those near the bottom of the social ladder, in the absence of sponsorship by a powerful chieftain, were defined as criminal acts and treated accordingly by the public authorities. For these men the solution was, as they said, "to fall into the *cangaço*," first by joining the bands of *cangaceiros-herói* and then by forming their own bands. When a handful of talented leaders emerged among them, recruiting gunmen in the villages and turning banditry into a professional enterprise, the new *cangaço* was born.

CANGAÇO: THE ENTREPRENEURSHIP OF VIOLENCE

The *cangaço* was an enterprise of select individuals, those who already stood above the rural masses' average levels of aspirations and personal independence. The leadership of the bands, for one thing, was of a slightly higher social origin, generally small proprietors, proud of their integrity

27 See, respectively, Walfrido Moraes, *Jagunços e heróis* (Rio de Janeiro: Editôra Civilização Brasileira, 1963); and Barbosa Lima Sobrinho, *A verdade sôbre a Revolução de Outubro*, (Rio de Janeiro: Edições Unitas, 1933). A political study of this period can be found in Moacir Palmeira, "Nordeste: mudanças políticas no século XX," *Cadernos Brasileiros* (October 1966).

even if they lived in virtual poverty; in the words of Labareda, an ex-chief of *cangaceiros*, what his family earned "sufficed, in those days, to live as human beings, not ashamed of our condition. We were poor but honest."[28] In fact, the respectable poor were exactly those who were less prone to bear an affront, especially if it came from the police. After all, they enjoyed a minimum of social prestige and were eager to preserve it. In this respect, the life stories of the various leaders of the *cangaço* are almost inevitably the same: Lampião, by far the most talented of all cangaceiros, is a typical example. Born in a family of small landowners, rendered influential by virtue of intimate relations with the clan of the Pereiras, he and two brothers murdered a neighbor in a dispute of minor importance. The police, backed by the clan of the Carvalhos, attacked soon afterwards and murdered his parents. Without protection, the family joined the band of Sinhô Pereira and Luiz Padre until 1922, when the leadership was assumed by Lampião.[29]

However, in contrast to the *cangaceiros-herói*, these men could not dream of resuming their normal activities. In 1922, for example Sinhô Pereira abandoned the *cangaço* and moved to another state, Goiás, where, assisted by his clan, he settled as a farmer. But the *cangaceiro*, deprived of influential and wealthy sponsors, could only survive by maximizing its sole power resource, violence. Faced with a weakened local power structure and an increasingly independent police, the *cangaceiros* were able to emerge as a third force in the backlands. In doing so they inaugurated a new channel of access to positions of power and prestige, not only because of their skillful employment of violence, but also because they could draw on a normative support, the local traditions that sanctioned violent actions for the defense of one's integrity. It did not require much effort on the part of those men to cast aside the traditional limits imposed on the use of violence; for, as was said of Robin Hood, "an outlaw, in those times, being deprived of protection, owed no allegiance."[30]

As a professional enterprise, the *cangaço* also subverted the status expectations prevalent in the patriarchal communities; there, the distribution of social rewards had much to do with a structure of dominant ascribed statuses. However, the access to such rewards via banditry required only one attribute, personal prowess. Joining a band became a means for achievement for all those who felt relatively deprived by virtue of a low ascribed

---

[28] Quoted from a recorded interview with Labareda, transcribed in Estácio de Lima, *O mundo estranho dos cangaceiros: ensaio biosociológico* (Salvador: Editôra Itapoã, 1965), pp. 177 ff.

[29] Ranulpho Prata, *Lampeão* (Rio de Janeiro: Ariel Editôra, 1934); and Optato Gueiros, *Lampeão: memórias de um oficial ex-comandante de fôrças volantes* (Salvador: Livraria Progresso, 1956).

[30] James Carter, *A Visit to Sherwood Forest, with a Critical Essay on the Life and Times of Robin Hood* (Mansfield: T. W. Clarke, 1875).

status.[31] Volta Sêca, a younger member of Lampião's band, exemplifies this point. He was eleven years old when he joined the band, first as a servitor and, shortly after, as a *cangaceiro*; until then, he sold candies at the village, living under his parents' stronghold. In the band, on the contrary, he could readily enjoy the rewards associated with older age. "I loved my new life," he recalled in 1958. "We were respected everywhere. Fearful peasants watched us pass by and that pleased me."[32]

The success of the *cangaço* was also a function of the type of group supports, internal and external, upon which it was organized. The band of Lampião serves as an illustration. Internally, the band was organized as a federation, topped by Lampião and his brothers. A number of subchiefs and their relatives, such as Corisco, Zé Bahiano, Virgínio, and Labareda, formed the second layer of leaders; chief and subchiefs constituted a highly cohesive group, intimately related to one another by ties of compaternity and friendship. Below them, and organized into smaller groups led by each subchief, came the *cabras*, the anonymous mass of bandits which shifted in number depending on the scope of the band's operations. Externally, the band was supported by a broad underground network, the *coiteiros*, a clientele of rural workers and small landowners who exchanged information for protection. Information about movements of police troops was essential for the band; but the *coiteiro* had other functions. For one thing, he was quite often the broker between the *cangaceiros* and the rural masses, either recruiting new members for the band or voicing complaints against the local chieftains and the police.[33] Notwithstanding, the *cangaço* was a professional enterprise, and it was carried on as such. Strategy, military and political, was of foremost importance. The band averaged eighty men, divided into twelve-man raiding units that undertook assaults within a range of no more than two hundred miles from the core unit led by Lampião. That was the band's exclusive territory, within which no other band was allowed to operate. The *cangaceiros'* strict discipline in combat was an

---

[31] A theoretical discussion of these propositions can be found in Lewis Coser, "Violence and the Social Structure," in *Violence and War*, ed. by Jules H. Masserman (New York: Grune and Stratton, 1963). This recruitment pattern explains, in part, the strong emphasis on racial factors as a cause of banditry that characterizes much of the literature on the cangaço. See, for example, Djacir Menezes, *O outro Nordeste* (Rio de Janeiro: José Olympio, 1937); and "Etnogênese das Caatingas e formação histórica do cangaço," *Cultura Política* (February 1942), pp. 31–42. The role of violence in the secularization of social relations in Colombia is discussed by Orlando Fals Borda, "Violence and the Breakdown of Tradition in Colombia," in *Obstacles to Change in Latin America*, ed. by Claudio Véliz (New York: Oxford University Press, 1965).

[32] Interview by Bruno Gomes, published in the newspaper *O Globo*. Quoted in Maria Isaura Pereira de Queiróz, *op. cit.*, p. 148.

[33] The role of the *coiteiro* is discussed by Prata, *op. cit.*, pp. 158 ff.

asset for the tactics of guerrilla warfare; highly mobile, familiar with the terrain, and careful to avoid direct confrontations, the raiding units inflicted serious defeats on the police troops. Data on thirty-seven incidents in Pernambuco and Bahia alone, during a period of fifteen years, show that the band held a favorable ratio of wins to losses, about two to one, in its encounters with police.[34]

Likewise, the selective and instrumental use of violence was the crux of the band's political strategy. Assaults on farms and villages—or even on cities of over ten thousand inhabitants, like Mossoró—provided only part of the band's economic profits. The other part came from extortion, ransom, "taxation" of commerce, and sale of "protection." The latter, especially, was an elaborate operation: Lampião compelled merchants and landowners to buy "safe passes," a card with his photograph and signature. In order to sustain these operations, the band had to be able to enforce their threats of violence in a discriminating manner. Refusals to pay for protection or ransom, abuses of his protegées, or a *coiteiro's* treachery were immediately punished with death. But the *cangaceiros* were careful not to alienate the support of actual or potential friends. As described by Labreda, "At our poor friends' shops we paid for everything we wanted. At our rich friends' shops we asked to be served. If not, they received a beating, a bullet, or some other petty cruelties as an example to others."[35]

By 1920 the *cangaço* had already attained autonomy in the backlands. However, the "official" acknowledgment of that status dates from 1926, when the Prestes Column invaded Northeast Brazil. The Prestes Column was born of a military rebellion against then-President Arthur Bernardes; it started as a barracks revolt in São Paulo, where it was rapidly subdued by the Army. As a last resort, the rebels formed a military column that raided the interior of the country, frustrating Army and police efforts to suppress it. In 1926, the situation was serious enough to compel the federal government into requesting the local chieftains' armed support, through the organization of "patriotic battalions" at some strategically located points, such as Juàzeiro, in Ceará. There, Padre Cícero, commissioned by the federal government, attested to the *cangaço's* autonomy, inviting Lampião to form one such battalion. Lampião's support was in fact bargained for, not commandeered; in exchange, he requested money, brand new armaments, and formally delegated powers to act against the Column. As a result, in April, 1926, he and two brothers were designated captain and lieutenants of the Army. As a matter of fact, he never fought the Column, and his reasons for not doing so were straightforward: "Banditry is a means of livelihood. If

[34] Gueiros, *op. cit.*, pp. 261–269.
[35] Estácio de Lima, *op. cit.*, p. 266.

I were to fire on all the *macacos* ["soldiers" or "policemen"] I come across, I would have been dead long ago."[36]

This new autonomy of the *cangaço* was paralleled by the increased commitment of public resources for its suppression. The local chieftains had set the tone of this enterprise: within their feuds, and as long as they were able to do so, all *cangaceiros* were executed. The state governments' actions followed the chieftains' strategy closely. For one thing, they feared that the *cangaço*, the exercise of uncontrolled private violence, might evolve into a broad civil revolt, such as the messianic wars of Canudos, in 1897, and Contestado, in 1916.[37] Governor Benjamin Barroso, for example, made sure that the state police's raids eliminated this threat through the physical elimination of bandits: "Have them summarily executed" were his orders to the commander of a military expedition to the backlands.[38] However, the state governments were in no position, at least until the late 1920s, to commit a significant amount of resources to the suppression of banditry, not only because their regulative powers were still limited, but also because the intrinsic instability of the coronelista bargain rendered the governmental apparatus unwilling to enforce impersonal rules in the administration of justice over all forms of private violence. Therefore, the impossibility of coping simultaneously with the landlords and the *cangaceiros'* violence led the state governments to endorse the violence of the *volantes*.

The *volantes* were semimercenary mobile police troops, loosely controlled by the state governments. The organization and direction of these troops were entrusted to police officers or commissioned members of the Army; but the troops themselves were a disparate collection of ex-criminals, policemen, and people seeking revenge on the *cangaceiros*. The *volante* of the Nazarenos is an example; it was thus named because a majority of its members were neighbors from Nazaré, a village harshly assaulted by Lampião. The *volantes* were, in general, only distinguishable from the *cangaceiros* in that their devotion to private violence was sponsored by the state governments. But, exactly for that reason, they were able to wage a war on the *cangaço* using similar tactics and weapons; they too created an exclusive clientele, sponsored blood vengeances, and resorted to terror as a means of securing the rural population's compliance. The soldiers' poor pay often led them to economic appropriations—looting properties of the *cangaceiros'* friends and the state governments' enemies. "We were not

[36] Gueiros, *op. cit.*, p. 110.
[37] On Canudos, see Euclydes da Cunha's classic study *Rebellion in the Backlands* (Chicago: University of Chicago Press, 1944). On Contestado, see Maurício Vinhas de Queiróz, *Messianismo e conflito social: a guerra sertaneja do Contestado, 1912–1916* (Rio de Janeiro: Editôra Civilização Brasileira, 1966).
[38] See Montenegro, *op. cit.*, p. 79.

saints," admitted Labareda. "We beat, we killed, we robbed; but, generally, in order to survive. But we also gave to the poor. [The *volantes*] did not give a thing to anybody: they robbed them. We did not have the government to supply us: they did."[39] The private feud between the *cangaço* and the *volantes* thus produced as many new recruits to one as to the other side: farmers and rural workers, embittered by police brutality, secretly or openly supported the *cangaceiros*, and vice versa. Furthermore, the spread of violence meant, at best, a permanent menace to the backlands' security and, at worst, a potential threat to the very integrity of the state.

Throughout this period, however, state regulative powers had been increasing at a slow but inexorable pace. And as they increased, so did the government determination to suppress private violence—patriarchal, professional, or mercenary.

THE REVOLUTION OF 1930 AND THE END OF THE *CANGAÇO*

As Max Weber observed:

If the coercive apparatus is strong enough, it will suppress private violence in any form. . . . Subsequently [the political community] engenders, more generally, a form of permanent public peace, with the compulsory submission of all disputes to the arbitration of the judge, who transforms blood vengeance into rationally ordered punishment, and feuds and expiatory actions into rationally ordered legal procedures.[40]

These were, indeed, the designs of the state. In 1922, a first effort was made to establish a pool of the state governments' coercive apparatus for the suppression of banditry. The oligarchies' fear of external intervention had long prevented the circulation of police troops across state boundaries; now, however, the threat of the *cangaço's* development imposed new conditions for more efficient police campaigns. The Inter-State Police Convention of December 1922 undersigned by the governments of Pernambuco, Ceará, Paraíba, and Rio Grande do Norte, permitted police troops to cross the border into a neighboring state in the pursuit of criminals, and established a close coordination between the state chiefs of police. However, the *volantes* were not disbanded; in fact, the agreement anticipated that each state would be responsible "for the damage his forces inflicted on private domiciles located in other states." In addition, it was careful to emphasize that "it was to be understood that these measures do not apply to political

---

[39] In Estácio de Lima, *op. cit.*, p. 239.
[40] Max Weber, *On Law in Economy and Society*, trans. by Edward Shils and Max Rheinstein and ed. by Max Rheinstein (Cambridge: Harvard University Press, 1954), p. 346.

persecution," that is to say, to local chieftains allied with the state governments.[41]

The threat of private violence became, nevertheless, unbearable. In 1930, the governor of Paraíba, one of the inspirers of the Revolution of October 1930 proposed another police convention to accomplish the final objectives of the Convention of 1922. His proposal, later to be incorporated into the Revolution's program, prescribed purging of criminal elements from the police forces, general disarmament of the rural population, prohibitive taxation on firearms and ammunitions, and extinction of the local chieftains' influence.[42] The governor, João Pessoa, murdered by an oppositionist chieftain, did not see the accomplishment of this task. In October 1930, however, the Liberal Alliance, a political coalition of rebel governors and Army officers, seized power and commandeered the destruction of the ancient regime. In Northeast Brazil, one of the first acts of the revolutionary government was the disarmament of all local chieftains and the arrest and demoralization of powerful landlords. During the first months of revolutionary rule, the new leaders made clear their designs for concentrating the governmental administrative and coercive apparatus in the hands of the state. A note of the government of Pernambuco, dated November 1930 prescribed that:

No prefect or any other person who may consider himself to have prestige in the political parties shall use the title of political chief. . . . The prefects shall limit themselves to the tasks of local administration, eliminating needless or excessive expenditures, retaining a minimum necessary number of public servants, and appointing public officers on a merit basis. . . . [And] the prefects shall not interfere with police matters, that, henceforth, remain an exclusive prerogative of police authorities.[43]

Subsequently, the revolutionary government replaced the prefects with appointed officers, established supervision and control on the municipal budgets, and promoted the centralization of justice. Finally under the Vargas dictatorship, from 1937 to 1945, all political parties and organizations were banned and the federal system was brought under the stronghold of the national government.

The suppression of patriarchal and mercenary private violence preceded the suppression of professional rural banditry by a few years. Backed by the Army and freed from local political interferences, the police forces embarked on a war of extermination of the cangaço. Commanded by the chief of police of Bahia, a pool of four northeastern state police troops was

[41] Montenegro, op. cit., p. 86.
[42] Ibid., p. 118.
[43] In Facó, op. cit., p. 196.

formed, some of which remained stationed at state borders, and all of which were organized into mobile forces equipped with radio transmitters. Repression of banditry was now a formidable enterprise; the evacuation of certain areas of the backlands, in 1931, exemplifies this point. This plan expressed the police assumption that the rural population's support was the main factor in the survival of banditry, thereby, under the supervision of Captain J. Miguel, an area within the range of almost three hundred miles from Paripiranga, in Bahia, was evacuated by the police, and some twelve thousand people were moved to villages and cities outside this range.[44] From 1931 on, thousands of bandits were arrested or executed, and in 1938 Lampião was killed. The remaining bandits surrendered to the police, with the exception of Corisco, killed in 1940. The government was careful to dissuade the reemergence of banditry; the bandits were decapitated and their heads exhibited throughout the backlands. The mummified heads rested until recently at the Nina Rodrigues Institute, in Salvador, as an example of the state's intolerance of private violence.

THE *CANGAÇO* AND ITS AFTERMATH

The *cangaço* never returned to the northeastern backlands. Among the peasants there remained the heroic tales of the bandits' lives and deeds, and a profound memory of the *cangaceiros*. The poems of the blind singers have kept alive the myth of the *cangaceiro* as a protector of the poor, an avenger of injustice, and an enemy of the rich and the powerful. They still tell the stories of the struggles of Lampião against the Devil, a Devil who keeps tax records, owns lands and cattle, and exploits the people.[45]

Conditions of life in the backlands remained very much the same during the past four decades. Under the same land tenure system, rural workers hardly experienced any significant betterment, and traditional work arrangements were still prevalent. After 1940, migration toward industrial southern Brazil siphoned off the most dynamic of the northeastern rural masses. Thus migration, rather than collective action, has been resorted to as a solution for unfulfilled aspirations.[46] Even those who challenged the dominant order in the past moved away from the backlands. Estácio de Lima collected data on twelve ex-*cangaceiros* and found that seven of them

[44] Prata, *op. cit.,* p. 193 ff.

[45] On the political content of the blind singers' poetry, see Amaury de Souza, "Traditional Media and Political Communication in Rural Brazil," Cambridge, mimeographed, 1968.

[46] On protest and migration as responses to rural poverty, see J. S. MacDonald, "Agricultural Organization, Migration, and Labour Militancy in Rural Italy," *The Economic History Review*, XVI, 1 (1963), 61–75.

are now skilled manual and clerical workers in large cities, while the other five are small farmers in the South.

The *cangaço* was an enterprise of men independent and ambitious enough to take their destinies in their own hands. They resorted to violence chiefly as a means for achievement and self-defense. But the conception of the *cangaceiro* as the champion of the people was not altogether mistaken. The *cangaço*, as Rui Facó pointed out, was also a rebellion of sorts against the dominant order. Social banditry was permeated by the rural masses' millenarian beliefs, a blend of equalitarian dreams and religious zeal. The bands had a modicum of organization and were capable of successful engagement in limited guerrilla operations. And the bandits could count on significant support from the rural workers. As a rebel, the *cangaceiro* could conceivably promote and assist peasant risings against the dominant order. Why, then, did the *cangaço* remain a political banditry?

The very environment in which the *cangaço* thrived prevented it from making effective revolt for the following reasons: first, because the *cangaceiros* catered to the peasants' support in exchange for protection, thus restructuring the traditional dependence and subordination relations between the bands and the rural masses; second, because the *cangaço* had no political aims radically opposed to those of the dominant order. The equalitarian aspirations of the millenarian movements were diluted by the bands' hierarchical conceptions into a diffuse rejection of existing society and government. For social banditry, as Eric J. Hobsbawn remarked, "protests not against the fact that peasants are poor and oppressed, but against the fact that they are sometimes excessively poor and oppressed."[47] The isolation of the backlands, the poverty and helplessness of the rural masses, and the traditional political outlook of the *cangaceiros* precluded the diffusion of urban-based, modern political ideologies and methods of effective organization—the essential ingredients for transforming primitive protest into effective revolt.

[47] Eric J. Hobsbawn, *Primitive Rebels: Studies in Archaic Forms of Social Movements in the 19th and 20th Centuries* (New York: W. W. Norton and Co., 1965), p. 24. Hobsbawn's work remains as the most important study of social banditry.

Chapter 7 The Entry of Padre Cícero into Partisan Politics, 1907-1909: Some Complexities of Brazilian Backland Politics Under the Old Republic

Ralph della Cava

[This study exemplifies the successful entry into politics of a maverick Catholic priest who was able to challenge the local church hierarchy and state oligarchy. The violence of the backlands that led to change and development in Juàzeiro and Crato was not necessarily the consequence of family feuds or decadent social structure but of changing economic and political conditions. For example, the inflexibility of the unitary political party structure of Ceará contributed to political violence during the period under consideration. In another vein, there is evidence that the penetration of international capitalism into the northeastern backlands also had an impact upon the traditional institutions of a region and the shifting relationship between landowners and merchants as that region prospered economically.]

Sometime between 1907 and 1909, Padre Cícero Romão Batista, a suspended Roman Catholic priest and leader of one of the Brazilian Northeast's most celebrated popular religious movements, drifted from the turbulent seas of religious controversy onto the equally seismic shores of backland politics. This transition was of no small significance. For Padre Cícero, it marked a rapid ascent on the political ladder: in 1911 and again in 1912, the onetime apolitical priest assumed public office, first at the local and then at the state level; in 1914, he nominally led an armed movement to depose a state governor; in 1926, he was elected to a seat in the Brazilian national congress. After his death in 1934 (at the age of ninety), Padre Cícero was reputed to have been the most influential political chief in the history of the Brazilian Northeast. For the suspended cleric's rather unorthodox religious movement, his entry into politics was of no less significance. Within a relatively short time, this movement—always an active vehicle of protest against the local Roman Catholic hierarchy and, on several occasions, a threat to the authority of the state—became integrated into the dominant political institutions of the Brazilian "Old Republic."

Despite these important personal and collective consequences, Padre Cícero's entry into politics has never been adequately examined. Early studies, inspired largely by rank partisanship, have attributed the cleric's decision (or, more accurately, series of decisions) to enter actively into politics to a variety of moral and sociopsychological factors. While recent studies demonstrate a much greater analytic sophistication, they often slight the actual historical record.

The purpose of this study is to remedy these shortcomings. In doing so, it seeks to retrace with historical accuracy Padre Cícero's entry into partisan politics during the critical years between 1907 and 1909, to illuminate the broader social structural factors that helped shape the cleric's new course, and to cast a fresh light on some of the complexities—especially the frequent recourse to violence and the impact of the international economy —that were attendant upon the political processes of the Old Republic in the first decade of the twentieth century.[1]

I

Before reexamining Padre Cícero's political course, two prior considerations are in order. Though briefly sketched here, these provide an indispensable framework within which the narrative may unfold more intelligibly.

[1] The present paper is based extensively on chapter vi of the author's unpublished doctoral dissertation, "Miracle at Joaseiro: A Political and Economic History of a Popular Religious Movement in Brazil, 1889–1934" (New York: Columbia University, 1968); published by Columbia University Press in 1970. A grant from the Foreign Area Fellowship Program financed the field research for the original study undertaken in Brazil during the latter part of 1963 and 1964.

A brief annotated bibliography on Padre Cícero and his movement is contained in Ralph della Cava, "Brazilian Messianism and National Institutions: A Reappraisal of Canudos and Joaseiro," Hispanic American Historical Review, XLVIII, 3, (August 1968), 402–420. (Ed. note: Joàzeiro or Joaseiro are old spellings of the city's name; for consistency, Juàzeiro is used in the text.)

Two outstanding interpretative works of recent publication are: Rui Facó, Cangaceiros e fanáticos (Rio de Janeiro, 1963); and Maria Isaura Pereira de Queiróz, O messianismo—no Brasil e no mundo (São Paulo, 1965). Still of value is the pioneering critical study of Joaquim Alves, "Juàzeiro, cidade mística," Revista do Instituto do Ceará (hereinafter cited as RIC), 62 (1948), 73–101.

The first consideration concerns Padre Cícero and the popular religious movement over which he presided. That movement originated in 1889 in the rustic hamlet of Juàzeiro, a *distrito* of the flourishing *município* of Crato, situated in the verdant Cariri Valley in the southernmost corner of the state of Ceará. The movement was sparked by a collective belief in a miracle, namely, that a host administered by the Catholic prelate to one of the hamlet's *beatas* had transformed itself into the blood of Christ.[2] After initial hesitation, the local Church hierarchy hotly contested the validity of this alleged miracle; and in 1892, Ceará's bishop, Dom Joaquim José Vieira, summarily suspended Padre Cícero from holy orders. Two years later, the Holy Office at Rome (the Inquisition) ruled the miracle a hoax and reconfirmed the prelate's suspension.[3]

A chief cause of the suspension was the persistence of an underground cult in honor of the alleged miracle which continued to spread throughout Juàzeiro and its environs despite repeated ecclesiastical prohibitions. Another was the unorthodox militance of two of the prelate's closest advisors. The one was José Marrocos, Padre Cícero's intimate friend and principal advisor, "theologian" of the prodigy and the key public advocate to persuade Rome to reverse its stand and declare the "vain and false events of Joàzeiro" a miracle. The other was José Lôbo, a pious and wealthy landowner who came to Juàzeiro in 1894 in order to organize backland believers and raise funds to propagate Juàzeiro's cause at home and abroad. Their activities, however, had the opposite effect: a long and bitter conflict between the Church and the dissident believers of Juàzeiro ensued. After 1892, censures from the bishop's palace in Fortaleza were relentlessly imposed upon Juàzeiro by Dom Joaquim's representatives in nearby Crato; meanwhile, the hope of revoking the suspension of the Patriarch of Juàzeiro dimmed.[4]

That suspension, it should be noted, significantly influenced the Patriarch's future. After 1892, the hitherto exemplary priest sought only to have it rescinded; his life's goal was now to regain in full his priestly status.

---

[2] For an account of the miracle and the subsequent ecclesiastical controversy, see Irineu Pinheiro, *O Joaseiro do Padre Cícero e a revolução de 1914* (Rio de Janeiro, 1938). Important documents are found in "Documentos sôbre a questão religiosa do Juàzeiro," *RIC*, 75 (1961), 266–297.

[3] Dom Joaquim José Vieira's four pastoral letters of 1893, 1894, 1897, and 1898 pertaining to Juàzeiro are published in Nertan Macêdo, *O Padre e a beata* (Rio de Janeiro, 1961), pp. 137–190. His letter of 1894 contains the decree of the Holy Office.

[4] An unflattering portrait of José Marrocos is found in Padre Antônio Gomes de Araújo, "Apostolado do Embuste," *Itaytera* (Crato, Ceará), II (1956), 3–63; a favorable view is presented by Padre Azarias Sobreira, *Em defesa de um abolicionista* (Fortaleza, 1956). José Lôbo's successful organizational activities were condemned by Dom Joaquim in his pastoral letter of 1898, cited in Macêdo, *op. cit.* 178–190. On Lobo's organization, see Eusébio de Sousa, "A vida da 'Legião da Cruz,'" *RIC*, 29 (1915), 315–322.

In 1898, thanks to the efforts of Marrocos and Lôbo, he even journeyed to Rome to confer with the Pope. But upon his return, his bishop revoked his conditional Roman reinstatement; in 1899, Dom Joaquim renewed the prelate's suspension *in toto* and even declared Juàzeiro under virtual interdict. Thereafter, return to the cloth became an obsession: it led the dissidents to defy systematically the authority of Ceará's bishop, while, at the same time, it encouraged them to appeal to the higher authority of Rome for the cleric's reinstatement.

The second consideration concerns the increasingly closer ties linking the Patriarch to the Carirí Valley's political chiefs, known as *coronéis*. That closeness was made possible by two factors. First, the upward trend in the valley's economic prosperity after 1900 had begun to depend in large measure on the cleric.[5] The priest was considered a miracle worker by destitute *sertanejos*, and religious pilgrims (known as *romeiros*) inundated "Padre Cícero's Joàzeiro." Thousands of them settled permanently there, as well as in the towns and on the estates of the neighboring *municípios* of Crato, Barbalha, Missão Velha, and Milagres. As a result, the verdant valley, whose natural fertility and perennial water sources stood in sharp ecological contrast to the surrounding arid *sertão*, did not experience a manpower crisis; unlike most of the Northeast, whose populations were migrating to the rubber forests of Amazonas, the Carirí—thanks to the Patriarch—showed a net gain in its labor supply.

Thanks also to the Patriarch, the cultivation of manioc, a staple in the northeastern diet, and *maniçoba* rubber, an important export at that time, were introduced on the plateaus, while traditional production of cotton, sugar, and cattle expanded on the valley floor. Production rose so rapidly (because of the local demographic boom and expanding exports both abroad and within the surrounding arid regions of the Northwest) that the Carirí was soon reputed to be the breadbasket of Ceará and the *sertão*. In addition, commerce, once limited primarily to the coast, began to expand in most interior cities. Nearby Crato became a potent mercantile emporium for the valley, while Juàzeiro itself gave birth to a variety of artisan industries. Under these conditions, the *coronéis* were more than willing to minimize the labor czar's reputed religious heterodoxy.[6]

Second, political changes in the Carirí rapidly transformed the *coronéis* into the Patriarch's active supporters. Between 1901 and 1910, there were recurrent eruptions of political violence in the valley: eight of the seven-

[5] Pinheiro, *op. cit., passim*. Also see Irineu Pinheiro, *O Carirí, seu descobrimento, povoamento, costumes* (Fortaleza, 1950), *passim*.

[6] The preceding discussion of the influence of the national economy on that of the Carirí region, as well as the emergence there of mercantile interests, is based upon Facó, *op. cit.*, pp. 29–37.

teen regional chiefs were deposed by armed force; several others narrowly escaped a similar fate.[7] Some of the causes of that violence are alluded to below; for the moment, it is sufficient to say that the increased economic and political rewards which a municipal perfecture accorded a *coronel* were sufficient incentives to make recourse to illicit force both desirable and more frequent. Another incentive was the assurance that the victor would not only be welcomed into the ranks of Ceará's unitary Partido Republicano Conservador-Ceará (PRC-C) but also be granted ample patronage by the state governor, Comendador António Pinto Nogueira Accioly, the celebrated "oligarch" who, for three decades, presided simultaneously over both the party and the state government.[8]

However, it is the consequences of the valley struggles upon Padre Cícero which are of concern here. As deposition followed deposition, political protagonists and antagonists sought out the Patriarch's good offices. Juàzeiro itself was soon transformed into a neutral haven where feuding *chefes* simultaneously sent their families and fortunes. Mediator, protector, and nonpartisan conciliator, the Patriarch pursued a "policy of neutrality" in valley affairs. In return for his neutrality, however, he readily received and accepted eager support from the *coronéis* for his own campaign to persuade an intransigent ecclesiastical hierarchy to reinstate him into the priesthood. To this end, after 1901, the Cariri's political "ins" and "outs" (*situacionistas* and *opposicionistas*) gratefully endorsed an endless stream of petitions, declarations, and character references. Drafted by the theologian-intellectual Marrocos and borne by the organizer-emissary Lôbo, these documents found their way to churchmen, politicians, and anyone else at home and abroad who might conceivably aid the suspended prelate to regain his orders.[9]

II

Let us now turn to the study proper, Padre Cícero's entry into partisan politics. No discussion of this is possible unless it is understood that the year 1907 marked the start of Juàzeiro's quest to win full municipal status from Crato. That initiative came not from Padre Cícero but from Major Joaquim Bezerra de Menezes, one of the *distrito's* wealthiest landowners, a direct descendant of the valley's founding family and a native son of Juà-

[7] Pinheiro, *O Joaseiro do Padre Cícero*, pp. 180–184.

[8] No monograph on Accioly's rule in Ceará exists. An invaluable, though hostile, account is Rodolpho Theophilo's *A libertação do Ceará: a queda da Olygarchia Accioly* (Lisbon, 1914). For an historical sketch of Ceará's political history, see the recent work by Abelardo Montenegro, *História dos partidos políticos cearenses* (Fortaleza: A. Batista Fontenele, 1965).

[9] On the "politics of neutrality," see della Cava, "Brazilian Messianism."

zeiro. Despite the landowner's pedigree, the Patriarch intentionally boy-cotted the rally scheduled that August at the Major's home to promote the elevation of Juàzeiro to municipal status. Padre Cícero's action effectively nipped the cause in the bud. Oddly enough, four years later, the Patriarch again undermined Major Joaquim's second bid for power: on the eve of Juàzeiro's inauguration as a *município* in 1911, the prelate reluctantly as-sumed the post of prefect in order to prevent the Major and native son from assuming that office.[10]

Although Major Joaquim's role in Juàzeiro's history is today all but for-gotten and although this study purposely excludes an account of the bitter partisan struggle after 1909 that led to Juàzeiro's autonomy, the incidents of 1907 and 1911 raise two important questions. First, why did the Patriarch "boycott" the Major's call for Juàzeiro's municipal autonomy in 1907? Second, why in 1911 did the prelate continue to oppose the landowner's personal political ambitions? The answers to these questions offer a glimpse into some of the structural determinants of the Patriarch's entry into poli-tics.

To answer the first question, it must be recalled that Juàzeiro was an ad-ministrative subunit (*distrito*) of the *município* of Crato. Elevation to mu-nicipal autonomy would require Crato to cede its rights to territorial and political jurisdiction over the hamlet. While the state legislature could con-ceivably have granted autonomy, such an action would most likely have alienated Crato's political chief, Colonel Antônio Luís Alves Pequeno, one of the most powerful *coronéis* of the Cariri: from his perspective, the auto-nomy of Juàzeiro would have meant a reduction in Crato's tax revenues and might have given rise to another political rival. However, in 1907 the Patriarch's "politics of neutrality" was in full force; just a year earlier, for example, Colonel Antônio Luís had lent his full prestige in his capacity as Crato's prefect and the valley's deputy in the state assembly to a petition urging Dom Joaquim to authorize Padre Cícero's reinstatement. Further-more, the Patriarch's closest advisors, José Marrocos and José Lôbo, con-tinued to place top priority on the cleric's struggle against the ecclesiasti-cal hierarchy. In politics, moreover, the apolitical Marrocos had long ad-vocated conciliation and cooperation among regional chiefs, not rivalry and dissension. Lôbo, for his part, had remained a monarchist and branded most cooperation with republican institutions a betrayal of the Catholic faith. Clearly then, Major Joaquim's 1907 plan for Juàzeiro's autonomy had little

[10] Data on Major Joaquim's 1907 bid for power is contained in Dra. Amália Xavier de Oliveira, "Inquérito do Juàzeiro" (unpublished manuscript, 1943), pp. 4–5. Padre Cícero's reasons for assuming the office of prefect in 1911 are contained in his last will and testament, *Cópia do testamento com que falleceu o Revdo. Padre Cícero Romão Batista* (Juàzeiro do Norte, n.d.), p. 3. Excerpts of the will are published in Macêdo, *op. cit.*, pp. 113–120.

hope of success. For Padre Cícero there was yet no sufficient reason either to scrap his successful policy of neutrality or to alienate friends such as Marrocos, Lôbo, and especially Colonel Antônio Luís, his most prestigious defender in present and future pleas before the churchmen for reinstatement.[11]

Why, however, did the prelate once again oppose Major Joaquim's bid for the office of prefect on the eve of Juàzeiro's inauguration as a *município* in 1911? On this occasion, the Patriarch explained in a hitherto unpublished letter that the Major "was totally unacceptable to the *people*, against whom he has always assumed a determinedly hostile attitude." Later, in the Patriarch's will of 1923, he added in hindsight that Major Joaquim had lacked both the knowledge and capability "to keep up the delicate balance of order" that until 1911 had been maintained by the prelate.[12]

In retrospect, the cleric's arguments indirectly pointed to the profound change that had gradually taken place in the "delicate" social balance of Juàzeiro, the political consequences of which had not escaped the Patriarch and were in fact to prove decisive in his opposition to Major Joaquim. Wherein lay the change? Over time, the inhabitants of Juàzeiro had become divided into two increasingly hostile groups: the *filhos da terra* ("native sons") and the *adventícios* ("newcomers"). The *filhos da terra* were not only those born in Juàzeiro but also those who had come from either Crato proper or other parts of the Cariri. On the whole, their social status had always been assured by their lineage, property, or birthright. The *adventícios*, in time the majority of Juàzeiro, comprised all the recent immigrants from the more distant regions and states. The term referred equally to prominent, recently arrived merchants, such as the Silva brothers from Alagôas and João Batista de Oliveira of Pernambuco, and to the lower class *romeiros* who had settled permanently in Juàzeiro. The prestige of the newcomers was determined far less by their origins or newly acquired wealth than by their social proximity to the Patriarch.[13]

This distinction between native sons and newcomers first became apparent in 1894, when Rome's condemnation prompted several native sons, es-

11 A 1906 petition to Ceará's bishop to reinstate Padre Cícero which Colonel Antônio Luís Alves Pequeno endorsed is found in the Arquivo do Colégio Salesiano "Dom João Bosco," Juàzeiro do Norte (hereinafter cited as ACS).

12 Padre Cícero to Comendador Antônio Pinto Nogueira Accioly, June 18, 1911, ACS. In this letter, Padre Cícero noted that Major Joaquim Bezerra de Menezes was "pressing for an official post once Juàzeiro was raised to municipal status." Padre Cícero's contention that the Major was unable to "keep the delicate balance of order" in Juàzeiro is cited in *Cópia do testamento*, p. 3.

13 On Juàzeiro's social divisions, see José Fábio Barbosa da Silva, "Organização social de Juàzeiro e tensões entre litoral e interior," *Sociologia*, XXIV, no. 3 (1962), 181–194, esp. pp. 181–187. Portions of my account are also based on Xavier de Oliveira, "Inquérito," pp. 43–47.

pecially the independently wealthy landowners such as Major Joaquim, to discredit the miracle; as a consequence, many other native sons undid the ties of intimacy which earlier had bound them to the prelate. It is true that some *filhos da terra*, especially merchants and the religiously zealous, retained the Patriarch's friendship for economic or religious reasons. They unstintingly supported this cleric, as did, for example, Pelusio Macêdo, the clever craftsman of church bells and tower clocks, who remained throughout his life the Patriarch's devoted friend. However, the 1894 decree undeniably forced the Patriarch, abandoned by some native sons, to rely increasingly on Juàzeiro's newcomers. It was the newcomer José Lôbo, for example, who organized the backland believers, while pilgrims' generous alms financed the many pleas to Rome. It was the business-minded merchant immigrants who became the prelate's steadfast supporters; not by coincidence was it João Batista de Oliveira, the hamlet's wealthy dry goods merchant from Pernambuco, who accompanied Padre Cícero to Rome in 1898. As the Patriarch came to favor the newcomers, resentment among the *filhos da terra* grew deeper.

The cleavage between the two groups also grew wider as Juàzeiro entered the twentieth century. In 1905, Pelusio Macêdo, then in charge of soliciting donations to pay the costs of one of the recent telegraphic appeals to Rome, astutely noted both the cleavage itself and one of its underlying economic aspects:

The population of the new Juàzeiro (I say new because among the old inhabitants one gets only a cold shoulder) . . . was astir in the streets having just raised the enormous sum necessary to pay for the cost [of the telegram] . . . . Never before have people given money with such punctuality and pleasure. . . . Those not accustomed [to doing so] appear to give more gladly . . . .[14]

Another economic aspect of this cleavage was the competitive spirit of newcomer merchants who frequently proved more successful in business affairs than did the native sons.

In 1907, the year of Major Joaquim's first bid for power, the division between the "new" and "old" Juàzeiro (in Pelusio Macêdo's words) began to harden, as evidenced by the mutually disrespectful nicknames that had come into vogue. Native sons called the newcomers *fanáticos* and *rabos de burro*; in turn, the newcomers labeled the native sons *cacaritos* or simply *nativos*, which nonetheless bore a most disrespectful connotation. Marriage was rarely contracted between "new" and "old" inhabitants, and even mem-

[14] The letter from Pelusio Correia de Macêdo to José Marrocos, January 24, 1905, is contained in the personal archive of Padre Cícero Coutinho, Juàzeiro de Norte (hereinafter cited as PCC). A biographical note on Pelusio Macêdo is Raimundo Gomes de Mattos, "Perece um gênio do sertão," *Unitário* (Fortaleza), May 12, 1955.

bership in Juàzeiro's religious organizations (*irmandades*) became discretely withdrawn from one or the other group.[15]

As hostility drove a wedge between native sons and newcomers, the Patriarch alone was able to bridge the gap; and for several decades he alone held together "the two Juàzeiros" in uneasy coalition. Partly for this reason he rejected Major Joaquim's 1907 bid for power. Had the prelate done otherwise, he would have shifted "the delicate balance of order" in favor of the *filhos da terra* minority. Similarly, in 1911, when the *adventícios* constituted Juàzeiro's overwhelming majority, the Major had understandably become, in Padre Cícero's words, "totally unacceptable" to the "people," that is, to Juàzeiro's newcomers, "against whom [the Major, a native son] had always assumed a definitely hostile attitude." Thus, to preserve harmony between the two Juàzeiros, the Patriarch "was forced to collaborate in politics" and in October 1911, became Juàzeiro's first prefect. However, this act was an unequivocal admission that the cleric had cast his lot with Juàzeiro's newcomers, on whom the success of his campaign for reinstatement had come to depend. That alignment had been in the making during the previous four years. During that time, the most astute *adventício* ever to come to Juàzeiro, Doctor Floro Bartholomeu da Côsta, rose rapidly to the apex of the "new Juàzeiro." His overwhelming influence over Padre Cícero has been widely argued by several authors as the chief reason for the Patriarch's entry into politics.[16]

III

Dr. Floro Bartholomeu da Côsta, a Bahia-born physician, came to Juàzeiro in May 1908. Before moving to Juàzeiro he had worked as a journalist, public notary, and itinerant doctor in the backlands of Bahia and Pernambuco. In 1907, he abandoned his full-time medical practice to join an expatriate French nobleman, the mining engineer Conde Adolpho Van den Brule, in the search for diamonds and semiprecious metals. Later that year, Conde Adolpho decided to return to the Cariri Valley, where he had earlier promoted a Paris-incorporated firm to exploit recently discovered copper deposits in the Coxá fields, not far from Juàzeiro. Prompted by rumors that unfriendly landowners intended to lay illegal claim to the area, the two adventurers made haste to the valley.[17]

[15] Barbosa da Silva "Organização social," p. 183; Xavier de Oliveira, "Inquérito," pp. 44–45. Interview with Amália Xavier de Oliveira in Juàzeiro, September 13, 1964.

[16] This viewpoint is sustained by Manuel Bergström Lourenço Filho, *Joaseiro do Padre Cícero* (São Paulo, 1926), pp. 79–84; Alves, *op. cit.*, p. 95. It is shared by Padre Azarias Sobreira, "O revolucionário," in *Revista do Cinqüentenário do Juàzeiro do Norte* (Fortaleza [?], n.d.), pp. 14–16.

[17] Biographical data on Dr. Floro Bartholomeu da Côsta (1876–1926) are scattered

Their first meeting with Padre Cícero in May 1908 was not a chance encounter. Some time before, the Patriarch had acquired property rights to most of the Coxá copper deposits. But, the adventurers argued, neither the Patriarch nor they themselves could develop the deposits until the ownership of the Coxá fields could be clearly determined. Impressed by the intelligence and persuasiveness of Dr. Floro and the technical skill and European contacts of Conde Adolpho, Padre Cícero soon agreed to petition the district court for the right to demarcate Coxá and thereby settle the question of ownership.

At the same time the Patriarch appointed Dr. Floro his legal proxy. During the ensuing months, the energetic physician scavenged the real estate records of Crato and other valley towns. In order to defend Padre Cícero's interests more effectively, he took up residence in July in Milagres and traveled often to Missão Velha, the two *municípios* under whose jurisdiction the Coxá mines fell. In mid-December 1908, when the district court at Milagres finally approved the prelate's request to demarcate the lands, no rival claim to Coxá had yet been filed. But Dr. Floro's satisfaction was short-lived. En route to Coxá on December 15, 1908, the Patriarch's representatives, led by Dr. Floro, narrowly escaped death by ambush. To retaliate, the Bahian adventurer immediately enlisted the support of the political chiefs of Milagres and Missão Velha, with whom he and the Patriarch had become increasingly more friendly. Provided with over fifty armed *capangas*, Dr. Floro boldly routed the band of assassins whose aim it was to prevent Coxá from falling into the hands of the Patriarch.[18]

The armed conflict nearly brought an abrupt end to Padre Cícero's politics of neutrality: the Patriarch was held responsible for Floro's armed counterattack. That action proved, furthermore, to be an unwanted declaration of war against Crato's powerful chief, Colonel Antônio Luís Alves

---

throughout his own published defense of Padre Cícero, one of the most interesting accounts written: Floro Bartholomeu, *Joàzeiro e o Padre Cícero, depoimento para a história* (Rio de Janeiro, 1923). Data are also contained in: Padre Azarias Sobreira, "Floro Bartholomeu—o caudilho bahiano," *RIC*, 64 (1950), 193–202; Hugo Víctor Guimarães, *Deputados provinciais e estaduais do Ceará* (Fortaleza, 1952), pp. 244–245; and the obituaries published in the *Correio do Ceará* (Fortaleza), March 10 and 11, 1926. Biographical data on Conde Adolpho Van den Brule are found in Bartholomeu, *op. cit.*, pp. 132–137, and Silvo Froes de Abreu, "Schisto Bituminoso da Chapada do Araripe, Ceará," *RIC*, 38 (1924), 363–377, esp. 363–364.

18 An account of the armed conflict at Coxá contained in an undated letter from Dr. Floro to Padre Cícero is found in Pinheiro, *O Joaseiro do Padre Cícero*, pp. 164–167, esp. 165, n. 30. A valuable account of the entire Coxá dispute was subsequently written by Dr. Floro Bartholomeu: "Minas do Coxá: ligeiras considerações para refutar os argumentos adduzidos pelo Illmo. Snr. Cel. José Francisco Alves Teixeira no 'Correio do Cariry' de 5 do corrente," a forgotten series of twelve articles published in Juàzeiro's first newspaper, *O Rebate*, between August 22, 1909, and July 25, 1910.

Pequeno, because it was with his tacit approval that his close relative, Colonel J. F. Alves Teixeira (who had long and guardedly coveted Coxá) had dispatched the band of assassins to stop Floro. Within months, these circumstances contributed forcefully to the Patriarch's decision to enter politics.

In sharp contrast to that decision, Padre Cícero's original entry into partnership with Dr. Floro and Conde Adolpho over Coxá was *not* motivated by political considerations. Rather, behind his eagerness to exploit Coxá lay his perennial obsession to regain priestly status. The failure of his repeated petitions led him to adopt a new strategy in 1908 with regard to the recalcitrant Church hierarchy. That strategy arose after reports reached Padre Cícero in 1907 that Rome intended to establish a new bishopric in the interior of Ceará State, a cause which the cleric claimed to have championed before the Holy Father in 1898. However, in 1908 the likely choice for the seat of the new diocese was Crato, from whence ecclesiastical censures and sanctions against Juàzeiro had emanated ever since 1892. Indeed, a new bishopric in Crato might forever dash Padre Cícero's hopes of clerical reinstatement, unless, of course, the new see could be erected in Juàzeiro! [19] Immediately the cleric set to work to lay the foundations of the "Diocese of the Carirí." In the press and before influential church friends in the south he argued that Juàzeiro, not Crato, was the very heart of the northeastern *sertão*, the principal center of convergence "from Alagôas to Maranhão." So sure was the Patriarch of success that he ordered an old two-story *sobrado* in Juàzeiro rebuilt as the future residence of the Carirí's first bishop.

Meanwhile, under pressure from the aging Dom Joaquim, Father Quintino, the Vicar of Crato, moved swiftly into action to win the honor for the "Pearl of the Carirí." On December 8, 1908, the feast of the Immaculate Conception, prominent Crato citizens solemnly met to plan a fund drive for the patrimony of the new diocese, with its seat in Crato.[20]

---

[19] Evidence that Padre Cícero had begun to work actively for the erection of the new diocese as early as 1907 is contained in [Manuel Benício], "Leandro Bezerra," *RIC*, 26 (1912), 206–214. Dr. Leandro Bezerra de Menezes, a native son of Crato, onetime imperial senator from Alagôas and intimate friend of members of the Roman Catholic hierarchy in Brazil, became one of the chief promoters in Rio de Janeiro and Niterói of the creation of the Diocese of the Carirí. That Padre Cícero earnestly believed that the new diocese ought have its seat in Juàzeiro is confirmed in the cleric's letter to Dr. Leandro Bezerra, September 25, 1908, ACS (Pasta do Bispado do Cariry): "There's no longer any doubt about the creation of the Diocese of the Cariry . . . in the very center of the different states that border on the Cariry. . . . Joaseiro is the key point . . . , the place desired and loved by all, appropriate for a great Chair of learning in civilization and Faith."

[20] On the meeting in Crato, see Irineu Pinheiro, *Efemérides do Carirí* (Fortaleza, 1963), pp. 175, 504–505.

This challenge, which contributed much to the later resentments between Crato and Juàzeiro, did not pass unnoticed. On December 10, 1908, the Patriarch telegraphed his influential contact before the Apostolic Nuncio in Petrópolis: "Spare no effort for the chancery seat in Juàzeiro, Ceará."[21] Five days later—exactly one week after the fund drive meeting in Crato—Dr. Floro set out to demarcate Coxá. There is no doubt that the Patriarch had earmarked the copperfields as the patrimony of the "Bishopric of the Cariri"—with its seat in Juázeiro![22] So convinced was the Patriarch that it was God's will to elevate Juàzeiro to an episcopal see—not a *município*—that the ominous political consequences of Dr. Floro's armed struggle at Coxá were totally lost on him. Instead, as the vision of the new diocese, and perhaps his own ensuing reinstatement, grew brighter, he decided to travel to Rio de Janeiro to promote the cause. On April 23, 1909, he left Juázeiro believing, "Divine Providence wants me to make the journey." On the eve of his departure he wrote to José Marrocos, whose unsung labors on behalf of the new diocese were as great as any he had ever undertaken: "Pray for me to the Most Holy Virgin that we may meet with success."[23]

IV

Two months later, *Unitário* (Fortaleza's libelous opposition daily to the Accioly oligarchy) reported Padre Cícero's hasty return from Rio de Janeiro. The Patriarch had disembarked in Salvador, Bahia—rather than in Fortaleza—and proceeded to the interior via the São Francisco River Railroad. As *Unitário* noted, the cleric had chosen "the shortest possible route" to the Carirí, from where he had been suddenly and "expressly summoned to put down a rebellion."[24]

In his absence, the events at Coxá had become a cause and pretext of a new and "serious threat to the peace of the Cariri": in May 1909, Dr. Floro's friends, the political chiefs of Milagres and Missão Velha, entered into a coalition with nearby Barbalha for the purpose of deposing Crato's Colonel Antônio Luís Alves Pequeno. He, rather than his relative, Teixeira Alves, was now charged with having ordered the ambush of Dr. Floro at

---

[21] Telegram, Padre Cícero to Leandro Bezerra, December 10, 1908. The orignial is in the personal archive of Leandro Bezerra's grandson, Dr. Geraldo Bezerra de Menezes, a resident of Niterói, Rio de Janeiro State.

[22] In a letter from the Benedictine Abbot at Quixadá, Ceará, Dom Ruperto Rudolph, to Padre Cícero, August 16, 1913, ACS, the friar stated that he had been aware of Padre Cícero's intentions to make the Coxá holdings "a part of the patrimony of the future diocese of the Cariry."

[23] Padre Cícero to José Marrocos, April 21, 1909, ACS (Pasta do Bispado do Cariry).

[24] *Unitário* (Fortaleza), June 29, 1909.

Coxá; it was this denunciation that became the nominal *cause de guerre* in the hands of Colonel Antônio Luís' trio of long-standing enemies.[25]

Chief among these enemies was the once-dominant Colonel Domingos Furtado, *chefe político* of Milagres. The real cause of Furtado's feud with Antônio Luís began not over Coxá in 1908, but over Crato politics in 1904.[26] That year, Antônio Luís, then a wealthy, apolitical merchant, entered into a "marriage of convenience" with Crato's otherwise hostile landowners and violently deposed the city's prefect, the merchant and competitor, Colonel José Belém de Figueiredo. Belém, an outsider who was born and raised in Milagres, was intensely disliked because neither his flukish rise to power in 1892 nor his subsequent control over Crato would have been possible without the prompt and continuing support of Furtado, his political mentor. In the following decade, after Belém became third vice-president of Ceará State, the Crato-Milagres axis saw to it that political power and wealth were evenly fed back into the predominantly commercial and pastoral-based economies of the two respective cities. When Antônio Luís and his landowner allies of Crato decided to move against Belém in 1904, Furtado rushed to the side of his protégé with several hundred armed henchmen. Even after Belém's bloody defeat on June 29, 1904, the vanquished ex-*chefe* and Furtado again joined forces to invade Crato with eight hundred men. But news of the secret plot leaked out. Crato's victorious new prefect, Antônio Luís, hastily mustered an "army" more than a thousand strong and forced Furtado into shameless retreat even before a single shot was fired. This humiliation, greater than defeat itself, and the subsequent cutback of power and wealth to Milagres once Belém was ousted from Crato, gnawed deeply at Furtado for revenge. Thus, vengeance and the desperate desire for Milagres' economic comeback at any price clearly accounted for Furtado's readiness to support Dr. Floro at Coxá in December 1908, as well as to assume the leadership in the three-sided coalition against Antônio Luís in May 1909.

Furtado's counterparts in Missão Velha (also a former ally of the ex-chief Belém) and Barbalha no less resented Antônio Luís' immense political power in valley affairs. This supremacy, the trio alleged, could not be attributed to Crato's more numerous electorate nor to the powerful post of deputy to the State Assembly that Antônio Luís had "inherited" from Col-

[25] Pinheiro, *O Joaseiro do Padre Cícero*, 183–184. The charge that Colonel Antônio Luís and not his relatives, Teixeira Alves, had ordered the attack on Floro at Coxá in 1908 was printed in the Barbalha newspaper, *A União*, and reprinted verbatim as "Inedictoriaes—os últimos acontecimentos," *O Rebate* (Juàzeiro), July 25, 1909.

[26] The following account of the 1904 conflict in Crato is based on the detailed study of José de Figueiredo Brito, "Maxixes e Malabares," *Itaytera*, IV (1959), 39–55. The interpretation, however, is my own.

onel Belém and had assumed and held in full regalia since 1905. To the contrary, contended the trio, the Crato chief's power as the state oligarchy's patronage-broker in the Carirí was due primarily to the special favors extravagantly accorded him by his first cousin, the governor of Ceará, Dr. Antônio Pinto Nogueira Accioly.[27]

Another cause for enmity can be traced to the traditional pastoral interests in the Carirí Valley, typified by Colonel Domingos Furtado, which attributed their declining fortunes to the growing wealth, power, and competitive expansion of Crato's merchants, symbolized by Colonel Antônio Luís, into many sectors of the valley economy. Furthermore, the merchant forces in the primarily agricultural-based *municípios* of Missão Velha and Barbalha entered the triple alliance with a view to increasing their own share of mercantile profits, once Crato was whittled down to size.[28]

These factors lay behind the three-sided coalition that planned to attack Crato in May 1909, in the name of Coxá and the absent Patriarch. Each side summarily proceeded to recruit more than a thousand armed henchmen from their usual sources of supply in the neighboring backlands of Pernambuco and Paraíba. As each faction made ready for the showdown, Padre Cícero was urgently summoned to return. However, the conflict never erupted. Thanks to the conciliatory initiatives of three Barbalha merchants, probably instigated at Governor Accioly's request, immediate violence was averted. However, a most tenuous and uneasy truce set in.[29]

The prevailing enmity was not the only change to greet the Patriarch upon his arrival in Juàzeiro on July 18, 1909. The first edition of O Rebate, the hamlet's first weekly newspaper had just rolled off the press that same day sporting a front-page portrait of the cleric. Under the editorship of Padre Joaquim de Alencar Peixoto, a maverick Crato priest and bitter political enemy of Colonel Antônio Luís, who had come to Juàzeiro in 1907, O Rebate's debut marked the yearnings of Juàzeiro's newcomer merchants for municipal autonomy.[30]

The appearance of O Rebate, like the political consequences of Coxá, had occurred without the Patriarch's awareness and, indeed, during his absence. Nonetheless, these two circumstances— "faits accomplis"—were por-

---

[27] On Colonel António Luís's familial relationship to Governor Accioly, see *ibid.*, pp. 47, 54–55. Biographical data on the Crato chief are found in Guimarães, *op. cit.*, pp. 184–186.

[28] The conflict between landowners and merchants in the backlands is suggested in a slightly different context in Facó, *op. cit.*, pp. 149–168.

[29] Pinheiro, *O Joaseiro do Padre Cícero*, pp. 183–184. On the truce negotiators, see "Inedictoriaes," *O Rebate* (Juàzeiro), July 25, 1909.

[30] An incomplete collection of *O Rebate*, published between July 18, 1909, and September 3, 1911, is located in the Biblioteca Nacional, Rio de Janeiro. A biographic sketch of Padre Peixoto appeared in the April 26, 1911, issue of *O Rebate*. Noteworthy is the fact that Padre Peixoto was a bitter political enemy of Colonel Antônio Luís's.

trayed by Padre Peixoto and Dr. Floro as irrevocable signs that only municipal autonomy could secure peace for Juàzeiro, the Coxá fields for the Patriarch, and full satisfaction for the hamlet's newcomer merchants whose expanding trade had placed them in their own opinion on an almost equal economic footing with Crato. The arguments evidently had merit, for within a week of his return, the Patriarch confidentially telegraphed Governor Accioly to request the hamlet's elevation to municipal status. The oligarch, however, cautiously deferred the decision to Crato's Antônio Luís, who in turn summarily refused to deal with the issue but tactically and tactfully promised to consider it the following year.[31]

Perhaps, unknown to the Patriarch himself, his exchange of telegrams with Governor Accioly marked his first steps into politics. But once again motivations other than political lay at the root of this decisive action. On the one hand, his journey to Rio de Janeiro had not met with the success that he expected Providence and the Virgin to accord him. To his dismay, the ailing and aged Dom Joaquim, who had sworn to defeat the prelate's goal, arrived unexpectedly in Rio de Janeiro during the Patriarch's stay. Once in the "marvellous city," the bishop earnestly and defiantly campaigned against the erection of a bishopric in Juàzeiro. On the other hand, despite Dom Joaquim's encouragement, Crato had not yet succeeded in raising sufficient funds for the patrimony. Since Rome was not likely to grant a benefice to paupers, there was only a slight chance that Padre Cícero might still succeed. These two considerations undeniably led the Patriarch to believe that Juàzeiro's political independence might conceivably increase his influence both in bringing the See to Juàzeiro and in ultimately winning back his clerical status.[32] The subsequent attitude adopted by the ecclesiastical hierarchy seems to have made the Patriarch's cautious entry into politics irreversible.

V

Less than two months after the Patriarch's return, new hostilities between him and the hierarchy erupted. On August 26, 1909, Dom Manuel Lopes, Ceará's coadjutor-bishop and aide-de-camp of the ailing Dom Joa-

[31] The exchange of telegrams among Padre Cícero, Governor Accioly, and Colonel Antônio Luís appeared in the following issues of O Rebate (Juàzeiro): July 25, August 15, and August 22, 1909. Also relevant is the editorial entitled "Quem não gostar que se morda" that appeared in the issue of September 25, 1910.

[32] The view that Padre Cícero entered politics in order to win reinstatement to the priesthood is expressed by Pinheiro, O Joaseiro do Padre Cícero, p. 166. Abelardo Montenegro contends the priest entered politics in order to prevent the Church from destroying his prestige before the masses; see his História do fanatismo religioso no Ceará (Fortaleza, 1955), p. 89.

quim, arrived in Crato on a pastoral visit. The following day orthodoxy fired the first volley in its new campaign against the Patriarch: one of the priests in the bishop's entourage, "a man otherwise intelligent and educated, mounted the pulpit erected in the square of Crato's mother church." Before thousands of persons assembled there for the week-long outdoor mission services, he "began his sermon in the following manner: 'Proud and noble people of Crato, I beg your permission to speak about the filthy rabble of Juàzeiro who live guided by Satan'." Thus, under the guise of a holy mission and episcopal visit, the hierarchy went to war against the "Satan of Juàzeiro," intent on defeating his bid for the Bishopric of the Cariri."

But the virulent diatribe did not go unchallenged. Under the *nom de plume* of Manuel Ferreira de Figueiredo, Dr. Floro, the one-time journalist, took to the pages of O Rebate. In three combative articles, impeccable in their logic, rhetoric, and militance, the Bahian physician roundly denounced the hypocrisy of the hierarchy and stoutly defended the Patriarch of Juàzeiro.[33]

The importance of Floro's "just defense," as he called the articles, lay less in their substance than in the political emergence of Dr. Floro: until his death in 1926, he was the most important single figure in Juàzeiro's history, second only to Padre Cícero. Understandably, Floro created many enemies who denounced his ascendency over the Patriarch and denigrated the newcomer as the cleric's "alter-ego." As such, Dr. Floro was depicted as an ambitious, self-seeking adventurer who, it was claimed, "rose to glory and national political prominence . . . behind the shadow of the most ancient cassock of the Cariry."[34] Dr. Floro's influence over the Patriarch is an undisputed fact. However, it cannot be accounted for simply in terms of Dr. Floro's ambition or Padre Cícero's gullibility. The former's ascent as the *de facto* political chief of Juàzeiro until 1926 was possible only because of a variety of circumstances that, summarized here, complete our brief survey of structural factors behind the Patriarch's entry into politics.

First of all, while Floro's multiple role in the Coxá enterprise—lawyer, researcher, and when necessary, armed defender—certainly made him indispensable to a Patriarch intent on erecting a diocese, it was not the sole cause fostering the early intimacy and friendship between the two unlike personalities. Perhaps of greater signficance was Floro's willingness to defend the cleric against the Church hierarchy, as he did for the first time during the course of 1908. That earlier defense was prompted by the in-

---

[33] The sermon is paraphrased in Bartholomeu, *Joàzeiro e o Padre Cícero*, p. 57. Dr. Floro's articles appeared in O Rebate (Joaseiro) on August 29, and September 12 and 19, 1909.

[34] The term "alter-ego" was popularized in one of the most scathing attacks on Dr. Floro by a native son of Juàzeiro, Padre Manuel Macêdo, *Joàzeiro em fóco* (Fortaleza, 1925), p. 10.

transigent refusal of the Church hierarchy to allow Padre Cícero to complete the erection of a chapel in Juàzeiro. The details of that episode need
not concern us here.[35] More important was Floro's disillusion with the in-
consistent and picayune stance of the Church toward the Patriarch; the latter's sole intent in erecting the new chapel was to fulfill a *promesa* to Our
Lady of Perpetual Help, whom the priest devoutly believed had cured him
of a near-fatal illness in 1906. Floro, considering this intention pure and the
Church's reticence hypocrisy, took it upon himself to construct the chapel
without waiting for the ecclesiastical authorities to grant him permission.
Years later, he recalled the episode in this way:

On that occasion, considering [the Church's attitude to be] nothing but buf-
foonery, I resolved to finish building [the chapel] without listening to another
consideration from Padre Cícero or anyone else. . . . I simply went ahead with
great satisfaction, quite ready to assume the responsibility for any consequences
which, for me, no matter how serious they might be, wouldn't bother me in the
least.[36]

Floro's defiance of the Church did not ingratiate him to the hierarchy;
it may even have widened the already irreconcilable breach between orthodoxy and dissidence. Yet Floro's seeming anticlericalism, in contrast to the
Patriarch's dissenting mysticism, had served in this instance to further what
the suspended cleric certainly considered a just cause, the fulfiillment of
a most orthodox *promesa*. Indeed, Floro's audacious stand was proof of his
fidelity to the Patriarch and sufficient grounds for Padre Cícero to bestow
upon this apparently selfless newcomer his lasting trust, friendship, and
gratitude.

A second factor helps explain why this newfound intimacy between Dr.
Floro and the Patriarch was at all possible: the priest's two surviving
friends and defenders, José Lôbo and José Marrocos, were becoming less
evident in his life. It is difficult to determine whether Floro subtly promoted
that rupture or whether the Patriarch's former associates decided to keep
their distance out of resentment toward the newcomer who now enjoyed
the aging cleric's favor, but the signs of that rupture are indisputable.

José Lôbo, for example, increasingly lived at home in virtual seclusion.
There, the onetime organizer and emissary devoted his time to answering
the hundreds of letters that daily arrived for the Patriarch from the poor
and abandoned *sertanejos* of the Brazilian Northeast. But as more and more
of the region's destitute came to Juàzeiro on pilgrimage, Lôbo's tasks be-

[35] A partial account is contained in Bartholomeu, *Joàzeiro e o Padre Cícero*, pp.
60–63.

[36] *Ibid.*, p. 62.

came less numerous and significant.[37] Shortly after Dr. Floro took up residence in the Patriarch's household in 1908, old "Zé" Lôbo either fabricated or indeed experienced a bitter coldness in his friendship with Padre Cícero. One day, Lôbo confronted the priest and demanded that unless this supposed coldness thawed, he would never again cross the Patriarch's threshold. The cleric, unaware of any change in his affections toward Lôbo, strongly denied that their friendship had altered. Days later, rumors, perhaps promoted by the jealousy of newcomers, alleged that Zé Lôbo had tried to poison the Patriarch. Padre Cícero publicly condemned the accusation as false and libelous; but Lôbo saw this as the "last straw." Thereafter, until his death in 1918, he never again set foot in the Patriarch's home.

For José Marrocos, the souring of an old friendship was as sudden as it was strange and unexpected. Before the Patriarch's journey to Rio de Janeiro in April 1909, it was Marrocos who had labored long, hard, and hurriedly to prepare the cleric's plan to bring the new diocese to Juàzeiro. It was to José Marrocos that Padre Cícero had confided his hope for success on the very eve of his departure. Then, on July 19, 1909, the day after the Patriarch returned and *O Rebate* made its debut, Marrocos plaintively wrote his longtime friend from neighboring Barbalha:

All day Saturday [July 17, 1909] I waited for the invitation to attend the inaugural celebration of Juàzeiro's newspaper: I wanted to seal with my presence the new progress of a place that I have always admired and for whose prosperity I have labored to the small degree that it was possible for me [to do]. I waited in vain; but disappointed if not most distraught, I accepted other obligations.[38]

Deeply wounded, Marrocos nonetheless attempted to regain his influence over the Patriarch. Later in 1909, he completed a scathing attack against Dom Joaquim which he intended to publish in the newspapers of Fortaleza. However, his attempt to win the Patriarch's favor by recalling the "past struggle against a common enemy" and by rekindling the controversy over the validity of the miracle of 1889 was anachronistic by comparison to the more persuasive rhetoric with which Floro contrasted the Patriarch's personal integrity to the hierarchy's hypocrisy, while deleting entirely the old thorn of the miracle. What is suggested here is that Floro's more intelligent strategy to help the cleric regain his orders had won the Patriarch's favor.

Marrocos, however, refused to succumb. In early 1910, the intellectual and famous educator of the Carirí closed down his private *colégio* in Barbalha and opened its doors in Juàzeiro. In greater proximity to his old

[37] This account of José Lôbo is based on an unpublished work by his grandson and a native of Juàzeiro, the late Senhor Octávio Aires de Menezes (1963), pp. 43, 68–72.
[38] José Marrocos to Padre Cícero, July 19, 1909, PCC.

friend Padre Cícero, Marrocos, it appears, may have regained some of his bygone influence; at least, on August 15, a political rally was scheduled to take place at his new *colégio* in Juàzeiro. The rally was never convened: on the afternoon of August 14, José Marrocos died suddenly. The coroner's report listed the cause of death as pneumonia, but Marrocos's state of apparent good health the previous morning later gave rise to rumors that Dr. Floro had poisoned the venerable professor. This accusation seems groundless because Dr. Floro was in Missão Velha the day Marrocos died; only on August 16 did he return to Juàzeiro for the sexagenarian's burial and on that occasion even delivered the principal funeral oration. The motive, attributed to Floro only many years later, was that Marrocos's repeated counsel had kept the Patriarch from entering politics, contrary to Floro's ambitions.[39] Whether or not this was true, it clearly illustrates that Floro's ascendancy caused or coincided with the rupture between the Patriarch and his former intimates; thereafter, politics rather than miracles became the order of the day.

A third and final factor accounting for Floro's ascendancy was inherent in the structural changes engendered by the steady penetration of modern capitalism into the *sertão* and especially into the Carirí Valley at the dawn of the twentieth century. Despite frequent economic setbacks caused by droughts, the growing European demand for *maniçoba* rubber, hides, and cotton, as well as for overseas markets capable of absorbing Europe's credit, banking and commercial services, its manufactures, telegraphs, and railroads sparked new economic life into the backlands between 1880 and 1920.[40] With the newfound riches of rural landowners, there was ushered into the backlands a new class of aggressive, money-oriented, small-town merchants; the *commerciantes*' growing profits soon enabled them to vie with the *fazendeiros* for local political power. As is known, the oligarchical politics of Governor Accioly had, since 1900, also invested the *município* with greater autonomy, new fiscal prerogatives, and an increased number of bureaucratic posts that precipitated, even within the same political party, often violent and bloody factional strife for control of local government.

This "new era" of republicanism and capitalist penetration necessarily altered the political style of backland politics. Alongside traditional methods of political coercion, intensified by the increase in the political spoils, the land-based *coronéis* were, per force, made to legitimize their power in terms of new republican laws and "rules of the game," in terms of the scat-

---

[39] This viewpoint, presumably based on oral history, was recently presented by Padre Antônio Gomes de Araújo, "A margem de 'A margem da história do Ceará,'" *Itaytera*, VIII (1962), 15, n. 25.

[40] For a general economic survey of Ceará, see Raimundo Girão, *História econômica do Ceará* (Fortaleza, 1947), esp. pp. 380–382, 401–460.

tered pockets of "public opinion" in the coastal cities, and also in terms of the demand for material advances that began to grow even among the small literate sectors of backland society. Increasingly, then, the backland *coronel* came to rely on the services of the rising numbers of the rhetoric-prone but talented *bacharéis,* graduates of the coastal university faculties of law and medicine. To these middle-class *bacharéis,* whose omnipresence and ambition marked the politics of the republican period and whose opportunism and corruption later led critics to attribute the subsequent decadence of the Old Republic to the "plague of the *bacharéis,*" service to the *coronel* opened the avenues to power, prominence, and success.[41]

The Carirí typified this social and political transformation of the *sertão* during the Old Republic (1889–1930). Lawyers such as Raimundo Gomes de Matos and Raul de Souza Carvalho became respectively the spokesmen of the political chiefs of Barbalha and Crato; while in Crato, the young physician, Dr. Irineu Pinheiro, served Colonel Antônio Luís Alves Pequeno well in economic matters as founder and director in 1921 of the city's first bank. Frequently, the intimacy between the *bacharel* and the *coronel* led to the former's marriage to a close relative of the latter: matrimony not only enhanced the professional's rise to success, but it also guaranteed the artless political chief of his ambitious aide's loyalty. In the first decade of the twentieth century, the principal task of the *bacharéis* was the verbal defense of their political chiefs. Everywhere throughout the Carirí, newspapers proliferated as political combat became increasingly rhetorical, less expensive (in both money and human life), and more imitative of the urban coast: between 1904 and 1909, more than eleven newspapers appeared in just three cities of the valley; of these, two in Crato, two in Barbalha, and *O Rebate* in Juàzeiro achieved considerable longevity and rarely missed the weekly publication date.[42]

Dr. Floro, a graduate of the faculty of medicine in Bahia, was a *bacharel* who had arrived in the Carirí at the moment of this transition. His profession gave him access into the homes of Juàzeiro's rich and poor; his clinic and pharmacy in Juàzeiro engratiated him to the villagers and to the Patriarch who had welcomed him not only as the hamlet's first resident doctor but as a sure sign of the *sertão*'s overdue right to progress. Dr. Floro's road to political success was typical of the backland physicians and lawyers of this period.[43] In addition, his earlier experiences as a journalist and public

[41] A critical view of *bacharelismo* is found in Sêrgio Buarque de Holanda, *Raizes do Brasil* (Rio de Janeiro, 1936), pp. 114–118. For a fictional treatment of the phenomenon in Ceará during the 1930s, see the novel by Jader de Carvalho, *Sua majestade, o juiz* (São Paulo, n.d.).

[42] Statistics on the press in the Carirí were culled from [Guilherme] Barão de Studart, *Para a história de jornalismo cearense 1824–1924* (Fortaleza, 1924), pp. 151–174.

[43] For a political scientist's discussion of the physician as an alternative type of

notary, as well as his personal qualities of ambition, audacity, and loyalty, were to serve himself, the Patriarch, and Juàzeiro admirably in the subsequent political struggle for independence from Crato. By 1909, that struggle was about to begin; it enjoyed the consent and blessing of the Patriarch of Juàzeiro, who had thereby irrevocably entered into the partisan politics of the backland.

VI

It is now possible to come to several conclusions in respect both to Padre Cícero's entry into partisan politics and to some complexities of the political system of his day. As for the cleric's entry into politics, it is clear from the preceding narrative that that decision or decisions, whether fully voluntary or not, can best be understood in the light of a number of important structural conditions. Those conditions might be identified as follows: (1) an ecclesiastical hierarchy that at one level (the Brazilian episcopacy) organized hostilities against the Patriarch, while at a higher level (the Roman curia and the Papacy) continually held out the possibility of reconciliation and reintegration. Thus, Padre Cícero could engage in defensive combat at the local level and at the same time sue for peace at the higher. Moreover, the pursuit of these objectives required the creation and maintenance of (2) a movement, composed on the one hand of ideologues and organizers (Marrocos and Lôbo; later, Dr. Floro) and on the other, of loyal supporters (the pilgrims, but especially the permanent settlers, i.e., the newcomers of Juàzeiro). The final significant structure can be simply identified here as (3) the outside economic and political reality represented for the most part by the *coronéis* of the Carirí (but in given moments, by Conde Adolpho and Governor Accioly). From changes within and between these units, the reasons for Padre Cícero's entry into partisan politics have been sought here.

The following series of observations, drawn from events that took place in the Carirí Valley, reveals some of the complexities inherent in backland politics during the Old Republic in our period of study.

First, incidents of actual political violence (such as the overthrow of Crato's Colonel Belém in 1904 and the ambush of Dr. Floro in 1908), as well as incidents in which the threat of violence occurred (such as the encirclement of Crato by the triple alliance in 1909), were political events explicable neither by the racist-inspired theory of the persistence of atavistic family feuds nor by the elitist doctrine of the inherent cultural inferiority of the backlands in comparison to the coast. In each of the incidents

---

"political chief" within the Brazilian politcal system, see Jean Blondel, *As condições da vida política no estado da Paraíba* (Rio de Janeiro, 1957), pp. 57–72, esp. pp. 70–72.

referred to, what was clearly at stake were economic and political gains of a relatively high magnitude.

Second, it is equally necessary to emphasize that violence or the threat of violence was made possible, if not encouraged by—among other factors —the contradictions inherent in the oligarchical political system of the Old Republic—at least in that prevailing in Ceará. On the one hand, oligarchic politics was centered on both (1) clientelism, by which political favors were reciprocally distributed between the state machinery and loyal followers at the local level, and (2) increased municipal autonomy, as a result of which the fruits of economic progress and increased taxation were reallocated more generously to local officeholders. On the other hand, the entire oligarchic structure, such as that in Ceará, was posited on a unitary party structure which by definition excluded any possibility of either local two-party rivalries or regular electoral transferences of power. Thus, there arose an inherent contradiction between clientelism and municipal autonomy on the one hand and the unitary party structure on the other. This contradiction greatly inspired frequent recourse to violence—always, it must be remembered, between members of the same party—as a relatively rational means of achieving power, prestige, and wealth.[44] That Ceará's oligarch, Governor Accioly, rarely intervened, except to award laurels to the victor and synecures to the vanquished, contributed also to the persistence of backlands conflict. Such conflict only subsided around 1910, when a powerful anti-Accioly faction, supported by a nationwide movement, emerged on the coast. That embryonic two-party system later forced a change in the political structure of the state. Also of influence was the influx of the *bacharéis* into politics; that partly contributed to altering the modes of political action from physical violence to a less costly form of symbolic violence.

The third and final observation pertains to a more indirect cause of the conflicts that unfolded in the backlands. The narrative clearly indicated that merchants had increasingly come to vie with landowners for power. This fact can be accounted for only by the rising economic prosperity which characterized life in the Northeast interior after 1880. In view of this fact, the backland violence and conflict of the first decade of the twentieth century must be understood not as a sign of decadence of Brazilian society, but rather as one of the many possible adjustments of a political system to

---

[44] This analysis of the causes of violence would seem to be most valid for Brazil between 1889 and 1914. Because, in this instance, much weight is given to the role of the unitary party, it might prove fruitful to compare Brazil with the tragic "violencia" in Colombia, where two-party allegiances at the grassroots level were of critical causal significance.

the increased integration of Brazil into the international capitalist economy that, in other underdeveloped nations during the same period, was also to wreak havoc on "traditional" institutions.[45]

[45] My analysis is slightly at variance with Merle Kling's 1956 classic, "Toward a Theory of Power and Political Stability in Latin America," republished in *Latin America, Reform or Revolution?*, ed. by James Petras and Maurice Zeitlin (Greenwich, Conn.: Fawcett Publications, 1968), pp. 76–93. Kling suggests that instability may clearly be a result of the high stakes to be won by controlling the political system independently of the economic one (pp. 90–91); the present analysis would indicate that the *motives* for seeking political power may very well derive from the desire of a newly emerging economic group—in this instance, merchants—to acheive either greater economic gains or political status appropriate to newly achieved economic gains.

Chapter 8 The Millennium that Never Came: The Story of a Brazilian Prophet

René Ribeiro

[This study of Cícero José de Farias and his movement in Northeast Brazil represents a particular contribution to general theories of messianism and charisma, the failures and success of messianic movements, and the violence and social disorganization that often characterize such movements. The failure of Cícero is attributed to changing economic conditions in Northeast Brazil in which messianic movements today are less likely to persist. Additionally, the movement's leadership was drawn from the urban middle class and was unable to recruit the rural peasantry. The prophet's introverted behavior undermined his charismatic appeal among the followers. Despite its lack of success, this movement is one small example of the fact that messianism continues to represent an alternative to social and economic conditions that make life so unbearably difficult for millions of people in Northeast Brazil. The ongoing development in that region has dramatically improved the life of only a small portion of the population. What might have been the consequences if Cícero had been able to attract rural lower-class elements and to focus his ideas and demands upon the socioeconomic problems that remain largely unsolved?]

INTRODUCTION

Brazil has offered to the sociologist and to the anthropologist a gamut of messianic and millenarian movements: native autochthonous movements—syncretic, antiacculturative or not, pre- and post-Columbian, and so forth (Terra-do-sem-mal, Santidades, Rio Negro, Canela); dramatic rustic movements—Sebastianist, chiliastic, and the like (Rodeador, Pedra Bonita, Canudos, Contestado, Mucker); secondary surgings of movements which had been suppressed or extinguished (Caldeirão, João Maria); movements accommodated or institutionalized (Velho Pedro, Padre Cícero, Yokaanan); urban movements of various types (Legião da Bôa Vontade, Sociedade Teosófica Brasileira); and some frustrated movements which have remained unperceived by students.

The literature concerning these movements is vast; several authors have classified the movements and studied their outstanding characteristics.[1] Certain frustrated messianic movements have been singled out by Sylvia L. Thrupp as being important, specifically those that "have not produced very clear-cut doctrines nor extremist leaders" and whose members were content "to await the consummation of their hopes quietly." [2] Roger Bastide has also been concerned with this type of movement, while Leon Festinger and his collaborators have analyzed reactions and rationalizations following the nonmaterialization of the hopes of a modern group of millenarists who hoped to take off in flying saucers in order to escape the end of the world.[3]

Although these movements are potentially most enlightening, they are difficult to understand fully because they have not progressed beyond mere attempts, or because they have failed totally or partly. The natural history of one of these movements, the evaluation of the charismatic qualities (or of the personality when possible) of its leader and of its followers, the means of communication used, and the nature of its message assume considerable importance when they are projected upon the general panorama of the socioeconomic setting and the system of values of the regional society and northeastern subculture. For it was within this context (in a previous era) that the characteristics of the various earlier movements emerged, characteristics that continue to serve as dynamic factors. Analysis of one such movement has both theoretical and practical importance (of evaluation and prevention) because, while there is not yet a theory that encompasses and explains all messianic movements, case study in this area still calls for methodological analysis, and because many movements, when successful, have resulted in violence and suffering and in personal and social breakdown.

Recently, I was able to study a frustrated messianic and millenarian

---

[1] See René Ribeiro, "Brazilian Messianic Movements," in *Millennial Dreams in Action*, ed. by Sylvia L. Thrupp (The Hague: Mouton and Co., 1962), pp. 55–59; Maria Izaura Pereira de Querióz, *O messianismo no Brasil e no mundo* (São Paulo: Dominus Editôra, 1965); and José Carlos Marão and Jorge Butsuem, "Yokaanan é um profesa," *Realidade*, II (1967), 92–101.

[2] Ribeiro, *op. cit.*, p. 14.

[3] See Roger Bastide, "Le messianisme râté," *Archives de Sociologie des Religions*, III (1958), 31–37; and Leon Festinger, Henry W. Rieken, and Stanley Schachter, "When Prophecy Fails," in *Readings in Social Psychology*, ed. by Eleanor E. Maccoby, Theodore M. Newcomb, and Eugene L. Hartley (NewYork: Holt, Rinehart and Winston, 1958), pp. 156–163.

movement through written documentation (manifestos and messages, printed or mimeographed, personal correspondence, etc.) and taped interviews with the principal followers and members of their families.

For Norman Cohn, the great specialist in medieval millenarian movements, the circumstances favoring such movements were: demographic expansion, accelerated industrialization, weakening or disappearance of traditional social ties, increase in the distance between rich and poor, and chiliastic hopes. These conditions produced in the population of the region between the Somme and the Reno, and in Central Germany, Holland, and Westphalia, collective sentiments of impotence, anguish, and envy which led to a confidence in Messiahs and a hope for wealth, comfort, security, and eternal power.[4] The social and economic setting in Northeast Brazil is obviously different from the circumstances present in Western Europe at the end of the Middle Ages. However, the circumstances enumerated by Cohn were present at the time in which the movement that concerns us was begun in a context of modern underdevelopment with coordinated efforts, both national and international, to overcome it.

THE PROPHET

The intractable inspirer and leader of the messianic movement that concerns us here, the New Israel (as he calls himself) was named Cícero José de Farias and was one of thirteen brothers whose family lived in an area bordering the semiarid zone (Canhotinho, Pernambuco) of Northeast Brazil. He and his relatives were middle-class agriculturists, artisans, and businessmen. His mother, who appears to have been the dominant figure in the family, learned the art of working leather and became a famous saddlemaker. Subsequently, all the family became dedicated to this art and to the making and selling of shoes. They achieved relative prosperity when they established themselves in Arcoverde, within the semiarid zone, one hundred and fifty miles from the coast.

By 1932 Cícero and his brothers had three shops but changed their line of work because of the decline of leatherworking. His brother said of him: "He was never a businessman and abandoned shoemaking" so that "he could begin to look for treasure, which he searched for here and there." [5] He used to go around the countryside wearing boots and an "engineer's hat" to see if he could locate lands rich in minerals. He arrived at neighboring villages and cities on foot, and it seems that he was already concerned with the su-

---

[4] Norman Cohn, *Les fanatiques de l'Apocalypse*, trans. by Simone Clémendat (Paris: Julliard, 1962), p. 42.

[5] Interview with Manuel Farias, October 29, 1967.

pernatural because "when he arrived he told what he had seen; people spoke with him. . . . Some believed, ... others said that he was mad." [6] Nothing happened to him, however, because "he was from a well-known family." [7] Also, "he heard certain voices." [8]

It was in this year, according to his brother, that Cícero, living in a small house in the suburb of Arcoverde, on a certain night with a full moon:

... saw a star which was different from the others, a little larger than the others. He began to watch that star, and it began to grow larger. It got to be the size of a lemon and then an orange, then a soccer ball, and at this point he found he couldn't tear his eyes away from the sight. He was attracted by that force. The star was coming nearer and nearer. Nearer, nearer, it got to the point where a face was visible and then a form. When it got closer, he saw that it was Jesus. It was the most beautiful thing in the world, and Jesus was much more beautiful than he is when seen in the pictures. He didn't bring any message.

However, Cícero did not remember well and ended by affirming that the vision pointed toward the North.

The prophet's secretary, Wyle Tenório, gave a more elaborate version of this vision: Having received a great quantity of wine, Cícero went out at night to see if it had been stolen. "When he got to the door of the house, he looked towards the east and saw a star in the sky become dislocated and come downwards over by a mountain which was behind the house; the star was growing, growing, and when it was as tall as a tree . . . he saw the star transform itself perfectly into Jesus, and the night became like day." The informant added that "then Jesus spoke" to Cícero "telepathically" and "showed him where the New Zion was to be, where the celestial court would be set up on the Earth, in a place in Arcoverde." According to the system elaborated, the "Tribunal of Justice" was to be in Juàzeiro (in the garden of Padre Cícero); "the judged and the absolved will come to Jerusalem and Zion which will be in Arcoverde"; and those who "attain the degree of saints" will go to a new Heaven which will be constructed in the municipality of Campina Grande (Livramento).[9] Tenório added that then Cícero was "very Catholic" and for this reason "went to the bishop and told everybody about it but gained no support" because he did not accept the "mission" implicit in the vision. Thus the result was that "he lost his reason through disobedience" (he showed signs of being mentally disturbed). In this Wyle is corroborated by the brother of the prophet himself, who reports that he stayed for some time after the vision "in an ecstatic state, and was not himself."

---

[6] Interview with Maria Anunciada de Farias, October 28, 1967.
[7] *Ibid.*
[8] Interview with Manuel Farias, October 29, 1967.
[9] Interview with Wyle Tenório, September 7, 1967.

After that, Cícero said that he had been given supernatural powers. According to his brother, although he continued on with the business in Arcoverde and with his search for minerals, "he would lay his hand on a person and he would become well"; never, however, was the subject cured of a serious illness—only of a headache or stomachache—so Cícero never became famous as a healer. For Wyle "the first mission that he received was spiritualist; he cured those he entreated with his hands." [10]

Little is known about the following twenty years of the prophet's life: it is known that his family dispersed, that he became a widower of his first wife, who abandoned him after five years of life together; that he married again and was also abandoned by his new wife. He then lived as an ascetic for a long time, and his brother says, "he was never very happy in marriage." He was also imprisoned in the Jaguaribe Valley (Ceará) because his activity of "digging up minerals" during World War II was thought suspicious.

In 1952 he appeared in Teixeira, some eighty miles northwest of Arcoverde. There he looked for the farm of an acquaintance, gathering some followers because "when a person comes from the outside and brings something new . . . especially in this matter of serious belief, of religion, then he attracts some people; by this means he got some initiates, a very few . . . . He never had a multitude with him." [11] Nor did he preach or develop public rituals. In this locale, Cícero limited himself to building two concentric fences. In the center he built a hut and dug a cave in which he lived, writing messages which he claimed he received telepathically from God. According to Wyle:

God ordered him to organize a group of men, lovers of God, that would set up a tabernacle of God on Earth. He brought people there, country people, who did not even have knowledge of the Bible, but he gathered them anyway. But when God began to apply the laws—no smoking, no drinking—people are used to doing these things, aren't they?—then they began to leave.[12]

The local ecclesiastical authority, having been informed, called the police and drove him away. It seems that he was held prisoner and then removed to Arcoverde as a madman. Part of the writings of the prophet were then lost and part were recovered. It was there, however, that God changed his name: from Cícero José de Farias, he came to be called Israel Farias because with this "mission" he would go on to be the second Israel—said his followers.

His next stopping place was Patos, about sixteen miles away. Little is known about his activity in this place because his faith healing did not earn

10 *Ibid.*
11 Interview with Manuel Farias, October 29, 1967.
12 Interview with Wyle Tenório, September 9, 1967.

for him a widespread reputation. It was at this time that he began his association with a family from Campina Grande and with Maria da Luz, from whose brother-in-law "he removed an obsession. He was almost crazy. When in crisis he would run around shouting."[13] They sent for the prophet in Teixeira and housed him at a farm in Patos, where he was able to treat the patient under the family's protection.[14] His brother Manuel confirmed that in Patos he "cured people rejected by doctors. Extraordinary cures. He cured any and every sickness."

Sometime in 1955 Cícero was hired to work on a farm in Paraíba, but he kept "walking around everywhere in his search for minerals." He got married in Rio Grande do Norte only to be abandoned because of religious disagreements five years after his failure in Juàzeiro: "She disbelieved in everything he did. She began to say he was a fraud, that it was she who supported him. She took another man as her mate."[15]

For three or four years Cícero stayed in Campina Grande and the surrounding area. He sent messages to friends and relatives announcing the Apocalypse. At the same time, he looked for enchanted treasures and remnants of past civilizations to use in the founding of his New Jerusalem. "Everyone in our family liked religious matters," said his brother Manuel, adding that their mother was "very religious," that she had taught the catechism to her children, and that everyone had read the Bible at home, as had been done since the time of his grandparents. Manuel found out, in 1958, that Cícero was receiving messages. He called him to Recife, where they shared their ideas.[16]

In Recife the prophet gathered some disciples. Among them were his brothers Manuel and Teodoro, who today are in Serra Branca, Paraíba. His wife began to compose various hymns.[17] Wyle Tenório "was affiliated with the Legião da Boa Vontade ["Legion of Good Will"]"[18] and was also a leader in the Sociedade Interplanetária ("Universal Interplanetary Society") founded by spiritualists of Pernambuco and Alagôas equally interested in the mystery of flying saucers. Sabino, Wyle's cousin twice removed, was also a student and an admirer of occultism, of occult sciences. Other disciples of the prophet were Manuel and João Caetano, now residents in Campina Grande; some "brothers" who were gathered together in one of the suburbs of the capital; and a novice from another borough whose garden was literally removed when the plants were transplanted to the Holy Gar-

13 Interview with Maria da Luz, October 20, 1967.
14 Interview with Maria da Luz, October 22, 1967.
15 Interview with Manuel Farias, October 29, 1967.
16 *Ibid.*
17 Interview with Maria da Luz, October 22, 1967.
18 A syncretic, spiritualistic, and theosophical movement founded in Rio de Janeiro by Zahrur.

den in Juàzeiro. There were some others, but all in all not more than twenty persons. There was no meeting of all the disciples. The leader, Cícero, entrusted his messages, which he said he received from God, to his brother Manuel who corrected the grammar while he sought out one or two followers at a time. Later on, that job fell to Wyle who, in 1959, said to a coreligionist : "Now I am in second place under Cícero in the Supreme Order." He said about his chief: "He is the True Prophet of God." [19]

The prophet revealed to a few initiates the next advent of the Messiah and prepared for this coming with a search for "enchanted" treasures and the hope for collaboration of the inhabitants of other planets presently living on Earth in caverns marked out by "hieroglyphics" and of those from the outer space who would come in their flying saucers—an indisguisable contribution of Wyle Tenório who, through his "knowledge" of the matter, was known in the Air Force as Planetinha ("Little Planet"). Wyle, second to the leader, then wrote to the brigadier commander of the II Air Zone, justifying his abandoning the job of civil specialist at the air base in Recife. He said he had to obey

the Voice of Jehovah, God of Abraham and of the Prophets as well as the Voice of his Divine Master, King and Judge, Jesus Christ who is now coming and who is speaking to the Earth to form a pact of Peace, Love, Life, and Fraternity with the Brazilian Government so that it can be united to the Cosmic Government and to the Planetary Government to found a New Jerusalem and to place the World a step ahead in the understanding of God . . . . In case the Brazilian Government accepts the alliance with the Cosmic or Celestial Government, the King of Jerusalem will pay the debts of Brazil in about twenty years and will open the doors of its dispensation so that all Brazilians might be satisfied in their needs and glorify God who is in Heaven.

These, he added, were "the Proposals of God revealed to his Prophet Cícero José de Farias." [20] To his father he set the advent of the "great reform of the world" for the end of the "cycle of Pisces with the beginning of the cycle of Aquarius," thus giving account of his activities:

These sheets that I am sending as a true testimony of the word of God correspond to pages 48 to 51 and 61 to 62 of a book revealed as the word of God the Father and God the Son and containing 143 questions and answers about the New Jerusalem and the Legião Jesuíta Cristã [Legion of Jesus Christ], of which I am a part. The questions are made by me to the Prophet and he responds being inspired with the word of God. I am nearly done writing it and organizing it into three parts. The first has questions and answers and gives all the explanations about the New Jerusalem and the Apocalypse. The second contains the revelations of Jesus Christ, Son of the Living God and gives all the clarifications

[19] Letter to Manuel Caetano, Campina Grande, May 23, 1959.
[20] Letter from Juàzeiro, April 10, 1959.

about the reform of the World, the foundation of Jerusalem, etc. etc. The third is the word of Jehovah, God of the Prophets preparing the New Kingdom of the spirit and the Life for the Third Millennium and creating the Empire of Jerusalem.[21]

This "revealed" book is today still being elaborated by the two and will be entitled: *Deus se revela ao mundo como levantamento do programa da fundação da Nova Jerusalém.* In 1959 Wyle told Sabino in confidence:

Cícero and I have worked for a long time on this book so that we can present to the world a healthy and clear work capable of being understood by all. On the other side, persecutions were terrible against the kingdom of God, and this has caused a great need of a weapon for our defense which will be this book. The Air Force sent two planes commissioned to investigate me and the Congregation.[22]

In the first months of 1959, Cícero, his brother Manuel, and the secretary Wyle went to Juàzeiro. There they located two owners of the lands that composed the garden which was famous at the time of the greatest religious fervor of the followers of the now dead miracle worker, Padre Cícero Romãno Batista.[23] They tried to obtain from them, as a donation, the area necessary for the erection of a Temple of Redemption which was to be made in the form of a pyramid under the true allegation that this "hill of the garden" (Genesareth Garden) had been reserved by Padre Cícero himself so that a church of the garden might be erected there. The owners, who at the beginning had made vague promises, refused because, when one of them consulted the Bishop of Crato, he said that this new mission "did not represent the truth." [24] Wyle says that they intended to found the Kingdom of the Second Advent of Christ, but "when we arrived there we were not well received by some religious groups" causing a situation of open hostility to the millenarists.[25] However, they were able to buy some land in a lot called "Tiradentes" behind the lagoon of Encanto, four miles from the center of the city.

Cícero and his followers tried to get some followers in Juàzeiro without any results:

[21] Letter from Campina Grande, May 19, 1959.

[22] Letter from Campina Grande, May 9, 1959.

[23] This is a mystical site located atop Catolé Hill, where Padre Cícero started to build a church (later stopped by the Bishop of Crato). In his will Padre Cícero wrote that it "ought to be completed following the blueprint brought from Rome and the maquette I leave on deposit in a safe place." See Edmar Morel, *Padre Cícero o Santo de Juàzeiro* (2d ed.; Rio de Janeiro: Editôra Civilização Brasileira, 1966), p. 190.

[24] Interview with Manuel Farias, October 29, 1967.

[25] Interview with Wyle Tenório, September 7, 1967.

Because no one believed. No one accepted. No one thinks that this is a true thing and that he is a true prophet. What is impossible?—that God doesn't speak to man. Disbelief, isn't it? A very extraordinary thing. It isn't for man to realize . . . . Who ought to realize it is God . . . . He will do it with the angels and not with man.[26]

They attempted to hold a mystical "Election of Jesus," and distributed notes in envelopes bearing the crest of the Legião Jesuíta Cristã, but did not receive one single answer from the population of the holy city.

Whether or not by coincidence with a prophecy of Padre Cícero's announcing that in 1960 extraordinary things would happen and signs would appear in the sky, our prophet sought to reunite his followers in Juázeiro for a new message to be received on New Year's Day. In December of 1959 his brother Manuel, Wyle, and two families from Campina Grande followed him. They built a cabin, which would shelter up to one hundred persons, and a type of tunnel which aroused suspicions that they were hiding arms. They tried to reunite "our people and the people of the city," but without any great result because the Franciscan brothers said hostile things about them until the pilgrims (followers of Padre Cícero) rose up against them: "Why did they think those things that we said were going to happen were not going to happen . . . . They would be realized through Padre Cícero. And that was his mission."[27] There was an uprising of common people armed with clubs, knives, and firearms which ended when one of the back rooms of the house was set on fire. Afterward, Cícero's house was searched by the police, and finally they were all threatened by the monks who told them to get out of the city. They still circulated a letter (the first one announcing the foundation of the New Jerusalem and the Second Advent). They were in Juàzeiro until July, when "they had an order" from the supernatural to return to their homes and to their interrupted activities. As to the expected supernatural facts, "there was a message, but it wasn't a definite one."[28] The group dispersed, the prophet went to Recife and later to Campina Grande where he soon discovered in the nearby town of Livramento indications that one of the agencies of the Kingdom of God ought to be located there.

The vicissitudes of the direct action and the secret nature of the mission (search for treasures, revelation of the designs of God, telepathic communications, etc.) gave preeminence to the missionary activity of the prophet and his secretary. Three "Letters of the Second Advent" (as one was entitled) were printed between 1960 and 1963, the first in Juàzeiro with 500

[26] Interview with Manuel Farias, October 29, 1967.
[27] Ibid.
[28] Ibid.

copies, the second in Recife with a thousand copies, the third again in Recife with two thousand copies. A fourth letter was mimeographed and dated from Livramento (1965).

The first of these letters was sent by mail to the heads of the government in three hundred countries; to the governor, to the bishop, and to the Protestant priesthood in each state of Brazil; to the ministers of state, presidents of legislative assemblies, federal and state, and to the mayors and municipal aldermen. "Seeing that the word of the Lord did not echo throughout the world, the world ignored [did not admit] the fact that God could speak to men." In reply to this absurdity, Wyle said, "the God of Israel sent a very loving message that was to be sent to all the nations of the earth to all languages and peoples inviting the people in general to the Bodas do Cordeiro at the Second Advent, *but this message was not heard* [italics mine]." [29]

In truth he seems to have had only two answers to these lettermanifestos. One came from Russia, "very uncivil"—Prime Minister Khrushchev sent "a rude answer to the Creator, and the Creator dismissed him from office and asked us to suspend the letters." [30] The other was from a Catholic bishop from the Territory of Rio Branco who thought the letter was from a delirant and said: "May God open your eyes to the light of Truth." [31] The third letter was largely distributed as a leaflet in Recife, among people with whom Wyle established contact, when, as a taxi driver, he awaited the divine call. [32]

The last letter was distributed only to the personal contacts of members of the group whom they judged were prospective adherents. The prophet became impatient with the lack of response to his movement and the slow coming of the Apocalypse and decided therefore that time had come when the "Friends of God ought to have two wives so as to make scandal and lead the world to sin even more and thus precipitate its own destruction." [33]

THE GROUP

Twenty-six people, almost all belonging to just one family, actually composed the body of loyal followers of the New Israel, or the apocalyptic prophet, Cícero José de Farias. Among these, twenty-four "elect" members

[29] Interview with Wyle Tenório, September 7, 1967.
[30] *Ibid.*
[31] Interview with Cassilda Tenório, August 20, 1967.
[32] It was this letter, moreover, that directed my attention to the movement on the eve of my participation in the meeting on "millenarism" on April 8 and 9, 1960, at the University of Chicago under the auspices of the editors of *Comparative Studies in Society and History*. See *Millennial Dreams in Action.*
[33] *Decreto para tirar descendência Israel.*

should be chosen to constitute the "Celestial Court on Earth." They would be the ones, in the words of the prophet, the appointed ones, to which the Apocalypse refers. The hierarchy of the group was not clearly defined, and there are several versions of it. One of them places Jehovah at the apex, constituting the "Supreme Tribunal for the Judgment Day." Then below are the Holy Spirit and Jesus Christ. Next come twelve members who compose the tabernacle of God with men. Finally there are twelve vice-kings and queens (which does not add up to twenty-four people because each member of a couple does not constitute a unity but only a band) whose functions remain equally obscure. Israel, the prophet, was to be the king of the New Jerusalem.

With the exception of Cícero, the prophet, and his secretary, Wyle, the rest of the adherents did not occupy definite positions. Wyle declared, for example, that each one should call himself Israel to confound their enemies, "because to persecute one, all must be persecuted." Maria da Luz seemed, however, not to accept this position. Not only did she never call him Israel the Second, but she pretended to have intuitions herself, adding that "When Israel [Cícero] goes out, I receive." These messages, however, came from lesser entities, Isaiah, Jeremiah, and other prophets of antiquity. By 1966 the order of sucession was the following: "Israel would be replaced by his brother Manuel who would bear this title. And God would care for him and if Manuel died Paulo Bezerra would succeed him. And if Paulo died, Manuel Bezerra will succeed him." [34] In the opinion of Wyle's wife, the brothers previously were identified with the apostles—Judas Thaddeus, John the Evangelist, Mark, and Peter—but "now everyone is a saint." [35] Those who had "some knowledge" constituted the generation of the New Israel, while the "initiates" composed the Legião Jesuíta Cristã. The position of the Sociedade Interplanetária Universal was not clarified since it was a component of the most esoteric of their conceptions. It is known that there would not be just one Jerusalem but several, and that each one of them would be structured into four classes: (1) the Trindade de Deus ("which is the pure Jerusalem—Father, Son, and Holy Ghost"); (2) the Coração do Povo ("what God sends within it; the anointed, sealed, and circumcised"); (3) "the people who are preparing themselves for this degree"; and (4) the manufactured class ("buildings that have to be constructed in Brazil as the greatest works of all times since people have existed on earth"). [36] This last part is what gave rise to the "archaeological" research because subterranean kingdoms exist which must be revealed. "These kingdoms will be used: the people and the fortune existing in those having in-

34 Deus se revela ao mundo, p. 61.
35 Interview with Cassilda Tenório, August 20, 1967.
36 Interview with Wyle Tenório, September 7, 1967.

habitants will be used for the edification of these works; and those which do not have inhabitants will be used to keep the seeds of God for the Third Millennium." [37]

The group suffered several defections. One was that of Pedro, whose family had princesses in the ministry and who was dismissed because his daughter refused to fulfill the restrictions imposed on the followers: "There are in our midst people who by not complying with the orders of God, have been dismissed." There was still dissension from Pedro Barros and his family who were residents in Campina Grande and had previously been very active members of the Brotherhood, and also from several other members announced by Wyle: "There was a break with some in the ministry who ignored the commandments of God, took another God and also who wanted to destroy the mission of Cícero." [38] In addition, a proselyte in Juàzeiro defected after stealing a bicycle and money from the group. Also, some boys in Recife admitted abandoning the group even as the suspicion of having tried to murder the prophet hung over them. God said through his prophet: "I am going to destroy the capital, Recife, and disband the congregation because there was an attempt to murder Israel." Wyle's wife, Vicente, Mário, Zuleide, and other members will be under "death sentences" [?] because "they want to destroy Jerusalem and Israel." [39] This made the existence of the group precarious (because it was surrounded with secrecy and suspicion). Its luck also varied because there were "many difficulties in getting followers," as is seen by "the present generation which does not understand these Biblical matters." [40]

The families of the closest followers of the New Israel were not unanimous in their adherence to the messianic beliefs. The wife of Manuel, brother of the prophet, did not follow him to Juàzeiro with her sons because "I didn't think that it would work." She compared the separation from her husband to death: "Life is like that, he dies, I don't have to die, isn't that right?" [41] Wyle's wife denounced the discordance between the predictions of the prophet and positive facts; and, when confronted with her husband's rationalizations, she commented, "There is always something changing." Regarding the impact of the movement, she said:

I think that it may be due to the way they preach .... I think it is a very aggressive manner—very—but ... as it is said, ... I think that every religion in which the word of God is preached has as an incentive, the love of God, of union, of tranquility, and of things .... They create a God for themselves and no one

[37] Ibid.
[38] Letter from Campina Grande, May 23, 1959.
[39] Deus se revela ao mundo, pp. 13–34.
[40] Interview with Wyle Tenório, September 7, 1967.
[41] Interview with Maria Anunciada de Farias, October 28, 1967.

likes this God. God comes to destroy, God doesn't come to give peace, God has to destroy these people, . . . this atomic bomb which is destroying the people . . . . God is going to make it . . . I mean that they have hardly any kind words or love of God. . . . Many things that they say are taken from the Bible, which is now said in their own way! [42]

She also opposed her husband when she was still living with him because he gave arbitrary interpretations to the Bible.

The neophyte did not need to undergo special initiation rituals to be received into the Legião Jesuíta Cristã, but became increasingly familiar with the "revelations" by means of progressive access to the literature produced by Cícero and Tenório. Participation in the ministry, however, brought rejuvenation and immortality as immediate payment: "God already removed all their sins" and gave them immortality; it was in the "enchanted kingdom of the Serra do Araripe where Cícero rejuvenated." [43] The appearance of Cícero, who was very well preserved for his seventy years, was given as proof of this.

A condition for entrance into the Confraria (as they called the group at times) was that one must be "a truly pacific man," as vegetarian as possible, who keeps Saturday and Sunday, does not drink, gamble, or celebrate Carnival, nor take part in strikes or wars, and one who follows the principles set down in the Sermon of the Mount.[44] The group also attempted to be endogamous ("It is not admissible for any reason for a member of the New Israel to marry with a member from outside") but actually accepted those already married even if their wives were disbelievers or only tolerant. Nevertheless, the prophet ordered them to take another wife so as to assure a "sanctified" descent. All were white and from the lower middle class.

All the information concerning Cícero's personality and his entrance into this ministry was obtained from third parties. His appearance, to judge by photographs, was of a man of medium height and a robust appearance that belied his seventy years. In one photo, he wore a dark suit of good quality, glasses, and a hat. In another, in which he was surrounded by girls of the Dantas family on a farm owned by this powerful backwoods clan, he wore the white clothes of the country, boots, and explorer's hat. Wyle's wife accused him of becoming refined in his habits: wore a tropical suit, carried an umbrella, had a portable radio, and slept "in a perfumed bed." He also had two wives, according to the *Decreto para tirar descendência Israel*. Extremely withdrawn, Cícero was afraid of contact with strangers and refused to preach in public because "if I went to the public square to

[42] Interview with Cassilda Tenório, August 20, 1967.
[43] *Ibid.*
[44] Interview with Wyle Tenório, September 7, 1967 .

have contact with the public, I would be crucified like Jesus." Another rationalization for this suspicious behavior is taken from another informant: "We know perfectly well that the true Pastor does not hear his voice in preaching." [45]

His prolificacy in producing "messages" caused wonder among disbelievers and adversaries: "At the same time that I have seen him as an exploiter of the people's credulity I have also seen that man write so many things that I don't know how an illiterate can fill up so much paper with so many things . . . horrible things." [46] The prophet pretends to communicate with God all the time—"The creator says telepathically what we ought to do every day"—and the enchantment of one of his proselytes is to follow him throughout the countryside and see him speak with the All-Powerful.[47]

His brother Manuel was one of his constant disciples. At the beginning he took on the job of revising and correcting the prophet's writings. He accompanied Cícero to Juàzeiro, participating there in the vicissitudes of the unsuccessful announcement of the Millennium (1960). Manuel's wife says that he was Catholic and took his children to the Catholic Church but that eventually "he separated from the Church and said that he had this mission." [48] Previously, he had been interested in spiritualism but had found some faults in it. Manuel was quiet and meticulous, having made himself notable in his work by the order and control he displayed in the distribution of gas to homes made by a large company. He was attracted by "the conviction that it is a movement from God himself." For him, "What will happen is an authentic repetition of Noah's case; only now it is not an ark; the ark now is different . . . a different catastrophe." He believed that there would be rains of stones and that atomic bombs would be detonated, and that their mission was "to separate this group of persons, to keep them in these determined places . . . and to form a new generation." All this would happen around the year 2100.[49]

The ultimate destiny of the group was explained thus by Manuel: "God will have to install his government on Earth, counting on them for a vast program" for paying the debts of Brazil, "to install a president by force if necessary; beyond this, works are to be constructed" where "the elect will be guarded from the catastrophe" because the rest of the world will be devastated. "Only those kept in these places will escape." This government will have eternal duration, Manuel declared, and added that then the

[45] Interview with Maria da Luz, October 22, 1967.
[46] Interview with Cassilda Tenório, August 20, 1967.
[47] Interview with Wyle Tenório, September 7, 1967.
[48] Interview with Maria Anunciada de Farias, October 28, 1967.
[49] Interview with Manuel Marias, October 29, 1967.

Earth will be rotating in another orbit; that twenty-six planets will compose "this new constellation" which, naturally, will have "its own light." In ample time "all will be constructed. Engineers will come from other countries" (three of them spared from the destruction and subordinate to the divine government) and also "from other planets by means of flying saucers." Ultimately the work of Israel, he said, would be to seek to find the sites where the new Jerusalems would be constructed and those where the "mines and treasures," indispensable to the financing of so ambitious a program, lay.[50]

The greatest expert on flying saucers, however, was Wyle Tenório, who entered the group after Manuel, in whose house he met the prophet. He was a slight, short man, forty-two years old, who easily inspired confidence. He was in the Navy during World War II and was admitted as an electrical technician in the Air Force. His imagination, said his wife, created miraculous and improbable stories: during the war he received warnings in his sleep and asked to be transferred from his ship, which was subsequently torpedoed; he saw Jesus more than once; and when he had an accident, Our Lady advised him not to submit to orthopedic treatment, which he feared. Also, he was for some time a participant in the Legião da Boa Vontade, a theosophical-spiritual movement originating in Rio de Janeiro.

By 1957 he was reading reports published in a weekly magazine of large circulation about flying saucers. He bought a book titled *Life on Mars and Flying Saucers*. "He began to study about them and this led to that story about the saucers; he said that he spoke with the people of Mars who were coming to earth." Afterward, a group of spiritualists from his state of birth (Alagôas) came together, founded a Sociedade Interplanetária Universal, and thought about discovering minerals which would cure cancer, speaking with the Martians, and receiving the flying saucers. Wyle then received warnings from the angel Gabriel: He traveled to the interior (after minerals) and to Maceió for spiritual sessions (he came from a spiritualist family, his father having faith in spiritualism and being greatly versed in the Bible), and he already believed in the "coming of the Promised Land." [51]

Wyle became a great reader of the Bible, especially of the Old Testament (he read in the morning, afternoon, and night), and together with Cícero he proposed to write a new Bible which "is going to be televised and the radio waves are going to be obliged to divulge his word." The informant added: "The translation that he is making of the Bible is com-

[50] *Ibid.*
[51] Interview with Cassilda Tenório, August 20, 1967.

pletely in his own way of thinking." [52] He neglected his job and came to be known by the nickname of Planetinha, because of his ideas.

Returning to Recife, Wyle resumed his contacts with Cícero and in 1960 announced to his wife the destruction of the world, urging her to accompany him to Juàzeiro with their children to take part in the Kingdom of God, or the New Jerusalem. He went alone (with a small group of loyal followers who accompanied the prophet) to the mystical city of Juàzeiro, where he was found by a medical board—bearded, Bible in hand, waiting for the Third Millennium and suffering from "confabulatory paranoia." When the awaited signs failed to appear and the predicted cataclysm did not come to pass, Wyle accepted all the moves from place to place justified by the prophet in the name of God and continued on, dedicated to the mission, certain that Brazil would be "the cradle of the future generation of the Third Millennium." [53]

After he entered the ministry, he confided:

I was very sick, but after I began to fulfill my mission, I was given health, vigor, vivacity, high intelligence, all of which I never had, and no man asked me anything that I couldn't answer in any field; I began to feel the spreading of the spirit of God; I became a happy man, marvelously happy, with peace of spirit for myself and for the others who desired it.[54]

Sabino was another adherent and a cousin twice removed of the prophet Cícero. A problem child, he left his family in the interior of Pernambuco at an early age and went to the big city, where he led an unsavory life which is not pleasant to describe. He traveled repeatedly to the south of the country as a driver, and there he acquired the accent and slang of the cariocas and paulistas. He joined the army, where he rose to the level of second-class specialist sergeant in maintenance and services. He obtained a discharge because of incapacity (spinal lesions in an accident that almost paralyzed him), then moved to Campina Grande with his wife and two children. Since about 1957 he has followed the movement, but he could not go to Juàzeiro in 1960 because of his army duty. It is said, however, that he was present at other "functions" (attempts at installing the New Jerusalem there). With affected modesty he claimed to be "little versed in occult sciences" and to be "predestined" to having visions. He was never a member of any religion, but he was a "thinker on various religions" (finding in all an obvious lacuna) and a "free thinker, who was very attracted to metaphysics." He claimed, "through occult sciences, from metaphysics, from spiritualism, and from yoga," to have obtained "a clear

[52] Interview with Cassilda Tenório, August 20, 1967.
[53] Interview with Wyle Tenório, September 7, 1967.
[54] Ibid.

conscience" of the part of his spirit which brought him an "objective and concrete clarity of God and his grandeur." However, he never did find "the fundamental truth of the objective of all things, which is God, until he took up with this man [Cícero] . . . ." He familiarized himself with the Legião Jesuíta Cristã and met with the prophet and Wyle in the house of his cousin Manuel.

With the exception of some letters (the third) which he distributed by mail to foreigners and of some ill-taken attempts to seduce the Spiritualists and Protestants, Sabino's activity in the company was slight, for he was not allowed to search for treasures. He showed himself to be, however, extremely zealous in the guarding of the secrets of the group and was hostile to curious strangers. Sabino brought to the group the spirit of barracks discipline ("the duty of all Israelites [followers of Israel] is to fulfill orders without fail"), a certain rationalism ("we do not only have faith; we are conscious"), and a pedantic and rudimentary scientism "because the greatest church that a man can build for God is his pure heart and in it is the will of God and not his own will." [55] He felt that participating in the movement was "the most perfect thing possible" because "we make ourselves part of the same society where, with a common unity of comprehension, we seek to obey our God." [56]

Maria da Luz, her husband, three brothers, and mother constituted a solid group of followers Cícero could count on in Campina Grande. Their loyalty was the result of the prophet's having cured an "obsessed" brother while in Patos. During one of these "curing" visits, he passed on the idea of the New Jerusalem to them. Maria da Luz preceded her husband in adherence. She was a Catholic but "felt no satisfaction" in the Catholic religion. She sought out the Presbyterian church and "felt somewhat better, but there was still something missing" until she encountered the "spirit of God" by means of Cícero. Her house became a center of meetings for the reading of the messages and a base for the comings and goings of the prophet to the interior, to Juàzeiro, to Rio Grande do Norte, to Recife, and so forth. Her husband, an automobile mechanic with a small local repair shop, was given to drink and remained outside as an observer. Finally, with the spiritual "prelections" of his wife, he acquired the new belief. In the same manner his mother ended up by seeing "that the small images of the saints on the walls were all wrong." Maria da Luz felt, with the new belief, a "joy within my heart," but she thought it "necessary for people to die because God will only accept mankind after all die." As to the elect, "We are awaiting God on Earth, the living God, a God like men," and

55 Interview with Sabino Pereira, September 7, 1967.
56 *Ibid.*

speaking of the everlasting life of the elect: "They will remain, those whom God accepts, in the manner of God; they are going to gather in Zion before the destruction of the world." [57]

In spite of the hierarchy outlined previously, there was a great feeling of equality among the followers of Cícero, but he kept somewhat reserved, aloof from intimacies and from contact with crowds or strangers. He did not transmit his messages verbally, only in writing; he did not preside over pious exercises nor go on pilgrimages. He was the indispensable intermediary between God and his followers because "God speaks to one and through inspiration to twenty-four" [58] and prefers gatherings with a few people who are progressively indoctrinated and involved in his ideas and secret research.

The number of the faithful was restricted and kept small for reasons of security. "We are close-mouthed about our meetings," said Maria da Luz. This was because they always expected persecutions or violence. The treasures were well protected, in the words of a member of the celestial court, by an electromagnetic belt; if this does not suffice, "whoever removes the treasure without the consent of God, will go mad." The same would happen to whoever opposed or persecuted the group.

Wyle was the only one who had access to the enchanted kingdom, which he entered through a secret door that opens in a stone in the mountain of Araripe.[59] Israel, however, could point to the site of the treasures:

The largest riches on Earth are at Pedra do Pinhão, by the road, in Mãe d'Agua de Fora, on the ridges of Serra do Teixeira. It is a diamond mine. It is deep. Dig; before you reach one meter the first diamond will be found. . . . The largest treasure in Brazil lies at São Caetano behind the Fiscal Post where there is a mound close to the road. Atop it, behind the last slab overlooking the post lies the treasure of the Andradas da Rasa Aria. . . . Another very large site rich in mineral wealth is at Sitio do Nunes, beyond Custódia at the main road between Recife and Juàzeiro. Before you reach the town, on your right there is a slab of medium size. North of this rock, by its base, there is a diamond mine.[60]

These treasures seemed to be a bait for loyalities. "Many people come after the promises of these treasures," [61] but the great hope was to increase their number by supernatural means. They were hoping to gain 144,000 new members—baptized at the Congregational church where a schism was being interpreted by them as an indication of a growing closeness to the

[57] Interview with Maria da Luz, October 22, 1967.
[58] Interview with Maria da Luz, October 22, 1967.
[59] Interview with Cassilda Tenório, August 20, 1967.
[60] *Deus se revela ao mundo*, pp. 55-56.
[61] Interview with Cassilda Tenório, August 20, 1967.

Legião. Sixty thousand workers would be needed for the erection of the New Jerusalem; they would come from the enchanted kingdoms of Agartha and Duat, or in saucers from Mars and Venus, and so forth.

THE MESSAGE

An analysis of the content of the messages announcing the new advent will clarify the nature of the beliefs that motivated this group of millenarists and their prophet. The printed letters have a peculiar sound molded in Biblical language, and their contents were obviously taken from the Apocalypse; the language is symbolic and, at times, obscure. Their logic leads them to announce that the distribution of the first letter, in the words of one of them, was responsible for the ecumenical movement of the Catholic Church: "There was a large reform in religion after these letters." [62]

The first letter, distributed in 1960, was presented as a revelation and was, consequently, of divine origin. It was announced in the letter that Jesus Christ was designated to govern a new humanity which would be established in a New Jerusalem after the Apocalypse, which was said to be already unfolding. The marvelous nature of the announced facts was accentuated, God was proclaimed the only one capable of producing them, and the localities of Juàzeiro and Arcoverde were identified as seats of the "government of the planetary system" soon to be inaugurated. Cooperation was asked of the churches and the governments, the New Advent was fixed for 1960, and redemption and rejuvenation were promised. The message was received "telepathically" by Cícero José de Farias in the role of "Promised Comforter," and the "coming of Jesus as King of Brazil and governor of the world" was announced as an invisible mystery because "he will not be seen to the naked eye."

The second letter, distributed in 1961, was also presented as the word of God, but its subtitle is much more pragmatic: "Operations of the Celestial Government." Its first paragraphs are energetic ("my will is firm and powerful," says Jehovah) and is directed to the civil, military, and religious authorities, announcing to them that the "Earth has come to be governed by Jesus." God continues, however, to be invisible, but his existence is recognized by "facts." The proclamation of Jesus Christ as "King of Brazil" is reiterated more than once, and the authorities are urged under the threat of the All-Powerful not to rise up against Jesus although politically they may be assured that "when God governs the Earth, he will

[62] Interview with Maria da Luz, October 22, 1967.

not remove the government from their power nor will he destroy the assemblies or the senates or the democracy of men." Moreover, the government will be "cosmic, theocratic, and theosophical."

The authority and continuity of the governments and churches being guaranteed, the supergovernment will, however, give them directives: to arm each person with a Bible, to combat witchcraft, to respect spiritualism, and to promote the love of God, peace, and human brotherhood; to punish the wicked and promote the regeneration of men, repaying them with the Kingdom of God and the peace resulting from the alliance between the cosmic government and the Brazilian government, a peace that will be secure for all people, all religions, for the clergy, for pastors, for spiritualists, for theosophical beliefs and doctrines, "for whoever believes in God and for whoever does not believe in God" as long as they live according to the will of God.

The reform of the Earth, it is said further on, will not be through "total destruction" but through a "metamorphosis of a general nature." The "Judge of the Judgement" will judge all in "a millenary advent" while Satan is imprisoned. The city of New Jerusalem "will be raised up from nothing by a new Noah" for the blessed once man is armed "with a Bible in his hand" and defends the way of God against the impious. Like the first, this letter had the crest of the Legião Jesuíta Cristã and the Sociedade Interplanetária Universal.

The third letter, distributed between 1962 and 1963, was the longest of all. The revelation was directed to the adversaries of God; over these was cast the Biblical threat of repudiation ("I will strike the dust from their sandals"). The desire for peace and the tolerance for other religions, were, however, reiterated jointly with the promises of world government and of measures that would lift Brazil "to the point of grandeur and of triumph as king of the countries of the Earth."

The Messiah was announced as having already come—his government would now no longer be in secret nor would he be "timid of those who do not know me"—and a "great moral struggle" was proposed. Whoever inquires into the reason of his choice of Juàzeiro for the founding of Jerusalem would be told: "The reason is because the pilgrims said that Padre Cícero Romão Batista was God," but "there is only one Savior for this generation," adding:

God was never touched by the hand of man and Padre Cícero, with his body here on earth, was subjected to the same conditions as other men. Today, at the side of the Son of Man, it is necessary to speak to his followers in a particular manner and to lead them on the path of knowledge of the Sacred Scriptures so that they may know how to say who is the Savior.

The Second Advent and the Millennium began in the year 1960. The city of Arcoverde was to be the heart of Jerusalem, and the coming of the Son of Man "needs to be revealed." The Catholic Church was criticized, as was the violence of the Franciscan brothers; enemies were threatened and obedience was advised for whoever "wants to be worthy of the Kingdom of God." Twenty-four commands were listed at the end of the document.

The fourth and the last letter began to be circulated in 1965 by the Office of the New Israel, City of Livramento, Paraíba. It was a "calling" from Christ for a "new alliance between God and men." Jesus as King of Jerusalem and of Brazil, addressed the chosen from the sky of Livramento "for the party of the sovereign monarchy" because Earth "will have a king capable of remedying the situation of Brazil." The spirit of this kingdom will be ecumenical, and the advent is often announced as already having been realized. Hope, however, will only be restored "in his empire" by struggle and suffering and by the punishing of those who have the misfortune not to accept the "new alliance of God." Also imminent "is the battle between good and evil, between God and the devil, to rectify the world which will come to be of God and of Christ." The end of anxiety with eternal felicity is then promised, in the conclusion of the letter, to those who "live according to the will of God" because the Earth will come to be "a paradise for the bold who will then be the shelter of God."

ANALYSIS OF A FAILURE

Socioeconomic change in Northeast Brazil seems to have been accentuated around 1930, the date of the last liberal revolution in that country. The social structures of that time, improperly labeled as "archaic" by Jacques Lambert,[63] underwent considerable transformation. Economically, the beginning of the disintegration of the *latifúndio* and the integration of the economy into the internal market undermined the artisanal and subsistence economy, extended the range of salaried work, fomented relationships of mercantile character, increased the internal market of consumer's goods and also the means of production, and determined the increase of average per capita income. Demographically, migrations to the industrial south or to the urban centers of the Northeast itself alleviated the pressure of overpopulation and freed the day laborers, the sharecroppers, the tenants, or semisalaried from the dominance of the landowners. Politically, central power was strengthened; the arbitrariness of the colonel was an-

[63] Jacques Lambert, *Os dois Brasis* (Rio de Janeiro: INEP, 1959).

nulled; and democratic processes and self-determination were implanted in the communities of the interior. Religiously, the penitents, the missions, and other forms of exacerbated religious expression gradually disappeared, thus weakening the prophetical-eschatological and chiliastic forms of religion common in the past. Educationally and culturally, the school network, the campaigns against illiteracy, and mainly, the mass media, the multiplication of the means for prevention and relief of disaster (droughts, floods, epidemics, calamities) all increased. Ideologically, a developmental mentality, the hope in technological progress, and a generalized confidence in the recuperation of this problem area were created.[64] All this led Rui Facó to affirm that it was no longer possible for redoubts of bandits and of *beatos* to subsist. He adds that a "change of mentality" has occurred in the Northeast and that customs are feeling the influence of contact with cultural groups of diverse origin.[65]

The failure of the New Israel must be interpreted, consequently, in terms of circumstance. Although conditions in the Northeast at the present time basically contain elements such as those enumerated by Norman Cohn (capable of leading the populations to reactions of a messianic type as on past occasions), they already encompass other elements which are capable of directing their hopes and their efforts in a compensatory manner to other paths, such as that of economic development. The movement was initiated by and had its membership made up of people of the middle class, urbanites, who never sought nor had any contact with the rural proletariat.

Past accumulated evidence also lends itself to the testing of other hypotheses which attempt to explain messianic movements. It was Norman Cohn, following Max Weber, who called attention to the role of the prophet in these types of movements. In his opinion, it is the prophet who adapts the traditional millenarian faith to a millenarian ideology and becomes the bearer of this resulting ideology. "If in addition," we are told, "the prophet possesses a suitable personality and is able to convey an impression of absolute conviction, he is likely in certain situations of emotional tension to become the nucleus of a millenarian movement." [66] The most credible information about our New Israel indicates that he is elusive,

---

[64] See Stefan H. Robock, *Desenvolvimento econômico regional, O Nordeste do Brasil*, trans. by José C. M. Cavalcante and Fernando B. da Silveira (Rio de Janeiro: Editôra Fundo de Cultura, 1963); and *Sudene: III plano diretor 1966–1968* (Recife: Sudene, 1966).

[65] Rui Facó, *Cangaceiros e fanáticos* (Rio de Janeiro: Editôra Civilização Brasileira, 1965), pp. 217 and 219.

[66] Norman Cohn, "Medieval Millenarism; Its Bearing on the Comparative Study of Millenarian Movements," in *Millennial Dreams in Action*, ed. by Sylvia L. Thrupp (The Hague: Mouton and Co., 1962), pp. 31–43.

suspicious, and fearful of exposing himself in public ("so that he would not be crucified"), and also that he received threats of assassination. At the same time, he developed hedonistic habits, such as that of only sleeping in a perfumed bed, dressing well, using motorized transportation (furnished by his "secretary"), and appreciating feminine company. He proposed to establish polygamy among his followers in order to benefit from it himself. From the very beginning of this movement he also assumed the role of an ethic prophet instead of that of an exemplary one.[67]

It is difficult and hazardous to classify his personality type only on the basis of the information collected, but it is certain that after the frustrated attempt of Teixeira, he abandoned his hermit inclinations, never dressing in sackcloth, nor making pilgrimages, nor exposing himself to the risk of gathering large crowds. Proceeding in this manner, he diminished to a large extent the charisma (he has recently given up his "curing" procedures) with which he could have dignified his prophetical figure. His reaction to the political hostility of the established church, contrary to other miracle workers and visionaries who were successful, was to organize a small, esoteric, and semiclandestine group of elect of his choice. This is in line with the findings of Leon Festinger and collaborators, who pointed out, in the two groups studied by them, the preoccupation of keeping these beliefs and activities secret and of limiting, egotistically, to a few (such as the elect of our example) the venture of the millennium.[68]

Secrecy and the search for secret treasures came to be an objective of the action of the group, thus making it difficult, when their hopes were not realized, for them to adjust to a new reality. Then too, tensions arose and culminated in the desertion of the prophet's second wife when she began attributing to herself supernatural powers greater than his. It can be observed, moreover, that the inner circle of the elect received little protection from the uninitiated members, the components of the Legião Jesuíta Cristã. These observations are in agreement with the conclusions of Harry B. Hawthorn in his study of the Doukhobors (British Columbia) in testing the hypothesis of George Simmel about secret societies.[69]

The persistence of the majority of the members of the movement in the expectation of the Second Advent and in the inauguration of the Millennium, in spite of successive postponements of the realization of the promises of Jehovah through his prophet, and the continuation of the work of proselytism at the same pace in spite of the repeated deception are phen-

[67] Max Weber, *The Sociology of Religion*, trans. by Ephraim Fishchoff (Boston: Beacon Press, 1967), p. 55.

[68] Festinger, Rieken, and Schachter, *op. cit.*, pp. 160–161.

[69] H. B. Hawthorn, "A Test of Simmel on the Secret Society: The Doukhobors of British Columbia," *American Journal of Sociology*, LXII (1956), 1–6.

omena that have been observed in other instances of millenarianism. Neither can be explained psychopathologically, because only one of the group proved to be abnormal while the others, however much they might be involved in the millenarist plans, seemed to be normal individuals when I interviewed them. These findings correspond to the peculiar functioning of these groups and to a particular form of reaction in face of deception. Leon Festinger and his collaborators observed the same thing among the millenarists who were the objects of his study. The explanation of this type of unexpected behavior, according to these authors, is found in their need to repudiate dissonance in the face of ambiguous nonconfirmation of these millenarian beliefs, which are then reinforced by coparticipation in the deception and support of other members of the group.[70]

Tactical errors committed by our prophet perhaps explain, in part, the small popular success of his movement. First, the hierarchy of the group adopted no insignias and avoided ritualism. Insignias and ritual reinforce belief and are very evident in most religious movements. Cícero and his followers ought to have felt this lack when, in affirming the existence of treasures and enchanted worlds and of communication with flying saucers, they exposed themselves to the criticism and derision of nonbelievers and to the skepticism of the uninitiated, including some of their own wives. Second, given the vulgarization of reports and the science fiction about interplanetary communication and the existence of other inhabited worlds, the appeal of our millenarists has not had much of an impact because their fantasies are within the grasp of all. In this respect they even lose originality in the face of the elaborate fantasies and of an existing temple for the New Christ, the Avatara Maitréya, constructed by the Brazilian Theosophical Society.[71] Third, we can place their attack upon the garden in the mystical city of Juàzeiro. It is possible that Cícero might have erroneously attempted to substitute himself for the miracle worker of this same name. He did not take into account that the movement of Padre Cícero had been institutionalized before his death and that the mystical profane *status quo* of Juàzeiro is under the watch of interests zealously defended by the Catholic Church and by the civil authorities. Fourth and last, the prophet's persistence in the use of pamphlets as a vehicle of his message, with a symbolic language obscure in the manner of the Bible, in a region in which 70 percent of the inhabitants were illiterate partially explains his failure to constitute the future cosmic government to be installed in Brazil.

Finally, it is necessary to take into consideration the range of choice for religious expression that is open to the individual in this region through religious pluralism and the reinterpretation of the components of various

[70] Festinger, Rieken, and Schachter, *op. cit.*, p. 162.
[71] *O Cruzeiro*, September 16, 1967.

religious traditions introduced here. Discounting the impact of ecumenism and of the Vatican II concerning the Catholic rituals and the attempt of this Church to recapture peoples who were previously solidly under its influence—which has brought a certain disturbance from the spirits and a certain revitalization of the beliefs of many individuals—the area of evangelical confessions (especially in the Congregational and Pentecostal churches), from spiritualism, from theosophism, and from African sects, is increasing in strength.

The movement just studied clearly shows the influences of several religions, such as Christian millenarism, in its free interpretation of the Bible (even with the rewriting of a new Holy Book), in the belief of its followers in reincarnation and in the existence of other inhabited planets, and in its prophet's use of telepathy and his belief in the transmission of thought in divine messages and in human relations. Pentecostalism, as explained in a previous work, offers respectability to the components of the African sects seeking social advance but is adverse to other religions which are not those of participation.[72] Spiritualism, by admitting the various Umbandist sects, opens the same opportunity to the descendents of the Africans; [73] at the same time, becoming an ethical and neotranscendental religion,[74] it attracts segments of the population, especially those individuals who wish a certain pseudoscientific rationalism in their religious belief.

Such possibility of choice among different religious systems having diverse degrees of gratification and terrestrial and extraterrestrial repayment evidently presents serious competition to any type of millenarism because the Pentecostalists, as well as the Jehovah's Witnesses, offer, door-to-door, their promises of salvation and their restrained millenarism.

[72] René Ribeiro, "Relations of the Negro with Christianity in Portuguese America," in *History of Religion in the New World*, reprinted from *The Americas*, XIV (1958), 118–148, esp. pp. 144–146.

[73] Luiz J. Rodrigues affirmed that "spiritualism of Umbanda represents today, in Brazil, the highest plane attained by the native Afro-Brazilian cult" (in *Muito além da morte: Didduk, satanás e Freud*, trans. by Hermínio C. Miranda [Rio de Janeiro, Livraria Freitas Bastos, 1962], p. 173). A chief of an Afro-Brazilian sect told us, "Any *pegi* becomes an Umbanda center; one only needs to set out *cachaça* [rum] and smoke a cigar for the *orisha* to give way to the *caboclos*."

[74] Interview with Major Z, August 2, 1967. See also David G. Mandelbaum, "Transcendental and Pragmatic Aspects of Religion," *American Anthropologist*, LXVIII (1966), 1174–1191, esp. p. 1189.

Chapter 9 Disunity and Discontent: A Study of Peasant Political Movements in Brazil

Shepard Forman

[This study focuses on mass peasant movements capable of realizing social goals and attempts to ascertain the conditions under which peasant grievances are channeled into a mass political movement. This paper thus moves beyond our earlier cases of generally restricted rebellions against local grievances which often lacked unity and effective organization. A basic hypothesis concerns the potential political radicalization of a peasantry through economic advances in urbanization, industrialization, and the subsequent commercialization of agriculture that result in improved transportation and communication and make mass recruitment of peasants possible. In the light of this hypothesis, particular contemporary peasant movements are examined. Special attention is given to the peasant leagues of Francisco Julião, which were organized into rural societies rather than unions to avoid bureaucratic law and were to be highly centralized with an urban base; also to the rural unions dominated by the Catholic Church. The Church unions spread quickly throughout Northeast Brazil, filling the vacuum left by the suppression of the peasant leagues and other organizations in 1964. As discontent increases in the countryside, the potential for mass unity and challenge to the oppressive conditions also increases.]

Peasant movements in Brazil are not a recent phenomenon but have recurred throughout the history of this essentially agrarian nation.[1] The earliest manifestations of peasant discontent were prepolitical movements

---

[1] I would like to thank Professors Robert Birrell, David Burks, Paul Doughty, and Joyce F. Riegelhaupt for their many useful suggestions. I am, nevertheless, totally responsible for all opinions expressed in this paper.

I would also like to thank Mrs. Emma Simonson, Latin American Librarian at Indiana University, and the librarian and staff at the Land Tenure Center Library, University of Wisconsin, for their help in locating bibliographic materials.

of both a religious and a secular nature.[2] They were primarily local expressions of immediate felt needs, temporary outbursts against misery and oppression. These were largely atomistic movements, confined in time and space, and characterized by a lack of unity and effective communication. More important, they were most often led by social deviates who were generally incapable of expressing realistic social goals that had appeal beyond the local group.

The primary task of this study is to discover the set of circumstances which will direct previously restricted peasant rebellions against local grievances into a mass movement capable of expressing realistic demands through articulate outside leadership and of applying pressures on the social system as a significant national lobby. In short, I am looking to the conditions that give rise to mass political participation in rural Brazil and, further, for an understanding of the forms such participation might take.

Attention will focus on peasant political movements as sociocultural phenomena which occur within a context of economic change over which the peasant himself has little or no control. The basic hypothesis is that urbanization, industrialization, and subsequent commercialization in agriculture create demands for increased production and consumption in rural areas which ultimately lead to a breakdown in traditional forms of behavior and to widespread discontent. Given the structure of Brazilian agrarian society, an influx of capital into the countryside results in further concentration of landholdings, in the increased proletarianization of the rural masses, and in the increased indebtedness of the rural masses. The accoutrements of a rationalized internal marketing system—vastly improved transportation and communications facilities—make mass recruitment of peasants, and thus mass movements, possible.[3] In essence, it is suggested that economic rationalization leads to political radicalization.[4]

The agrarian history of Brazil is characterized by the exploitation of

[2] E. J. Hobsbawn, *Primitive Rebels* (New York: Norton, 1959). For an introduction to prepolitical movements in Brazil, see: Rui Facó, *Cangaceiros e fanáticos* (Rio de Janeiro: Editôra Civilização Brasileira, 1965); Maria Isaura Pereira de Queiróz, *O messianismo no Brasil e no mundo* (São Paulo: Dominus Editôra, Editôra do Universidade de São Paulo, 1965); and Maurício Vinhas de Queiróz, *Messianismo e conflito social* (Rio de Janeiro: Editôra Civilização Brasileira, 1966).

[3] Charles Wagley, "The Brazilian Revolution: Social Changes since 1930," in *Social Change in Latin America Today*, by Richard Adams et al. (New York: Vintage Books, 1960), p. 207; and CIDA, *Posse e uso da terra e desenvolvimento socio-econômico do setor agrícola–Brasil* (Washington, D.C.: Pan American Union, 1966), p. 13.

[4] In *The Social Origins of Dictatorship and Democracy* (Boston: Beacon Press, 1966), pp. 454–469, Barrington Moore has done an exceptional comparative study of the role

commercial export crops on large-scale plantations. Labor for these agricultural establishments was provided first by slaves and later by freemen tied to the land in a number of ways. The boom cycles of sugar, coffee, cacau, and cotton, and the speculative orientation of landed elites are too well known to need further explication here. Although large cattle ranches and numerous small holdings operated by owners, sharecroppers, and renters who provided foodstuffs and other commodities for a growing internal market grew up alongside the export-oriented commercial enterprises, the dominant pattern throughout Brazil was and remains that of the *latifúndia.*

According to the Brazilian Institute of Agrarian Reform (IBRA), 76 percent of the properties registered in Brazil's most recent cadastral survey belong to small holders, or *minifundiários*. Thus, approximately 2.5 million properties are sharing a land area of only some 40 million hectares, or less than 14 percent of the total land area registered in private property. At the other extreme, a total area of some 32 million hectares is held in private property by only 150 large landowners, each of whose land area totals more than 100,000 hectares.[5] Emphasizing the gravity of the agricultural crisis in Brazil, Frank estimates that in 1950, 62 percent of the people dependent upon agriculture for their livelihood were landless agricultural workers. If those whose land was not economically viable are included, the number of *de facto* landless agricultural laborers climbs to 81 percent.[6]

The conditions of poverty, illiteracy, disease, and early death, which are concomitants of this agrarian structure, have existed in Brazil for almost 500 years, and by themselves fail to explain adequately why the peasant political movement has garnered such strength across the nation in the past two decades.[7] Similarly, statements which attribute the peasant political movement to feudal and semifeudal conditions, to archaic land systems, and to "centuries-old injustices" fail to demonstrate the factors that differ-

---

of commercialization in agriculture in transforming agrarian societies into modern industrial states based on either democratic capitalism, fascism, or Communism. Moore rejects the traditional explanations regarding peasant political participation in revolutionary movements and concentrates instead on the ways in which peasantry and dominant landholding classes adapted themselves to economic changes in rural areas.

[5] Brasil, Instituto Brasileiro de Reforma Agrária (IBRA), *A estrutura agrária brasileira* (1967), p. vi. IBRA estimates that there are approximately 3.8 million properties in Brazil with a total of some 350 million hectares, representing only about 40 percent of the Brazilian land mass (*ibid.*, p. v). Less than 20 percent of the total land mass is being effectively utilized in agriculture (*ibid.*, p. 37).

[6] André Gunder Frank, *Capitalism and Underdevelopment in Latin America* (New York: Monthly Review Press, 1967), p. 249.

[7] There can be no empirically validated absolute degree of misery below which a peasantry will cease to be resigned. Degrees of misery and oppression are relative to the kinds of superordinate-subordinate relationships in which they are embedded.

entiate the contemporary political movement from previous prepolitical movements in Brazil.[8]

Traditionally, the Brazilian peasant participated only vicariously in the political process by exchanging his vote for the favor of a *patrão*.[9] He was insulated from the pressures of the outside world by the *noblesse oblige* meted out to him by the plantation master. Communication was unidirectional, passed down along the rigid lines of the social hierarchy. Alternative courses of action for the rural masses were few. Grievances could only be aired to the *patrão* or through open rebellion. The recent peasant political movement in Brazil is, at least in part, an attempt to open up new lines of communication where traditional patterns have failed. Still, the breakdown in the *patrão* system alone does not fully explain the advent of peasant politicalization, since it too is a symptom and not a cause of social change.[10]

It is also essential to avoid the pitfall of simply attributing the contemporary peasant movement in Brazil to mass media and political mobilization. It is true that the breakdown in traditional patron-client relationships has exposed the peasant to the political appeals of urban leaders who have responded to the possibility of representing a potentially powerful electorate. Nevertheless, the root causes of peasant discontent are not to be discovered in political demagoguery.

The Brazilian peasant is clearly integrated into the national economy both as a commodity producer and as a consumer of manufactured goods.[11] He has always been a contributing member of a national, as well as international, capitalist system,[12] and he is now demanding full participation in

[8] An understanding of the mass political movement that developed in Brazil after 1940 cannot be gleaned from descriptions of traditional or static agrarian systems, especially since the movement fed on the extreme tensions resulting from socioeconomic changes within an expanding capitalist system.

[9] For a discussion of political *coronelismo* in rural Brazil, see Víctor Nunes Leal, *Coronelismo enxada e voto* (Rio de Janeiro: Livraria Florense, 1949). Other accounts of political life in rural areas can be found in: Edilson Portela Santos, "Evolução da vida política no município de Picos, Piauí," *Revista Brasileira de Estudos Políticos*, 10 (1961), 160–183; Belden Paulsen, "Local Political Patterns in Northeast Brazil: A Community Case Study," (Research Paper No. 12; Madison, Wis.: Land Tenure Center, 1964); and Marvin Harris, *Town and Country in Brazil* (New York: Columbia University Press, 1956).

[10] A common explanation for the failure of the peasant leagues to make inroads in the state of Alagôas is that the plantation owners are resident there and that the patrão system prevails. Yet the fact that Alagoan history is replete with social banditry and that Alagoans swelled the ranks of the religious pilgrims to Juàzero of Padre Cícero renders such an explanation less tenable. I would suggest that the failure of the peasant leagues to make headway in Alagôas reflects the attenuated development of the internal marketing system in that state as compared to others. Church-sponsored rural unions did make some inroads among the rural proletariat in the northernmost part of the state.

[11] I cannot agree with Oberg that the peasant in Brazil is "an economic zero . . . for he sells little and he buys little" (Kalervo Oberg, "The Marginal Peasant in Brazil,"

that system. The movement that embodies these demands is far more than a new wave in Brazilian politics.[13] It is a response to intensified socioeconomic pressures which are pervading the Brazilian countryside along with the spread of a rationalized internal marketing system.

The effect of the world market on salaried workers and peasants is generally well known.[14] For example, the expansion of sugarcane plantings in the Brazilian Northeast during the postwar boom forced rural workers from their subsistence plots and created widespread discontent in the coastal zone.[15] However, very little attention has been paid to the processes by which economic and social change affect peasants—small owners, sharecroppers, tenant farmers—who are not engaged in commercial export crop production and who have always comprised a significant proportion of rural Brazilian society. Far too little consideration has been given to the internal marketing system for foodstuffs, that is, to the commercial aspects of rural production and consumption and to their effects upon peasant political participation in Brazil.

Elsewhere it has been suggested that the growth of urban centers in Brazil has made extreme demands on the system of agricultural production

---

American Anthropologist, LXVII [1965], 1417–1427). Brazilian peasants are an integral part of national patterns of food production and consumption. Their produce feeds a nation and their labor produces its wealth. On the way in which the backward and advanced sectors of traditional economies are articulated in symbiotic fashion, see Eric Wolf, "Reflections on Peasant Revolutions" (paper presented at the Carnegie Seminar on Political and Administrative Development, Indiana University, Bloomington, Ind., April 3, 1967).

12 See Frank, *op. cit.*, for an illuminating discussion of the capitalist development/ underdevelopment syndrome in Brazil and of the myth of feudalism in Brazilian agriculture.

13 For a fruitful discussion of the peasant movement in Brazil as a reflection of the mass appeal of "new guard" politics, see Anthony Leeds, "Brazil and the Myth of Francisco Julião," in *Politics of Change in Latin America*, ed. by Joseph Maier and Richard Weatherhead (New York: Praeger, 1964), pp. 190–204. Leeds contends that the movement merely substitutes new patrons for the old. Another discussion of the paternalistic aspects of the movement can be found in Benno Galjart, "Class and 'Following' in Rural Brazil," *América Latina*, VII (July-September 1964), 3–24: and a reply by Gerrit Huizer, "Some Notes on Community Development and Rural Social Research," *América Latina*, VIII (July-September 1965), 128–144. Another refutation of this position can be found in Aníbal Quijano Obregón, "Contemporary Peasant Movements," in *Elites in Latin America*, ed. by Seymour Martin Lipset and Aldo Solari (New York: Oxford University Press, 1967), pp. 329 ff. For a complete account of national political events in Brazil since 1930, see Thomas E. Skidmore, *Politics in Brazil: 1930–1964* (New York: Oxford University Press, 1967).

14 Celso Furtado, *Diagnosis of the Brazilian Crisis* (Berkeley, Calif.: University of California Press, 1965), pp. 148–149.

15 CIDA, *Posse e uso da terra*, p. 336; and Manuel Correia de Andrade, *A terra e o homem no nordeste* (Rio de Janeiro: Editôra Brasiliense, 1963), p. 246.

and distribution.[16] Urban demands for a greater and more continuous food supply at lower prices have begun a process of rationalization of the internal marketing system which is having serious consequences on the system of production and land tenure in rural areas. Foodstuffs have begun to follow the model of commercial export crops in a direct line to urban centers through large warehouses located strategically in hub cities in the interior.[17] Thus the crops bypass the traditional peasant marketplace, which comes to serve primarily as a terminal point in the downward flow of finished consumer goods. The multiplicity of middlemen who move minimal units of goods as highly functional components of the peasant marketplace are replaced by commercial elites who are capable of moving produce in bulk.

This rationalized internal marketing system in turn imposes further demands for increased production, involving a rate of investment in the land which the peasant producer is incapable of supporting. Food prices continue to rise, but this benefits the intermediaries and not the producers. At the same time, increased land values drive rents upward and force the renters off the land.[18] The small owner is unable to compete with the *latifúndia*, and there is further intensification in the concentration of landholdings.[19] The peasants are losing what little land they had.

Another concomitant of the rationalized internal marketing system is the demand made on the rural worker for increased consumption. Manufactured goods find their way to the most remote weekly markets and create a rise in expectations which are not easily met.[20] The salaried worker

[16] Shepard Forman and Joyce F. Riegelhaupt, "Market Place and Marketing System: Toward a Theory of Peasant Economic Integration," *Comparative Studies in Society and History*, vol. XII, no. 2 (1970).

[17] High food prices benefit the intermediary rather than the producer and attract commercial elites to the marketplace. From 1950 to 1960, prices for consumers went up sixteen times, compared to thirteen for the producer, reflecting the monopolization of internal marketing for foodstuffs in Brazil. Price incentives thereby lead large landholders to speculate on the land rather than to increase production of foodstuffs (CIDA, *Posse e uso da terra*, pp. 33–34). For a discussion of the commercialization of the internal marketing system in Brazil, see "O problema do abastecimento alimentar," *Desenvolvimento e Conjuntura*, VIII (December 1964), 79–125.

[18] Furtado, *op. cit.*, pp. 148–149.

[19] CIDA, *Posse e uso da terra*, pp. 106–107. According to a recent study, the price of land in Brazil is not high in relation to income and capital invested, but it is prohibitive to small property owners and landless rural workers (*ibid.*, p. 11). The same study indicates that large landholdings dominate the production of goods destined for the internal market, such as rice and corn. Other crops, such as cacau, were often witness to the violent replacement of small holdings by large ones.

[20] According to Caio Prado Júnior, "Commercial-type exploitation characteristic of all the principal sectors of Brazilian farming and livestock raising . . . always tends to expand and absorb most of the profitable lands, eliminating independent workers, landowners or not, as well as their subsistence plots. Consequently, the living conditions

and the peasant are constantly being exposed to more merchandise. Yet, while salaries are going up,[21] they do not keep pace with inflation, and real wages are going down. In reality, capital is being injected into the system, but it is being stopped at a level above the small-scale producer and rural worker, who do not reap the benefits of economic change.

THE DEVELOPMENT OF THE PEASANT MOVEMENT

It is not mere coincidence that the peasant political movement has grown up in the decades since 1940. The years between 1940 and 1960 were marked by tremendous urban growth in Brazil, followed by rapid industrialization.[22] Population shifts brought great pressures to bear, not only on urban areas but also in the countryside. Recent social tensions in Brazil are a concomitant of this development. However, population pressures alone do not explain peasant discontent. As Furtado notes, the process of increasing political awareness in Northeast Brazil accelerated greatly in the late 1950s and early 1960s and penetrated most deeply in rural areas close to large urban centers.[23] The rapid proliferation of peasant and rural worker associations during this period coincided with an increasing commercialization in agriculture and the rationalization of the internal marketing system.[24] State federations of rural unions held meetings across the country, and the I Congresso Nacional dos Lavradores e Trabalhadores

---

of the rural working population worsened; their reward, either wages or a share of the main crop, is always less than the relative price of the kinds of necessities which the workers are obliged to buy in the market—generally an exploitative market due to the very conditions created by the process of largescale production" (Caio Prado Júnior, "The Agrarian Question in Brazil," *Studies on the Left*, IV [1964], 83).

21 CIDA, *Posse e uso da terra*, p. 308.

22 Urban population grew from 31.2 percent in 1940 to 45 percent in 1960 (CIDA, *Posse e uso da terra*, p. 61). See also Wagley, *op. cit.*, p. 189; and T. Lynn Smith, *Brazil: People and Institutions* (rev. ed.; Baton Rouge, La.: Louisiana State University Press, 1963), pp. 593–601.

23 Furtado, *op. cit.*, p. 162.

24 A law of rural unionization was passed as early as 1903, but only thirteen unions resulted from the legislation (Robert Price, *Rural Unionization in Brazil* [Research Paper No. 14; Madison, Wis.: Land Tenure Center, 1964], p. 6). Moreover, these unions had little meaning with regard to the formulation of demands, since they grouped employers and employees together in the same associations (Mary E. Wilkie, "A Report of Rural Syndicates in Pernambuco," Rio de Janeiro: Centro Latinoamericano de Pesquisas em Ciências Sociais, April 1964 [mimeographed], p. 5). For a discussion of rural labor legislation in Brazil, see J. V. Freitas Marcondes, *First Brazilian Legislation Relating to Rural Labor Unions: A Sociological Study* (The Latin American Monograph Series, No. 20; Gainsville, Fla. University of Florida Press, 1962). Price's *Rural Unionization in Brazil* offers the most complete account of rural labor legislation and unionization.

Agrícolas met in the city of Belo Horizonte in 1961.[25] Because of the intense interest in the organization of rural workers, the Ministry of Labor—once the fly in the ointment of unionization—published a pamphlet in 1962 containing instructions for union organization.[26] In addition, the Agency for Agrarian Reform, or SUPRA, was created in 1962 precisely to work with the peasant movement. By 1963, five hundred unions with over a half million members were grouped under a Confederação Nacional dos Trabalhadores na Agricultura (CONTAG).[27]

In reality, there was not one peasant movement in Brazil but several, differentiated in terms of the rural subcultural groups which comprised their membership and of the leadership through which they voiced their demands. The CONTAG was made up of such diverse groups as the Church-sponsored rural unions, the peasant leagues, the radical Catholic Agrarian Front of Paraná and Rio Grande do Sul, the Movimento dos Agricultores Sem Terra (MASTER) in Rio Grande do Sul, the União dos Lavradores e Trabalhadores Agrícolas do Brasil (ULTAB) in São Paulo, and the Federação das Associações dos Lavradores e Trabalhadores Rurais in the state of Ceará. In addition, between 1960 and 1963, associations sprang up in the states of Goiás, Bahia, Santa Catarina, and Minas Gerais.

These diverse organizations can be grouped for analytical purposes into two major divisions: (1) reformist movements which appeal primarily to salaried rural workers and include the Church-sponsored rural unions; and (2) potentially revolutionary movements which appeal primarily to tenants and small holders and include the well-known peasant leagues. In between, a residual category might be made for radical Catholic and independent peasant associations which appeal primarily to salaried workers but which have adopted a more militant reformist stand.[28] The goals each

[25] For reports on several of these state and national conventions, see: Manoel Silva. "I Congresso dos Trabalhadores Rurais do Paraná," *Revista Braziliense*, 33 (1961), 56–62; Nestor Vera, "O II congresso camponês em Maringa," *Revista Brasiliense*, 37 (1961), 62–65; Nestor Vera, "O congresso camponês em Belo Horizonte," *Revista Brasiliense*, 39 (1962), 94–99; and I Congresso Nacional dos Lavradores e Trabalhadores Agrícolas, "Declaração . . . sôbre o caráter da reforma agrária," *Estudos Sociais*, 12 (April 1962), 433–437.

[26] Brasil, Ministério do Trabalho, *Sindicalização rural*, Portária Ministerial, No. 335-A (1962).

[27] "A situação social de agricultura em 1963, "*Desenvolvimento e Conjuntra*, VIII (February 1964), 33–34. The National Confederation was made up of ten federations with 270 unions, but thirty-three more federations with 557 unions were waiting for recognition at the time (Brazil, Superintendência de Política Agrária, *Sindicatos rurais*, Relação No. 1 [December 31, 1963], p. 17). Huizer, *op. cit.*, p. 129, says that the Confederation includes twenty-nine federations from nineteen states and 743 rural unions. In addition, an inestimable number of peasants were obviously sympathetic but feared to join the movement.

[28] This breakdown corresponds substantially to a recent typology of peasant political movements in Latin America elaborated by Quijano in "Contemporary Peasant Move-

of these groups espouse are different because the needs of their membership are different and because commercialization in agriculture and the rationalization of the internal marketing system are having differential effects on the variety of rural types in the Brazilian countryside.[29]

THE PEASANT LEAGUES OF FRANCISCO JULIÃO

Francisco Julião, the self-styled leader of the peasant leagues in Northeast Brazil, was aware that different land tenure systems and productive arrangements produced different subtypes of peasants who could be expected to react differently to appeals for political mobilization. He divided the rural population into: the proletariat, or rural salaried workers; the semi-proletariat, or workers in temporary labor service arrangements on the land; and the peasants, or those who have some sort of effective control over the land, either as sharecroppers, renters, squatters, or small property owners.[30] It was the peasants, he believed, who presented the best conditions for waging a protracted struggle against the *latifúndia*, and he appealed to them to join together in the building of an effective agrarian society.[31]

Indeed, the ranks of the peasant leagues were to be filled by peasants who were unable to compete with the expanding *latifúndia*. There is every reason to believe that it was a desire to transform a plantation which had been subdivided into numerous rented plots into an expansive cattle-raising operation which led to the eviction of the peasants of the *fazenda*

---

ments." Noting that his classification might be lacking in empirical underpinnings, Quijano proceeds to treat the peasant leagues in Brazil as a monolithic organization, including them in all three categories of peasant movements (*ibid.*, p. 308). We have already noted that the peasant leagues are definitely not a monolithic organization and that the name is best treated as generic rather than a specific referent for the movement as a whole.

[29] Regional and even subregional ecological conditions in Brazil have historically given rise to a variety of land tenure patterns and different productive arrangements. Attempts to classify Latin American peasantry can be found in Charles Wagley and Marvin Harris, "A Typology of Latin American Subcultures," *American Anthropologist*, LVII (1955), 428–451; Eric Wolf, "Types of Latin American Peasantry," *American Anthropologist*, LVII (1955), 452–471; and Richard Adams, "Rural Labor," in *Continuity and Change in Latin America*, ed. by John J. Johnson (Stanford, Calif.: Stanford University Press, 1964), pp. 49–78. In *An Introduction to Brazil* (New York: Columbia University Press, 1963, Wagley attempts to refine these earlier typologies for Brazil.

[30] Francisco Julião, *Que são as Ligas Camponesas?* (Rio de Janeiro: Editôra Civilização Brasileira, 1962), p. 11. Julião's typology bears some resemblance to Lenin's, although the latter is not cited in Julião's basic treatise on the peasant leagues.

[31] Julião believed the landed peasant to be more effective than the rural proletariat because under Brazilian law his rights fell under the civil code exempting him from

Galiléia.[32] Julião's defense of these peasants and the subsequent expropriation of the plantation and its distribution among the sharecroppers was, in effect, the first act in the ten-year drama of the Brazilian peasant leagues.[33]

Still more evidence points to the far-reaching effects of commercialization in agriculture on the formation of the leagues. The first league founded in Sapé, in the state of Paraíba, in 1959, resulted in part from the eviction of its leader from his land. João Pedro Teixeira was put off the land he occupied without indemnification after the owner sold it to one of the commercial elites from the city who was to use it for speculative purposes.[34]

Generally, the leagues spread most quickly in the *agreste*, the transitional mixed farming zone of small landholdings which was under a constant threat from the expanding *latifúndia* in the coastal lowlands and in the cattle-raising *sertão*.[35] For example, the vast majority of agricultural workers in Sapé farmed their own small plots [36] but had to compete for land with the large sugar mill located in the county. Even when the peasant leagues operated within the sugarcane zone itself, they were apparently

---

the rigid bureaucracy of the Labor Ministry, because he could pay for legal defense with the fruits of his labor, and because he could take the offensive in a struggle by occupying land and withholding rents and shares (*ibid.*, pp. 58–62). Juridical proceedings proved ineffective in protecting the rights of salaried workers who lacked the financial resources for legal defense and the minimal economic conditions necessary to resist the landowner (*ibid.*, pp. 50–57). Furthermore, while the relationship between salaried worker and employer is essentially economic since it is based on a wage, the relationship between peasant and landowner concerns itself with rights, thus assuming a political character from the beginning (*ibid.*, p. 64). Nevertheless, Julião also appealed to rural salaried workers to join unions, although he recognized a fundamental difference between urban and rural workers and believed that the model for urban trade unionism could not simply be transplanted in the countryside (*ibid.*, pp. 46–47).

[32] Antônio Callado, *As industriais de sêca e os "Galileus" de Pernambuco* (Rio de Janeiro: Editôra Civilização Brasileira, 1960), p. 35; and Timothy Harding, "Revolution Tomorrow: The Failure of the Left in Brazil," *Studies on the Left*, IV (1964), 36. It has been noted that one of the prime incentives to the consolidation of landholdings throughout Brazil is the growing market for cattle (CIDA, *Posse e uso da terra*, p. 240; and Salamão Schattan, "Estrutura econômica da agricultura paulista," *Revista Brasiliense*, 37 [1961], 75).

[33] Some additional references on the peasant leagues of Julião not cited elsewhere in this paper are: Lêda Barreto, *Julião, nordeste, revolução* (Rio de Janeiro: Editôra Civilização Brasileira, 1963); Antônio Callado, "Les Ligues Paysannes," *Les Temps Moderns*, XXIII (1967), 751–760; Gondim da Fonseca, *Assim falou Julião* (São Paulo: Editôra Fulgor, 1962); Francisco Julião, *Escucha campesino* (Montevideo: Editôra Presente, 1962); Francisco Julião, "Brazil, A Christian Country," in *Whither Latin America?*, ed. by Carlos Fuentes (New York: Monthly Review Press, 1963), pp. 103–110; and Novais Sodré, *Quem é Francisco Julião* (São Paulo: Redenção Nacional, 1963).

[34] João Pedro Teixeira was shot and killed on April 2, 1962, and the new owner of the plantation on which he lived was implicated in the crime (CIDA, *Posse e uso da terra*, p. 338). A large manifestation was organized in the state capital on May 1, 1962, to honor Teixeira.

[35] Furtado, *op. cit.*, pp. 148–149.

[36] CIDA, *Posse e uso da terra*, pp. 319–320.

appealing to the large numbers of peasant farmers who inhabit these areas and not specifically to the limited numbers of agricultural wage earners at the mills.

A Brazilian journalist has written that "The [peasant] league begins in the marketplace, goes to the notary, and takes over the world." [37] Actually, the traditional marketplace did play a role as the physical locus of the encounter in the recruitment of peasants in Northeast Brazil. However, the quote might better read "The peasant league comes to the marketplace . . . ," for it was there, at the weekly *feiras*, that the leagues' urban organizers found a ready audience among the usually dispersed peasantry. It was to the marketplace that they came to tell the story of Galiléia and of Francisco Julião and to offer legal advice and medical assistance. It was in the marketplace that the peasant traditionally listened to the troubadour spin his tales and sing his songs of culture heroes and newsworthy events. And it was through the troubadour that Julião carried his "Letter of Liberation of the Peasant" to the countryside.[38]

The peasant political movement in Brazil, as elsewhere, has clearly been led from outside the peasant stratum.[39] Julião quite explicitly called for the organization of a highly centralized peasant movement with a base in urban areas where it could be insulated from the landholding class.[40] At the same time, he preferred to organize the leagues into rural societies rather than into unions subject to the bureaucratic rigors of the unionization law.[41]

On a visit to the peasant league headquarters in Recife in 1962, I was im-

[37] Fragman Carlos Borges, "O movimento camponês no nordeste," *Estudos Sociais,* XIV (1962), 255.

[38] Julião's letter to the peasant (Julião, *Que são as Ligas Camponesas?* pp. 62 ff.) was rendered into popular song and sung in the countryside (Rafael de Carvalho, *Carta de alforria do camponês* [Recife?: Editôra Jotape, 1962]). For a description of an actual league meeting and the content of the message carried to the peasant by the league organizers, see Shepard Forman, "Os sinos de São José dobraram em Surubim," *Cadernos Brasileiros,* V (1963), 48–53.

[39] Quijano, *op. cit.,* p. 321, contends correctly that the confederation of peasant "bands" in Brazil grew out of strength in the countryside. However, there is no doubt that the movement was organized by urban elites. Carneiro tells us that the original leaders of the league in Sapé were not peasants but workers with union experience in the cities, although the movement later came to be run almost exclusively by the peasants themselves (CIDA, *Posse e uso da terra,* p. 338).

[40] Julião, *Que são as Ligas Camponesas?* pp. 46–47.

[41] Labor legislation in Brazil was always concerned primarily with the urban worker (J. V. Freitas Marcondes, "Social Legislation in Brazil," in *Brazil, Portrait of Half a Continent,* ed. by T. Lynn Smith and Alexander Marchant [New York: The Dryden Press, 1951], p. 399), and the unionization of rural workers was inevitably to bear the mark of Vargas's syndicalist state. The rigid hierarchical organization of territorially based noncompeting unions into state federations and a national confederation of rural workers subordinated to the Ministry of Labor would place control over the unions in the hands of the government bureaucracy.

pressed by the lack of any formal bureaucratic structure. Housed in rather modest facilities donated to the leagues by the Brazilian Socialist Party (which Julião represented in the Federal Chamber of Deputies), the headquarters were open to the comings and goings of students and peasants, who intermingled freely, discussing their needs, the movement, and Francisco Julião, their leader.[42]

During several days of conversations with the young student organizers of the leagues, I was struck by their lack of any clearly defined ideological position. As they told of their projected plans, their individual differences became apparent. They failed to share any clearly defined goals other than that of making the peasant "aware of social justice and of his rights." Openly critical of the lack of any organization that would make the peasant leagues a cohesive unit on the national level, they believed that they had to pique the social consciousness of the nation before they could begin to structure and define the movement. They questioned Julião's leadership abilities and admitted that his image had been largely inflated by the foreign and domestic press, but they still clung to him loyally as their charismatic and devoted standard-bearer.

Julião's appeal to the peasant members of the leagues was based on a strange combination of mystique and faith. I had occasion to interview a tenant farmer at a peasant league meeting in the interior of Pernambuco in 1962. When I asked him why he joined the leagues, he responded: "I want a defense in life, for medicine, if one should fall sick among us . . . for advice." His opinion of Francisco Julião was clear: "He is the Prince of Life, who is going to give us the resources to live." When queried as to how Julião would do this, the peasant quipped, "I don't know because I am ignorant. I am waiting for an explanation and then I will follow."

Julião did demand a serious agrarian reform. The "Ten Commandments of the Peasant Leagues for the Liberation of the Peasant from the Oppression of the *Latifúndia*" included demands for a progressive land tax, a constitutional reform enabling the expropriation of land with payment in long-term bonds, regulation of rents and crop shares, production and consumption cooperatives, strict limitations on monopolistic land concentration, development of colonization projects, extension of labor legislation to rural workers, elimination of the abuses of the intermediary in the marketing system, restructuring of the sugar economy, and the creation of national peasant leagues which would "represent Law and Order against the anarchy and disorder which are the *Latifúndia*."[43] While he advocated land invasions and the possible use of violence, Julião strongly urged prior

[42] The student organizers of the peasant leagues insisted that the only connection between the leagues and the Brazilian Socialist Party was Francisco Julião himself.
[43] Andrade, *op. cit.,* pp. 250–252.

use of the juridical process. Perhaps the motto of the peasant leagues, "within the law or by force," best sums up Julião's own view of the possible strategy of a movement which clearly had radical potential but which lacked radical leadership.[44]

A great deal has been written about Julião's personal convictions. The descriptions vary from caustic criticism to highly romanticized sketches.[45] While he undoubtedly clamored for radical and even revolutionary change,[46] it is questionable whether Julião indeed ever intended to undermine the system of which he was so much a part. All indications are that he was appealing to an audience which appeared radical by the very nature of its demands for changes in the agrarian structure, but which he intended to use merely as his power base in the established system of order.[47] It must be remembered that Julião was himself the son of a large plantation owner,[48] and there is no evidence that a peasant league meeting ever took place within the county in which his family's property is located even though it was the area of greatest agitation in the state. There is every likelihood that Julião was interested primarily in the establishment of a firm electoral base among the peasantry. He explicitly stated that one of the basic reasons for working with peasants rather than with the rural proletariat was that sharecroppers, renters, and small owners greatly outnumbered the rural wage laborers. Indeed these peasants were to be very telling in Julião's success at the polls.[49] In fact, Julião was at one point taken to task by a spokesman of the Communist party for neglecting the peasant

[44] There is an indication that once he was in exile from Brazil, Julião's position became more radical. In a recent statement from Mexico, he wrote, "We believe that you cannot win the peasant masses from the top down, from the city to the country. You must live with the peasants, undergo the same problems they meet every day, fight with them as one of them" (Francisco Julião, "Interview with Alfonso Gortaire Iturralde," *CIF Reports*, V [November 1966], 167, trans. from *Comunidad*, I [September 1966]).

[45] See Callado, *As industriais;* Callado, "Les Ligues Paysannes"; and Irving Louis Horowitz, *Revolution in Brazil* (New York: Dutton, 1964).

[46] Callado, "Les Ligues Paysannes," contends that Julião was willing to use violent means, but in an interview with league organizers in 1962 I was told that Julião believed in the possibility of peaceful revolution.

[47] Leeds, *op. cit.*, p. 196.

[48] Horowitz, *op. cit.*, p. 21, attempts to show Julião's humble origins; yet there can be no doubt that he is a member of the national elite. See Julião, *Cambão; la otra cara de Brasil* (Mexico: Siglo XXI, Editores, 1968).

[49] Julião, *Que são as Ligas Camponesas?* p. 67. Julião noted that in Brazil there were about 40 million peasants and only about 5 million rural salaried workers (*ibid.*). In the 1958 elections for state assembly, Julião polled 3,216 votes; in the 1962 election for the Federal Chamber of Deputies, he won an easy victory, with 16,200 votes (Price, *op. cit.*, pp. 42–43). According to Andrade, *op cit.*, p. 250, there were 30,000 to 35,000 league members in the state of Pernambuco in 1963 and some 80,000 in the Northeast. Wilkie, *op. cit.*, p. 7, estimates some 40,000 members in 1964 in Pernambuco.

and concentrating his political energies in the cities.[50] There is further evidence suggesting that Julião was intent on extending his influence beyond the state of Pernambuco and obtaining leadership of the peasant leagues as a whole.[51] However, it should be noted that there were a number of autonomous peasant associations in Northeast Brazil which never did pay homage to Julião as their leader. The peasant leagues that professed allegiance to Julião as their leader were largely confined to Pernambuco State.

Although the peasant leagues were founded with the help of the Communists,[52] it is important to point out that Julião and the Brazilian Communist party had their very serious differences.[53] In part, these resulted from the Communists' interest in the rural salaried worker and their strong belief that agitation for agrarian reform should be subordinated to efforts to extend labor legislation to rural areas.[54] Indeed, the major concern of the Brazilian Communist party since establishing the first peasant league in the Northeast in 1945–1946 has been with making minimal demands for legal aid, schools, medicines, and burial funds, rather than with making an appeal for radical agrarian reform.[55]

The Communists were evidently suspicious of the autonomy of the leagues and of Julião's independence. They distrusted his use of the peasant movement for personal aggrandizement and feared his emergence as a charismatic leader.[56] They insisted that the success of the movement depended not on individual leadership but on organization and legalization,

[50] Borges, *op. cit.*, p. 259.

[51] Julião eventually broke with Assís Lemos, the leader of the Paraíba league at Sapé, because of a political question which arose between the two. Lemos criticized Julião's violent stand, but the real issue seems to have been the control over the league (CIDA, *Posse e uso da terra*, pp. 330–340). Part of the attraction was certainly the strength of the Sapé league, which boasted some 10,000 members, one-quarter of the total membership in the state (*ibid.*, p. 341).

[52] See Callado, "Les Ligues Paysannes," and Price, *op. cit.*, p. 45.

[53] A good deal has been said about Communist party infiltration into the peasant movement. While the Communist party would certainly like to take credit for the movement (see Borges, *op. cit.*, p. 260), and their influence cannot be denied in some areas, it would be blatantly wrong to classify the independent peasant associations as generally Communist.

[54] The Communist orientation to rural salaried workers was obviously a reflection of their bias for an urban proletarian revolution. They criticized Julião for making the workers' movement an appendage of the peasant movement and for excluding the Communist party from a role in the direction of the movement (*ibid.*, p. 259).

[55] *Ibid.*, p. 253. These first peasant leagues died out when the Brazilian Communist party was declared illegal in 1947. However, the Communist activity in rural areas began again in 1962 (*ibid.*). In 1954, the Communist party founded ULTAB, which is active in the states of São Paulo and Ceará. In São Paulo it is aligned with the Agrarian Front, a radical Catholic group.

[56] Borges, *op. cit.*, p. 259.

and they sought to register the leagues as unions.[57] Again, it must be emphasized that the Communist party was organizing not among the peasants but among the rural proletariat and that this placed them in competition with the Catholic Church rather than with Julião,[58] whose leagues operated among the landholding peasantry when within the sugarcane zone. Their argument with Julião was essentially that his appeal for political support provoked radical demands on the part of the peasantry which could be detrimental to the Communist party. They were concerned that radical action might upset the slow gains made possible through legislation by provoking an extreme reaction from the landed upper class.[59]

THE RURAL UNIONS

The Catholic Church has also been hard at work since early 1960 trying to extend its influence among workers in agricultural enterprises throughout Brazil. Church-sponsored rural unions can be found in a number of states, but they are particularly strong in Rio Grande do Norte, Pernambuco, and São Paulo, and to a lesser extent in Paraná, Rio Grande do Sul, Santa Catarina, and Minas Gerais. Like the other peasant movements, the Church-sponsored unions are highly centralized, with leadership coming from the ranks of more enlightened members of the clergy.[60]

[57] Borges (*ibid.*, p. 257) claims that the weakest leagues from an organizational point of view were in Pernambuco.

[58] The principal influence of the Communist party in Pernambuco seems to have been in the largest labor unions of the sugarcane zone, where they were better organized than the Church (Price, *op. cit.*, pp. 51–52). The Church, the Communist party, and the peasant leagues sometimes appear to be in competition in the same area; however, it would seem that they were appealing to different population segments within that area. Obviously, further research into the precise composition of the membership of various peasant unions and leagues is necessary.

[59] The Communist party might well have feared a crackdown, since an earlier movement had been shut down in 1945–1946, as had one in Paraná in 1951 (Silva, "I Congresso dos Trabalhadores Rurais do Paraná," pp. 56–57). After the 1964 military *coup d'état*, Celso Furtado said that the Communists also criticized Goulart for moving too fast, fearing that he might provoke the military into action (personal communication). Skidmore notes, in *Politics in Brazil*, p. 225, that "the Brazilian Communist Party was working to force a more nationalist and democratic government within the existing structure."

[60] The rural unions actually originated in 1949, in the state of Rio Grande do Norte, when Bishop Eugênio Sales founded the Rural Assistance Service. By 1963, there were 48 rural unions in the state, with a total of 48,000 members (Price, *op. cit.*, p. 49). According to Wilkie (*op. cit.*, p. 7), 61 of the 62 rural unions in the Pernambuco Federation, which claims some 200,000 members, were Church sponsored. Feitosa Martins reports tremendous growth in the movement in São Paulo between 1961 and 1962 (Araguaya Feitosa Martins, "Alguns aspectos da inquietação trabalhista no campo," *Revista Brasiliense*, 40 [1963], 136–137). See also Ibiapa Martins, "Proletariado e inquietação rural," *Revista Brasiliense*, 42 (1962), 62–81.

It has been said that the Church-sponsored rural unions in Brazil developed as a response to the peasant leagues; it is probably true that the clergy was attempting to counterbalance a secular political force in the countryside. Yet it is important to emphasize that until very recently the clergy operated almost exclusively among the rural proletariat. Inspired by the papal encyclical "Mater et Magistra," the Church has defined its role in the peasant movement as primarily reformist and conciliatory, stressing improvements in living conditions for the salaried worker, cooperation with the federal government, and the inapplicability of the concept of the class struggle.[61] Its primary concern has been with the promotion of labor legislation for the rural salaried worker.[62]

Padre António Melo, an outspoken parish priest from Cabo, Pernambuco, has criticized the Catholic Church for its conciliatory role in the peasant movement. In an interview in August 1967, Padre Melo accused the Church of disguising its real motives in organizing rural unions, noting that its historic ties with the *latifúndia* made it an unlikely advocate of a real agrarian reform. He criticized the clergy for working primarily with trained union leaders rather than with the peasants themselves and suggested that a strong grass-roots organization is necessary to press for real reforms.[63] Speaking out strongly against the use of violence, Padre Melo advocated the strike as the most effective weapon for change.

The young priest noted that in 1963 he led a successful strike in the

[61] For a statement of the mixture of social, religious, and economic goals of Church-sponsored rural unions in São Paulo State, see Frei Celso de São Paulo, *Os cristãos e o sindicato na cidade e no campo* (São Paulo: Editôra Saraiva, 1963); and Feitosa Martins, *op. cit.* Dumoulin notes that the primary stress of the unions in Rio Grande do Norte was on basic education, agricultural extension, and the development of good citizenship (Diana Dumoulin, "The Rural Labor Movement in Brazil," Land Tenure Center, University of Wisconsin, [mimeographed], p. 16. Their interest in processing land disputes was so slight that they only employed one lawyer. A further statement of the goals of the movement and its nonpolitical nature can be found in Julieta Calazans, *Cartilha sindical do trabalhador rural* (Natal: Editôra Serviço de Assistência Rural, 1961).

[62] In 1943, the Consolidation of Labor Laws extended to rural workers the minimum wage, the right to annual vacations, regulation of the labor contract, provisions regarding the payment of salaries, and the right to prior notification of termination of the labor contract (Price, *op. cit.*, pp. 7–8). The serious problem is to see that such legislation is made effective in the countryside.

[63] In the same interview; Padre Melo sharply criticized Bishop Dom Helder Câmara and Padre Paulo Crespo, spokesman for the Church-sponsored Rural Orientation Service of Pernambuco (SORPE), for their policy of directing rural unionism from above, working primarily with the leaders of the movement and not with the peasants themselves. For further insights into the different positions of Padre Melo and Padre Crespo, see Padre Paulo Crespo, "O problema camponês no nordeste brasileiro," *O Síntese*, XVII (1963), 55–66; and Fanny Mitchell, "Padre Crespo and Padre Melo: Two Approaches to Reform," Institute of Current World Affairs Letter FM-17, November 9, 1967 (mimeographed). Everywhere the rural unions have attempted to train local leaders (see Wilkie, *op. cit.*, p. 8; and Feitosa Martins, *op. cit.*, p. 139). However, as

sugarcane zone of Pernambuco which culminated in a collective work contract and an 80 percent salary increase for 200,000 rural workers.[64] While the strike can be an effective weapon in the hands of the rural proletariat, it should be clear that such advances depend on a variety of factors which are again outside the workers' sphere of influence. Furtado leaves no doubt that the success of this strike coincided with decreased opposition on the part of the landlords because of a concomitant rise in international prices for sugar from 1962 to 1963.[65] Those landowners who did not want to pay the increased wage merely ignored the provisions of the agreement, laid workers off, or, in some instances, closed down their operations.

In addition to the strike, Padre Melo believes that pressure can be placed on sugar mill owners by correcting the balance of supply and demand on the labor market. He suggests withdrawing large pools of labor by resettling rural workers in colonization projects and on half-hectare plots around rural towns and cities. In this way, he believes, the sugar mills will be required to make technological improvements in their operations, leading to increased profits and to a willingness to increase salaries. At the same time, he maintains that garden plots encircling populated areas will greatly alleviate the problem of urban food supply. Thus, while Padre Melo certainly works for changes within the prevailing system, he has distinguished himself from a more conservative Church organization by pressing demands for land for the peasant and rural worker.

INCREASED RADICALIZATION AND OFFICIAL REACTION

The distinction between rich, middle, and poor peasants, each having different access to adequate land and the means of production, is well known.[66] The rich peasant is the commodity producer who farms com-

---

Wilkie notes (*op. cit.*, p. 10), outside leadership continued to be important among the rural unions in Pernambuco; the federation's administrative assessor even recommended candidates for the president and council.

[64] These salary increases stimulated activity in rural marketplaces in the state.

[65] Furtado, *op. cit.*, p. 138.

[66] This distinction was used by Lenin, who believed that the middle peasant would be swept away in the capitalist economy, leaving the extreme groups to rural proletariat and capitalist farmers (V. I. Lenin, "The Differentiation of the Peasantry," in *Collected Works*, I [Moscow, Foreign Languages Publishing House, 1960], p. 181). Lenin also notes that the market is a key factor in the ability of the small farm to compete with the highly capitalized farm (V. I. Lenin, *New Economic Developments in Peasant Life*, in *ibid.*, III, 37). For an application of this typology to rural São Paulo State, see Moisés Vinhas, *Operários e camponeses na revolução brasileira* (São Paulo: Editôra Fulgor, 1963). From a strictly empirical perspective this typology might be considered insufficient. In reality, the rural types are constantly intermixed, so that one man may be an owner, renter, sharecropper, employee, and wage earner

mercially, utilizing hired labor. The poor peasant is so bereft of land that he is forced to sell his labor on the market. The middle peasant, however, is in the most precarious position because his land is adequate for subsistence only in the best years, and he is under constant pressure from above to sell his labor also.

Eric Wolf suggests that it is precisely this "middle peasant" who suffers the greatest strains from the pressures of the marketing system and its effects on rural populations.[67] It is this stratum of peasant society, led by middlemen in the system, that is most likely to participate in peasant revolutions.[68] It is precisely this sector of Brazilian agrarian society which has given a radical tone to the peasant movement as a whole. It is not the salaried worker who makes radical demands for changes in the system but the tenant farmer and the sharecropper threatened with the loss of their land.[69] The salaried worker is primarily concerned with his share of increased production and the benefits of an increased wage. His demands, theoretically, can be met by legislation and do not pose a threat to the system per se. The peasant, on the other hand, knows that he is an unlikely competitor in the new market arena. He is being displaced by a rationalized system of production and distribution, and he seeks fundamental changes in the prevailing agrarian structure. His demands for adjustments in the land tenure system are radical by their very nature and are bound to provoke a far more extreme reaction.

In Brazil separate rural movements with different ideologies developed

---

at the same time on different agricultural properties. Souza found six different types of renters in the São Francisco Valley and three different types in São Paulo State (João G. de Souza, "Some Aspects of Land Tenure in Brazil," in *Land Tenure*, ed. by Kenneth H. Parsons, Raymond J. Penn, and Philip M. Raup [Madison, University of Wisconsin Press, 1956], pp. 283–289). CIDA, *Posse e uso da terra*, pp. 192 ff., offers a description of the variety of peasant types in rural Brazil. There are also regional variations.

[67] Wolf, "Reflections on Peasant Revolutions," p. 8.

[68] *Ibid.*, p. 9. I would like to suggest that it is the local middleman (who is being forced out of the internal marketing system by commercial elites) who shares common goals with the peasant whose tenure on the land is being threatened. Years of tension between peasant fishermen and local elites in the county of Coruripe, Alagôas, in Northeast Brazil, broke into armed conflict when policemen tried to force them to sell their fish to consumers directly on the beach at lower prices. The village women, led by a fishhawker, attacked and killed eight policemen, thereby ensuring their place in the local market.

[69] According to Harding, "Combative peasant organizations appear not in vital coffee, cacau, sugar, and cattle sectors, but where paternalism had broken down and the conflict was most intense between peasant and landowner: in marginal *fazendas* that were hard-pressed to compete with more modernized commercial sectors in agriculture; and in frontier areas and land near cities, where, because of the rise in land values, speculators and commercial farmers were moving in to grab land from squatters who had cleared and farmed the land" (*op. cit.*, p. 36).

from this fundamental fact. Yet, these divergent organizations did manifest solidarity on a number of occasions. The general trend was obviously toward an increased radicalization, and leftist Catholic groups were in the vanguard in pressing demands for a real agrarian reform. This trend has been attributed to Communist infiltration of the movement.[70] However, another alternative should be suggested: that the demands of the peasant, aligned to the rural worker, had become the dominant ones in the rural movement. Thus, while only a few priests had supported the extreme demands of the Declaration of the I Congresso Nacional dos Lavradores e Trabalhadores Agrícolas in Belo Horizonte in 1961,[71] by 1963 the once conciliatory group led by priests in Rio Grande do Norte was also calling for basic agrarian reform.[72]

The development of the peasant movement in the state of Paraná met in 1960 in apparent harmony with government officials and political and economic elites. The tone of the meeting was substantially nationalistic but decidedly reformist and nonrevolutionary.[73] By 1961, however, peasant leaders were denouncing armed conflict between workers and landlords' private police. The second congress, held in Maringa in 1961, had a far different tone, calling for radical agrarian reform and the liquidation of the landowners as a class.[74] It is important to note the effects of the expanding coffee economy on the character of these meetings. The late 1950s was a period of general prosperity in the state of Paraná. The agricultural frontier was expanding rapidly and salaries were actually higher than the legal minimum, a fact that attracted large numbers of agricultural workers to the region.[75] Yet there is evidence that here, too, land speculation and frequent consolidations by resale were displacing small holders in a general trend toward land concentration.[76] The plight of the peasantry, not the demands of the rural proletariat, led to violence and the increased radicalization of the rural movement in Paraná.

[70] Price (*op. cit.*, pp. 64–65) states that by 1963 the Communist-oriented ULTAB group had acquired control of CONTAG.

[71] Vera, "O congresso camponês em Belo Horizonte," pp. 94–95. For the content of this declaration, see I Congresso Nacional dos Lavradores e Trabalhadores Agrícolas, "Declaração."

[72] The manifesto of the Natal meeting called for a radical reform based on the expropriation of land payable in government bonds over a long term and calculated on the declared tax value of the property. Additional demands included voting rights for illiterates, establishment of cooperatives and price guarantees for production and warehousing, long-term credit arrangements, and extension of social security benefits to all rural workers (I Convenção Brasileira de Sindicatos Rurais, *Mensagem . . .* [July 15–20, Natal, 1963]).

[73] Silva, *op. cit.*, p. 61.

[74] Vera, "O II congresso camponês em Maringa," pp. 63–64.

[75] CIDA, *Posse e uso da terra*, p. 324.

[76] Frank, *op. cit.*, pp. 198, 231.

Government and landlord receptivity to the demands of the rural proletariat emboldened the peasant movement as a whole. In part, this was the
result of the prevailing national political climate. President Goulart viewed
the movement as a means of solidifying his political base.[77] The Rural
Labor Statute of 1963 demonstrates that he was not willing to let the
movement get out of hand. While the statute attempted to restate previously ignored provisions of rural labor legislation,[78] it also sought to
reestablish government control over the peasant movement.[79]

The Rural Labor Statute was quite clearly directed to the demands of
the rural proletariat rather than to the problems of a true agrarian reform.[80]
The hierarchical structure of the union organization and the legal requirements involved in obtaining federal recognition placed the peasant movement under extreme bureaucratic controls. The arbitrary division of rural
types into two broad categories of workers and employers failed to come
to grips with the sociological realities of the Brazilian countryside.[81] For
example, small property owners were lumped together with salaried workers, renters, and squatters. Furthermore, the inclusion of the sharecropper
as an independent worker removed the possibility of his negotiating with
his landlord as an employee.

Under the statute the unions were recognized to deal with the economic
activities of the laboring class, and political activity was strictly forbidden,
at least in theory. The strike as a weapon was made illegal, and arbitration
councils were established to redress grievances in rural areas.

Despite Goulart's playing both sides, he failed to satisfy either peasants

[77] From 1946 to 1960 only six rural unions received the recognition of the Ministry
of Labor. Under the government of João Goulart, however, 266 rural unions were
recognized (Brazil, SUPRA, *Sindicatos rurais*, p. 18). While it is obvious that formal
recognition of the unions depended on the receptivity of national political leaders, the
movement was evidently well under way before Goulart took office. He by no means
created the demands of peasantry; but capitalized on them when they became highly
audible.

[78] Price, *op. cit.*, p. 12.

[79] The Rural Labor Statute was essentially a complement to the Consolidation of
Labor Laws of 1943 (*ibid.*, pp. 7–8; CIDA, *Posse e uso da terra*, pp. 302–309). It had a
long history in Brazilian congressional committees, having originated in a bill sent to
Congress by President Getúlio Vargas as early as 1954 (Price, *op. cit.*, pp. 9–10).
Ferrari recounts the legislative events surrounding the presentation of the bill (Fer-
nando Ferrari, *Escravos da terra* [Pôrto Alegre: Editôra Globo, 1963]). For conditions
leading up to the Rural Labor Statute and an explanation of it, see Adriano Campan-
hole, *Legislação do trabalhador rural e estatuto da terra* (São Paulo: Editôra Atlas, S.
A., 1963); and Sagadas Viana, *O estatuto do trabalhador rural e sua applicação* (São
Paulo: Livraria Freitas Bastos, 1963).

[80] Prado, "O estatuto do trabalhador rural," *Revista Brasiliense*, 47 (1963), 6.

[81] Similar criticism has been levied against the earlier Consolidation of Labor Laws
(CIDA, *Posse e uso da terra*, pp. 329 ff). See also Price, *op. cit.*, p. 16; J. V. Freitas
Marcondes, "O estatuto do trabalhador rural e o problema da terra," *Cadernos
Brasileiros*, IV (1963), 56; and Prado, "O estatuto do trabalhador rural," p. 3.

or landlords in rural Brazil. Apparent receptivity in the presidential palace gave the peasant class and its leaders the courage to press for more radical reforms. Yet there were limits to the permissiveness of the landowning class. At a massive rally on March 13, 1964, Goulart issued the now-infamous SUPRA Decree, enabling the expropriation of all underutilized properties of over twelve hundred acres located within six miles of major routes of communication, and lands of over seventy acres which were within six miles of federal dams or irrigation or drainage projects.[82] Since no constitutional amendment had been passed to provide for payment in bonds for expropriated lands and there was no money in the treasury for such expenditures, the application of such a decree would have meant the outright seizure of the property of the landowning class. The lines of battle had been clumsily drawn.

Landowner opposition to the peasant movement had long been a fact of life. The strong agrarian interests represented in Congress successfully resisted rural reform for many years. The same Consolidation of Labor Laws which provided for rural unionization also legitimized the Rural Brazilian Confederation of Landowners which was organized for collective action in their own behalf. Their early opposition to Goulart's plan for rural reorganization had helped to oust him as Vargas's minister of labor in 1954.[83] They again vigorously protested the rural labor movement in 1963.[84] In short, the landed elite were lobbying for the *status quo* in rural Brazil.[85]

In addition, the threat of land invasions and assaults on local markets by starvation-driven peasants put the landholding class on constant alert. Private and sometimes public police forces carried out reprisals against the peasants in every region of the country. In the northeastern state of Paraíba, the dreaded Syndicate of Death stood ready to execute the *patrão*'s most dire requests. In the state of Alagôas, resident landowners banded together to defend themselves against any encroachment of the peasant leagues. They proudly showed the arsenals they kept in their plantation houses to "stem the tide of Communism" in Brazil. Their fears were reinforced by exaggerated press reports, and they began to react with

[82] Goulart simultaneously called for the nationalization of all privately owned oil refineries.

[83] Wilkie, *op. cit.*, p. 6.

[84] This association came to be known as the National Confederation of Agriculture after the Rural Labor Statute was passed in 1963. It has been held that the movement was a weak organization. At the end of 1961 there were 1,711 such associations, with 240,120 members, mostly in the south, east, and Northeast ("Agricultura em 1963," p. 33).

[85] In 1961, the Federation of Rural Associations of São Paulo prepared fourteen position papers on agrarian questions, ten more on rural unions, thirteen on labor legislation, and eleven on agrarian reform (Feitosa Martins, *op. cit.*, pp. 137–138).

violence at the slightest provocation. The peasant league meeting I attended in 1962 ended with an armed assault on the humble gathering in the town square. The meeting had been called to peacefully protest the destruction of a tenant's manioc crop by a landowner trying to evict her from her plot. The local parish priest, from the sanctity of his Church, directed the townspeople in a violent counterdemonstration which left one peasant wounded and a twelve-year-old boy dead, a bullet in his head.

CONCLUSIONS

The coup that ousted João Goulart from the presidency on April 1, 1964, carried its purge down to the level of the local peasant political movement. The peasant leagues and independent associations were disbanded, and many of their leaders were arrested. Francisco Julião spent several months in a military prison before making his way into exile in Mexico. The Church-sponsored rural unions were allowed to continue, but with government interventors in leadership roles.[86] The political plowhands had been removed and the team muzzled and bridled. Nevertheless, it was clear to all that legislation against peasant movement leaders would not cause the movement to disappear.

The direction that the peasant movement now takes will obviously depend on the responsiveness of the military regime to a policy for agrarian reform. According to the president of IBRA, the political climate before April 1964 was both sensationalist and demagogic, but the "revolutionary government . . . opted for a democratic solution based on stimulating private property, on the rights of the farmer-owner to the fruits of his labor and, naturally, on increased production, reintegrating property into its natural social function and conditioning its use for the general welfare." [87] To this end, the Castelo Branco regime enacted an agrarian reform bill in 1964 which empowered the federal government to: carry out a complete cadastral survey in Brazil, to institute a progressive land tax, exercise control over rural labor contracts, survey and demarcate public lands, expro-

---

[86] Padre Melo's rural union in Cabo, Pernambuco, was left untouched because, according to the priest, the military was afraid of his tongue. In 1966, the movement was returned to clerical leadership, but the government maintains strict control. The weakening of the rural unions is evidenced by the fact that collections from rural workers for the unions have fallen considerably. In 1964–65, 1,691 patrons collected union contributions from their workers, while in 1966–67 only 555 collections were made (Serviço de Orientação Rural de Pernambuco, "Os trabalhadores rurais querem ser agentes do desenvolvimento do nordeste plantando dos hectares," Recife, 1967 [mimeographed]).

[87] César Cantanhede, *Palestra proferida na Escola Superior de Guerra* (Rio de Janeiro: Instituto Brasileira de Reforma Agrária, 1967), p. 7.

priate land with payment in bonds,[88] colonize and establish cooperatives, and provide general assistance and protection to the rural economy.[89] In addition, Castelo Branco extended the right to strike to rural workers. According to a presidential decree of 1965, every rural worker in the sugar-cane zone was entitled to have, after one year of continual service, up to two hectares of land near to his house "sufficient to plant and raise live-stock to an extent necessary for his and his family's subsistence."[90]

Nevertheless, the government's stated goals of transforming the rural workers, renters, and sharecroppers into a rural middle class, of stimulating the development of small properties through cooperatives, and of mod-ernizing and democratizing medium and large plantations [91] are still no-where in sight. Land speculation and concentration of landholdings continue throughout Brazil—even on the open frontiers.[92] Commerciali-zation in agriculture moves faster than government planning, and peasants are still being evicted from their land, thus "abandoning subsistence agri-culture which supplies foodstuffs to the market places." [93] The agricultural sector of the Brazilian economy continues in a cycle which the govern-ment appears unable or unwilling to break.

During a trip through the Northeast in 1967, I noticed that Church-sponsored rural unions were again spreading throughout the entire coun-tryside, filling the vacuum left by the demise of the peasant leagues and independent associations.[94] Regardless of the ideology of the new Church leadership, it is clear that the demands of the peasant membership remain substantially the same. Discontent continues to mount in the Brazilian countryside, and now it threatens to lead the rural masses into a terrifying unity.

[88] Skidmore, *op. cit.*, p. 318, notes that ample protection was provided for the land-owners, including guarantees against currency depreciation for the holders of govern-ment bonds. Perhaps the most significant aspect of the agrarian reform bill was the beginning of IBRA's cadastral survey in 1965.

[89] Cantanhede, *op. cit.*, p. 12.

[90] Serviço de Orientação Rural de Pernambuco (SORPE) "Os trabalhadores rurais querem ser agentes do desenvolvimento do nordeste plantando dos hectares," Recife, 1967 (Mimeographed).

[91] Cantanhede, *op. cit.*, p. 8.

[92] CIDA, *Posse e uso da terra*, p. 104.

[93] Reported to *Jornal de Commercio* (Recife), August 13, 1967, p. 133.

[94] Significantly, the Federation of Rural Unions in Pernambuco, originally com-prised almost exclusively of rural workers, was reported to have split after 1964 into three federations—one of wage earners, one of sharecroppers and fixed tenants, and one of small holders who are not employees.

Part II   An Overview

Chapter 10   Portugal's Contribution to the Underdevelopment of Africa and Brazil

Marvin Harris

[This essay focuses on Portugal's role in the underdevelopment of its territorial possessions and posits the thesis that Portuguese Africa and Brazil are examples, with different results, of colonialism and imperialism. Similarities between the two areas are superficial although a comparative approach is recognized as useful. Accordingly, differences in the patterns of Brazilian and African history and culture are emphasized: in the evolution of the slave trade and the cash-crop slave and wage-labor plantations; in the successes and failures of military conquest and colonial domination; and in technoeconomic developments. Thus the rhetoric of "civilizing mission" and official claims to the lusotropical thesis and to resemblances between the areas are abruptly dismissed. Additionally, the pattern of race relations in Brazil is contrasted with that in Portuguese Africa. Finally, Portugal's continued presence in African territories is explained as a consequence of the mother country's own underdevelopment.]

Current interest in foreign area studies is associated with doctrines and policies which stress the global nature of contemporary sociocultural events. It is generally understood, for example, that the political economy of Euro-America constitutes a globally integrated system: that fluctuations in the world market prices of such commodities as copper, sugar, coffee, and petroleum exert an enormous force upon the political stability of dozens of countries; that the political and military confrontations of the great powers, as in Vietnam, shake the foundations of society on a planetary scale. But many regional and disciplinary specialists erroneously attribute the systemic nature of intercontinental relations to recent improvements in transport and communications. Indeed, the platitudinous quality of so much that is heard about our sudden emergence into "one world" status actually obscures the causes of the different and unequal forms of participation in the world historical process. Satisfactory analysis of the system of present-day intercontinental conflict and change cannot be achieved unless the immediate conditions of growth, stasis, and regression are viewed in their maximum space-time extension.

Analysis of the differential trajectories of development in Africa and Latin America is especially dependent upon macrocosmic perspectives. The reason for this is not simply that the European powers held far-flung colonial possessions in both Africa and the New World. It is, rather, that from the sixteenth century onward the destinies of Africa, Europe, and the New World were locked together as part of a single system of political economy. This system was initially based on slave labor. The rise of monocrop, slave plantation agriculture along the Atlantic littoral not only provided the basis for the Euro-American exploitation of Africa, but fixed the patterns of development and underdevelopment for centuries to come. Participation in various aspects of the slave system created divergences among colonies yoked to a common power and convergences among those under separate dominion. Indeed, the characteristic result of plantation slavery was the emergence of maximum sociocultural and developmental contrast between the African and American territories.

In the case of Portuguese Africa and Brazil, the question of the degree of resemblance produced as a result of common metropolitan policies and traditions has acquired considerable ideological significance. Despite official claims to the contrary, the resemblances between Portuguese Africa and Brazil that can be attributed solely to the fact of Portuguese dominion are only superficial. As an antidote to politically inspired interpretations of Portugal's "civilizing mission" in the tropics, it would be well to stress without delay the fact that Portuguese Africa and Portuguese America are categorically and irreconcilably opposed examples of the consequences of Euro-American colonialism and imperialism. This contrast does not diminish the need for a comparative approach; the differences involved are those that pertained among the elements of a single organism or ecosystem. That is, the differences between the patterns of Brazilian and African history are aspects of a single demographic, technoeconomic, and technoenvironmental complex in which Africa and America discharged separate but mutually interdependent functions.

I

The salient feature of this relationship is that Africa was the breeder and supplier of the laborers whose work on cash-crop slave plantations determined the development trajectory of vast portions of the circum-Caribbean, and of tropical and semitropical North and South America. Yet in Africa itself, the cash-crop slave plantation or its wage-labor analogues did not develop until the late nineteenth century. The most important questions that can be asked concerning the relationship between Africa and the New World aim at penetrating the intercontinental significance of this situation: Why did the exploitation of African labor assume the form of slavery? Why were the plantations established in the New World and not in Africa? More specifically, in reference to the Portuguese experience: Why were there no sugar plantations in Africa?

David Birmingham has formulated this problem somewhat more broadly, making no mention of plantations, sugar, and slavery, and asking "why the Portuguese (and subsequently all the other European powers) found it more expedient to foster the development of American colonies with African labour rather than encourage direct production in Africa." [1] Birmingham suggests two lines of explanation, the first being that Africa had a higher density of population along the margins of the ocean shared with the Americas. Given the technical essentials of African food production, this density could not be raised; hence, according to Birmingham, there existed in effect a condition of "land shortage" which discouraged European productive enterprises.

It is, of course, quite correct that aboriginal population density along the Brazilian coast was less than that which the Portuguese encountered along the African coast (except in the Mauretanian and Southwest African latitudes). Yet in the sixteenth century a much higher population density existed in the Mexican and Andean highlands than was to be found anywhere along the African littoral. [2] Instead of posing obstacles to the European efforts to organize agricultural, mining, and commercial enterprises in the nuclear American highlands, these dense populations provided the manpower that guaranteed the continuing interest of colonial adventurers, missionaries, and crown authorities. It should also be made clear that the relationship between African subsistence patterns and population density could easily have been improved by the introduction of European and American agricultural technologies. Indeed, it is generally recognized that an incidental result of the Portuguese presence in Africa was the rapid spread of New World food crops, principally maize and manioc, which

[1] David Birmingham, *Trade and Conflict in Angola* (Oxford: Clarendon Presss, 1966), p. 14.
[2] See Julian Steward and T. C. Faron, *Native Peoples of South America* (New York: McGraw Hill, 1959); Henry Dobyns, "Estimating Aboriginal American Population," *Current Anthropology*, VII (1966), 395–449; and Robert Stevenson, *Population and Political Systems in Tropical Africa* (New York: Columbia University Press, 1968).

did increase the productivity and carrying capacity of African subsistence practices.[3] If the introduction of these crops failed to raise the density of African populations during the period between 1500 and 1850, it was because the advantages of maize and manioc were canceled by the monumentally disruptive effects of the slave trade on production, distribution, and social organization.[4]

Birmingham's second line of explanation is more significant: "the ability of Africans and African kingdoms to resist encroachments on their sovereignty." [5] As Birmingham demonstrates, the Portuguese confronted strong military resistance in Africa, and they were "militarily" incapable of establishing a secure hegemony over the African hinterlands. But this was true only in a relative sense. The problem was not simply military, for it also involved the comparative costs of winning battles in the New World as compared with winning them in Africa.

In Brazil, the Portuguese faced an enemy whose armaments belonged largely to the Stone Age. Even among the most advanced Amerindian groups, metal weapons were limited to a few bronze or copper maces. For the Aztecs, the obsidian-edged wooden club and the stone-tipped javelin hurled from the *atl-atl* were the principal combat weapons.[6] Similarly, the common soldier of the Inca armies depended primarily upon stone-headed clubs, wooden knives, and an occasional bronze or copper-tipped spear.[7] The steel armor of the *Conquistadores* could not be penetrated by most of these weapons. The European soldiers were able to use crossbows, muskets, and steel lances with devastating result. Mounted on armored horses, they constituted veritable equestrian tanks, and in Spain's conquest of both Mexico and Peru, cavalry played a decisive role. But the specific comparison that concerns us here is not the ineffectual resistance offered by the great massed armies of the Aztec or Inca. The question is rather, where in Africa could the Portuguese find a prey so vulnerable to their horses, steel, and gunpowder as the Tupi-Guaraní village Indians of the Brazilian littoral? The military cost of destroying these sparse populations living in acephalous, egalitarian, semisedentary villages was negligible. Adapted to a subsistence base of shifting horticulture, fishing, hunting, and collecting, their response to European colonization was to retreat back into the abun-

---

[3] Marvin P. Miracle, "The Introduction and Spread of Maize in Africa," *Journal of African History*, VI, no. 1 (1965), 39–55.

[4] Karl Polanyi and A. Rotstein, *Dahomey and the Slave Trade* (Seattle: University of Washington Press, 1966), pp. 22 ff.

[5] Birmingham, *op. cit.*, pp. 14–15.

[6] George Vaillant, *Aztecs of Mexico* (New York: Doubleday, Doran and Co., 1941), p. 210.

[7] J. Alden Mason, *The Ancient Civilizations of Peru* (Baltimore: Penguin, 1957), p. 192.

dant unoccupied vastness of the interior. Those who remained near the coast and yet managed to escape the Brazilian slavers were finished off by microbial "weapons" even more devastating than cavalry and bullets: smallpox, measles, and the common cold, against which most precontact Amerindian populations lacked immunity.[8]

Thus Africa confronted the Europeans with a relatively expensive task. Let us for the moment define the Europeans' ultimate objective as some unspecified form of conquest and subsequent investment in profit-making activities. What were their opportunities south of the Sahara? From Guiné to Dahomey, they were confronted with highly stratified, populous, well-organized native states capable of raising large armies, whose weaponry was based upon metallurgical techniques. Iron-tipped lances, iron-pointed arrows, and double-edged broadswords raised the material cost of military engagement far beyond anything the Iberians had to face in the New World. Furthermore, north of the Congo, wherever cavalry could operate, that is outside the tropical forest and tse-tse fly areas, the Africans themselves were mounted.

These facts help to answer another question posed by Birmingham, namely, "Why in the whole of Africa, was it Angola which became the site of the one major attempt at European conquest?"[9] It is precisely in Angola that the military situation once again suggested the prospect of relatively cheap and easy conquest. Here were groups politically less well organized than in the Congo, lacking any considerable development of iron weaponry, in a habitat suitable for mounted operations, yet into which the Sudanic horse complex had not yet penetrated. Even so, as Birmingham's reconstruction of the campaigns of the late sixteenth and early seventeenth centuries reveals,[10] the Portuguese seriously miscalculated their military possibilities. Expeditions into the Angolan highlands against the Ngola and the Imbangala were repeatedly turned back with great loss of material (trade goods) and European lives. One of the problems was that in Africa it was the Europeans who suffered most from the *de facto* biological warfare which accompanied the contact of diverse populations. Strains of malaria to which the Europeans had developed no immunity took their toll before, during, and after battle. The Africans, on the other hand, appear to have enjoyed considerable immunity to smallpox and the respiratory infections which were the scourge of the Amerindians. In addition, the Portuguese faced a foe in Angola who, unlike the Brazilian Indians, could not retreat into remote, unoccupied areas. Indeed, the most

[8] Darcy Ribeiro, "Convívio e contaminação," *Sociologia*, XVIII (1956), 56; and Dobyns, *op. cit.*, p. 410.

[9] Birmingham, *op. cit.*, p. 15.

[10] *Ibid.*

humiliating Portuguese defeats were experienced at the hands of warriors who were part of migratory movements emanating from the regions to the east and north of Angola. Far from fleeing the Portuguese, these groups may actually have been motivated in part by the expectation of getting closer to the source of trade goods flowing from the coast and of asserting control over it.

These military factors, however, should be placed in their larger techno-economic and technoenvironmental context. It is inadequate to assume, as we have been doing up to this point, that the Europeans were interested in an unspecified variety of profitable arrangements. Hence the significance of the slight difference in wording between Birmingham's formulation and my own, namely the specification in one instance and not in the other that the transport of African labor was destined to facilitate the production of plantation crops, or to be even more specific, of sugarcane. That is, the answer to our basic question approaches the self-evident if we wonder why African labor was not put to work in textile factories, vineyards, silver mines, or steel mills. To such inquiries we may respond at once: either the enterprise in question was competitive with metropolitan interests, required unavailable amounts of capital, or was ruled out by the absence of crucial raw materials (as in Portuguese attempts to exploit the nonexistent silver mines of Cambambe). Actually, even in these self-evident examples of noninvestment there are important lessons concerning the nature of the relationships between Portuguese officials, soldiers, missionaries, and entrepreneurs and the Africans with whom they interacted. Despite the rhetoric of the "civilizing mission," which has retrospectively become one of the central themes of the ideology of the colonial period, the material gifts the Portuguese were prepared to bestow upon Africa were as non-existent as the Cambambe mines. The utility of these oft-made observations is simply that they remind us once again that the Portuguese, to-gether with all the other European powers who followed them, acted in conformity with their own short-term material interest, regardless of the consequences for the Africans. If benefits of any sort flowed from Euro-peans to Africans, it was as a result of temporary lapses, ambiguities in the interpretation of self-interest, or other manifestations of "noise" in the system (the introduction of New World cultigens, for example).

None of these considerations, however, is specific enough to explain the transport of African labor to the Brazilian *engenhos de açucar*. For this enterprise there was evidently sufficient capital—enough to finance the slave raiders, the slave ships, the slaves, the mills, and the sugar boats.

There is of course no question that many areas of Angola were clima-tologically and edaphically suitable for cane production (in 1960, 60,000 tons of cane were milled in Angola). The possibility of establishing an

Angolan sugar industry on the model of the Brazilian sugar *fazendas* was explicitly considered and repeatedly proposed during the four centuries that preceded the actual beginning of large-scale production. Furthermore, there was no need to look to Brazil for the technical and organizational precedents of the sugar industry. Indeed, the precedent of the Brazilian industry itself was to be found in Africa, in the early fifteenth century slave plantations of the island of São Tomé.[11]

Two characteristics of sugar production must now be mentioned: first, the large amount of labor required for the cutting and hauling operations, a condition dictated by the rapid loss in sucrose content if milling is delayed; [12] second, the relatively long growing period—eighteen months to two years—required for optimal maturation. The significance of the first characteristic is that if the need for large man-hour inputs was to be met by African labor, that labor had to be slave labor. Given the absence of a money economy, the alternative sources of subsistence open to the African, and the scarcity or high cost of trade commodities brought from Portugal, there were no price-market inducements for large numbers of African laborers to surrender a portion of their surplus product to European entrepreneurs. Furthermore, given the incomplete formation of the aboriginal state apparatus in Angola, the necessary labor contingents could not be aggregated through centrally administered corvées. This alternative —the one actually pursued by Spain in Mesoamerica and the Andes—would have required the very conquest and political reorganization that we have seen was unobtainable without a relatively high investment in military operations. Once the politicoeconomic balance governing the nature of the labor input in cane production tipped in the direction of slave labor, the fate of the two continents was sealed, and their respective roles in the underdevelopment system determined, for five hundred years to come.

But why send the slaves overseas? The flow of slaves into the European maw was achieved, as is well known, through the mediation of African slave hunters and African raiding parties. This supply was directly proportional to the amount of warfare and intergroup hostility, and in one way or another, deliberately or tacitly, the Portuguese with their hunger for labor subsidized the prolongation and intensification of conflict and political unrest. The maximization of the slave supply depended upon maximizing treachery, insecurity, and hostility. The greater the anarchy, the greater the percentage of violable persons. One does not set out a crop, especially a crop that needs a long maturation period, plus heavy invest-

---

[11] James Duffy, *Portuguese Africa* (Cambridge: Harvard University Press, 1959), p. 53.

[12] Rolf Knight, "Why Don't you Work Like Other Men Do," unpublished Ph. D. dissertation, Columbia University, 1968.

ments in buildings and machinery, in such a country. It is all too risky.

Moreover, how does one prevent the slaves from attempting to make their way back to their homelands? While the chances are good that they will be intercepted along the route by a group of slave hunters, the temptation to escape will be irresistible. From the owner's point of view, it is of little consequence that the escape has failed, for his loss of capital cannot be recovered in the absence of firm political control over the hinterland. In this light it is perfectly clear why the island of São Tomé was the center of the African sugar industry prior to the late nineteenth century. For a man without a boat, nothing is more conducive to resignation than an ocean between himself and his homeland.

Thus it happened that Africa became the labor supplier for the plantations of the New World. The consequences of this arrangement for Angola and Moçambique are not exhausted when we have noted that the slave trade kept the interior in a state of turmoil and caused incalculable suffering to the slaves and their families. From the point of view of the development of underdevelopment, we must assign priority to the almost total absence of European investment for agricultural production, mining, or manufacture. Thus the significance of the European-stimulated slave trade was that it subverted the trajectory of aboriginal political and economic development. It is fully in accord with the known historical facts to state that conduct of the slave trade prevented Angola and Moçambique for 350 years from taking the first steps toward achieving technological and political parity with Europe.

II

The havoc wrought by the commitment to the slave labor system was not confined to Africa. The wealth created by slave-produced sugar temporarily gave rise to a colonial society in Brazil which, during the eighteenth century, almost achieved parity with Southern European techno-economic standards. But the slave plantation fatally compromised Brazil's capacity to develop further as international capitalism moved into its industrial phase. Slavery's ideational and motivational profiles were incompatible with the requisites of industrialization. The slave plantation left as its heritage a mass explicitly trained to be illiterate, explicitly trained to be apathetic, and explicitly trained to be dependent. This mass was deficient in both agricultural skills and the mechanical arts. The slave system also left an elite trained in oratory and otiose consumption, with neither the experience nor the motivation for organizing industrial production. This handicap was intensified by Portugal's own ill-fated commitment early in the eighteenth century to a future based on colonial tribute rather than on the development of domestic manufacturing industries. By the Treaty of Methuen (1703), Portugal voluntarily bowed out of the European competition for textile manufacture in return for a monopoly of the English wine trade. It was the textile industry that provided the principal techno-economic foundation of the industrial revolution. The stage was thus set for Portugal's decline to the status of a third-rate power, a condition which was confirmed at the end of the Napoleonic wars by the Brazilian secession. While Portugal ceased to be directly responsible for the relative stagnation of the Brazilian economy during the nineteenth century, the trajectory to which the slave plantation system had committed Brazil proved difficult to alter. Because Brazil lacked the rudiments of a manufacturing complex of its own, Brazilian trade fell captive to European, especially English, capital. Brazil remained a source of agricultural (or even merely collected) products, at the mercy of world market prices, confronted with ever-expanding ranks of competitors growing the same products throughout the vast European colonial domains. That this situation has not endured to the present day, that Brazil is now among the most important industrial powers in the southern hemisphere, is a fact utterly and wholly unattributable to Portugal's contribution to Brazil's technoeconomic, social, demographic, or ideological makeup. Indeed, it was the Portuguese legacy that constituted the main obstacle to the belated utilization of Brazil's vast national resources on behalf of its own industrial growth. The tide turned, as is well known, when hundreds of thousands of Italian, Polish, and German immigrants streamed into southern Brazil at the end of the nineteenth century, bringing with them the same pent-up drive, skills, and technical know-how that were simultaneously laying the basis for the emergence of the United States as a first-rank world power. Despite the strides that Brazil began to make toward industrial self-sufficiency, the pace of development within the United States with its head start in the slave-free North of over one hundred years, was far beyond Brazil's competitive capacities. The result of this disparity in economic strength was that by the 1930s Brazil's economic life had virtually become a reflex of its balance of payments with the United States. After World War II, United States influence penetrated the Brazilian political process and subverted the political and economic reforms that are the necessary condition for bringing the Brazilian standard of living up to parity with the fully industrialized nations.

For fifty million Brazilians the effects of the slave plantation linger on. Throughout the Northeast, the main sugar region of colonial times, illiteracy remains over 60 percent; per capita income, under $300; infant mortality, about 200 per thousand. The desperation and ignorance of this population are illustrated by the recurrence of revitalization movements which have periodically swept millions of the region's inhabitants into cruelly ineffectual, illusory, and diversionary solutions to their material problems.

Better communications, more effective intelligence, and modern political-military control will probably prevent recurrence of millenarian movements on the scale associated with nineteenth-century António Conselheiro and early twentieth-century Padre Cícero. On the other hand, peasant movements aimed at land reform have begun to appear for the first time during the past decade. These movements, with their unprecedented political and legal defiance of the landowning oligarchies, might have resulted in a fundamental restructuring of Brazilian society had they been permitted to achieve expression in free elections. Not the least of the adverse consequences of the coup of 1964 was the suppression of these peasant movements through the jailing or exiling of their elite organizers, the murder of their peasant cadres, and the suspension of electoral processes.

III

One of the most interesting by-products of Brazil's role in the slavery system was the development of a distinctive pattern of race relations. The main features of this pattern are: (1) an absence of structurally significant groups whose membership is defined by racial criteria; (2) a multitude of individualized "racial" categories extending across a broad spectrum of gently intergrading nuances; (3) a high degree of referential ambiguity; (4) no apartheid-like segmentation or discrimination.

A considerable amount of politically inspired mythologizing has taken place with respect to this pattern. As previously indicated, the attempt to prove the importance of a common heritage of Portuguese traditions in Africa and Brazil has acquired political significance for both Brazilians and Portuguese. The central claim is embodied in the so-called lusotropical thesis: Brazil has remained free of apartheid because of the lack of racial prejudice among the Portuguese colonists and plantation owners.[13] This proposition has served to enhance Brazil's prestige and influence in the international community. At the same time it has helped Portugal to defend its self-appointed civilizing mission in Africa, especially since the attempt, initiated in 1953, to pass off the African colonies as "overseas provinces."

It is simply and wholly false, however, that the Portuguese in Africa and Brazil, or present-day Brazilians, lack prejudices directed against dark-

[13] Gilberto Freyre, *O mundo que o português criou* (Rio de Janeiro: Livraria José Olympio Editôra, 1940).

skinned and Negroid physical types. Studies carried out by historians,[14] sociologists, social psychologists,[15] and anthropologists[16] have repeatedly confirmed the existence of powerful and uninhibited defamatory stereotypes and attitudes directed against Negroid types in both Brazil and Portuguese Africa. All scientific sources agree that there is a Brazilian gradient of preference in which Caucasoid types occupy one extreme and Negroid types the other. This pattern of prejudice is common to all countries in which blacks were enslaved by whites. The distinctive patterns of race relations in Brazil arise not from a lack of racial prejudice but from the non-existence of structurally significant racial groupings and from the cognitive ambiguities associated with racial identity.

It is absurd, therefore, to claim that Brazil's system of race relations is a heritage Portugal has bestowed on Brazil and of which Africa is to be the next beneficiary. The formative factors in the development of Brazilian race relations were the demographic shortages of the colonial period, the slow and delayed emergence from the slave-plantation economy, and the virtual absence of poor white homesteaders until the end of the nineteenth century. Lacking significant currents of European homesteaders, the Portuguese had no alternative but to permit the emergence of a large, eventually preponderant, mass of free racially mixed types. Unlike the situation in the United States, free people of color, representing every conceivable biotype resulting from the mixture of Amerindian, Negroid, and Caucasoid, greatly outnumbered the endogamous Caucasoid elite throughout the colonial period and into the twentieth century. This group was the functional equivalent of the poor whites in the United States. It was they who tended the cattle, raised subsistence crops, fought in the militia, served as retainers for local politicians, and carried out the marketing, transportation, and other activities that supported the main plantation interests. It was they who filled all of the social and economic niches that could not be filled by slaves. Thus during the formative phases of the slave system, the structural basis for Brazil's avoidance of apartheid was already present,

[14] Charles Boxer, *Race Relations in the Portuguese Empire, 1415–1825* (Oxford: Oxford University Press, 1963); Stanley Stein, *Vassouras* (Cambridge: Harvard University Press, 1957); and David Brion Davis, *The Problem of Slavery in Western Culture* (Ithaca: Cornell University Press, 1966).

[15] Octávio Ianni, *As metamorfoses do escravo; apogeu e crise da escravatura no Brasil meridional* (São Paulo: Difusão Europeia do Livro, 1962); Florestán Fernandes, *A integração do negro à sociedade de classes* (São Paulo: Faculdade de Filosofia, Ciências e Letras da Universidade de São Paulo, 1964); and Donald Pierson, *Negroes in Brazil* (Chicago: University of Chicago Press, 1942).

[16] Charles Wagley, ed., *Race and Class in Rural Brazil* (Paris: Unesco, 1952); Thales Azevedo, *As elites de côr* (São Paulo: Companhia Editôra Nacional, 1955); and Marvin Harris, *Town and Country in Brazil* (New York: Columbia University Press, 1956).

even though these foundations were opposed to the explicitly formulated ideological principles of Brazilian plantation society.[17] Throughout the eighteenth century, attempts to prevent the emergence of free mulatto groups in conformity with prevailing slavocratic doctrines were defeated by these structural conditions.[18]

The lusotropical thesis is even more inadequate to the history and present circumstances of Portuguese Africa. Here, as in Brazil, the thesis is in error because the Portuguese colonists manifest racist stereotypes. But the Portuguese African territories lack every other aspect of the fundamental Brazilian pattern described above: (1) These territories have structurally significant groups determined by racial criteria. The groups are Africans, assimilated Africans, *mixtos*, and white Portuguese settlers. Despite recent legal "reforms" aimed at confusing the international community, these groups exist both *de facto* and *de jure*, and they are associated with differential state-enforced privileges and penalties. Nothing like them has existed in Brazil since the abolition of slavery. (2) Racial categorization conforms not to the complex, free-ranging idiosyncratic Brazilian pattern, but consists rather of three or four sharply defined and widely recognized types. (3) The applicability of the categories of racial identity to specific individuals exhibits none of the ambiguity and indefiniteness characteristic of the Brazilian system. (4) And finally, except for a slippery veneer of egalitarian sentiment laid down by Lisbon to cover up the embittered racism of the white settlers, there is almost complete conformity to the structural conditions for which the heartlands of apartheid are appropriately infamous.

The racist configurations in the Portuguese African territories arose as a consequence of the system of corvée labor, which was in turn a consequence of the nineteenth-century political-military conquest of the African hinterlands. In a more fundamental sense, both the corvée system and the penetration and subjugation of the hinterlands were by-products of the steadily widening technological gap between nineteenth-century Europe and nineteenth-century Africa. Paced by Great Britain, the nineteenth-century powers competed among themselves for markets and for new outlets for investment capital. To the most advanced and efficient producer, namely Great Britain, all restrictions on the free flow of goods and labor were detrimental. Slavery and the slave trade soon became one of the prime targets of the attempt to create a completely open world

[17] See Marvin Harris, *Patterns of Race in the Americas* (New York: Walker and Co., 1964).

[18] See Charles Boxer, *The Golden Age of Brazil* (Berkeley and Los Angeles: University of California Press, 1962).

market in which price alone would regulate the nature of production and exchange. While there were losses to British planters in the Caribbean, the main thrust of British foreign policy lay in the direction of pressing its advantage through the expansion of free-trade opportunities. The suppression of the slave system was thus an act of British imperialism which benefited Britain both economically and politically. As the slave system came to an end, Europe, led by England, Germany, France, and Belgium, prepared to penetrate the interior of Africa for the first time and to usurp or take over the indigenous political institutions.[19]

The timing of these invasions and conquests was, to a considerable extent, a secondary reflex of the technological advances that lay at the root of the whole capitalist explosion. Among the technological advances associated with the industrial revolution were many items that helped to increase Europe's military advantage over the world's preindustrial peoples. Several new weapons, especially repeating rifles and machine guns, drastically altered the military balance between African and European armies. At about the same time, the vulnerability of the Africans was intensified by the neutralization of one of their strongest allies, the malaria plasmodium. This occurred as a result of the isolation of quinine as the active ingredient in cinchona bark and the establishment of large-scale plantations of cinchona trees in the Dutch East Indies at mid-century. Meanwhile, few of the products of the industrial revolution had flowed into Africa; least of all, the new weapons.

Pushed from behind by the competitive threat of the great powers and lured from ahead by the promises of easy military victories against a foe whose relative capacity for resistance had now at last been reduced to that of the Stone Age Indians of the Brazilian coast, the Portuguese also made their move to establish total political control over their African territories. One of the most remarkable consequences of the differential effects of the slave system is that this process had not yet been completed in parts of Moçambique and Angola as late as the 1920s, and that the period of full-scale colonialism that ensued did not last more than forty years before it began to crumble under renewed military resistance by the Africans.[20]

With effective political control established, capital investments were secure, and entrepreneurs, both foreign and domestic, were invited to make use of the conquered African laborers. Outright slavery was politically impossible. On the other hand, wage labor at free-market prices was

19 (Ed. note: While suppression of the slave trade was a manifestation of British imperialism, the abolition campaigns were viewed by liberal segments of British society as moral issues and waged as crusades.)
20 See Paul Bohannon, *African and Africans* (New York: Natural History Press, 1964), pp. 121–122.

too expensive, since the Africans continued to enjoy access to their subsistence farms. There remained corvée. And this form of labor exploitation dominates the history of Angola and Moçambique from 1900 to the present. The corvée contingents have been gathered by various direct and indirect means: by outright impressment, by raising taxes to the point that migratory wage work must be sought even at wages below marginal utility, and by imposing compulsory quotas for nonsubsistence crops such as cotton and coffee.[21]

The period of direct European political control in Africa has been remarkably brief. Maximum return on investments could best be achieved by developing agricultural and industrial skills among the Africans and by enlarging the Africans' share of consumption and production. Despite more or less effective barriers set up against educated elites, such elites inevitably emerged, even in Portuguese territories, passing in some instances through veritable eyes of needles. These elites became more and more troublesome; they demanded a share in the surplus production and in the management of their political affairs. After World War II the politicoeconomic cost of direct control over the Africans swung back once again in the Africans' favor. Most of the European powers gave up their attempts to exploit the Africans through administrative devices. In most instances, however, the withdrawal of the political apparatus has not disturbed the basic economic subordination of the new African nations to European capital, technological know-how, and European markets. The pattern of relationship between Europe and its former African colonies is thus for the first time strongly convergent with the pattern that has characterized the relationship between the United States and Latin America since the beginning of this century.

Portuguese territories, on the other hand, have thus far constituted a conspicuous exception to these trends. One of the reasons for Portugal's apparently irrational insistence upon political control in the face of these on-going, large-scale guerrilla wars is that Portugal herself remains an underdeveloped country, lacking the industrial and financial strength that would assure the dependency of Angola and Moçambique after the withdrawal of its political-military apparatus. Adriano Moreira, a former overseas minister, states the facts quite bluntly: "We know that only political power is a defense against the economic and financial invasion of our territories by . . . former colonial powers."

The Portuguese investment in the three wars now being waged is additionally forced upon them by an unique circumstance not alluded to by Moreira. Angola and Moçambique constitute an essential buffer zone be-

[21] Marvin Harris, "Labour Emigration Among the Mozambique Thonga: Cultural and Political Factors," *Africa*, XXIX (1959), 50–64.

tween the revolutionary movements in the Union of South Africa and the black African regimes sworn to the task of wiping out apartheid. The offer of independence to Moçambique or Angola would have to be made with the knowledge that South Africans would attempt to move in either militarily or by political infiltration. In their stubborn adherence to an obsolete form of colonialism, the Portuguese may yet render their greatest contribution to the development of Africa. The wars of liberation in the Portuguese territories are providing black Africans with their first opportunity to learn how to compensate for their centuries-old military disadvantages. By learning how to wage guerrilla warfare, the Africans in the liberation armies of Moçambique and Angola are injecting a wholly unprecedented ingredient into the balance between Euro-American imperialism and the prospects for African independence and development. Thus, by providing the opportunity for prolonged military confrontation between apartheid and black nationalism, the Portuguese, contrary to their intentions, actually hasten the end of white domination in southern Africa and of imperialist control throughout the rest of the continent.

Chapter 11   Lusotropicology, Race, and Nationalism, and Class Protest and Development in Brazil and Portuguese Africa

Roger Bastide

[Focusing on the weaknesses and contradictions in the science of lusotropicology, Bastide analyzes the impact of religion, in particular Portuguese Catholicism, upon colonial and subjected peoples in Brazil and Portuguese Africa.[1] Messianic and syncretic movements of resistance are examined. Urbanization and industrialization are viewed in the light of nationalism. Nationalism that emanates from a rural or urban milieu relates to development, but economic development accompanies a widening of the gap between classes, between urban and rural labor, between white and black.]

Gilberto Freyre's "science" of lusotropicology claims that Portuguese civilization evidences distinctive characteristics when it is confronted with slavery and colonialism.[2] To think so is to overlook the lesson of sociology: that social systems have their own internal logic and that the functioning of their processes depends on the conjunction of circumstances. In this sense, there is a system of slavery which results everywhere in domination and exploitation by the white man, and there is a system of colonialism which always results in the alienation of the man of color. What is founded

[1] Roger Bastide's study was translated by Virginia Conlou of the African Studies Center, University of California, Los Angeles.
[2] Gilberto Freyre, *O mundo que o Português criou* (Rio de Janeiro: Livraria José Olympio Editôra, 1940); and Gilberto Freyre, *Aventura e rotina* (Rio de Janeiro: Livraria José Olympio Editôra, 1953).

on force can only be maintained by force, the force of arms or, more insidiously, the force that corrupts souls. Neither Brazil nor Portugal is an exception to the rule: Brazil with her policies concerning the Indian and the slave who worked in plantation or mine; [3] and Portugal with her policies regarding the natives of Angola and Moçambique, formerly the object of a system of slave trade and today, of a system of forced labor.[4] But what one can retain from the science of lusotropicology is that slavery and colonization have differed in their operation:

First, according to the "cultures" within which they may be found—Portuguese, Spanish, French, or Anglo-Saxon—although they cover basically the same phenomenon [5] (Gilberto Freyre himself admitted that he found in the American South a very similar atmosphere to that prevailing in Northeastern Brazil [6]).

Second, according to historical events, in the transition from a trade-based economy to one based on colonialism, and in the transition from mercantile capitalism to industrial capitalism, which provoked the metamorphosis of the slave into the free proletarian. In Brazil, this transformation was the result of the prohibitive cost of slavery for a nascent industry.[7] In Portuguese Africa, the same historical evolution ended the period of diplomatic exchanges and religious conversions and initiated a period in which Angola was looked upon as the reservoir for a slave trade. Did not Angola, at the beginning of the nineteenth century, go so far as to conceive of seceding and annexing itself to Brazil when the slave trade on which it subsisted was threatened? [8] And then, when it could no longer exploit its human resources by slavery did Angola not turn to cultivating the land with a new policy of forced labor? [9]

To a certain extent, lusotropicology presents us with seemingly correct facts. The importance of cultural differentiation is brought to light, but it is more applicable to Brazil than to Africa and more to the Brazil of old than to contemporary Brazil. Lusotropicology becomes false, how-

[3] Roger Bastide, *Les religions africaines au Brésil* (Paris: Presses Universitaires de France, 1960).

[4] Guy de Bosschere, *Autopsie de la colonisation* (Paris: A. Michel, 1967).

[5] M. Wilhelmine Williams, "The Treatment of Negro Slaves in the Brazilian Empire: A Comparison with the United States of America," *Revista do Instituto Histórico e Geográfico Brasileiro*, IV⁰ Congresso de História Nacional, I (1950), 273–292.

[6] Gilberto Freyre, *Casa grande e senzala* (Rio de Janeiro: Livraria José Olympio, 1933). English translation: *The Masters and the Slaves* (New York: Knopf 1946).

[7] Florestán Fernandes, *A integração do negro à sociedade de classes* (São Paulo: Editôra da Universidade de São Paulo, 1965); Fernando Henrique Cardoso, *Capitalismo e escravidão* (São Paulo: Difusão Européia do Livro, 1962); and Octávio Ianni, *As metamorfoses do escravo* (São Paulo: Difusão Européia do Livro, 1962).

[8] José Honório Rodrigues, *Africa e Brasil: outro horizonte* (Rio de Janeiro: Editôra Civilização Brasileira, 1961).

[9] Bosschere, *op. cit.,* pp. 188–192.

ever, when it ignores the historical dimension. Freyre is compelled to differentiate the "paradise" of Northeastern Brazil from the industrial cities of southern United States where racial prejudice is evident in the competition that exists between races and ethnic groups in the labor market. For Portuguese Africa, he differentiates between the underdeveloped regions ("lusotropicales") and those of industrial development.[10] But because the new industrial society refuses to accept this "science," lusotropicology changes from a cultural, nonsociological description of events into a sentimental ideology of underdevelopment by ascribing value to the vestiges of a past era.

In sum, our point of departure is the distinction between social systems, with their own internal logic, and cultural systems (which may impede the development of social systems but which, in the final analysis, must submit to them). Unlike social systems, cultural systems are characterized by their internal inconsistencies or contradictions. As far as lusotropicology is concerned, Freyre's analysis consists of three elements: an anthropological element—the adaptability of the Portuguese to a tropical climate; a sexual element—the high value assigned to the woman of color (explained by the original scarcity of white women and by the sexual exploitation of the slave woman by the white master); and a religious element—a Portuguese Catholicism that is more social than mystical. The last two elements are by nature in conflict. Lusotropicology appears, therefore, to be a dynamic interaction between three heterogenous cultural elements. Of the three mentioned, only the religious element will be considered.

I

Freyre argues that religion, not race or skin color, constitutes the criterion for discrimination in the Portuguese Empire.[11] The correctness of this claim is not our concern here; what is important is that Freyre's statement involves a series of dichotomies: the Savage Indian (the struggle to enslave him being perfectly acceptable) and the Pacified Indian (controlled and protected by the Jesuits); the pureblood Pagan Negro and the baptized Creole Negro; the Negro and the Mulatto; the Plantation Negro (harshly treated) and the Household Negro (linked affectionately to the master); the Tribal Member in Africa and the Black Citizen; and finally, at times partaking of the dichotomies and at times the means of defining them, the Christian Indian or Negro and the Pagan. The demographic expression of these dichotomies—the opposition of a large group (the dom-

[10] Freyre, *Aventura e rotina*.
[11] Freyre, *Casa grande*; and Bastide, *op. cit.*

inators) to a smaller one (the dominated)—is the logical result of a colonial or slave-based system.

Portuguese policy has always been, from its origins to the present day, to "select" a smaller group from a larger one. "Selection" is a kind of filtering process in which an elite of color, true to its social function, is set up as the arbitrator or, more exactly, as the "absorber" of tensions. Criteria for passing from one group to the other include skin color (the mulatto being more acceptable than the dark-skinned Negro), eroticism (the master's Negro concubine and her children), and finally, religion. The Portuguese claim they are free of prejudice because they accord full citizenship to all Negroes in Angola and in Moçambique who have been assimilated and Christianized. Citizens of color, however, constitute only a minute minority of the total tribal population, for education is meted out parsimoniously and primary school is taught in native dialects. In Angola, less than one native in one hundred was a citizen in 1950.

Strictly speaking, then, religion has created dichotomies only in association with other criteria. Moreover, the role of religion has varied according to the historical context.

When proselytism had multiplied the number of converted pureblood natives, a dual Catholicism emerged: a Black Catholicism and a White Catholicism. In other words, the creation of a "second-rate" Catholicism became necessary when the smaller group tended to overcome the larger one.[12] Passage from one group to the other (as in eighteenth-century Brazil) was based on Christianization. However, only certain Christians were chosen—those set off by their physical beauty, their health, their intelligence, or their devotion as household slaves, craftsmen, or foremen. Religion played a minor role, whereas today in Portuguese Africa it plays a major role. Any onlooker must inevitably raise certain questions: What is meant by "religion"? In this assemblage of dichotomies, barriers, and channels of social ascension, can religion really be defined as the agent of dichotomy for the colored man, or is its meaning purely symbolic? The Portuguese do not differentiate between Christianity as a religion and Christianity as an essential element of the white man's civilization. The mere fact of becoming a Christian is not, in itself, decisive. Christianity only serves to open the door through which will enter, little by little, the rest of this civilization. It is only when the "black-man-with-a-white-soul" of the old adage has been produced that the black man will be accepted. This kind of Christianity is the very opposite of a mystical religion, one transcending all civilizations. The Portuguese use religion as an instrument of cultural alienation.

12 Bastide, *op. cit.* (chapter on the two Catholicisms).

The Indian and the Negro became citizens with the demise of the two systems of slavery formed around them: the Indian first, beginning in the seventeenth century, followed by the Negro, beginning in the second half of the nineteenth century. Christianity once more furnishes the model, that of the protector; and Catholicism again plays less the role of a faith than of a kinship system (spiritual kinship). This phenomenon is understandable in vast Brazil where social organization was founded, until recently, on the extended family and the clan. Membership in a family-based society could not be had via an as yet theoretical citizenship, but only through the establishment of the new kinship links. The structures of Catholicism, therefore, serve exclusively as social structures, incorporating into the same tribe as the white masters all the "poor cousins" of color in order to control them and to bar their social ascension. Nevertheless, social ascension remains an individual phenomenon; it becomes collective only with the arrival of industrial capitalism.[13]

As Catholicism has come to symbolize a certain social status, that of the poor cousin, political and economic opposition will also be cloaked in apparently religious garments, but resistance, as may be guessed, will really be more social than religious.

In the course of time, and depending upon the ethnic groups involved, resistance takes different forms. For the Indians, resistance began in the early days of colonization, taking the form of a messianic movement, the "Santidade." Seeking a Land of No Evil like that which prevailed before the arrival of the white man, social groups moved either vertically (through dance which lightens the soul) or horizontally (by moving toward the ocean or toward the Andes).[14] When the Indian was forced to become sedentary, resistance movements turned to advocating the overthrow of the existing social situation: the Land of No Evil became the land where the Indian was master and the white man, slave. The religious aspects of the Santidade, with its mixture of paganism and Catholicism, are of less concern here than are its economic functions. Documents dating from the Inquisition indicate that some large landowners participated in the Indian religion, thus encouraging its growth. By forcing the nomadic Indian to stay in one place, the Santidade movement provided the big landowners with a servile labor force cemented by a common cult.[15] Thus the initial phase of resistance ended with the integration of the Indian, as a serf, into the society. Social integration did not end conflict; however, the

---

[13] Roger Bastide, "The Development of Race Relations in Brazil," in *Industrialisation and Race Relations,* ed. by Guy Hunter (London: Oxford University Press, 1965), pp. 9–29.

[14] Alfred Métraux, *La religion des Tupinambás* (Paris: E. Leroux, 1928).

[15] "Confissões" and "Denunciações" of the Inquisition at Bahia.

class struggle still strives to integrate the proletarian into the total society.

Lack of historical documents makes it impossible to compare the evolution of the Indian messianic movement with the transformation of the pureblood Indian through the *mestiço* or *caboclo* stage into the "Catimbo" of today. Historians have studied only the bloody moments of the transformation, such as the holocaust of Pedra Bonita.[16] This incident shows the continuing desire for the creation of a Land of No Evil, incorporating traits of Portuguese Sebastianism as well as remnants of Indian religions, a land seen as the antithesis of the political and economic organization of white Brazil. In any event, it is striking to note that all of the Indian or mestizo messianic movements are more techniques devised to solve actual problems than simple pipe dreams: they belong more to the realm of the "praxis" than to that of theology. By the invention of adequate rituals, sorcerers are cast out and the world reformed.

These movements, therefore, are not so much the expression of a social crisis as a reflection of the dichotomy between the haves and the have-nots in an immobile society. Religion can be an aspect of "differentiation" because it defines a social group and because the mysticism inherited from the Indians—and those gradually Christianized—provides an identity for those who feel rejected.

These movements advocate social reform and also manifest a desire for social integration. As they become secularized, the peasant messianic movements serve as vehicles of social and economic progress. The movements of Canudos and Padre Cícero demonstrate this kind of evolution. António Conselheiro founded a sacred city, a city that also, however, fed its people, provided them with an agricultural cooperative, businesses, and craft industries. Padre Cícero created a flourishing town where miracles were put to work for interregional trade. It could be said that these messianic movements furnished a model for the only agricultural revolution which has succeeded in Brazil. The charismatic leader was able to do something that the bureaucracy of the central state could not do. He was able to spark the transition from an agricultural economy, based on the system of private property, to a cooperative economy held together by prayer; from subsistence production (dependent on the *minifundium*, or "small private property") to a market economy (necessary to support the masses drawn by the prophet or the messiah).[17] Certainly no one will negate Euclydes da Cunha's emphasis on "resistance" or "revolt": the wastelands of the *sertão* are in stark opposition to the more progressive coastal regions. In the last

[16] A. Attico de Souza Leite, *Fanatismo religioso, memória sôbre o reino encantado na comarca de Villa Bello* (Juiz de Fora, 1898).

[17] This point has been skillfully elucidated by Maria Isaura Pereira de Queiróz in all of her studies on the messianic movements of the Brazilian peoples, especially in her *Sociologia e folclore* (Bahia, 1953).

analysis, however, this revolt was really one that sought the integration of a rejected group into a total society where all the different elements of the population would find the place in which they belong by right. A new religious culture, that of a folk Catholicism (retaining certain elements of the messianic Indian movements or of Sebastianism), has replaced the archaic one and has provided the definition and identity of a group. In contrast to an intellectual, urban, priest-controlled Roman Catholicism, it regroups the most forsaken segments of the rural population into a movement aspiring toward the re-creation of the world, a world where faith in the messiah will strengthen arms and where working arms will give riches to the poor.[18]

With urbanization and industrialization new phenomena have appeared in Brazil. Since the abolition of forced labor the blacks have moved to urban centers, thus escaping the control of the whites by losing themselves in the anonymity of the large cities. But they have no training. They are nothing more than unskilled laborers; and in the slums, the *favelas*, they form a sort of subproletariat, not a true proletariat. In the Northeast and, especially, in Rio de Janeiro, the new arrivals, only partially Christianized, find well-organized African fraternal organizations which have remained faithful to the indigenous religion. These sects become therapeutic centers, so to speak, which permit the new arrivals to adapt more easily to the society around them. First, they help the newcomers avoid the frustrations that would necessarily accompany their failure to integrate into the society at large, a society that would abandon them to their unhappy lot. The sect is at the same time a mutual help society, a hospital, and a gathering place for religious festivities; it gives support to a whole portion of the population, and, by the same token, it has a "secularizing" influence.[19] Second, the African sects are made up of a whole series of hierarchical positions, from the *ekedy*, or "servant of the gods," to the *iyalorisha*, or "supreme priestess" for the women; from the *Ogan* to the *babalorisha* for the men.[20] Thus, inside their own organizations the blacks are able to aspire to the upward social mobility refused them by whites on the outside, class-structured society.[21] But it is apparent that these sects (*Candomblés, Xangô, Macumba*, etc.) do not integrate the individual into the urban milieu, al-

[18] Maria Isaura Pereira de Queiróz, *La 'Guerre Sainte' au Brésil: le mouvement messianique du Contestado*, São Paulo: Boletim 187, Faculdade de Filosofia, Ciências e Letras da Universidade do São Paulo, 1957.

[19] Luís A. da Costa Pinto, *O negro no Rio de Janeiro* (São Paulo: Companhia Editôra Nacional, 1953), chap. vii.

[20] Roger Bastide, *Le Candomblé de Bahia* (The Hague: Mouton, 1958).

[21] René Ribeiro, "Cultos Afrobrasileiros do Recife: um estudo de ajustamento social," *Boletim do Instituto Joaquim Nabuco*, Recife (1952); and René Ribeiro, "As estructuras de apôio e as reaçôes do Negro ao Cristianismo na América Portuguesa," *Boletim do Instituto Joaquim Nabuco*, Recife (1957), pp. 59–80.

though they permit his adaptation to it. Herein lies the reason for the attacks made against them by capitalist and Communist alike: the sects facilitate the development of a preindustrial mentality which, in the eyes of the former, discourages national productivity and, in the eyes of the latter, stifles any hope for progress (seen as the exclusive product of revolutionary trade unionism).[22]

As the country becomes more industrialized, however, the blacks are gradually evolving from a subproletariat to a proletariat; a small black middle class will even develop. The African religions will not disappear, but they will undergo certain transformations. First, as the working class, whatever its ethnic origin, becomes more and more conscious of its existence, the sects will evolve from ethnic-based ones (Nagô, Dahomey, Angola, Congo, Caboclo, or Indian) to syncretic ones, adopting African cultural traits or combining these traits with white cultural traits (Catholicism, centered around a cult of the saints, and spiritism, centered around communion with the dead). The *macumba* of Rio de Janeiro is an example of this first evolutionary type.[23] But as the black workers, who are competing in a labor market where the whites take the best positions, become more and more aware of the forces blocking their integration into a class-structured society, a new phenomenon will appear: the spiritism of Umbanda.[24] Nationalism is one of the two characteristic features of this spiritism. The Catholic religion and the spiritism of Allan Kardec are imported, "foreign" religions, a sequel to colonialism, whereas the religion of Umbanda is the only national religion. By combining the spirits of the Indians, the gods of the Africans, and the saints of Catholicism, it expresses the uniqueness of Brazil, the fruit of the union of three races: the Indian, the Negro, and the white. The second characteristic trait of Umbanda is the will to promote the social and economic development of the multiracial proletarian class, as well as of the small mulatto middle class, against the forces of discrimination and pluralism.

Thus, two new ideas begin to take form which will have a growing importance in the present day: nationalism and development. They appear first in a religious context and take on differing traits depending on the milieu, urban or rural, that nurtures them. In the rural areas revolt springs from within the messianic movements—in other words, from within the folk Catholicism—and its growth is a function of the charismatic authority of certain leaders. In the cities, revolt develops outside any messianic or

[22] This is the subject of *Jubiabá* (3rd ed.; São Paulo: Livraria Martins, 1944), the excellent novel by Jorge Amado.

[23] A. Ramos, *O negro brasileiro* (Rio de Janeiro: Editôra Civilização Brasileira, 1934).

[24] Bastide, *Les religions africaines* (see the chapter entitled "Naissance d'une religion").

prophetic movements; it takes form inside organized African religions, and its development depends directly upon the will emanating from the base, the faithful, who constantly remold the religious superstructures in accordance with nonreligious values.

A study of these two ideas must not omit their secular development. The concepts of nationalism and development were elaborated by the white elite of the country, principally bankers and industrialists. But the mass media were necessary for these ideas to reach every Brazilian, and practical results could be had only by generalizing these concepts in the forms of ideals: patriotism and progress. By definition these are nonracist ideologies; recent surveys of Brazilian society no longer specify skin color, only economic stratum.

It is the place the Negro is to hold in Brazilian society that is of interest here, and several comments need to be made. Economic development is always accompanied by a widening of the gap between classes: between the urban proletarian class (protected by excellent labor laws) and the rural class of day laborers, tenant farmers, and small landholders, whose poverty increases daily; or in the city, between the whites at the top of the pyramid, who are becoming richer and richer, and the blacks, unskilled laborers working mainly in construction and therefore subject to all the uncertainties of urbanization; or again, the gap between the whites and the racially mixed rural population who are drawn to the big city but only "camp" there rather than being integrated into it.[25] The black man, who is more aggressive than the mestizo, accepts "nationalism," for he has learned that his own economic development must necessarily take that route. Nationalism does present disadvantages, however, a result of slavery and of the survival of stereotypes. White nationalism is an Aryan ideology, postulating the progressive disappearance of the black race, to be brought about by the higher mortality rate among blacks, by the whitening of the race through miscegenation, and by the influx of European immigrants. The black nationalist ideology, on the other hand, as expressed by the Negro sociologist in Brazil, Guerreiro Ramos, argues that Brazil's people are a "Negro" race, and that it is the vanguard of all the Negro countries.[26] To accept Brazilian nationalism is to reject the black nationalist ideology—and the traumatic situation of the Negro becomes immediately apparent.

The desire for economic and social progress hidden under religious garbs in the spiritism of Umbanda turns into a secular demand in São Paulo, the

[25] We have borrowed the term "camp" from A. Comte, who applied it to the European proletariat; it has been employed more generally for the Negro and the *caboclo* by the Positivist Church in Brazil.

[26] G. Ramos, *Relações de raça no Brasil* (Rio de Janeiro: Editôra Quilombo, 1950); and Guerreiro Ramos, "O problema do negro na sociologia brasileiro," *Cadernos de Nosso Tempo*, I (1954), 189–220.

largest industrial center in Latin America. Interviews with the Negro leaders of São Paulo revealed the same themes: it is through education, job training, and the acceptance of Western values that the Negro can rise in the society. The tactics developed to reach this goal include: (1) forming, in harmony with the power structure, pressure groups to encourage the promulgating of self-help laws (awarding scholarships, opening technical high schools to the Negro, etc.); and (2) in the economic sector, going on strike for better salaries. (The Negro learned a valuable lesson, one he did not forget, from the successful strikes of the Italian immigrants.) [27]

The economic development of the Negro, however, is hampered, first by his precarious living conditions, next by the state of his health (and public hospital facilities are inadequate), and lastly by his lack of education (in order for the family to survive, children must begin working at an early age). Feelings of frustration thus arise which account for the growing success, even in the industrial center of São Paulo, of a rational conception of the world as found in the spiritism of Umbanda. The state of Guanabara, with its housing developments for workers, the ports of Santos and São Paulo, and the southern region of the state of Rio Grande do Sul have all become the meccas of this African-influenced spiritism, an expression of the failure of a colored proletariat.

II

Is the situation in Portuguese Africa analogous? Historians and travelers have commented on the contrast between Portuguese colonization in Brazil and in Africa. There were, of course, historical reasons for predicting an association between Portugal and Africa, for example, the famous alliance between the king of Portugal and the king of the Kongo. Portuguese culture would have been freely accepted then by the Africans in an atmosphere of racial equality. However, economic pressures modified the original policy, which had embodied qualities considered to be characteristic of Portuguese colonialism. In Brazil, plantations and later gold mines required a growing number of slaves, and Angola thus became the center of a slave trade; mercantile interests took precedence over the original "missionary" intentions.

The first period, which lasted until the beginning of the nineteenth century, was accompanied by the first form of indigenous resistance: messianic movements similar to those originating among the Amerindians in Brazil during the original period of colonization. The white man's lack of interest, however, accounts for the paucity of knowledge of African

[27] Roger Bastide and Florestán Fernandes, *Brancos e negros em São Paulo* (2d ed.; Africa, 1958).
São Paulo: Companhia Editôra Nacional, 1959).

prophetic movements of that era. The only one for which there is any information at all is the Antonin movement in northern Angola, in which a prophetess claimed to be St. Anthony resurrected. She announced the vanishing of the white man and the return to the golden age of the ancestors led by Ntotila, the king of São Salvador.[28]

The slave trade naturally brought ruin to the entire country, even if it did enrich dealers and, to a lesser extent, *pombeiros*, mulattos or Africans who conducted expeditions into the interior to bring back slaves to the coastal ports. With the end of the slave trade, the Portuguese found themselves in possession of an economically worthless country. Yet Angola served to nourish the thoughts of grandeur which had not ceased to haunt the Portuguese, a people who had at one time possessed the greatest empire in the world, only to see it fall before stronger adversaries.

This state of mind generated a period of military colonization during the nineteenth century which aimed at building a new empire from the Atlantic to the Indian Ocean. Troops were to proceed inward from the coastal regions of Angola and the few ports of Moçambique (former stations along the route to the Portuguese Indies). English opposition effectively halted the project but was not the only cause of its failure. The inhabitants fiercely resisted penetration, and it was not completed until 1918. Portuguese colonization could not, therefore, develop here as successfully as it did in Brazil. Nevertheless, was there not a "Luso-African" cycle during this period analogous to the "Luso-Brazilian" cycle? The Portuguese colonial who followed closely upon the military had not altered his mentality; he came without women, took Negro concubines, and mixed with the surrounding population; but the soldier remained by his side. The novels of Castro Soromenho, which depict the end of this period, give a dismal image of a stagnating society. It has been said that Angola experienced an "archaic" type of colonization, that the lack of economic development and advancement for the native peoples prevented its progression beyond the first stages of Brazilian colonization.[29] The modern system, however, which marks twentieth-century Portuguese colonization in Africa, emerges during this period. The system works approximately in the following manner: a planter notifies his government that he needs a certain number of men; they are supplied by the *chef de pôsto*, or district officer in the region. Native recruiters travel through the villages and gather together the necessary number of men to be sent to the planter.[30] In this system, which can be called Luso-African, forced labor replaces the slave

[28] Mgr. J. Cuvelier, *Relations sur le Congo du Père Laurent de Lucques (1700–1797)* (I.R.C.B., 1953).

[29] Perry Anderson, *Le Portugal et la fin de l'ultra-colonialisme* (Paris: F. Masperó, 1963); and Basil Davidson, *Black Mother* (London: V. Gollancz, Ltd., 1963).

[30] Marvin Harris, *Portugal's African Wards* (New York: American Committee on

labor typical of Brazil; but the system did not have the same effects as in Brazil, either because the number of whites was too small, or because the Portuguese colonial lost his particular trait of lusotropicology. The fact that in the region of most intense racial intermingling, the *luanda*, there are only 16,000 mulattos for 74,000 whites and 230,000 blacks exemplifies the difference between Portuguese Africa and Brazil, whose population becomes progressively whiter through miscegenation.

Resistance in this second period again took the form of messianic movements, although of a new sort, very different from those found in Brazil in the nineteenth century. The Kuyoka, a fetish-burning sect, appeared in the late 1800s. The Africans—the Ba-Kongo of Angola and the Ba-Kongo of French and Belgian Congo—quickly realized that the white man's strength resided in his religion. With this realization the messianic movements abandoned their dream worlds to enter the domain of practicality: "It is a classical form of iconoclasm which is translated by a need for renovation and for social reform, and which is principally obsessed with the struggle against sorcery." [31] This kind of movement continued up through World War II with the sect of Tonsi, in northern Angola. [32] The African saw his civilization threatened and his society torn apart through contact with the white man. He sought to fight his growing sense of alienation and the putrefaction in which he lived, after having tried, in vain, the expedient of force. He sought new techniques of renovation through a pseudo-Catholic religion which quickly acquired political overtones. The German Kaiser became the third and ironic element in the trinity which was to bring liberation to an Africa colonized by other European nations.

The twentieth century has been a century of progress. Portugal rapidly noticed that all her European neighbors were expanding economically while she floundered in misery. Her colonies appeared to be her only salvation, the only possible road to wealth. They were to provide two services: homes for the overflow of peasants, who could no longer eke out a living in the motherland; and centers of economic opportunity. By the end of World War II, more than 100,000 colonials had arrived in Angola and Moçambique, drawn by the rapid rise in value of colonial products. They were given the best lands, which they cultivated by a system of forced labor. These men did not resemble the old-style Portuguese colonial in either their mentality or their actions; they were peasants motivated by the desire for gain, and they were aloof from the Negro. They had no

---

[31] A. Doutreloux, *Prophetisme et leadership dans la société Kongo* (Louvain: Desclée de Brouwer, 1961), pp. 67–81.

[32] For information on this sect, see V. Lanternari, *Les mouvements religieux des peuples opprimés* (French translation; Paris: F. Masperó, 1962), p. 33.

money to invest and had to resort to outside help.[33] Names of companies in Portuguese hide the reality of world economic imperialism: the Companhia de Diamantes de Angola, whose "policy of violent and rapid extermination of indigenous culture" was denounced by Freyre, is a subsidiary of the Anglo-American Diamond Corporation, Limited; 70 percent of the Companhia Lobito Fuel Oil is controlled by the Compagnie Petrofina, a Belgian firm; A. Therese Berman controls the manganese production; Pechiney, the aluminum; the Dutch company Billiten Mautschappij, the bauxite; and the Krupp trust. Outside interests penetrate even as far as the agricultural sector: the Companhia Agrícola de Angola is controlled by the French Banque Mallet; and the Companhia Geral de Algodões do Moçambique, by the Société Générale de Belgique. All of these trusts have created a new Portuguese mentality, one that does not hesitate to uproot workers through forced labor or to seek additional resources by selling black labor to the mines in South Africa.

The Portuguese government will undoubtedly try to clothe this new kind of colonial mentality in the vestments of its old ideology of the "civilizing" influence of colonization. Balandier's statement in his *Sociologie actuelle de l'Afrique Noire* comes immediately to mind: "If the Portuguese government conceives of assimilation as a condition of equality, it is either because they know it is impossible to bring about or because they control it severely." The state handed over to the Catholic Church by contract the responsibility of primary-level education. However, classes are taught in the native language, thus preventing the rapid assimilation of the black man; and only a small minority benefits from educational facilities (90 percent of the population was illiterate in 1965).[34] As Marcello Caetano puts it, "the black man in Africa must be considered for the moment as a source of production" and not as a future citizen of Lusitania. It is not surprising, then, to see Brazilian immigrants to the Portuguese colonies return home so embittered. Waldir Freitas Oliveira is a good example of this kind of person. His judgment is unequivocal: "The Portuguese colonial failed in Angola because he could not build a multiracial society like the one which exists today in Brazil." [35]

How do the Africans react to this third and last stage in the history of Portuguese colonization? Those who remained in the bush are moving in increasing numbers to the cities. (This is, moreover, a general trend for all of Africa.) They hope to earn better salaries but meet instead with the

[33] On white colonization, see J. Denis, "Une colonie agricole en Afrique Tropicale: Cela, Angola Portugais," *Bulletin Agricole du Congo Belge*, II (1956), 387–424.

[34] Buanga Fele, "Crise de l'enseignement dans les colonies portugaises," *Présence Africaine* 7 (April-May 1956), pp. 85–93.

[35] W. Freitas Oliveira, "Brancos e pretos em Angola," *Afro-Asia* (Centro de Estudos Afro-Orientales, Universidade de Bahia), I (December 1965), 33–40.

resistance of a growing number of "poor whites" who monopolize even the lowest forms of employment, including positions as shop boys and waiters, and, of course, of the white-collar workers. Thus for the Africans a life of unemployment begins; they will waste away in the suburbs in miserable huts on unpaved streets with no water, electricity, or sewers. But contact with the white man and his religion leads to the creation of a folk religion, the Ilundo, which presents many analogies with the spiritism of Umbanda in Brazil, and with movements like the Macumba. An occultist religion, the Ilundo combines Bantu animism, spiritism, and Christianity. Sessions are held to invoke the spirits, who manifest themselves through the body of the entranced medium. Therapeutic magic is practiced (white medicine is expensive), as is sorcery (in order to seize the enemy's soul).[36] Like the spiritism of Umbanda, the Ilundo may gradually transform itself into a nationalist ideology; but this will not occur in the near future, for a Negro proletariat does not yet exist. The Negro remains outside the class-structured society.

The Ilundo is still an African religion; it is not a meeting place for the Negro, the mulatto, and the poor white. Resistance, therefore, takes place outside any religious framework. It is above all a movement of intellectuals who had believed in assimilation and who had been the first to feel—and painfully so—the discrimination against the colored laborer.[37] Included in this group are the poets of *Mensagem* in Angola and those of *Brado Africano* in Moçambique. But resistance movements eventually became more violent, taking up arms to combat a system of forced labor which often resulted in the tearing away of laborers from their homes and in their exile to regions in which work was found. (Fifty percent of the Negroes of São Tomé and Príncipe have been brought in from the outside—from Cape Verde, Angola, Moçambique—to work in the large plantations there.)

III

The image of lusotropicology upon which this argument has been based is a very ideal and internally consistent one. However, the reader has been thrown into a reality of chaotic, heterogenous, and sometimes contradictory facts: contradictions in space between the Brazilian process and the African one; contradictions in time between the different periods of colonization and Brazilian history. In concluding, it must be seen whether a rapid survey of these chaotic data will not, nevertheless, reveal some

[36] Oscar Ribas, *Ilundo* (Luanda: Museu de Angola, 1958).
[37] A. Margarido, "Incidences socio-economiques sur la poésie noire d'expression indigène," *Diogène*, XXXVII (1962), 53–80.

number of constants upon which to construct a theory. Lusotropicology consists in giving preference to a certain type of interethnic or interracial relations, of which Brazil offers us the most accurate model; but these relations are perceived and elaborated by whites. In order to study the reactions of the Indian or of the African slave to Portuguese colonization, the point of view of the victims has been taken, in which friction and tension were manifest and in which lusotropicology was exposed in its demystified form. Colonization served the economic interests of the mother country, which sought wealth first in fields of sugarcane and then in gold mines, but such financial gain remained inseparable from the two-fold vocation of "civilizing" and of "Christianizing." In the same manner, the reactions of the victims of colonization were first of an economic nature (against slavery or forced labor for the Indian, and against slavery for the Negro); but reaction also took the form of antiacculturation movements (Palmares, Santidade, etc.) and of "religious" resistance movements (the messianisms of Brazil and Portuguese Africa). This is the first constant: as long as Portuguese colonization remains "archaic," religion continues to be the focal point both for economic imperialism and for the resistance which it generates.

Amid all these tensions, however, a certain state of *modus vivendi* had to arise, dominated by one of the races involved. The movements of religious resistance in Brazil evolve from the initial messianic "dream" period to a "social adaptation" period marked by the desire for economic and social progress. (In Portuguese Africa these movements advanced no further than the first period, because of the halt in economic development and the subsequent transformation of the country into a warehouse and salesroom for the slave trade.) In short, resistance is not directed against adaptation to a multiracial society; it is, on the contrary, the very tool of adaptation and development. This is the second constant. Although it has been documented here only for Brazil, with the passage from a purely ethnic-based messianic movement to a folk messianic movement after the period of miscegenation, Engels's analysis of similar movements in Germany need only be recalled as evidence of such a constant.

In this kind of archaic colonial situation, nationalistic sentiment develops outside any religious context. It expresses the feeling that the mother country hinders economic development to the advantage of an alien few. But nationalism becomes a clear force only with the birth of an industrial society and the subsequent supremacy of the city over the countryside. As a result, this phenomenon appeared earlier in Brazil than in Portuguese Africa; it came at the end of the eighteenth century, provoked by the growth of cities, which in turn resulted from the growth of the mining industry. All that can be said when comparing Angola to Brazil is that the former is still in the period of intellectual revolt led by the poets and of a more spontaneous than organized revolt of the colored masses. It is not the task of this paper to study the origins and the growth of Brazilian nationalism: it was an affair between white men, an outgrowth of the opposition of the creoles to the Portuguese. This paper has considered only the role that the man of color was to play in this new ideology. Here again, it would seem, a number of constants have been unearthed:

1. Although a century late, nationalistic sentiment developed among blacks in the same manner and for the same reasons as it did among whites. It was retarded first by slavery and then by the effects of slavery. The black man uses nationalism as the basis of a program of social reform when he becomes aware that he is discriminated against—both racially and economically—to the advantage of another class. The greatness of the country requires an acceleration of his development. This is the first constant: there is a correlation between the concepts of nationalism and development.

2. Religion, which played such an important role in the primitive forms of social adaptation, ceases to be an essential factor. However, the new system retains certain characteristics of the old in the countries of Portuguese colonization where resistance movements (the *catimbó* of the Indian and the *candomblé* of the Negro) were the crystallization of a determined effort to cling to the indigenous and African religions against a Catholic religion which was more social than mystical. The spiritism of Umbanda appears to be a movement of newly realized proletarian unity behind a banner of social progress. It seeks to restore dignity to the man of color and strives for the unity and fraternity of all Brazilians inextricably bound together by the intermingling of bloods and religions. An analogous religion, the Ilundo, appeared in the Negro suburbs of the cities of Angola, perhaps to play an analogous role in the future. The constants in a multiracial society, during the first stages of industrialization before the appearance of a true trade-union force, the "people"—the folk—are inseparable from the "proletariat."

The question is whether Catholicism can avoid being the object of the revolution in social structure brought about by industrialization. Will it grasp the opportunity presented to it to develop a Christian trade unionism and to organize Christian socialist parties?[38]

---

[38] In this paper we have considered the role played by industrialization only from the point of view of the colored classes. The growth of the industrial society had, of course, as far-reaching effects for the white colonial: Portugal's present-day policies in tropical Africa are the inevitable consequences of the passage from mercantilism to industrial and financial capitalism. If lusotropicology does not wish to remain the nostalgic expression of a "glorious" past, it must transform itself by creating a new model of democratic cooperation among racial groups which have become social classes.

Part III　Conclusion

Chapter 12 Protest and Resistance in Brazil and Portuguese Africa: A Synthesis and a Classification

Ronald H. Chilcote

This conclusion is an attempt to provide a very general framework which not only embraces the individual studies in this volume but also incorporates the broad range of movements of protest and resistance which are identifiable throughout many centuries of history in Brazil and Portuguese Africa. No effort is made to include every instance of protest and resistance, but a simple classification is provided. Two classification outlines accompany the text. They are included to aid the reader in sifting through the many examples, but the breakdown employed should be used only as a guide. Many of the examples, events, and ideas are superficially classified. The categories, illustrated with prominent historical examples, are not meant to be mutually exclusive but do allow for a synthesis of the ideas and patterns found in the available literature. Extensive reference to the literature is made to lead the reader to some of the major primary and secondary source material. In general I confirm the identification of a vast number of protest and resistance movements, both in Africa and Brazil, but I also note on the African side a dearth of secondary material in the form of books, monographs, and articles. My primary objective thus is to conclude this volume with a critical bibliographical essay and a synthesis of ideas which I hope will point the way for future research by social scientists on prenationalist movements of protest and resistance.

I

BRAZIL

My classification of Brazilian movements is broken into several major categories and subcategories. All categories are exemplified by a variety of historical examples as listed in outline 1. My objectives in the following section are twofold: to identify, classify, and analyze each category and type of resistance and protest; and to support this discussion with extensive bibliographic reference to the literature.

Outline 1
Classification of Brazilian Movements
of Protest and Resistance

I. Indigenous forms of resistance to alien influence
  A. Indian response
    1. Migratory: traditional, mythical, and religious (Tupi-Guaraní)
    2. Traditional, pacific protest against colonialists (1539, 1562, 1569, and 1605)
    3. Messianic and magicoreligious movements of violent resistance (*Santidades*: Confederação de Tamoios, 1563; Santidade de Jaguaripe, 1584; 1626–1627; 1635–1637; 1778; 1779; and 1892)
    4. Other insurrections: Cabanagem (1833–1836); 1857; and 1880
  B. Afro-Brazilian response
    1. Refuge of escaped slaves to the *quilombo* (Palmares, 1630–1695; Rio de Janeiro, 1659; Alagôas, 1671; São Paulo, 1737–1787; Minas Gerais, 1756 and 1769; Santa Catarina, 1839)
    2. Muslim revolts (Bahia, 1807–1835)
    3. Armed popular insurrections (War of the Cabanos; Balaiada, 1838–1839)
II. Movements of Sebastianism, messianism, social banditry, and incipient social protest
  A. Sebastianist movements
    1. Rodeador, Pernambuco (1817)
    2. Pedra Bonita, Pernambuco (1839)
  B. Fanatical movements with millenarian ideology
    1. Canudos (1893–1897)
    2. Os Santarrões in Rio Grande do Sul (1872–1898)
    3. Contestado, Santa Catarina (1910–1914)
    4. Movement of Pedro Batista da Silva (1942–   )

C. Social banditry
    1. José Brilhante de Alencar e Souza and Jesuíno Brilhante (nineteenth century)
    2. António Silvino (1896–1914)
    3. Lampião (1918–1938)
D. Catholic resistance and protest
    1. Folk Catholicism and mysticism (Padre Cícero, 1889–1934; Beato Lourenço, 1933–1946)
    2. Protest and organization among socially conscious clergy (Ação Popular and rural syndicates)
E. Military protest and uprising in rural areas (Prestes Column, 1924–1927)
F. Peasant leagues and rural workers unions
    1. Communist (1928, 1946–48, and ULTAB, 1954–1964)
    2. Ligas Camponesas and Francisco Julião (1959–1964)
    3. Church-supported rural workers unions
III. Popular rebellions and discontent
A. Nationalist-oriented rebellions
    1. War of Mascates (1710–1715)
    2. Inconfidência Mineira (1789)
    3. Inconfidência da Bahia (1798)
    4. Revolution of Pernambuco (1817)
    5. Confederação do Equador (1824)
    6. War of Cabanos, Pernambuco, and Alagôas (1832–1835)
    7. Cabanagem (1833–1836)
    8. Republic of Farrapos (1835–1845)
    9. Sabinada, Bahia (1837)
    10. Balaiada, Maranhão (1838–1839)
    11. Praieira Revolution, Pernambuco (1848–1849)
B. Military coups and attempted coups in urban areas
    1. Rio (July 1922)
    2. São Paulo (July 1924)
    3. Revolution of October 24, 1930
C. Radical left and Communist-inspired revolts (Natal, Recife, and Rio in November 1935)
D. Labor disorders

INDIGENOUS FORMS OF RESISTANCE TO ALIEN INFLUENCE

The movements in this category divide racially into two groups, Indian and Afro-Brazilian. The resistance of the first is identifiable throughout periods both before and after the penetration in Brazil of the white European. The second group is associated with the slave trade and the repercussions of life on the sugar plantations, as well as with the tensions emanating from the friction and fusion of indigenous African with imposed European values and traditions.

The Indian movements, traditional in nature and based on mythical and religious inspiration, are documented in the early writings of Portuguese missionaries and colonial travelers and explorers who recorded the precolonial periodical migrations of Tupi-Guaraní tribes, first from the interior to the coast and later northward along the coast.[1] The dream of paradise (the *terra sem males,* or the "land without evil"), and the prophecy of a native leader, usually the medicine man, provided the mythical basis for these mass Indian migrations which, unlike later movements, were not provoked by population pressures, war, famine, or disease.[2]

Traditional Indian movements also were found after the European's arrival to Brazil; they manifested pacific forms of protest against the resulting conditions of deprivation and suppression which accompanied the social and religious order imposed by the colonial rulers. There were, for example, peaceful migratory movements in Pernambuco and Bahia, including that of 1539 (from the Brazilian coast to the Peruvian village of

[1] In his classification of movements in Africa, James S. Coleman suggests three basic categories: traditional, syncretistic, and modern. His two types of traditional movements, spontaneous resistance and nativistic or messianic, and one of his three types of syncretistic movements, separatist religious groups, are relevant to the following discussion. See his "Nationalism in Tropical Africa," *The American Political Science Review,* XLVIII (June 1954), 406; also see Ralph Linton, "Nativistic Movements," *American Anthropologist,* XLV (April–June 1943), 230–240.

[2] A thesis supported by René Ribeiro, "Brazilian Messianic Movements," in Sylvia L. Thrupp, *Millenial Dreams in Action* (Leiden: Comparative Studies in Society and History [Supplement II], Mouton and Company, 1962), pp. 55–57, and others who describe these early movements. Ribeiro cites two sources I have not examined: Kurt Nimuendaiu Unkel, "Legenda de la creación y juicio final del mundo," (São Paulo, 1944, mimeographed), in which the author based his analysis on information from a twentieth-century tribe that was continuing its ancestral migrations; and León Cadogan, *Ayvu Rapyta: testos míticos de los Mbyá-Guaraní del Guairá* (São Paulo: Boletim 227, Faculdade de Filosofia, Universidade de São Paulo, 1959), which presents further evidence of myths and legends collected among Indians on the Brazil-Paraguay border. Similar myths were documented among the Urubu Indians of the Gurupi River in northeastern Brazil; see Darcy Ribeiro, "Uirá vai ao encontro de Maira," *Anais, II Reunião Brasileiro de Antropologia* (Salvador, 1957), pp. 17–28. An updated version of Ribeiro's earlier study is his, "Movimentos messiânicos no Brasil," *América Latina,* XI (July-September 1968), 35–56.

Chachapoyas), brought about through the promises of a medicine man, Viaruzu, as well as those of 1562 (an abortive attempt of three thousand Indians in Bahia) and 1569 (in the region of Rio Real in Bahia). In 1605 some twelve thousand Indians sought refuge from the Portuguese and migrated to Maranhão, returning to Pernambuco only after the death of their native prophet. Four years later sixty thousand Tubinambás reached refuge on the island of Maranjó.[3]

Additionally, there was evidence of movements, usually of messianic and magicoreligious character, which violently resisted European domination or revolted against the imposition of new institutions and forms of coercion.[4] Often these were syncretistic movements or separatist religious groups that declared their independence from European religion; while stressing old tribal organization, custom, and ritual, they also tended to incorporate some elements of Catholicism. The *Santidades*, mass movements of Indians in the sixteenth century, were of such character. They sprang up among Indians subject to Jesuit discipline and forced acculturation, and their leaders promised not only freedom but restoration of old Indian traditions and religious ritual. Reacting against the social and religious order imposed by their colonial master, the leaders were followed into the interior where the search for the *terra sem males* could be continued without fear of interference by missionary and colonial authorities. Two movements are particularly noteworthy. The first, known as the Confederação de Tamoios, emerged in 1563 as an alliance of Indian groupings whose objective was to attack and exterminate the Portuguese invaders. Although details and documentary evidence are sparse, the movement has been characterized as a xenophobic insurrection of great significance which permitted formerly hostile tribes to unite in a common cause to confront the presence of the white man.[5] The second significant movement, the Santidade de Jaguaripe, occurred in 1584. Led by Tupanassu, the movement fused Indian and Catholic belief, and its ritual consisted of

---

[3] Maria Isaura Pereira de Queiróz, *O messianismo no Brasil e no mundo* (São Paulo: Dominus Editôra, Editôra da Universidade de São Paulo, 1965), pp. 142–146, gives detail on these and other movements discussed below. Other relevant sources include Alfred Métraux, *A religião dos Tupinambás* (São Paulo: Companhia Editôra Nacional, 1950); José Anchieta, *Cartas, informações, fragmentos históricos e sermões* (Rio de Janeiro: Civilização Brasileira, 1933); and Florestán Fernandes, *Organicão social dos Tupinambás*, 2d ed.; São Paulo: Corpo e Alma do Brasil (XI), Difusão Européia do Livro, 1963).

[4] Violence, prompted by messianic native prophets, occurred in São Paulo State, at Piratininga in April 1557 and at Pinheiras about 1590. See Queiróz, *op. cit.*, p. 146.

[5] Queiróz states that perhaps this was the first manifestation of indigenist nationalism. A brief discussion of the *Santidades* is in Estevão Pinto, *Muxárabis e balcões e outros ensaios* (São Paulo: Companhia Editôra Nacional, 1958), pp. 79–88; especially useful are the references cited on pp. 85–88.

songs, dances, prayers, prophecy, and confession, while the rite of baptism was requisite to entrance in the sect.

Other movements manifesting violence and syncretistic in nature were recorded, generally by Jesuit and Franciscan missionaries in southern Brazil. These accounts refer to the fame of a native prophet in the region of the Paraná River about 1626–1627; to Yaguacaporo who rallied escaped Indian slaves against Jesuit missions about 1635 to 1637; and to the native chief, Guiraverâ, who, in the area between the Incay and Ubay rivers, commanded a large center of resistance against the Jesuits. Other examples include the movements of the Chiriguano who resisted Franciscan attempts at colonization in southern Brazil: in 1778 (led by an unknown prophet against whom were sent several expeditions); in 1779 (led by a prophet who called upon his followers to abandon their European clothes and ways to seek a new world); and in 1892.[6]

During the nineteenth century several movements were active in Pará and Amazonas. The insurrections known as the Cabanagem (1833–1836) were led by Indians who had been sold as slaves and were the principal source of labor in an area where Africans were scarce. These Indians were able to seize power temporarily and maintain a popular government (this case, which is really more representative of a transitional than a traditional movement, is discussed briefly below). At the confluence of the Negro and Amazon rivers a mestizo named Cristo Alexandre revolted against the Brazilian government, and in 1857 a Venezuelan Indian, Venácio, formed a syncretistic movement. In the same region emerged the movements led by the Indian, Aniceto; Basílio Melguerio (in 1857); and Vicente Cristo (about 1880). All demanded the expulsion of the white settlers and officials.[7]

The causes for the many centuries of Indian resistance are perhaps obvious. First the Indian was forced to submit to a new pattern of economic life on the plantations; he became servile to a system of intense monocultural agricultural exploitation oriented to colonial exploitation. Second, the native was a victim of an imposed social structure in which he was re-

---

[6] See Queiróz, op. cit., p. 191, and Documentos para la historia Argentina Vol. XX (Buenos Aires, 1929), pp. 299–300, 348.

[7] Twentieth-century movements (the Mbüa tribe, for example, which migrated from Paraguay to São Paulo to the Brazilian coast during the period 1924 to 1946) have been noted by Egon Schaden and others; see his Aspectos fundamentais da cultura guaraní (São Paulo, 1954), and A mitologia heroíca de tribos indígenas do Brasil (Rio de Janeiro; Ministério de Educação e Cultura, 1959). A recent work that focuses on racial friction and tension is Roberto Cardoso de Oliveira, O índio e o mundo dos brancos: a situação dos Tukuna do Alto Solimões (São Paulo; Corpo e Alma do Brasil, Difusão Européia do Livro, 1964). A classic work on Indian culture is Estevão Pinto's Os indígenas do nordeste (São Paulo: Companhia Editôra Nacional, 1935); this book deals lightly with Indian resistance, however (see p. 195, for example).

duced to inferior status in a stratified society. These conditions led to reaction and protest, accompanied by reverence in the prophets or medicine men who gave to the movements a mythology and a dream of paradise, as well as instructions of how to get there. At the same time the Indians attempted to attain freedom and individual perfection through practice of old tribal customs and traditions. Enhanced authority was vested in the prophets whose promises and instruction were accepted by the lay chiefs. Thus the Indian was made conscious of his inferior social position in an alien white society. Seminomadic and accustomed to long journeys, he sought escape to the interior, where messianic authority could weld the formerly detribalized groups into a pantribal confederation; there both tradition and spirit could long endure.[8]

The reaction of the black African in Brazil was to the system of slavery, as well as to imposed alien cultural influences and a discriminating social class structure. Three forms of resistance and revolt can be suggested: first, the escape of black slaves from the coastal sugar plantations to the inland forests and the refuge of the *quilombo*; second, the revolts, organized to seize power, of Muslim slaves in Bahia; and third, occasional armed insurrections of a popular and spontaneous nature.[9]

The first type is best exemplified by Palmares, situated in the old captaincy of Pernambuco in the Serra da Barriga of present-day Alagôas. Palmares was significant for its successful repulse of dozens of white expeditions between 1630 and 1695, although it is not a unique instance in the history of black resistance.[10]

[8] Additional background information on the causes of Indian resistance is in Herbert Baldus, "Métodos e resultados de ação indigenista no Brasil," *Revista de Antropologia,* X (June-December 1962), 27–42; Eduardo Galvão, "Estudos sôbre a aculturação dos grupos indígenas do Brasil," *Revista de Antropologia,* V (June 1957), 67–74; Egon Schaden, "O problema indígena," *Revista de História,* XX, no. 42 (April-June 1960), 455–460. An attempt to document the seizure of Indian lands in Pernambuco is in Fragmon Carlos Borges, "As terras dos Indios," *Estudos Sociais,* 3–4 (September-December 1958), 399–404.

[9] These patterns, clearly identifiable in Brazilian history, are discussed briefly by Edison Carneiro in *Antologia do negro brasileiro* (Rio de Janeiro: Editôra Globo, 1950), especially in the introduction to Part IV, "As reações do negro," pp. 211–237. In his *Religiões negras: notas de etnografia religiosa* (Rio de Janeiro: Editôra Civilização Brasileira, 1936), pp. 2–3, Carneiro affirms that throughout national history "the Negro refused to submit to the social and political tyranny of the white man" and that "his reaction has been violent, at times armed insurrection." An interesting but superficial synthesis of the revolts is Aderbal Jurema, *Insurreições negras no Brasil* (Recife: Edições da Casa Mozart, 1935). Two forms of resistance open to black slaves in Brazil, both of which are inappropriate to the above discussion, were suicide and infanticide.

[10] Nina Rodrigues writes: "Como Palmares no Brasil, eram cidades ou estados compostos de escravos fugidos e aventureiros Atakpamê nos Ewês, Abeokutá no Egbá, mas sobretudo Aguê ou Ajiogô no Pequeno Pôpô, onde libertos do Brasil concorriam com mais epulsos do Dahomey, com Nagôs repelidos do centro e americanos da

The first Brazilian *quilombo*, organized in the interior of Bahia and destroyed about 1575, was not of great importance.[11] Others were founded in the *sertão*, but none was so celebrated as the Republic of Palmares, known as the "Tróia Negra."[12] Palmares was established at a time when Portugal, weakened under Spanish Hapsburg rule, was challenged by Dutch advances in colonial possessions in Brazil and Africa. The repercussions were twofold: the colonial administration and military were weakened by a scarcity of financial and human resources, and internal struggles characterized Portuguese rule in Brazil. This unstable situation allowed the successful escape of many slaves from sugar plantations, especially in Bahia and Pernambuco.

The black Africans, rejecting their role as slaves, were able to maintain order and organization through many decades of resistance to attempts to

---

Libéria. Mais estreitas são, porém, as suas analogias com Farabana no Bambuk, alto Senegal" (*Os Africanos no Brasil* [São Paulo: Companhia Editôra Nacional, 1932], pp. 119–120).

[11] The word *quilombo*, Angolan in origin, refers to "a house in a forest where fugitive Negroes are sheltered." Palmares was a refuge for twenty thousand blacks whose villages were protected by fortifications. In the surrounding area they cultivated mandioca and maize, raised animals, engaged in basket weaving, and in general preserved their traditional economic ways; see Gustavo Barroso, *Segredos e revelações da história do Brasil* (2d ed.; Rio de Janeiro: Edições O Cruzeiro, 1961), pp. 58–59. Aderbal Jurema described Palmares as an African state with "African agriculture, indigenous political organization, a well-organized police and internal defense network, and techniques of land cultivation." See his *Insurreições negras no Brasil* (Recife: Edições Mozart, 1935), p. 39.

[12] Among the major studies on Palmares are Edison Carneiro, *O quilombo dos Palmares, 1630–1695* (São Paulo: Editôra Brasiliense Limitada, 1947), an interpretative history plus documents of the period; Ernesto Ennes, *As guerras nos Palmares: subsídios para a sua história* (São Paulo: Companhia Editôra Nacional, 1938), comprising a collection of ninety-five documents selected by a Portuguese writer from colonial archives in Lisbon; and M. M. de Freitas, *Reino negro de Palmares* (Rio de Janeiro: Ministério da Guerra, Companhia Editôra Americana, 1954), a two-volume history. Less useful are a school text by Sérgio D. T. Macêdo, *Palmares, a tróia Negra* (Rio de Janeiro: Distribuidora Record 1963); a novel for young people by Lêda Maria de Albuquerque, *Zumbí dos Palmares* (Rio de Janeiro: Companhia Editôra Leitora, 1944); and a short novel containing historical inaccuracies by Jayme de Altavilla, *O quilombo dos Palmares* (São Paulo: Melhoramentos de São Paulo, 192[?]); (a musical, *Arena contra Zumbi* by Augusto Boal and Camargo Guarnieri was based on the historical event and presented with popular acclaim throughout Brazil during 1966 and 1967); see also Altavilla's "O quilombo dos Palmares . . . " in his *História da civilização das Alagôas* (4th ed.; Maceió, 1962). Useful and occasionally scholarly articles of varying quality are in the periodical literature, including Mário Behring, "A morte do Zumby," *Revista do Instituto Arqueológico e Geográfico Alagoana*, XIV, no. 57 (1930), 142 ff.; João Blaer, "Diário da viagem do capitão João Blaer aos Palmares em 1645," *Revista do Instituto Arqueológico e Geográfico Pernambucano*, X, no. 56 (1902), 87–96; Provina Cavalcanti, "A república negra," *Revista do Brasil*, 1st phase, 68 (August 1921), 395–398; Duvitiliano Ramos, "A posse útil da terra entre os quilombolas," *Estudos Sociais*, I, no. 3–4 (September-December 1958), 393–398; and R. K. Kent, "Palmares: An African State in Brazil," *Journal of African History*, VI, no. 2 (1965), 161–175.

destroy their republic. Although detailed information on political structure is scant, the refuge was constituted of *mocambos* or villages where local authority was vested in each chief. These chiefs represented a kind of elite or oligarchy which banded together in times of war and crisis to deliberate major issues. Such meetings were held in Macaco, the largest *mocambo*, which housed five thousand blacks and the supreme chieftain.[13] Each *mocambo* apparently had a judicial system and allocated land to families. Being largely self-sufficient, each *mocambo* based its economy on the raising of sugarcane, maize, and bananas, and on handicraft industries such as basket weaving or pottery making.

Trade with neighboring settlements frequently degenerated into armed fighting, and black raids on plantations and towns yielded supplies and escaped slaves. The *quilombo* enticed the slave to rebel, escape, and fight for freedom. The response of white settlers and government officials was retaliation in the form of *entradas*, or military expeditions, to the relatively unknown interior with the objective of conquest and "pacification" of the former slaves, but the terrain was rugged and roads did not exist over which supplies could be transported. The rebels' strategy was essentially defensive, and when attacked, they usually retreated and established their *mocambo* elsewhere.

Palmares evolved through three phases.[14] A first phase, initiated about 1630, terminated in 1644–1645 with the Dutch seizure and burning of *quilombos* near Pôrto Calvo. The expulsion of the Dutch from Pernambuco in 1654 accompanied the reestablishment of Palmares into a confederation of small villages, united under one chief; the reconstituted Palmares, however, was again overcome, this time by a series of Portuguese expeditions sent by the governor, Dom Pedro de Almeida, during 1675 to 1678. The Palmares experiment, however, was not finally crushed until 1695, by the combined force of six thousand soldiers and *bandeirantes*, or armed bands of early explorers.[15]

Other quilombo insurrections are identifiable in Brazilian history.[16] Au

---

[13] Carneiro, *O quilombo*, p. 12, describes Palmares as dominated by an oligarchy of chiefs, more or less despots, comprising "the Master de Campo Ganga-Muiça, the president of the Conselho Gana-Zona, the Mocambo chiefs, Amaro and Pedro Capacaça, the 'potentate' Acaiuba, the military chiefs Gaspar, Ambrósio, and João Tapuya—headed by the King, Ganga-Zumba and later by the 'military general,' Zumbí, chief of the *Mocambo* and nephew of the king."

[14] A description of these phases and early documentation is in Rodrigues, *op. cit.*, pp. 109–143; on pp. 115–16 he cites names and the specific location of various refuges.

[15] Carneiro, *O quilombo*, p. 26, identifies two Dutch (in 1644 and 1645) and fourteen Luso-Brazilian (between 1667 and 1694) expeditions sent against Palmares.

[16] The first of the *quilombos* is usually identified as that destroyed in Bahia in 1575. Others were reported in existence in 1597 and 1607. Scattered references to these rebellions and others mentioned above are in Miguel Costa Filho, "Quilombos,"

thorities viewed with alarm the *quilombos* established outside Rio de Janeiro by runaway slaves and, although in 1659 a military expedition under Manuel Jordão da Silva destroyed *quilombos* then in existence, black Africans sought a new refuge and reportedly continued to harrass the neighboring population.[17] *Quilombos* appeared in Alagôas in 1671; along the São Francisco River during the first quarter of the eighteenth century; and in São Paulo State during 1737–1787. *Quilombos* in Minas Gerais, with a population of perhaps twenty thousand blacks, were well-organized and certainly second in importance only to Palmares; a black revolt against white landowners occurred on April 15, 1756, and the ensuing retaliation destroyed many *quilombos*, including one at Sabambaio in 1769.[18] Destruction of other *quilombos* included that of Carlotta in Mato Grosso in 1770, São José de Maranhão in 1772, two in São Paulo State during 1778, and one in Cachoeira, Bahia, in 1798. During the nineteenth century a *quilombo* was discovered in Linhases, São Paulo, in 1810; another in Minas, formed by fugitive blacks from São Paulo, in about 1820; several near Recife known to exist by 1828 and led by a chief, Malunguinho; one known as Maravilha in the Amazon and destroyed in 1855. Perhaps the most important of the nineteenth-century *quilombos* was that of Manoel Congo in the forests of Santa Catarina near Petrópolis, destroyed in 1839.[19]

A second form of black resistance, that of Muslim revolts organized against white authority with the objective of seizing power and abolishing Christianity, occurred in Bahia during 1807 to 1835. The black Muslims, or *malés*, were motivated by more than politicoreligious considerations, however, for like their predecessors, they were primarily rebelling against oppressive slavery and economic conditions.[20] Like Palmares and the seventeenth- and eighteenth-century *quilombo* insurrections, the rebellions of the *malés* coincided with general instability in Brazil, marked by the Pernambuco revolt of 1817, independence in 1822, the Confederação do Equador in 1824, and the later Cabanos and other popular uprisings.

The period of revolts divides into three principal phases.[21] The first phase comprised a series of revolts by Haussás, runaway slaves originally

Estudos Sociais, III, no. 7 (March 1960), 334–360; III, no. 9 (October 1960), 95–109; III, no. 10 (July 1961), 233–247; and Roger Bastide, *Les religions africaines au Brésil* (Paris, 1960), pp. 126–135.

[17] See "Quilombolas no Rio de Janeiro," in Carneiro, *Antologia do negro brasileiro*, p. 213.

[18] Nina Rodrigues, *Os africanos no Brasil*, pp. 143–147, and Bastide, *op. cit.*, p. 129.

[19] Under the pseudonym of Marcos, Carlos Lacerda focused on this movement in *O quilombo de Manoel Congo* (Rio de Janeiro: R. A. Editôra, 1935).

[20] Conflicting interpretations of the political, religious, and economic character of the revolts is discussed by Edison Carneiro, *Religiões negras: notas de etnografia religiosa* (Rio de Janeiro: Editôra Civilização Brasileira, 1936), pp. 104–105.

[21] Useful sources of the *malé* revolts are Nina Rodrigues, *op. cit.*, chap. ii, "Os Negros Mahometanos no Brasil," pp. 59–107; and Abelardo Duarte, *Negros Muçul-*

from Central Africa. A small outbreak on May 28, 1807, was followed by scattered disturbances throughout 1807 to 1809. A second revolt occurred on January 6, 1809, with Haussás allied with Nagôs, former rivals. The third and largest of the revolts took place on February 28, 1813, resulting in the death of eight whites and the burning of houses and plantations. Four major uprisings and the establishment of a *quilombo* in the forests of Urubú by Nagôs marked a second phase. The four uprisings took place in Pirajá on December 17, 1826; on the sugar plantations of Recôncavo in April 22, 1827; near Pirajá on March 11, 1828; and on April 10, 1830, when some twenty blacks mounted an attack. A final phase revolved about a major revolt of January 24, 1835, led by a Nagô, Guilhermina; the objective of the fifteen hundred rebels was the establishment of a Muslim state, but their uprising was overcome by Bahian police.[22]

A third type of black African resistance emerged in the unstable period of empire and struggle for independence during the first half of the nineteenth century. In Pernambuco the decline in the sugar economy affected the lives of slaves who occasionally rebelled. Economic problems also affected a large group of free mulatto artisans who were participants in a number of revolts. A plot by black slaves in 1814 may have influenced the rebel leaders of the 1817 revolution to recruit hundreds of slaves into their ranks.[23] In the essay in this volume, Manuel Correia de Andrade discusses the role of the Afro-Brazilian in the War of the Cabanos.[24] Black slaves also participated in the Balaiada revolt in Maranhão during 1838 and

manos nas Alagôas: os Malés (Maceió: Edições Caeté, 1958), which contains a short selection on the Bahia revolts, pp. 29–35, as well as a discussion of a planned *malé* revolt in Alagôas in 1815, pp. 42–50. One of the best sources which contains analysis and twenty-five documents is Clóvis Moura, *Rebeliões da senzala: quilombos, insurreições* (São Paulo: Ediçoes Zumbí, 1959). Another documentary source is Silva Barros, "Chronica dos acontecimentos da Bahia, 1809–1828," *Anaes do Arquivo Público da Bahia*, XXVI (1938), 49–95.

22 Querino states that the Arquivo Público de Bahia holds two hundred and thirty-four trial records of rebellious Africans, including those of one hundred and sixty-five Nagôs and twenty-one Haussás; see Manuel Querino, *A raça africana e os seus costumes* (Salvador: Livraria Progresso, 1955), pp. 112–113. Moura, *op. cit.*, pp. 184–188, identifies a "forgotten" uprising in 1844, suggesting that this is the termination date of the *malé* rebellions. The historian, Pedro Calmon has written a novel about the events of 1835, *Malés: a insurreição das senzalas* (Rio de Janeiro: Pro Luce, 1933).

23 See L. Borges, "A participação dos homens de côr na Revolução de 1817," *Estudos Sociais*, III (April 1962), 485–498.

24 In addition to Andrade's writings cited below, see "Documentos dos quilombos de Goiana, Catucas," *Revista do Instituto Histórico de Goiana*, 2d ser. I (1947–1948), 7–31, which includes twenty-one documents dated 1829. Interestingly, the participation of the Afro-Brazilian in the Cabanos and other revolts coincided roughly with one of the most famous of slave rebellions in the United States, that of Nat Turner. See, for example, the monograph by Herbert Aptheker, *Nat Turner's Rebellion* (New York: Humanities Press, 1966). The Turner rebellion was very different in nature from the Cabanos revolts, however.

1839. Nearly half the population of the state was black, yet the leadership of the rebellious movement was unable to draw this black element into the fighting force. Instead the slaves resorted to sporadic and disconnected revolts; and, once escaped, they moved to *quilombos* along the coast.[25] Like the Indian, the African in Brazil resisted the slave conditions of the colonial period. He frequently opposed the inferior status to which he was relegated in Brazilian society. Palmares, the establishment of other *quilombos*, the *malês* insurrections, and Afro-Brazilian involvement in nineteenth and even twentieth-century revolts were responses to such conditions in an alien society. Nevertheless, Brazilian writers have emphasized the integration of the African into Brazilian society. Nina Rodrigues and Artur Ramos contributed the pioneer studies of the African element in Brazil, and Gilberto Freyre followed with studies of the role of the slave in the transitional phase of Brazilian society from a rural to an urban patriarchy.[26] Brazilian culture and literature have been strongly influenced by the African,[27] but the thesis of racial harmony, which is so much a part of Freyre's lusotropical conceptions,[28] has been discredited by recent empirical evidence despite the prevailing myths that continue even today.[29] That sharp distinctions prevail between black and other Brazilians helps us to understand the persistence of black religious sects in the coastal urban life, so aptly analyzed by Roger Bastide in his essay in this volume.[30]

[25] See Caio Prado Júnior, "A revolta dos Balaios," in Carneiro, *Antologia do negro Brasileiro*, pp. 227–229. Brief reference to the role of the Negro in the revolts of Bahia is made in Luiz Vianna Filho, *O negro na Bahia* (Rio de Janeiro: Livraria José Olympio Editôra, 1946), especially pp. 110 ff.

[26] The leader of a sailors' rebellion in 1910, for example, was João Cândido, a black Brazilian; see Edmar Morel, *A revolta da Chibata; subsídios para a história da revolta na Esquadra pelo marinheiro João Cândido em 1910* (Rio de Janeiro: Irmãos Pongetti Editôres, 1959).

[27] Among Gilberto Freyre's important studies are *The Mansions and the Shanties: The Making of Modern Brazil* (New York: Alfred A. Knopf, 1963), and *The Masters and the Slaves* (abridged, rev. from 2d ed.; New York: Alfred A. Knopf, 1964).

[28] See, for example, the analysis and bibliography in the special issue of *African Forum*, II, no. 4 (Spring 1967), 1–109, entitled "The Negro and Brazilian Literature," especially the bibliographic essay by Manuel Diegues Júnior, pp. 90–109.

[29] See, for example, Gilberto Freyre, *The Portuguese and the Tropics* (Lisbon, 1961).

[30] Evidence of racial distinctions is presented by Marvin Harris and Conrad Kotak, "The Structural Significance of Brazilian Categories," *Sociologia*, XXV (1963), 203–208. Evidence of racial prejudice is extensively presented in the results of a survey, "Começo de conversa: nosso tema não é o preconceito, mas a fraternidade," *Realidade*, II, no. 19 (October 1967), 21–60.

Additionally, see Roger Bastide and Florestán Fernandes, *Brancos e negros em São Paulo* (2d ed.; São Paulo: Brasiliana [305], Companhia Editôra Nacional, 1959); and Fernando Henrique Cardoso and Octávio Ianni, *Côr e mobilidade social em Florianópolis . . .* (São Paulo: Brasiliana [307], Companhia Editôra Nacional, 1960). René Ribeiro, whose essay on messianism is included in the present volume, has focused attention on the African cults; see, for example, his *Cultos afrobrasileiros do Recife*

MOVEMENTS OF SEBASTIANISM, MESSIANISM, SOCIAL BANDITRY, AND INCIPIENT PROTEST

An overview of protest movements in rural Brazil reveals a variety of types, including movements of Sebastianistic inspiration, millenarian ideologies, social banditry, Catholic resistance, military struggle, and peasant organization.

Sebastianistic movements have been based by their leaders on the belief that Sebastião, the Portuguese king lost in the battle of Alcáçer Kebir in 1578, would return to punish the wicked and lead the faithful. Many such movements existed both in Portugal and Brazil.[31] Two important movements emerged during the nineteenth-century Brazil. The first occurred about 1817 at Rodeador in the southern part of the northeastern state of Pernambuco and was led by Silvestre José dos Santos, the prophet and ex-soldier who, with some four hundred followers, established his "City of the Terrestial Paradise." This collective society included religious organization under Santos's direction and that of a lieutenant and twelve "wise men." Subordinate to these twelve men was an army, and the existence of such a force apparently prompted the state governor to take suppressive action, resulting in the massacre of the movement on October 25, 1820, with Santos managing to escape.[32] The second movement was known as the "Enchanted Kingdom" of Pedra Bonita and also evolved in Pernambuco. João Antônio dos Santos was the early leader of the movement, but after he was dissuaded from continuing, his brother-in-law, João Ferreira, assumed command. In prophesying the return of Sebastião, the prophet called for human sacrifice, and on May 14, 1838, his own father was the first to be slaughtered. Three days later, thirty children, twelve men, eleven women, and fourteen dogs met a similar fate; finally, "King" Ferreira was sacrificed, and immediately thereafter local authorities suppressed the movement, dispersing and imprisoning many of its followers.[33]

. . . (Recife: Instituto Joaquim Nabuco, 1952). Also Waldemar Valente, "Influências islâmicas nos grupos de culto afro-brasileiros de Pernambuco," *Boletim do Instituto Joaquim Nabuco de Pesquisas Sociais*, 4 (1955), 7–32. For comparative perspective and insight into black oppression, see Frantz Fanon, "The Ordeal of the Black Man," in *Social Change: The Colonial Situation*, ed. by Immanuel Wallerstein (New York: John Wiley and Sons, 1966), pp. 75–87; and Eldridge Cleaver, *Soul on Ice* (New York: McGraw-Hill Book Company, 1968).

[31] An historical synthesis of the origins and evolution of Sebastianism is in J. Lúcio de Azevedo, *A evolução do sebastianismo* (2d ed.; Lisbon: Livraria Clássica Editôra, 1947), pp. 181, especially the brief discussion of movements in Brazil, pp. 113–120.

[32] The best analysis of Rodeador is René Ribeiro, "O episódio da Serra do Rodeador (1817–1820): um movimento milenar e sebastianista," *Revista de Antropologia*, VIII, no. 2 (December 1960), 133–144. There is also a brief account in Queiróz, *op. cit.*, pp. 198–200.

[33] For details and analysis of Pedra Bonita, see Nina Rodrigues, *As collectividades*

Sebastianism was also an element in other fanatical movements in which a millenarian ideology was paramount. The leaders of such movements usually assumed the role of messiah or prophet or a new saint to lead the followers in the belief that they would be saved on the day that the world would end and a new kingdom be established. Three characteristics generally are evident in millenarian movements: first, the total rejection of the present evil world and a longing for another and better one; second, an ideology usually in the context of Judeo-Christian messianism; third, a vagueness about how the new society will evolve.[34]

Canudos is a conspicuous example of such a millenarian movement, although influences other than Sebastianism played a part. Canudos was established in the backlands of the Northeast by a religious fanatic, Antônio Vicente Mendes Maciel, better known as Antônio Conselheiro, whose followers included peasants, thieves, and prostitutes, all of whom lived in poverty and were alienated from society. Together they were to found a heaven on earth. With the overthrow of the emperor and the establishment of a republic, Antônio injected into his preachings criticism of the new government and its policies. The authorities immediately perceived Canudos as a threat and federal troops were sent to assure order. Canudos never surrendered. Its population was completely eliminated by the fourth expedition sent in 1897, the earlier three having suffered defeat and failure. Although Canudos fell, the people fought fiercely and stubbornly; their early victories over the federal troops had signified for the illiterate peasants of the backlands that they could resist the *status quo* and seek an alternative to their plight. Antônio had offered the people salvation, and they had resisted the authorities magnificently. The end of the world that Antônio preached did not come, but the example of powerful resistance remained with the *sertanejos*. Antônio's ideas were religiously and fanatically inspired, yet his actions became socially and politically very significant.

---

anormaes (Rio de Janeiro: Civilização Brasileira, 1939), especially pp. 135–139; Artur Ramos in a note to this work cites a monograph by Antônio Atico de Souza Leite, *Fanatismo religioso. Memória sôbre o reino encantado na camarca de Villa Bella, com um juizo crítico do Conselheiro Tristão de Alencar Araripe* (2d ed.; Juiz de Fóra, 1898). A novelistic account is in José Lins do Rego, *Pureza, Pedra Bonita, Riacho doce* (Rio de Janeiro: Livraria José Olympio Editôra, 1961). See also Antônio Atico de Souza Leite, "Memória sôbre a Pedra Bonita ou Reino Encantado na camarca de Vila Vela, província de Pernambuco," *Revista do Instituto Arquelógico e Geográfico de Pernambuco*, LX (December 1903), 217–248. See also T. A. Araripe Júnior, *O reino encantado, chronica sebastianista* (Rio de Janeiro: Typographia da Gazeta de Notícas, 1878).

[34] Hobsbawm, *Primitive Rebels: Studies in Archaic Forms of Social Movements in the 19th and 20th Centuries* (Manchester, England: University of Manchester Press, 1959), pp. 57–58.

From Euclydes da Cunha's classic study of Canudos we can draw some interesting observations.[35] First, Canudos constituted a primitive, barbarian social collectivity—integrated, unified, and homogeneous. Newcomers turned over to the community some 90 percent of what they brought with them; this was then "an absolute community of land, pastures, flocks, and herds, and the few cultivated products, the landlords receiving merely their quota, while the rest went to the 'society.' " Second, this community was inbued with a common sense of destiny and identity—for "all ages, all shades of racial coloring." A sense of will, motivation, and consciousness was instilled in the people in their attempt to escape materialistic life and seek new values in religious destiny. Canudos, for example, became a sanctuary for criminals and others who, in turn, became rehabilitated and converted to the common cause. Third, Antônio's charismatic fanaticism seems to have been the essential element that allowed Canudos to evolve as a unified community. His attack on the Republic may well have been a means of maintaining his charisma and authority internally. As the community perceived the exogenous threat to its existence, its internal cohesion strengthened.[36]

[35] Euclydes da Cunha, *Rebellion in the Backlands* [*Os sertões*] (Chicago: University of Chicago Press, 1944), especially pp. 143–169.

[36] An account of Canudos and the psychological aspects of Antônio's behavior is in Nina Rodrigues, *As collectividades anormaes*, in the chapter entitled "A loucura epidémica de Canudos," pp. 50–77. A romantic account is in R. B. Cunningham Graham, *A Brazilian Mystic: Being the Life and Miracles of Antônio Conselheiro* (London: William Heinemann, 1920). A useful annotated bibliography has been compiled by José Calasans, "Contribuição ao estudo da campanha de Canudos," *Revista Brasiliense*, 17 (May–June 1958), 176–190. Among useful other works consulted by this writer, see several books about Cunha and his work, including the sympathetic and well-documented study by Olímpio de Sousa Andrade, *História e interpretação de "Os Sertões,"* (São Paulo: Edart Livraria-Editôra, 1960); Francisco Venâncio Filho, *A glória de Euclydes da Cunha* (Rio de Janeiro: Brasiliana, 5th ser. [193], Companhia Editôra Nacional, 1940); Eloy Pontes, *A vida dramática de Euclydes da Cunha* (Rio de Janeiro: Coleção Documentos Brasileiros [13], Livraria José Olympio Editôra, 1938); and Sylvio Rabello, *Euclides da Cunha*, (2d ed.; Rio de Janeiro: Editôra Civilização Brasileira, 1966). An attack on Eloy Pontes is in Dilermando de Assis, *A tragédia da piedade. Mentiras e calúnias da "A vida dramática de Euclides da Cunha"* (Rio de Janeiro: Edições O Cruzeiro, 1952). An attack on Cunha by Dante de Mello, *A verdade sôbre "Os Sertões"* (Rio de Janeiro: Biblioteca do Exército-Editôra, 1958), is rebutted by Luiz Viana Filho in *A margem d' "Os Sertões"* (Salvador: Livraria Progresso Editôra). Works focusing on military events include: Tristão de Alencar Araripe, *Expedições militares contra Canudos, seu aspecto marcial* (Rio de Janeiro: Imprensa do Exército, 1960); Henrique Duque-Estrada de Macêdo Soares, *A guerra de Canudos* (Rio de Janeiro: Typografia Altina, 1902); and J. de Costa Palmeira, *A campanha do Conselheiro* (Rio de Janeiro: Calvino Filho, ed., 1934). José Calasans has collected the popular poetry of the backlands in *No tempo de Antônio Conselheiro* (Salvador: Livraria Progresso Editôra, n.d.); and Paulo Dantas has romanticized Canudos in a novel, *Purgatório* (São Paulo: Editôra Piratininga, n.d.), and in an essay, *Quem foi Antônio Conselheiro?* (São Paulo: Empresa Gráfica Carioca, 1966). Hundreds of

Two other messianic movements stand out in Brazilian history. One, known as the Mucker movement, or "os Santarrões," emerged along the Sinos River in the state of Rio Grande do Sul. The movement of João Jorge and Jacobina Maurer evolved in conditions quite different from those of the Northeast. Here the climate was not dry and the population comprised mostly European immigrants and their descendents. Religious instruction was lacking and doctors were scarce. João was an illiterate carpenter and a healer of the sick. His wife suffered from fits of epilepsy which led her followers to believe that she possessed special powers. On May 19, 1872, she announced to a large gathering that she was Christ reincarnated and then chose twelve disciples, the first being her husband, Jorge. When authorities and an armed force attempted to suppress the movement a few years later, violence and bloodshed ensued; Jacobina was killed, but her followers, isolated in small groups, carried on until about 1898.[37] The other movement, known as Contestado, also was in Southern Brazil in the backlands of the state of Santa Catarina. There a messianic movement developed during the period 1910 to 1914. In late 1913, José Maria, the "brother" of a famous prophet, João Maria, founded a "Holy City" in the town of Taquaraçu. The local *coronel*, or landowner–political boss, fearful of losing his power, alerted the governor who in turn dispatched a force of soldiers in late December to dislodge José Maria and his followers. A first attack failed in the face of the defenders' tactic of remaining in the forests as guerrilla fighters. A second government attack two months later dispersed the rebels, who retreated to the interior. Later in 1914 the rebel force issued a Monarchist Manifesto and called for the launching of a "Holy War" on September 1. The complaints of local landowners prompted the government to send another force of troops; after a month's battle, these troops finally penetrated the defenses of the rebels' stronghold, lo-

---

articles have been written, including Pedro Muniz Aragão, "Canudos e os monarquistas," *Revista do Instituto Arquelógico e Geográfico de Pernambuco*, XXXIX (1944), 205–254; Fernando Azevedo, "O homen Euclides da Cunha," *Revista de História*, III (January–March 1952), 3–30; João Cruz Costa, "Euclides da Cunha e os filósofos," *Revista Brasiliense*, 24 (September–October 1959), 110–120; Paulo Dantas, "Cancioneiro de Lampião," *Revista Brasiliense*, 29 (May–June 1960), 210–211, and "O drama de Antônio Conselheiro," *Revista Brasiliense*, 13 (September–October 1957), 125–132, and "Viagem definitiva a Canudos," *Revista Brasiliense*, 21 (January–February 1959), 141–161; Rui Facó, "A guerra camponesa de Canudos," *Revista Brasiliense*, 20 (November–December 1958), 128–151, and "A guerra camponesa de Canudos," *Revista Brasiliense*, 21 (January–February 1959), 162–183; Noel Nascimento, "Canudos, Contestado e o fanatismo religioso," *Revista Brasiliense*, 44 (November–December 1962), 63–67; Francisco Xavier de Oliveira, "Reminiscências da guerra de Canudos," *Revista do Instituto Geográfico e Histórico da Bahia*, LXVIII (1943), 102–107. A recent publication is Nertan Macêdo, *Antônio Conselheiro (A morte em vida do beato de Canudos)* (Rio de Janeiro: Colecção Presença Brasileira, Gráfica Record Editôra, 1969), pp. 181.

[37] The Mucker movement is described in detail by Queiróz, *op. cit.*, pp. 220–230.

cated strategically in the Serra de Santa Maria. The rebel chiefs fled, some continued the struggle, and others abandoned their cause. By 1915 most of the rebel commanders were imprisoned. Traces of the movement persisted, however, and a reunion of families was held in Taquaraçu as late as 1954 in anticipation of the return of João Maria.[38]

In 1942 another messianic movement appeared under the leadership of Pedro Batista da Silva, known as a healer of the sick, in the backland interior of Alagôas, Sergipe, and Pernambuco. Having been expelled by authorities from municipalities in which he had been making pilgrimages, Pedro moved south to the poverty-stricken and isolated Bahian town of Santa Brígida. There Pedro became a landowner and merchant dedicated to caring for the thousands of pilgrim visitors and settlers. As the town prospered, eventually it became a district and later a municipality. Pedro's followers believed him to be the reincarnation of Padre Cícero, the famous priest of Juàzeiro in Ceará, and the community spirit reminded many that a new Canudos was in the making.[39]

Social banditry constituted another form of protest movement in backlands rural Brazil, especially in the Northeast. As Amaury de Souza emphasizes in his essay in this volume, the rise of the banditry contributed to the decay of the patriarchical order in the backlands, and rural violence provided the masses with an alternative to their traditional dependency on the local chieftain. The bandit, known variously as *cangaceiro, jagunço, bandido,* and *capanga,* was organized into professional bands most of which maintained strict order and discipline, murdering loyally at the command

[38] It should be noted that Contestado refers to the area in which these events took place and that the area was a "contested" border region claimed by both Santa Catarina and Paraná, but policed by neither. The major writings on Contestado include a firsthand account by a military participant in the war, Herculano Teixeira d'Assumpção, *A campanha do Contestado (as operações da Columna do Sul)* (2 vols.; Belo Horizonte: Imprensa Oficial do Estado de Minas Gerais, 1917). Two definitive monographs are Maurício Vinhas de Queiróz, *Messianismo e conflito social: a guerra sertaneja do Contestado, 1912–1916* (Rio de Janeiro: Editôra Civilização Brasileira, 1966); and a doctoral dissertation by Maria Isaura Pereira de Queiróz, *La "Guerre Sainte" au Brésil: le mouvement messianique du Contestado* (São Paulo: Boletim 187, Faculdade de Filosofia, Ciências e Letras da Universidade de São Paulo, 1957), and in her "O movimento messiânico do Contestado," *Revista Brasileira de Estudos Políticos,* 9 (July 1960). 118–139. Also see Oswaldo R. Cabral, *João Maria, interpretação da Campanha do Contestado* (São Paulo: Companhia Editôra Nacional, 1960), and Brasil Gerson, *Pequena história dos fanáticos do Contestado* (Rio de Janeiro: Ministério da Educação e Cultura, 1955). A brief synthesis is in Queiróz, *O messianismo no Brasil,* pp. 246–260. A useful and recent article is Noel Nascimento, "Contestado, guerra camponêsa do Brasil," *Revista Brasiliense,* 50 (November-December 1963), 86–88.

[39] Details of this movement are in Queiróz, *O messianismo no Brasil,* pp. 272–283. Queiróz focuses on another example of messianism in the state of São Paulo in "Tambaú, cidade dos milagres," pp. 131–193, in Queiróz et al., *Estudos de sociologia e história* (São Paulo: Editôra Anhêmbí, 1957).

of a landowner or bandit chief, looting villages and *fazendas* as a "right" of war, but otherwise disdaining robbery as a disgraceful practice.[40] His activity was similar to the social bandit behavior described by Eric Hobsbawn: "a rather primitive form of organized social protest . . . regarded as such by the poor, who consequently protect the bandit, regard him as their champion, idealize him, and turn him into a myth."[41] A person becomes a social bandit because he has done something legally wrong but not considered as criminal by local tradition. He is likely to be protected by the population, persecuted by the authorities.

Several causes have been identified to explain the emergence and persistence of the social banditry. Early studies attributed the banditry to racial and genetic factors.[42] Other studies emphasize psychic disorders, sometimes related to the racial miscegenation of black, brown, and white peoples.[43] Still others explain banditry and rural violence as a response to the tensions emanating from Brazil's dualistic society divided into primitive rural and modern urban elements.[44] Simpler explanations attributed the banditry to the sociocultural backwardness of the backlands, the lack of communications, and the inability to guarantee justice.[45] Some studies make reference to the geological structure of the Northeast, its excessive heat and recurring droughts, and the corresponding failure of administrative authorities to remedy the social and economic difficulties that are a consequence of these physical conditions.[46] Perhaps to some degree all

[40] Without exception most *cangaceiros* who were imprisoned were eventually released for exemplary conduct and all were able to integrate satisfactorily into society, usually as leaders in their respective vocations. This information based on an interview with Estácio de Lima, October 26, 1967. See also his interesting book which relates his personal experience with those *cangaceiros* imprisoned in Salvador; the Nina Rodrigues Institute contains the heads of Lampião and others. Lima's book is entitled *O mundo estranho dos cangaceiros* (Salvador: Editôra Itapoã, 1965).

[41] Hobsbawm, *op. cit.,* 13. The social bandit is one of several types of rebels discussed by Hobsbawm whose examples are Robin Hood in England, Janosik in Poland and Slovakia, and Diego Corrientes in Andalusia. Hobsbawm's *Bandits* (New York: Delacorte Press, 1969) also is useful for an analysis of the social bandit.

[42] See, for example, Djacir Menezes, *O outro nordeste* (Rio de Janeiro: Livraria José Olympio, 1937), especially pp. 186–205; and his "Etnogênese das caatingas e formação histórica do cangaço," *Cultura Política*, II (February 1942), 31–42.

[43] Euclydes da Cunha emphasized psychic disturbances generated by miscegenation. So too did Nina Rodrigues in *As collectivadades anormaes* and other works. See also Waldemar Valente, *Misticismo e região* (Recife, 1963), pp. 18–19.

[44] Queiróz in her *O messianismo no Brasil* emphasizes the rural and urban societies that react and interact with each other. The notion of dual society has led many writers, including Communists, to emphasize feudal society and conditions as the basis for reaction and protest among traditional elements of the population. This "myth" of feudalism is attacked by André Gunder Frank, *Capitalism and Underdevelopment in Latin America* (New York: Monthly Review Press, 1967); and by Caio Prado Júnior, *A revolução brasileira* (São Paulo: Editôra Brasiliense, 1966).

[45] Orlando da Cunha Parahym, *Homens e livros* (Recife, 1967), p. 134.

[46] Basílio de Magalhães, *O folclore no Brasil*, (Rio de Janeiro, 1960), p. 157, n. 160.

these considerations help to explain the phenomenon of social banditry. They should be examined, however, in the context of a society in which institutionalized violence and a patriarchical order prevailed and in which social banditry became the means of liberating the alienated poor of the backlands.

Social banditry probably existed well before the nineteenth century, but it fully established itself as a phenomenon of some significance during the nineteenth and twentieth centuries. Gustavo Barroso presented a number of case studies of bandit chieftains who were related to or under the patronage of distinguished families and tied to the patriarchical order. These included the important Cunha family of Boqueirão, located on the Jaguaribe River in Ceará; and the Cacundos, Mourões, Moquecas, Liberatos, Guabirabas, Brilhantes, Limões, Suassunas, Viriatos, and other families also from Ceará.[47]

Three bandit heroes are particularly significant in peasant folklore and in Brazilian history. Perhaps the most famous of social bandits of the early nineteenth century was José Brilhante de Alencar e Souza. His son, Jesuíno Brilhante, later formed his own band which fought the Limões and the Viriatos. During the famous drought of 1877, he assaulted rich convoys and distributed the contents among the rural peoples.[48]

A second legendary figure was Manoel Baptista de Moraes, better known as Antônio Silvino, who began his professional bandit career seeking revenge for his father who had been assassinated in 1896. Like Jesuíno Brilhante, Silvino distributed his booty among the needy lower classes. He imposed taxes on commerce and rail cargoes. Pernambucan by birth, Silvino roamed the backlands with a small band of the most notorious of bandits, including Godê, Balisa, João de Banga, Rio Preto, Cocada, Dois Arroz, Tempestade, Ventânia, Nevoeiro, Barra Nova, and Relâmpago. His imposing taxes on commerce and rail cargoes impeded construction of the Great Western Railway in Pernambuco during 1906. Finally in 1914 he was wounded and captured, tried, and imprisoned.[49]

The third figure was Virgulino Ferreira da Silva, nicknamed Lampião, one of the most notorious bandits of the Northeast. His band of some eighty members was divided into small units of a dozen men which oper-

---

[47] Gustavo Barroso, *Heróis e bandidos: os cangaceiros do Nordeste* (Rio de Janeiro: Livraria Francisco Alves, 1931). Studies focusing on these families include Nertan Macêdo, *O bacamarte dos Mourões* (Fortaleza: Editôra Instituto do Ceará, 1966), and his *O clã dos Inhamuns. Uma família de guerreiros e pastôres das cabeceiras do Jaguaribe* (2d ed.; Fortaleza, 1967). A useful article reference is Abelardo F. Montenegro, "José Antônio do Fechado e o banditismo político," *Revista Brasileira de Estudos Políticos*, 1 (December 1956), 159–169.

[48] Barroso, *op. cit.*, pp. 161–192.

[49] The story of Silvino's capture and imprisonment is in *Diário de Pernambuco*, nos. 300 to 331 (November 29 to December 31, 1914), and *Jornal do Recife*, nos. 328 to 347 (November 29 to December 18, 1914).

ated within a radius of two hundred miles of the core unit, headed by Lampião. Lampião began his professional banditry about 1918. Six years later, with some one hundred and fifty *cangaceiros,* he occupied the city of Souza in Paraíba. In 1926 political chieftains employed his services to fight the Prestes Column which had reached Ceará. A year later the famous bandit attacked the city of Mossoró in Rio Grande no Norte.[50]

The *cangaceiros* of the late nineteenth and early twentieth centuries subjected themselves to strict discipline and employed tactics of guerrilla warfare. Armies and state police encountered great difficulty in containing these backlands heroes.[51] For agreeing with Juàzeiro's chieftains to ward off the Prestes Column, Lampião was recognized with the rank of army captain. The 1930 revolution, however, stripped the local chieftains of their armaments and allowed the bands of *cangaceiros* free reign against

[50] There are hundreds of books and articles on the famous bandit Lampião. Among the more useful and interesting are Eduardo Barbosa, *Lampião, rei do cangaço* (Rio de Janeiro: Edições do Bolso, n.d.), a romanticized account with poetry and photographs; Gustavo Barrozo, *Almas de lama e de aço. Lampeão e outros cangaceiros* (São Paulo: Melhoramentos de São Paulo, 1930?) a popular version; João Bezerra, *Como dei cabo de Lampeão* (Rio de Janeiro, 1940), a detailed account by the captain of the Alagoan police force which finally brought an end to Lampião's exploits; Bezerra e Silva, *Lampião e suas façanhas* (Maceió, 1966), a narrative of principal events; Rodrigues de Carvalho *Serrote prêto, Lampião e seus sequazes* (Rio de Janeiro: Sociedade Editôra e Gráfica, 1961), a detailed and romanticized summary; Nelly Cordes, *O rei dos cangaceiros* (São Paulo: Clube do Livro, 1954); Optato Gueiros, *Lampeão, memórias de um oficial excomandante de forças volantes* (3rd ed.; 1953), the memoirs of an official who fought Lampião; Luiz Luna, *Lampião e seus cabras* (Rio de Janeiro: Editôra Leitura, 1963), with a focus on specific episodes; Raimundo Nonato, *Lampião em Mossoró* (2d ed.; Rio de Janeiro: Irmãos Pongetti, 1956), including considerable documentation on Lampião's presence in Rio Grande do Norte; Ranulfo Prata, *Lampião, documentário* (São Paulo: Editôra Piratininga, n.d.); Melchiades da Rocha, *Bandoleiros das caatingas,* (Rio de Janeiro: Editôra A Noite, n.d.), and Algae Lima de Oliveira, *Lampião, cangaço e nordeste,* 2d ed. (Rio de Janeiro: Edição O Cruzeiro, 1970). Lampião and other *cangaceiros* have been romanticized in Brazilian literature. Some outstanding examples are Mário de Andrade, *O baile das quatro artes* (São Paulo: Livraria Martins Editôra, 1963); Américo Chagas, *O cangaceiro Montalvão* (São Paulo, 1962); Paulo Dantas, *O Capitão Jagunço* (São Paulo: Editôra Brasiliense, 1959); Carlos Dias Fernandes, *Os cangaceiros, romance de costumes sertanejos* (3rd ed.; São Paulo: Monteiro Lobato, 1922); José Lins do Rêgo, *Cangaceiros, romance* (Rio de Janeiro: Livraria José Olympio Editôra, 1953); Nertan Macêdo, *Capitão Virgulino Ferreira Lampião* (Rio de Janeiro: Editôra Leitura, 1960?); Verissimo de Melo, *O ataque de Lampeão a Mossoró através do romanceiro popular* (Natal, 1953); Leonardo Motta, *No tempo de Lampeão* (Rio de Janeiro: Oficina Industrial Graphica, 1930); and Rachel de Queiróz, *Lampião, drama em cinco quadros* (Rio de Janeiro: Livraria José Olympio, 1953). See also the article by Paulo Dantas, "Cancioneiro de Lampião," *Revista Brasiliense,* 29 (May-June 1960), 210–211.

[51] See Eduardo Santos Maia, *O banditismo na Bahia* (Salvador, 1928); Manoel Cândido, *Factores do cangaço de 1910 a 1930* (Pernambuco, 1934); and Pedro Baptista, *Cangaceiros do nordeste* (Paraíba do Norte: Livraria São Paulo, 1929). See also Walfrido Moraes, *Jagunços e heróis* (Rio de Janeiro: Editôra Civilização Brasileira, 1963), especially chapters 20 and 21.

the defenseless population. Once in power, the revolutionary government was able to mobilize its forces and concentrate its attention on the suppression of the banditry. Lampião was finally contained and killed in battle in 1938. Only one of his bands under its chief, Corisco, survived and continued to operate until his death. Although the deaths of Lampião and Corisco symbolized the end of the heroic battles of the *cangaceiro*, a few instances of social banditry were reported thereafter. One such instance was that of Antônio Batista da Cruz, known as Antônio de Dina, who, in January 1963, was trapped and killed by Bahian police in Iapecá, Bom Conselho.[52] Newspaper reports described Dina's relations with a crime syndicate centered in the state of Alagôas. The syndicate had become in the sixties a modern version of the organized violence that previously had swept the backlands. Linked with politicians and wealthy ruling families, it too manifested social overtones.[53]

The emergence of a social banditry and its confrontation with established authority produced a number of significant consequences. The *cangaceiro* represented a sharp reaction against societal injustice and the existing social structure. The response of official authority—the police and army—indiscriminately affected large segments of the rural population whose sympathy for the elusive bandit heroes evolved into a certain consciousness of the dilemmas and problems of national society. As such they became potentially revolutionary and a threat to the semifeudal and capitalistic economic system whose prosperity was based on a surplus of labor at low wages. Eventually the intensive challenge of the *cangaço* contributed to the gradual decline of patriarchal order. In the process the *cangaceiro* disappeared; the absolute control of the local chieftain over his rural workers weakened, as did his power and control over violence.[54]

Catholic resistance and protest took two essential forms. One, based on the folk Catholicism of the backlands, related to many of the examples described above. The folk Catholicism and the mystique that imbued so many movements of protest often were tied to a charismatic leader whose appeal rested upon spiritual authority. Such was true of Padre Cícero Romão Batista and his Juàzeiro, analyzed by Ralph della Cava in this

[52] A detailed account is in the Recife daily, *Ultima Hora*, no. 198 (January 7, 1963), pp. 1, 2; no. 199 (January 8, 1963), p. 1; and no. 200 (January 9, 1963), p. 1. Banditry in the state of Goiás was reported by Luiz Gutemberg in a series of articles "Roteiro do cangaço: do nordeste a Goiás," in *Jornal do Brasil*, May 9, 1967, May 10, 1967, and May 11, 1967.

[53] The Alagôas crime syndicate was allegedly involved in the assassination of the mayor of Marechal Deodoro which became a celebrated case in October 1967; see *Diário de Pernambuco*, October 12 to November 11, 1967.

[54] This interpretation is modified from that of Rui Facó, *Cangaceiros e fanáticos*, pp. 44–46.

volume. The other form of Catholic resistance and protest evolved among progressive priests who, in the 1950s and 1960s, undertook the task of organizing rural workers.

Padre Cícero's movement developed after a series of miracles had occurred between March 1889 and 1891 during which a *beata*, or pious woman, Maria de Araújo, bled from her mouth after taking communion from the hands of the Padre. Although the miracle was denounced by the Church hierarchy, Cícero's fame spread quickly throughout the backlands, and Juàzeiro became a center of pilgrimage. Claiming veracity in the miracle, Cícero finally was able to refer his case to the Vatican, which ruled that he be removed to a parish some distance from Juàzeiro and be denied the right to preach and hear confessions; called to Rome, he repented and was allowed to return to Juàzeiro but without his priestly rights.[55]

Juàzeiro prospered thereafter from the influx of pilgrims and a rapidly growing population. Cícero collaborated with the local oligarchs, amassing a fortune in landholdings. By 1907 he had began a career in politics and by 1911 he had become the first mayor of Juàzeiro. Meanwhile, he had established contact with a Bahian physician, Floro Bartolomeu da Costa, who was to become the real political boss of the town. In 1912 an alliance between the oligarchs of the Cariri Valley, where Juàzeiro was situated, and the Nogueira Accioly family was broken by a popular uprising in Fortaleza and the ouster of Nogueira Accioly from the state governorship. The new governor was unacceptable to the Cariri bosses, and Floro Bartolomeu was sent to Rio to confer with national heads of the dominant Partido Republicano Conservador. A decision to establish a second government in Ceará with its headquarters at Juàzeiro also resulted in the proclamation of Floro as provisional governor. A military struggle ensued between a battalion of state militia sent to end the dissidence at Juàzeiro and the fervent supporters of the Padre. The battalion was repulsed, the neighboring town of Crato sacked, and other towns seized, and by late February 1914, Cícero's forces were on the outskirts of Fortaleza. The governor resigned, and Cícero became the patriarch of all the Northeast until his death in 1934.[56]

---

[55] An excellent synthesis of the Padre's emergence is in Queiróz, *O messianismo no Brasil*, pp. 231–246.

[56] The best descriptions of Padre Cícero and developments at Juàzeiro are Otacílio Anselmo, *Padre Cícero: mito e realidade*, (Rio de Janeiro: Editôra Civilização Brasileira, 1968); M. Bergström Lourenço Filho, *Joaseiro do Padre Cícero, scenas e quadros* (São Paulo: Companhia Melhoramentos de São Paulo, n.d.); Irineu Pinheiro, *Joaseiro do Padre Cícero e a Revolução de 1914* (Rio de Janeiro: Irmãos Pongetti Editôres, 1938); Xavier de Oliveira, *Beatos e cangaceiros. História real, observação pessoal e impressão psychológica de alguns dos mais célebres cangaceiros do nordeste* (Rio de Janeiro, 1920); and Reis Vidal, *Padre Cícero, Joàzeiro visto de perto. O Padre Cícero Romão Baptista sua vida e sua obra* (Rio de Janeiro, 1936). In contrast to the above, Edmar Morél in *Padre Cícero o santo do Joàzeiro* (Rio de Janeiro: Empresa Gráfica

Religious fanaticism did not end with the death of Cícero.[57] One of his *beatos*, José Lourenço, founded a communal sect at Caldeirão in the Serra do Araripe near Juàzeiro. Lourenço and his two confidants, Severino Tavares and Isaías, were able to attract some five thousand to Caldeirão between 1933 and 1935. When ordered by police to disperse and to return to their place of origin, the people of Caldeirão refused to leave. Then police, in November 1936, systematically destroyed the town, forcing Lourenço to move elsewhere with many of his followers. There Severino proposed to attack Crato and to retake Caldeirão, a plan opposed by Lourenço who chose to retire to a farm in Pernambuco where, with some of his followers, he remained until his death in 1946.[58] After being attacked by the police and bombed by airplanes during May 1937, Severino took his followers to Pau de Colher, near Casa Nova in the state of Bahia. In January 1938 the new site was devastated by a Pernambucan force, resulting in the death of four hundred, mostly women and children.[59]

The second current of Catholic resistance was evident among socially and politically conscious clergy who remained closely attached to the Church as an institution. Their protest was in the tradition of the anti-colonial dissent of António Vieira, who attacked Portuguese colonization in the mid-seventeenth century, and Frei Joaquim Caneca, whose separatist movement culminated in the Confederação do Equador, which embraced six independent provinces in 1824. During the early 1960s the left wing of the Church manifested its concern for social and economic problems through the Ação Católica and Ação Popular, which became influential among workers and peasants, and through the Partido Democrata Cristiano, which gained support in politics. Several priests, including Francisco

O Cruzeiro, 1946), presents a critical and negative portrayal of Cícero. Rodolpho Theophilo in *A sedição do Joàzeiro* (São Paulo: Monteiro Lobato, 1922), presents a firsthand account of the events of 1914. For Floro Bartholomeu's views, see his *Joàzeiro e o Padre Cícero, depoimento para a história* (Rio de Janeiro: Imprensa Nacional, 1923), based on his speech to the Brazilian Chamber of Deputies on September 23, 1923. Some of the more interesting and useful articles include Joaquim Alves, "Joàzeiro, cidade mística," *Revista do Instituto do Ceará*, LXII (1929), 73–101; Rui Facó, "Juàzeiro e o Padre Cícero," *Revista Brasiliense*, 38 (November-December 1961), 108–124; José Fábio Barbosa da Silva, "Organização social de Juàzeiro e tensões entre litoral e interior," *Sociologia*, XXIV (September 1962), 181–194; Lívio Sobral, "O Padre Cícero Romão," *Revista do Instituto do Ceará*, LIV (1940), 136–141; and Padre Azarias Sobreira, "Floro Bartolomeu, o caudilho baiano," *Revista do Instituto do Ceará*, LXIV (1950). See also Padre Azarias' strong defense of Padre Cícero in *O patriarca de Juàzeiro* (Juàzeiro, 1969).

[57] A series of cases of religious fanaticism is described in Abelardo Montenegro, *História do fanatismo religioso no Ceará* (Fortaleza: Editôra A. Batista Fontenele, 1959).

[58] Queiróz, *O messianismo no Brasil*, pp. 260–272.

[59] Facó, *Cangaceiros e fanáticos*, pp. 200–210.

Laja and Alípio de Freitas, were condemned for subversive activities by a military court after the coup of 1964.[60] The archbishop of Recife and Olinda, Dom Helder Câmara, emerged as the spokesman of progressive forces in the mid-sixties.[61] Most important, Church progressives became especially active among peasants; and, under the direction of young radical priests, rural labor unions were organized, first to combat the rapidly increasing influence of the Ligas Camponesas in the early sixties and later to increase peasant support for Church unions after military intervention in 1964 had destroyed most of the organized peasant movement (see below). As such, the Church favored policies of land reform, raising the living standard, and founding cooperative banks to aid farmers.

Some types of military protest have affected rural peoples of the Brazilian backlands, the major twentieth-century example being the famous army column of Luiz Carlos Prestes. The formation of the column and its long marches were related to the emergence of *tenentismo*, an urban-inspired movement of army lieutenants who participated in the 1922 abortive revolt of Fort Copacabana in Rio de Janeiro and the military uprising in São Paulo during July 1924. This movement was directed against federal machine politics, especially in the states of São Paulo and Minas Gerais, and its primary objective was to establish representative government for the Brazilian political system. Eventually the *tenentes* were able to usher Getúlio Vargas into power in 1930.[62]

After holding São Paulo for nearly three weeks, the rebels withdrew with arms and munitions and moved westward, distributing issues of a newspaper, *O Libertador*. By late August this column of soldiers reached Iguaçu Falls in Paraná State to the south. From there João Cabanas led his

[60] A brief synthesis of Church protest from the sixteenth century to the present is in Departamento de Pesquisa, "As bandeiras negras de revolução," *Jornal do Brasil*, May 11, 1967, Section B, p. 1. An important piece on the contemporary church is Emanuel de Kadt, "Religion, the Church, and Social Change in Brazil," in Claudio Veliz, *The Politics of Conformity in Latin America* (New York: Oxford, 1967), pp. 192–220.

[61] For a discussion of clerical nationalism, see Ralph della Cava, "Ecclesiastical Neo-colonialism in Latin America," *Slant*, III, no. 5 (October-November 1967), 17–20.

[62] The development of *tenentismo* is the focus of several important studies. The classic work is Virginia Santa Rosa, *O sentido do tenentismo* (Rio de Janeiro, 1933), also published in a second edition as *Que foi o tenentismo?* (Rio de Janeiro: Cadernos do Povo Brasileiro [22], Editôra Civilização Brasileira, 1963). Among important articles on the movement, see Robert J. Alexander, "Brazilian 'Tenentismo,'" *Hispanic American Historical Review*, XXXVI (May 1956), 229–242; Ann Quiggins Tiller, "The Igniting Spark—Brazil, 1930," *Hispanic American Historical Review*, XLIV (May 1964), 161–179; Jordan Young, "Military Aspects of the 1930 Brazilian Revolution," *Hispanic American Historical Review*, XLIV (May 1964), 180–196; and John D. Wirth, "Tenentismo in the Brazilian Revolution of 1930," *Hispanic American Historical Review*, XLIV (May 1964), 161–179.

"death" column through large landholdings, bringing terror to the countryside.[63] Juarez Távora set off to Rio Grande do Sul to join Prestes (then an army engineer) and other *tenentes*. By late 1924, Prestes had become the top revolutionary commander, and he began a march to a point near Iguaçu Falls, where he joined the Paulista rebels at the end of March 1925. From there, the united column began the "long march" of fourteen thousand miles through the vast Brazilian interior, reaching Goiás in June 1925, Minas and Bahia two months later, and finally the northern states of Maranhão and Piauí where the revolutionaries received support from anti-government politicians, and Ceará, where they were opposed by Padre Cícero in alliance with Lampião and his band. Eventually they were forced to move south again, finally reaching Mato Grosso and exiting into Bolivia in February 1927.[64]

The impact that the Prestes Column had upon the rural population is difficult to assess. The presence of the rebel soldiers in the oligarchic-dominated backlands was a threat to the wealthy *coronéis*, especially in the Northeast. Although both Padre Cícero and Lampião contributed significantly to the breakdown and decline of the traditional patriarchal order, they too had to combine forces with federal troops to ward off the column. Eventually, the decisive blow to the patriarchal order was the 1930 revolution, for one of the new government's first acts was to disarm the local chieftains.

The experience of the column brought political consciousness and an awareness of Brazil's social problems to some of the *tenente* leadership. After distinguishing himself as a remarkable leader, Prestes moved to Buenos Aires where he came into contact with Argentine Communists, went to the Soviet Union where he became a member of the executive committee of the Communist International, and eventually returned to Brazil where he became head of the Partido Comunista do Brasil (PCB).[65]

---

[63] See the memoirs of João Cabanas in his *A columna da morte sob o comando do Tenente Cabanas* (6th ed.; Rio de Janeiro: Livraria Editôra Almeida e Torres, 1928).

[64] Interesting personal accounts of the famous march are those of the former Italian artillery captain, Italo Landucci, *Cenas e episódios da Columna Prestes* (São Paulo: Editôra Brasiliense, 1947); and the secretary to the column, Lourenço Moreira Lima, *A Columna Prestes: marchas e combates* (São Paulo: Editôra Brasiliense, 1945), including letters and documents. Two accounts of particular event, respectively in Rio Grande do Norte and Paraíba, are Raimundo Nonato, *Os revoltosos em São Miguel, 1926*, (Rio de Janeiro: Editôra Pongetti, 1966); and Manuel Otaviano, *Os mártires de Piancó* (João Pessoa: Editôra Teone, 1955). Other personal accounts include João Alberto Lins de Barros, *Memórias de um revolucionário* (Rio de Janeiro: Editôra Civilização Brasileira, 1954); and Juarez Távora, *A guisa de depoimento sôbre a revolução brasileira de 1924* (São Paulo, 1927).

[65] In 1927 the Central Committee of the PCB resolved to send its secretary general, Astrojildo Pereira, to Bolivia to discuss with Prestes the possibility of his leading an

Two *tenentes*, Trifino Corrêa and Agildo Barata, also became Communists.[66] A number of *tenentes*, Miguel Costa and João Cabanas for example, became socialists.

A recent type of rural protest evolved with the organization of peasants into leagues and unions, the subject of Shepard Forman's essay in this volume. Since the 1930s, several changes have affected the traditional relationship between the small farmers, tenants, sharecroppers, and laborers, on the one hand, and the large landowners, on the other. Large numbers of landowners left their farms and plantations for urban life. Higher wages and a better life attracted many peasants to the cities, and the landowner, generally, increasingly became dependent on migrant labor. Additionally, agriculture became increasingly commercial, and regional monopolies developed because of poor communication and difficulties in transportation; producers and wholesalers sometimes limited distribution of their produce, and the increase in demand led to price increases. Also, industrialization in the towns and cities benefited from the export of commercial agricultural products. At the same time rampant inflation isolated the rural workers from the national market while they were prohibited from organizing unions and unable to receive social security benefits. Paternalism tended to break down, especially in frontier areas and on the marginal farms, and conflict intensified between landowner and worker.[67]

These developments influenced four types of peasant organization: that formed by the Communist party; that which evolved under the leadership of a radical lawyer from Recife, Francisco Julião; that promoted by young Catholic priests; and finally that sanctioned by the Brazilian government.

Communists were the first to attempt to organize dissident peasants. One of their early efforts to organize a peasant league occurred in São Paulo State about 1928 in the zones of Sertãozinho and Ribeirão Prêto, where peasants, under the leadership of Teotônio de Sousa Lima, marched in protest on the large coffee farms.[68] The Pernambuco branch of the party

alliance between the party and the petty bourgeoisie. Pereira recalls this experience in his book, *Formação do PCB, 1922–1928* (Rio de Janeiro: Editorial Vitória, 1962), pp. 105–109.

[66] Agildo Barata's memoirs are in his *Vida de um revolucionário: memórias* (Rio de Janeiro: Editôra Melso, n.d.).

[67] That Brazilian agriculture has in fact been oriented to production for export and sale abroad tends to undermine the traditional theses, abundantly posited in PCB documents, that the Brazilian land system is and always has been feudal. An interesting analysis is developed by André Gunder Frank, "A agricultura brasileira: capitalismo e o mito do feudalismo," *Revista Brasiliense*, 51 (January-February 1964), 45–70; and Caio Prado Júnior, "Contribuição para a análise da questão agrária no Brasil," *Revista Brasiliense*, 28 (March-April 1960), pp. 165–238, and "The Agrarian Question in Brazil," *Studies on the Left*, IV (Fall 1964), 77–84, as well as his *A revolução brasileira* (São Paulo: Editôra Brasiliense, 1966).

[68] Octávio Brandão, "Combates da classe operária," *Revista Brasiliense*, 46 (March-April 1963), 78.

actively organized peasants into leagues during 1946 to 1948.[69] About 1954 the PCB formed a rural workers' organization known as the União dos Lavradores e Trabalhadores Agrícolas do Brasil (ULTAB) which aggregated sharecroppers among coffee and some sugar workers in São Paulo State. ULTAB tended to engage in collective bargaining, pressuring for trade-union type legislation and protection for workers in the countryside.[70]

A second type of peasant organization appeared in the Northeast where Francisco Julião, a lawyer and state deputy in the Pernambuco assembly, defended in court a group of peasants of the Galiléia plantation, located near Vitória de Santo Antão in the transitional *agreste* zone between the wet coastal sugar lands and the dry cattle interior lands. Julião fought and won the case for the peasants and later succeeded in pressuring the state governor to expropriate the property which in 1959 became a cooperative.[71] The Galiléia association thus became the first Liga, and thereafter, other peasant leagues were organized in other municipalities, generally west of the populous sugar lands in the states of Pernambuco and Paraíba. The movement also spread to other states.[72] The Ligas directed attention to the prevention of rising rents, the abolishment of the *cambão* (the obligation of sharecroppers and tenants to work a certain period for the owner at lower than average wages), the enforcement of existing legislation, and the implementation of land reform.[73]

Led by progressive priests, the Catholic Church offered a third alternative. Focused on the rural proletariat rather than on the peasantry, the Church-supported unions had their origin in the state of Rio Grande do

[69] Information on the Communist peasant leagues in the Northeast is in *Fôlha do Povo* (Recife), scattered issues between no. 114 (April 6, 1946) and no. 715 (March 23, 1948).

[70] By 1962 ULTAB claimed to have nine federations, three hundred and nineteen associations, and 500,000 workers, according to a report by its Communist leader, Lyndolpho Silva, "Divisionismo e tração dentro do movimento camponês," in *A Hora* (Recife), June 2–8, 1962, p. 7.

[71] See details on the Galiléia developments in Francisco Julião, *Que são as Ligas Camponesas?* (Rio de Janeiro: Cadernos do Povo [1], Editôra Civilização Brasileira, 1962), p. 24; also see Antônio Callado, *Os industriais da sêca e os 'Galileus' de Pernambuco: aspectos da luta pela reforma agrária no Brasil* (Rio de Janeiro: Editôra Civilização Brasileira, 1960), especially pp. 33–44. The legally registered name of the first Liga was Sociedade Agrícola e Pecuária dos Plantadores de Pernambuco. See also Francisco Julião, *Cambão: la otra cara de Brasil*, translated from Portuguese into Spanish by Jorge Asencio (Mexico: Siglo XXI Editores, 1968), pp. 208.

[72] According to an army source, by late 1963 there were two hundred and eighteen peasant leagues, including sixty-four in Pernambuco and fifteen each in Paraíba and São Paulo. See Inquérito Policial Militar No. 709, *O comunismo no Brasil*, Vol. IV (Rio de Janeiro: Biblioteca do Exército, 1966), pp. 280–281.

[73] Julião advocated ten "commandments" for the Ligas Camponesas; these were described by Manuel Correia de Andrade in *A terra e o homem do Nordeste* (São Paulo: Editôra Brasiliense, 1963), pp. 247–249.

Norte under Bishop Eugênio Sales de Araújo. In 1961 young priests, inspired by Bishop Sales's work, decided to initiate a training program in Pernambuco and to form legally recognized rural unions. By 1963 there were forty-eight legal rural unions in Rio Grande do Norte, apparently all Catholic-oriented, and sixty-two unions in Pernambuco of which sixty-one were Church-sponsored.[74] The Church also was particularly aggressive in organizing rural unions in São Paulo with lesser activity in Minas Gerais and the southern states of Paraná, Santa Catarina, and Rio Grande do Sul. The major effort was led by two parish priests, Padres Antônio Melo of Cabo and Antônio Crespo of Jaboatão, two municipalities in the depressed sugar belt around Recife.[75]

The Church movement was spurred by the government's recognition of numerous rural unions, especially after 1962, and the establishment of the Confederação Nacional dos Trabalhadores Agrícolas (CONTAG) in 1963.[76] There was, however, general indifference on the part of the federal government to rural unionization, resulting in maneuvering for control by such populist politicians as Miguel Arraes, governor of Pernambuco during 1963–1964, and by the Communist-dominated ULTAB. After the military coup of 1964, the peasant leagues, the Communist unions, and other unofficial organizations were banned, and their leadership, imprisoned or exiled. The "official" unions were allowed to continue, although in many instances they too were intervened by government officials. With their competitors eliminated, Padres Melo and especially Crespo moved to strengthen their unions. Although a Church-government *modus vivendi* appeared to prevail after 1964, the Catholic organizers were only moderately successful in the face of an increasingly conservative military government.

One other type of rural protest is guerrilla warfare. The organization of "Groups of Eleven," or Grupos dos Onze, was a conspicuous example of such a movement. Launched on October 25, 1963, by the leftist politician, Leonel Brizola, these groups were "to serve as the principal means and the advance vanguard of the revolutionary movement that will liber-

[74] Mary E. Wilkie, "A Report on Rural Syndicates in Pernambuco," Rio de Janeiro, Centro Latinoamericano de Pesquisas em Ciências Socias, April 1964 (mimeographed), p. 7.

[75] An excellent report on the two priests is in Fanny Mitchell's "Padre Crespo and Padre Melo: Two Approaches to Reform," Letter FM-17 to the Institute of Current World Affairs in New York, November 9, 1967, p. 12.

[76] A review of legislation on the rural unions is in Robert E. Price, "Rural Unionization in Brazil," Land Tenure Center, University of Wisconsin, August 1964 (mimeographed). For Pernambuco, see Mary E. Wilkie, "A Report on Rural Syndicates in Pernambuco," especially pp. 5–6. Under a 1903 law thirteen short-lived unions were founded and dominated by landowners. Based on decree 7038 of 1944, individual unions were established in 1946, 1952, 1955, 1956, and 1957.

ate the country from international capitalist oppression and its internal allies with the objective of establishing in Brazil a government of the people, by the people, and for the people." [77] Brizola and his movement were associated with a series of guerrilla and revolutionary activities which alarmed Brazilian authorities. Allegedly he was behind a plot in November 1964 to seize the state governments in Rio Grande do Sul, São Paulo, Guanabara, and Goiás. He also was linked by the anti-Communist press to a renegade army colonel and his band who were captured in early 1967 after attacking a military outpost near the Uruguayan border; to a guerrilla band broken up in March and April in a mountainous area inland from the port city of Vitória in the state of Espírito Santo; to an armed group arrested during August in Mato Grosso, not far from the Bolivian border; and to another guerrilla force captured near Uberlândia during September. In December a small guerrilla force was arrested near Manaus.[78] In general, however, these activities had little impact upon the military government which, through a sensationalist Brazilian press, was able to rally some support with the ensuing widespread anxiety that pervaded the nation.

POPULAR REBELLIONS AND DISCONTENT

Four types of revolt are especially distinguishable: nationalistic-oriented rebellions, military coups, Communist revolts, and labor disorders. Although they frequently were spawned in rural areas, these movements generally were urban-oriented.

Among the many revolts we can label as nationalist in orientation are the War of Mascates (1710–1715), the Inconfidência Mineira (1789) and the Inconfidência de Bahia (1798), the 1817 Revolution of Pernambuco, the Confederação do Equador (1824), the War of the Cabanos in Pernambuco and Alagôas (1832–1835), the Cabanagem (1833–1836) in Pará and Amazonas, the Republic of Farrapos (1835–1845) in Rio Grande do Sul, the Sabinada in Bahia (1837), the Balaiada in Maranhão (1838–1839), and the Praieira Revolution of Pernambuco (1848–1849). Discontent and rebellion were linked to the prevailing colonial system. The historian, Caio Prado Júnior, has identified and described the conditions that provoked internal protest and revolution against the prevailing authority. First, the idea that Brazil would become independent from the mother country was formulated well before the event actually occurred. Second, it was evident by

[77] Brizola's pronouncement is reprinted in Inquérito Policial Militar No. 709, *O comunismo no Brasil*, Vol. IV, pp. 393–395.

[78] These events are described in *Jornal do Brasil*, May 5 and 11, 1967; and by Fialho Pacheco, "O diário do chefe guerrilheiro," in *O Cruzeiro*, XXXIX (April 22, 1967), 15–18.

the eighteenth and nineteenth centuries that complete disintegration was the result of colonization, the obvious evidence being the impoverishment of lands by primitive agricultural techniques and the exhaustion of mineral resources. Third, there was an increasing number of people "condemned to a marginal existence outside the normal productive activity of colonization." Fourth, the colonial system was too deeply rooted in the organization of the Portuguese monarchy, and Portuguese policy was not oriented toward carrying out any substantial reforms.[79] Identification of such conditions allows us to lump the above revolts into a "nationalist" category and to suggest common patterns and links among the various examples.

The War of the Mascates was a reflection of profound class differences between the elitist landed proprietors and the *mascates*, or "immigrant merchants," who, through hard work, had amassed some wealth and attempted to use their money to rival the social prestige of the free-spending Brazilian-born colonists. The *mascates* succeeded in monopolizing the colony's trade and thus threatened to deprive their rivals of a livelihood. In Pernambuco the struggle evolved between creole planters and the merchant middlemen who controlled the distribution of sugar, as well as the credit that sustained the planter aristocracy. Sugar was the source of most income, but changing patterns of production and capital formation in the seventeenth century brought tensions, violence, and confrontation between the rural and urban forces. The result was the growth of a new urbanized class at the expense of the rural landowning aristocracy.[80]

The Inconfidência Mineira and the Inconfidência da Bahia were unsuccessful attempts, apparently, to achieve independence and were largely inspired by the independence of the English colonies in North America. The Minas Gerais plot to overthrow the Portuguese regime in 1789 was organized by a man nicknamed Tiradentes ("the Toothpuller") who was executed after the conspiracy was leaked to authorities.[81]

---

[79] Caio Prado Júnior, *The Colonial Background of Modern Brazil* (Berkeley and Los Angeles: University of California Press, 1969), pp. 417–423.

[80] Details, description, and analysis and interpretation are in Guilherme Auler, *Mascates e Bernardo: um episódio da história pernambucana*, reprint from *Revista Tradição*, November 1940, pp. 263–269; Barbosa Lima Sobrinho, *Guerra dos Mascates* (Recife: Universidade do Recife, 1962), a brief monograph based on a lecture to the Instituto Histórico de Olinda; Vicente Ferrer, *Guerra dos Mascates* (Lisbon: Livraria Ventura Abrantes, 1914); Mário Melo, *Afirmações nacionalistas: a guerra dos Mascates* (Rio de Janeiro: Imprensa Nacional, 1942), reprinted from Terceiro Congresso de História Nacional, *Anais*, V, pp. 617–668, and his *A guerra dos Mascates como afirmação nacionalista* (Recife: Imprensa Oficial, 1941), studies by the late eminent Pernambucan historian; and Amaro Quintas, "Prodromos da guerra dos Mascates" (Recife: Cadernos de História [1, 2] Universidade Católica de Pernambuco, March 1967).

[81] There is a prolific literature on the Minas conspiracy. Among those works I consulted are: Assis Cintra, *Tiradentes: perante a história, revolações sôbre a Inconfi-*

The Pernambuco conspiracy of 1817 was directed against absolutism, centralized control, and Portuguese administrative and economic influence. Further, it was aggravated by the decline of the sugar industry, by slave revolts, and by the participation of free mulatto artisans. Once in power the rebels formed a provisional government and abolished some taxes and initiated other reforms.[82] One of the leaders, Frei Caneca, also participated in the 1824 uprising, a second revolt in Pernambuco known as the Confederação do Equador. While the rebels in 1817 proposed progressive emancipation of slaves, freedom of the press, and religious toleration, in 1824 they called for a republic and the abolition of the slave trade.[83]

dência Mineira (São Paulo: L. Marrano, 1933); Brasil Gerson, Tiradentes. Herói popular (Rio de Janeiro: Edições Horizonte, 1946) a popular account; Augusto de Lima Júnior, Pequena história da Inconfidência de Minas Gerais (Belo Horizonte: Imprensa Oficial do Estado de Minas Gerais, 1955); Luiz Pinto, Tiradentes: uma interpretação da Inconfidência Mineira (Rio de Janeiro: Editôra Alba Limitada, 1961); Amaro Quintas, Atualidade da Inconfidência (Recife: Editôra Nordeste, 1952), an essay; Antônio Torres, As razoens da Inconfidência, obra histórica (3rd ed.; Rio de Janeiro: A. J. Castilho, 1925); and Luíz Vanderley Torres, Tiradentes a áspera estrada para a liberdade (São Paulo: Obelisco, 1965), a detailed, documented study. Three useful journal articles are Alexander Marchant, "Tiradentes in the Conspiracy of Minas," Hispanic American Historical Review, XXI (1941), 239–257; Manoel Cardozo, "Another Document on the Inconfidência Mineira," Hispanic American Historical Review, XXXII (November 1952), 540–545; and Aires da Mata Machado Filho, "Tiradentes e as mulheres," Revista do Brasil, 3rd phase, III, no. 26 (August 1940), 23–24. On the Bahia conspiracy see Mário Behring, "Introdução" and "A Inconfidência da Bahia in 1798," Biblioteca Nacional, Annaes, XLIII-XLIV (1920–1921), pp. 1–11 and 85–225; Luiz Vianna Filho, "Homens e cousas da revolução baiana de 1798," Terceiro Congresso de História Nacional, Anais, IV, pp. 641–663; and Affonso Ruy de Souza, A primeira revolução social brasileira (São Paulo, 1942).

[82] Analysis of the 1817 revolution is in Francisco Muniz Tavares, História da revolução de Pernambuco em 1817 (2d ed.; Recife, 1883?), the standard work on the subject; Amaro Soares Quintas, A génese do espirito republicano am Pernambuco e a revolução de 1817 . . . (Recife: Imprensa Industrial, 1939), one of the better contemporary studies; Sylvio de Mello Cahú, A revolução nativista pernambucana de 1817 (Rio de Janeiro: Biblioteca do Exército, 1951), a brief description of the event; Alipio Bandeira, O Brazil heróico em 1817 (Rio de Janeiro: Imprensa Nacional, 1918), which includes biographical analysis of seven "heroes" of the revolution; and Mário Melo, A loja maçonica, seis de março de 1817 ao oriente do Recife (Recife: Typografia Recife Graphico, 1921), which examines the influence of the masons in the revolt. Two brief studies on events of 1817 outside Pernambuco are Luiz Teixeira de Barros, A revolução de 1817 no Ceará (Recife: Tradição, 1944); and Luís da Rosa Oiticica, Aspectos da revolução de 1817 (Recife: Editôra Nordeste, 1953). Also an article by Carlos Studart Filho, "Revolução de 1817 no Ceará," Revista do Instituto do Ceará, LXXIV (January-December 1960), 5–91. On Alagôas, see Abelardo Duarte, "A revolução Pernambucana de 1817 e a emancipação política de Alagôas," Revista do Instituto Histórico de Alagôas, XXI (1940–1941), 146–155.

[83] See Ulysses de Carvalho Soares Brandão, A Confederação do Equador (1824–1924) (Pernambuco: Secretaria Technica da Repartição de Publicações Officiaes, 1924), and his Pernambuco versus Bahia: protesto e contra-protesto (Recife: Imprensa Official, 1927). Also see Angelo Jordão Filho, A influência de Frei Caneca na Confederação do

The War of the Cabanos ensued and, in part, was related to the fact that the regime of independence under Pedro I (1822–1831) brought only nominal relaxation of traditional colonial policies. It also was linked to Pedro's abdication, as were other revolts that followed until the middle of the century. In the present volume Manuel Correia de Andrade has written a case study with description and analysis of the Cabanos war.[84]

The Republic of Farrapos (1835–1845) was the result of a republican and federalist civil war in the state of Rio Grande do Sul; it has been given considerable attention by Brazilian investigators.[85] The insurrections (discussed above) in Pará and Amazonas known as the Cabanagem (1833–1836) have received little attention, even though one historian has characterized the event as "one of the most, if not *the* most notable popular rebellion in Brazil." [86] The Cabanagem was particularly important because lower-class indigenous elements were able to seize power and to temporarily maintain a stable, popular government. Their response was reaction to the barbarous practices against Indian slaves captured in Maranhão and sold in Pará. Since Negro slaves were rare in that part of Brazil, the Indians became the principal source of labor and subsequently contributed much to the agitations and insurrections.

Both the Cabanagem and the Farrapos revolts stemmed from the repercussions of the nine-year regency government after Pedro I's abdication; [87]

Equador (Recife: Cadernos do Instituto de Ciências Políticas [4], 1961). See the article by Mário Melo, "Uma episódio da Revolução Pernambucana em 1824," *Revista do Brasil,* 1st phase, 52 (April 1920), pp. 307–310.

[84] Manuel Correia de Andrade has produced the best writings on the War of the Cabanos; see his *A Guerra dos Cabanos* (Rio de Janeiro: Coleção Temas Brasileiros [7], Conquista, 1955), and a brief essay, *Pernambuco e a revolta de Pinto Madeira* (Recife: Editôra Nordeste, 1953), as well as an excellent article, "As sedições de 1831 em Pernambuco," *Revista de História*, XIII, no. 28, (October-December 1956), 337–407. See also Milton F. de Mello, *A setembrizada* (Recife: Directória de Documentação e Cultura, 1951).

[85] On the Farrapos revolt, see Alfredo Varela, *História da grande revolução: o cyclo farroupilha no Brasil* (Pôrto Alegre, 1933); Dante de Laytano, *História da república riograndense, 1835–1845* (Pôrto Alegre, 1936); and Basílio de Magalhães, "Guerra dos farrapos," *Estudos de história do Brasil* (São Paulo, 1940), pp. 165–202.

[86] See Caio Prado Júnior, *Evolução política do Brasil e outros estudos* (2d ed.; São Paulo: Editôra Brasiliense, 1957), p. 71. On the Cabanagem, see also Jorge Hurley, *A Cabanagem* (Belém: Livraria Classica, 1936); and Basílio de Magalhães, "A Cabanagem," *Estudos de história do Brasil* (São Paulo, 1940), pp. 203–243. A classic study is Domingos Antônio Raiol, *Motins políticos ou história dos principais acontecimentos políticos da província do Pará desde o ano de 1821 até 1835* (3 vols.; Belém: Universidade Federal do Pará, 1970).

[87] See the analysis by Stanley J. Stein, "The Historiography of Brazil, 1808–1889," *Hispanic American Historical Review,* XL (May 1960), 243–245. This excellent bibliographical essay appears also in *Revista de História,* XXIX, no. 59 (July-September 1964), 81–131.

so too did the Sabinada revolt in Bahia.[88] That Bahian uprising commenced in November 1837, but represented the culmination of a series of revolts (in 1798 and 1821 especially) which made Bahians particularly sensitive to imperial absolutism.[89] Led by Sabino Vieira, the revolutionaries proclaimed the independence of Bahia, but the rebel government was overcome four months later by the imperial navy which transported troops to the scene of battle, blockaded Salvador, and crushed the revolt.

The Balaiada uprising took place in the state of Maranhão. In the village of Vila da Manga, bands of backlands peoples gathered under the leadership of a creole named Balaio. They overcame a force of government troops sent to disperse them, then marched on the commercial city of Caxias, encircled the city, and eventually occupied it in late June 1839. Reacting to this crisis, government troops were able to recapture the city in September only to be forced out the following month. Balaio was killed in battle, and at the same time other rebel leaders abandoned the movement. Not until early 1841, however, was the government able to announce that the region was pacified.[90] The failure of this mass movement was attributable to its lack of organization, its alliance with some moderate elements within Caxias, and its failure to align with the thousands of black slaves of the *fazendas*, most of whom sought refuge in *quilombos* along the coast.[91]

The Praieira Revolution of 1848–1849 has been carefully studied, especially by the historian Amaro Quintas.[92] Like the other major Pernambuco revolts since 1817, the Praieira rebellion sought an end to the empire. The

[88] On the Sabinada, see Braz do Amaral, *A Sabinada: história da revolta da Cidade da Bahia em 1837* . . . , special issue of *Revista do Instituto Geographico e Histórico da Bahia* (Bahia: Typografia Bahiana, 1909); Luiz Vianna Filho, *A Sabinada, a república bahiana de 1837* (Rio de Janeiro: Livraria José Olympio Editôra, 1938), a popular account; and Bahia, Publicações do Arquivo do Estado da Bahia, *A revolução de 7 de Novembro de 1837 (Sabinada)* (5 vols.; Salvador, 1937–1948), containing the documentation of the state archives. Also see José Wanderley de Araújo Pinho, "A Sabinada," *Revista do Instituto Histórico da Bahia*, CVI (1930), 635–793.

[89] Stein, *op. cit.*, p. 247.

[90] Two useful works on the Balaiada are Rodrigo Otávio, *A Balaiada, 1839* (Rio de Janeiro, 1942); and Astolfo Serra, *A Balaiada* (2d ed.; Rio de Janeiro: Bedeschi, 1946). A novel on the events was written by Viriato Corrêa, *A Balaiada, romance do tempo da regencia* (São Paulo: Companhia Editôra Nacional, n.d.).

[91] Caio Prado Júnior, *Evolução* . . . , pp. 74–75.

[92] The writings of Quintas on the Praieira Revolution include his important *O sentido social da Revolução Praieira* (Rio de Janeiro: Editôra Civilização Brasileira, 1967) which incorporates earlier studies such as "Considerações sôbre a Revolução Praieira," *Revista do Arquivo Público* (Recife), vol. V (1948), pp. 113–130; *Notícias e anúncios de Jornal*, (Recife: Departamento de Documentação e Cultura, n.d.), including bibliographic references and documents from the press of the period; *A Revolução Praieira* (Recife, 1949); and "O sentido social da Revolução Praieira . . . ," *Revista de História*, IX (July-September 1954), 131–178.

conflict also contained the manifestation of nationalistic feeling against Portuguese administrators and merchants, tensions between urban merchants and slaveholding planters, and antimonarchist resentment over neglect of regional interests. Quintas appropriately focuses attention on the "social significance" of the revolt. He also suggests that there existed "an intellectual elite prone to the comprehension of socialist principles" shaped by Antônio Pedro de Figueiredo ("one of Brazil's first socialists") and the magazine, O Progresso.[93] Nevertheless, the movement was unable to arouse mass support. Nor was it able to give much impetus to the independence movement.[94]

Military coups or attempted coups have constituted a form of urban protest against established authority. Prominent examples in the twentieth century include the revolts of 1922, 1924, 1930, and 1932. The first three were related to a basic objective of obtaining representative government through the overturn of federal machine politics based on an electoral arrangement between Brazil's two wealthiest states, São Paulo and Minas Gerais, which took turns supplying presidents. The decision of Rio Grande do Sul to oppose the presidential choice of Minas and São Paulo in 1922 set the stage for a period of turmoil. In addition, many army officers and especially the Military Club in Rio had opposed the dominant political machine during 1921–1922. Their opposition led to the abortive revolt of Fort Copacabana, led by a young, ambitious lieutenant, Antônio de Siqueira Campos, in July 1922.[95] Expecting an amnesty, the young lieutenants who participated in the 1922 outbreak instead were condemned to

[93] Amaro Quintas added a preface to a reedition of O Progresso (Recife: Impresna Oficial, 1950), and also has written of Figueiredo in "Antônio Pedro de Figueiredo, o cousin fusco," Revista de História, XVI, no. 34, (April-June 1958), 287–304.

[94] Other writings on the Praieira include Barbosa Lima Sobrinho, A Revolução Praieira (Recife, 1949), based on a lecture in the Instituto Histórico Brasileiro; Edison Carneiro, A insurreição Praieira (1848–1849) (Rio de Janeiro: Temas Brasileiros [3], Conquista, 1960); João Peretti, O movimento Praieiro, ensaios sôbre a revolta de 1848 (Recife, 1950); Eládio dos Santos Ramos, A rebelião Praieira (Recife, 1949), based on a lecture in the Teatro Santa Isabel; General Mello Rego, Rebellião Praieira (Rio de Janeiro: Imprensa Nacional, 1899); and Fernando Segismundo, História popular da Revolução Praieira (Rio de Janeiro: Editorial Vitória, 1949). Article references include Jamil Almansur Haddad, "Castro Alves e a Revolução Praieira," Revista de História, IV, no. 13 (January-March 1953), 211–221; Edison Carneiro, "O Partido da Praia," Estudos Sociais, I (July-August 1958), 190–214; Olívio Montenegro, "Aspectos da Revolução Praieira," Revista do Arquivo Público, V (1948), 103–112; Mauro Mota, "Amaro Quintas, um intérprete da Revolução Praieira," Revista do Arquivo Público, V (1948), 721–725; and Eládio dos Santos Ramos, "A rebelião Praieira," Revista do Arquivo Público, V (1948), 93–102.

[95] For a popular account of these events, see Glauco Carneiro, O revolucionário Siqueira Campos. A epopéia dos 18 do Forte e da Coluna Prestes ... (2 vols.; Rio de Janeiro: Gráfica Record Editôra, 1966). 2 vols.

prison. The *tenente* movement emerged to carry on with the struggle thereafter.

The São Paulo uprising of 1924 was the turning point for the *tenentes*. It began on July 5 and was led by a group of conspirators, including Siqueira Campos, who had escaped from a military hospital, Eduardo Gomes, and the brothers Joaquim and Juarez Távora; all had rebelled two years earlier. Also, there was Miguel Costa, as well as the head of the movement, Isidora Dias Lopes, a retired colonel known for his participation in an 1893 uprising. Surprisingly, on July 8 São Paulo fell into the hands of the revolutionaries, but attacked by a large and well-reinforced federal force, the revolutionaries chose to withdraw on July 27, and with an abundant supply of arms they moved southward to form the Prestes Column.[96]

The *tenente*-led revolts of 1922 and 1924 and the march of the Prestes Column until 1927 provided a basis for the outbreak of revolution on October 24, 1930, and the coming to power of Getúlio Vargas as head of the provisional government on November 3. Before Vargas had consolidated his regime, however, he was challenged by the unsuccessful *constitucionalista* revolution in São Paulo during July 9 to October 2, 1932. São Paulo had emerged as the center of industry that survived the delayed effects of the ending of World War I, anti-inflationary policies during the 1920s that encouraged foreign capital investment, and the world financial crisis of 1929. These economic conditions brought disaffection to the oligarchies of São Paulo and other states and encouraged conspiracies among middle-class politicians and military officers. Thus, the abortive revolt of 1932.[97]

Vargas's revolution did not bring immediate social, economic, and political change. It did end the republican structures established at the end of the nineteenth century and it did result in experimentation to bring about ambitious plans of economic and social change despite agitation caused by the São Paulo revolt, a new constitution, a popular front, a fascist movement, and an attempted coup.

The attempted coup occurred during November 1935 and was representative of a new form of urban protest, manifested by the left and the Par-

[96] For a description of the 1924 events and aftermath, see Nelson Tabajara de Oliveira, *1924, a revolução de Isidoro* (São Paulo: Companhia Editôra Nacional, 1956). Also see J. Nunes de Carvalho, *A revolução no Brasil, 1924–1925; apontamentos para a história* (3rd ed.; Rio de Janeiro: Typografia de Terra de Sol, 1931).

[97] These developments and conditions are described by Caio Prado Júnior, *História econômica do Brasil* (8th ed.; São Paulo: Coleção Grandes Estudos Brasiliense [2], Editôra Brasiliense, 1963), pp. 263–274. An important bibliography on the 1932 São Paulo Revolt is Aureliano Leite, "Bibliografia da Revolução Constitucionalista," *Revista de História*, XXV (July-September 1962), 125–166.

tido Comunista do Brasil (PCB). The uprising began on November 23 with a barracks' revolt in Natal, the capital of Rio Grande do Norte. Rebel soldiers, joined later by peasants and workers, many of whom were unemployed, occupied strategic parts of the city, including the military police headquarters. Two days later, the Comitê Popular Revolucionário, the rebel governing committee, ordered a reduction in streetcar fares and bread prices, and closed the local neofascist Integralista head quarters. The Natal revolt collapsed on November 27 about the same time as an outbreak in Rio and three days after an uprising in Recife. On November 24 a suburban military barracks in Recife was occupied, but the rebels failed to attack strategic communications centers and military arsenals. Further, they were joined by only a few dozen civilians. When the arrival of loyalist reinforcements a day later forced the rebel commanders to order a full retreat, the rebellion collapsed. The Rio revolt was headed by Captains Alvaro Francisco de Souza and Agildo Barata. After the rebels in Rio had seized the Praia Vermelha garrison and the School of Military Aviation at Campo dos Afonsos, they also were overcome by government troops.[98]

There has been considerable speculation on the timing of the revolt and whether the rebels acted on their own, according to plan, or by mistake. Most writers agree that Moscow was involved through the sending of important Comintern agents to Brazil and that the PCB and the popular front movement of which the PCB was a part, the Aliança Nacional Libertadora (ANL), as well as the Vargas police, were aware of preliminary instructions for the uprising. A major view suggests that the Natal revolt was touched off by a police message ordering the revolt to commence two weeks before the planned date. Another view interprets the revolts as the culmination of an evolving political confrontation between the Vargas government and the ANL and the labor movement. A slightly different interpretation suggests that the individual revolts were closely related to local conditions, and that the decision to revolt in Natal came directly from military leaders there. Most writers agree that the revolts served Vargas with a pretext not only for crushing the PCB but also for assuming extraordinary emergency powers.[99]

[98] João Medeiros relates details of the Natal revolt and his capture and includes police documentation in his *Meu depoimento: sôbre a revolução comunista e outros assumptos* (Natal: Imprensa Oficial, 1937). The three revolts are described by Robert M. Levine in "The Vargas Regime and the Politics of Extremism in Brazil, 1934–1938," unpublished Ph.D. dissertation, Princeton University, 1967. The official police version of the Rio events, including documents and useful biographical details of the rebels, is in Eurico Bellens Pôrto, *A insurreição de 27 de novembro* (Rio de Janeiro: Polícia Civil do Districto Federal, Imprensa Nacional, 1936).

[99] In the Soviet Union Prestes had convinced the Comintern of the necessity of a military coup and the establishment of a popular front government under his leader-

Labor disorders among the working class are representative of another form of urban protest. The degree of labor protest has been somewhat dependent on ideology, organization, and leadership. Before the Russian Revolution two ideologies dominated. One, socialism, provided the early roots of contemporary radicalism, especially in the intelligentsia. The other, anarchism and anarchosyndicalism, was particularly significant in the period from 1906 to about 1920. These ideologies were accompanied by organizational activity and the aggregation of intellectuals and workers who favored reforms and alternatives to oligarchic rule. Despite many weaknesses and failings, these early radical ideologies not only provided a basis for a Communist movement after 1917 but also influenced early efforts to organize and defend the working class. From 1848 to 1917 the labor movement organized sporadically at the local level, especially in Rio and São Paulo. During that period, sixteen major protests occurred, including fourteen labor-organized strikes in Rio, São Paulo, Santos, Pôrto Alegre, and Fortaleza. In only five instances were labor demands satisfied and the strikes successful: in one, wages were increased; and in the others, the daily number of working hours was reduced.[100]

Established in 1922, the Communist party drew most of its leadership and membership from organized labor, and throughout its evolution the party concentrated on establishing and maintaining its influence in labor. During the 1920s the party supported important labor strikes and the formation of several workers' confederations, as well as an electoral front with workers and peasants. Communist influence declined under the Vargas-imposed system that allowed government arbitration between capital and labor and the maintenance of control through a paternalistic labor code and a vast program of social welfare. The end of the Vargas dictatorship in 1945 did not free labor from official control, and the corporativist

---

ship. The Vargas government was aware of the plans, however, because one of its agents, Antônio Maciel Bomfim, had become secretary general of the PCB after the imprisonment of the top leadership in 1932 and had even traveled to Moscow to support Prestes's coup plans. Bomfim, also known as Miranda, as Adalberto de Andrade Fernandes, and as Américo de Carvalho, had been a leader of the Liga de Ação Revolucionária and was elected secretary general at the PCB's First National Conference in 1934. Details of these developments are in Leôncio Basbaum, *História sincera da república* (2d ed.; São Paulo: Coleção Temas Brasileiros, Editôra Edaglit, 1962), Vol. III, pp. 87–89.

[100] This analysis of labor protest is based on a synthesis of Evarardo Dias, *História das lutas sociais no Brasil* (São Paulo: Temas Brasileiros [8], Editôra Edaglit, 1962); Hermínio Linhares, *Contribuição à história das lutas operárias no Brasil* (Rio de Janeiro: Baptista de Souza, 1955), and "As greves operárias no Brasil durante o primeiro quartel do século XX," *Estudos Sociais*, 2 (July-August 1958), 215–223; Astrojildo Pereira, *Formação do PCB, 1922–1928* (Rio de Janeiro: Editorial Vitória, 1962); and Jover Telles, *O movimento sindical no Brasil* (Rio de Janeiro: Editorial Vitória, 1962).

organization remained intact while the Labor Ministry continued to control labor through the union tax and the threat of intervention. Communists therefore adopted the tactic of working within the government-established unions rather than forming a rival organization.[101]

With the formation of the unofficial but powerful Confederação Geral dos Trabalhadores (CGT) in 1961, union leaders were able to maintain a degree of independence from the government as they won concessions, including substantial wage increases, for every strike they initiated and supported. These wage increases, along with rapid inflation and increasing anxieties by conservatives who believed that the João Goulart government was too dependent on labor, tended to polarize left and right political forces, prompting military intervention in 1964.[102]

II

PORTUGUESE AFRICA

Unlike Brazil, which attained independence in the early nineteenth century and became a republic in 1889, Portuguese Africa as of 1970 in theory remained integrally tied to Portugal. The Portuguese empire and colonialism long have caught the attention of scholars, and the available literature generally reflects an exaggerated view of Portugal's role in Africa. The African perspective is relatively little known although historians Edward Alpers, David Birmingham, and Jan Vansina have recently completed important works which reflect the African's role in shaping indigenous developments.[103]

Our examination of African resistance and protest attempts to parallel our previous discussion of Brazil. Various movements are classified into

[101] See Teotônio Júnior, "O movimento operário no Brasil," *Revista Brasiliense*, 39 (January-February 1962), 100–118. For a general account of the evolution of labor and its organization, see Robert J. Alexander, *Labor Relations in Argentina, Brazil, and Chile* (New York: McGraw-Hill, 1962).

[102] See Timothy F. Harding, "Revolution Tomorrow: The Failure of the Left in Brazil," *Studies on the Left*, IX, no. 4, (Fall 1964), 30–54, but especially pp. 37–44.

[103] See Edward Alpers, "The Role of the Yao in the Development of Trade in East-Central Africa, 1698– c. 1850," unpublished Ph.D. dissertation, University of London, 1966; David Birmingham, *Trade and Conflict in Angola, the Mbundu and their Neighbors under the Influence of the Portuguese, 1483–1790* (Oxford: Clarendon Press, 1966); and Jan Vansina, *Kingdoms of the Savanna* (Madison: University of Wisconsin Press, 1966). Douglas Wheeler also has contributed two biographical sketches of African leaders in his "Gungunyana," in *Leadership in Eastern Africa*, ed. by Norman Bennett (Brookline: Boston University African Research Studies [9], Boston University Press, 1969), and "A Nineteenth Century African Protest: Prince Nicolas of Kongo," in *The Journal of African Historical Studies*, I (March 1968). See also M. D. D. Newitt, "The Massingire Rising of 1884," *Journal of African History*, XI, no. 1 (1970), 87–105.

simple, often overlapping, categories in an effort to achieve perspective and synthesis of a broad range of developments over several centuries in time. It is clear from outline 2 that the major events, linked with black

Outline 2
Classification of Portuguese African
Movements of Protest and Resistance

I. Indigenous forms of resistance to alien influence
   A. Spontaneous rebellions against Portuguese conquest, occupation, and pacification
      1. Portuguese Congo or the Kongo kingdom*
         a) Mpanzu a Nzinga or Mpanza a Kítima revolt of 1506 in Mbanza
         b) Revolt of Jorge Muxuebata against King Affonso I and the Portuguese
         c) General violence against the Portuguese in the 1560s
      2. Angola kingdoms
         a) Mbundu attack on Portuguese military force, 1578
         b) Cafuxe Cambara and Kissama forces attack Portuguese, April 1594
         c) Series of campaigns led by Queen Nzinga Mbandi initiated in 1625
         d) Revolt of Dembo Ambuíla, 1631
         e) Dembos wars, 1872–1919
      3. Benguela highlands and kingdoms to the south
         a) Soba Bongo destroyed presidio at Caconda, 1684
         b) Resistance of Kapango I, 1660
         c) Resistance of *soba* of Huambo, 1698
         d) Cuanhama revolt, 1904–1906
      4. Portuguese Guiné or Guiné (Bissau)
         a) Attack by Papéis at Bissau, February 1753
         b) Bijagós attack Bolama, 1792
         c) Papéis attack at Cacheu, May 1824
         d) Papel uprising in Bissau, 1842 and 1844
         e) Mandinga attack at Farim, 1846
         f) Uprising at Gêba, 1855
         g) Felupe massacre of Portuguese military at Bolor River, December 1878

* (Ed. note: the spelling Kongo refers to the African kingdom while the use of Congo is related to Portuguese [as well as former Belgian and French] controlled territory.)

    h) Attack on Buba by Fulas and Mamadú Paté, 1880

    i) Wars waged by Mussá Moló, 1886 and thereafter

  5. Moçambique

    a) Namarrães rebellions, 1898–1906

    b) Mataka III Bonomali and Yao tribesmen wage resistance, 1889–1904

B. Resistance to Portuguese cultural domination

  1. Kongo revolt in 1506 against Catholic Portuguese and Affonso I

  2. Affonso I antagonism to King Manuel's regimento

C. Revolts against outside political interference

  1. Assassination of governor of Bissau, 1871

  2. Alliance of Ngola with Alvaro II of the Kongo and the Jagas of Matamba, 1590–1600

  3. Alliance of Queen Nzinga with Ndongo, Mtamba, Kongo, Kassanje, Dembos, and Kissama, 1630?

  4. Coalition of kingdoms, led by Tchiyaka, attacked fortress at Caconda, 1718

  5. Soshangane and Ngoni tribes attack Inhambane in 1834 and Sofala in 1836

  6. African insurgents against Lourenço Marques, 1894

D. Reaction to foreign penetration and domination of indigenous economies

  1. Slave trade repercussions

    a) Ngola Kanini attack on Portuguese, last half of seventeenth century

    b) Wars launched by Papel chief, Incinhate, late seventeenth century

  2. Disruption of local markets and introduction of new commodities

    a) 1886 alliance between Bié and Bailundo

    b) Struggle of Numa II, king of Bailundo

    c) Rebellion of Muta-ya-Kevela of Bailundo, 1902

    d) Uprisings in Cacheu by Mata and Mompataz, 1679

    e) Rebellion of Chombe in the Sena region of the Zambeze Valley

    f) Changamire attack on Dambarare, 1693

  3. Opposition to Portuguese control of minerals

    a) Resistance at Cambambe until 1605

    b) Reaction of Gatsi Rusere in early seventeenth century

    c) Resistance of Monomotapa Capranzine until 1628

  4. Labor revolts

    a) Alvaro Tulante Buta revolt in Congo (1913–1914)

    b) 1953 rebellion on São Tomé

II. Secret societies and nativistic or messianic mass movements
   A. Secret societies (Nevemba, Kimpási, Ndêmbu e Nkimba, Mbumba, Nkita, and Ngôngi)
   B. Nativistic or messianic mass movements
      1. Simon Kimbangu
      2. Simon Peter Mpadi
      3. Simon Lassy
      4. Andrew Grenard Matswa
      5. Simão Toko
      6. Other prenationalist religious movements (Movimento Tônsi, Movimento Maiange or Nlênvu, Movimento Tonche or N-Tonche, and the Grupo Saint Esprit or Dibundo Mpeve ia Londo)
III. Written and organizational protest
   A. Assimilado protest writings
      1. José de Fontes Pereira (1823–1891)
      2. António de Assís Júnior
      3. Other writings, including *Voz d'Angola clamando no deserto* and articles in the colonial press of the 1920s
      4. *A Mensagem* and *A Cultura* (1948?)
   B. Protest through organization
      1. Partido Pro-Angola (early 1920s); Liga Nacional Africana (1921); Grêmio Africano (1929) or Associação Regional dos Naturais de Angola
      2. Sports and Recreation Association (Guiné, 1954)
      3. Grêmio Africano of Moçambique or Associação Africana; Instituto Negrófilo or Centro Associativo dos Negros de Moçambique
      4. Alvaro Tulante Buta in Portuguese Congo (1913–1914)
      5. Strike at Bissau, August 3, 1959
      6. Uprising at Luanda, February 4–6, 1961

African resistance and protest, tended to be sporadic, spontaneous, and often unorganized responses to Portuguese conquest, colonization, pacification, and economic exploitation. The following section elaborates on these events and the organizations that occasionally evolved from them and at the same time attempts to identify some of the principal bibliographic sources that have been useful to this writer and to many of the contributors to this volume.

INDIGENOUS FORMS OF RESISTANCE TO ALIEN INFLUENCE

Reviewing the history of African resistance in Angola, Portuguese Guiné or Guiné (Bissau) and Moçambique, one notes four overlapping patterns of response: sporadic and sometimes spontaneous rebellions against the Portuguese conquest, occupation, and pacification; revolts against Portuguese cultural penetration and domination; revolts against political interference in African affairs; and reaction to foreign domination of the native economies. These responses and their consequences are the concern of David Birmingham in the present volume.

Sporadic rebellion has predominantly characterized the pattern of resistance among African tribes and groupings in the three territories. In Angola, this resistance was centered in the major kingdoms of three important areas, known as the Congo or Kongo, Ndongo or Angola, and the Benguela highlands to the south. Occasionally the Portuguese presence resulted in factional disputes over the royal succession. In the Kongo the Portuguese attempt to convert the king and his sons to Christianity during the late fifteenth century was disrupted by the king himself and a son, Mpanzu a Nzinga or Mpanza a Kítima, who in 1506 briefly occupied the capital until being overcome by a rival brother, Affonso I. The reign of Affonso I (1507 to 1543?)was marred by the revolt of Jorge Muxuebata at Mbanza who apparently desired the expulsion of the king's Portuguese allies. In the 1560s there was further violence when Portuguese residents assassinated the people's choice of a successor to the monarchy and attempted to name their own candidate; the people of Mbanza revolted, apparently killing many Portuguese. About 1570 Mbula Matadi led an unsuccessful popular revolt against the Kongo king, Alvaro I, and his Portuguese supporters.[104]

---

[104] All these revolts and many of those mentioned in the following discussion are included in the provocative analysis of the Centro de Estudos Angolanos, Grupo de Trabalho História e Etnologia, "História de Angola (Apontamentos)" (Algiers: Centro de Estudos Angolanos [2], July 1965, mimeographed). The preliminary report by a group of Angolans studying in Algiers is one of the first serious efforts to identify and synthesize African resistance as a basis for a reformulation of historical developments in the Portuguese territories. Although incomplete and occasionally in error, it nevertheless provides an outline for study and publication. The Kongolese revolts are referred to on pages 42 to 47. Additionally helpful and available in English is Ernst George Ravenstein, "A Sketch of the History of Kongo to the End of the Seventeenth Century," Appendix II in Andrew Battel, *The Strange Adventures of Andrew Battel of Leigh, in Angola* . . . (London: Hakluyt Society, 1901), pp. 102–137. See also Jan Vansina, "Notes sur l'origine du Royaume de Kongo," *Journal of African History,* IV, no. 1 (1963), 33–38. Other basic works that provide leads to African resistance but focus generally on Portuguese policy and activities are Filippo Pigafetta and Duarte Lopes, *A Report of the Kingdom of Congo* . . . (London: John Murray, 1881); Visconde de Paiva Manso, *História do Congo* (Documentos), (Lisbon: Typographia

Resistance in the Angola kingdoms is also identifiable. We know, for example, that in 1578 a Mbundu chief captured a detachment of Portuguese soldiers, killing twenty of them and returning the others for ransom. This was one of the early African responses to the militant Portuguese policy charging Paulo Dias de Novaes or Novais with the task of conquering and colonizing Angola. In April 1594 an African force led by a powerful Kissama chief, Cafuxe Cambara (Kafuche Kabara or Kafushe) ambushed and massacred a Portuguese force at a new fort on the site of the Kissama salt mines, and later victories left the Portuguese confined to the unhealthy lowlands and unable to penetrate the plateau country. About 1625 Queen Nzinga Mbandi (Jinga and at one time baptized as Anna de Souza Nzinga) initiated a series of campaigns against the invading Portuguese. About 1631, Dembo Ambuíla, a prestigious chieftain of the Dembos region, launched an abortive revolt against the Portuguese. Sporadic resistance continued throughout the seventeenth and eighteenth centuries, and by the late nineteenth century, African hostility appeared to be as strong as three centuries earlier.[105] The Dembos region, northwest of Luanda, resisted Portuguese expeditions sent to the interior and was especially troublesome after 1850. War broke out in 1872, but only after military campaigns of 1907 and 1908 could the Portuguese claim effective occupation of the region. Complete "pacification" and access to the Congo frontier were achieved with the Dembos military operations of 1918 and 1919.[106]

African resistance in the Benguela highlands was marked by the destruc-

---

da Acadêmia, 1877), an invaluable collection of 211 documents on the early years; Jean Cuvelier. *L'ancien royaume de Congo: fondation, découverte* . . . (Bruges, Paris: Desclée de Brouwer, 1946); and G. A. Cavazzi de Montecucollo, *Istorica descrizzione degli tré regni Congo, Angola, e Matampa* (Bologna, 1687). A more recent work is Hélio A Esteves Felgas, *História do Congo Portugûes* (Carmona, Angola, 1958).

[105] David Birmingham, *Trade and Conflict in Angola*, presents one of the most incisive syntheses of the Angolan wars, including considerable detail. His shorter work, *The Portuguese Conquest of Angola* (London: Institute of Race Relations, Oxford University Press, 1965) is also useful. Vansina, in *Kingdoms of the Savanna*, covers the rise of Angola in chapter 5, pp. 124–154. Other works of importance on the early centuries are Ralph Delgado, *História de Angola, 1482–1836* (4 vols.; Benguela: Tipografia do Jornal de Benguela, 1948–1955); Alfredo de Albuquerque Felner, *Angola* . . . (Coimbra: Imprensa da Universidade de Coimbra, 1933), including a useful appendix of documents; and an especially important work of the period despite some erroneous interpretation by António de Oliveira de Cadornega, *História geral das guerras angolanas* (3 vols.; Lisbon: Agência Geral das Colónias, 1940–1942). A useful history is Elias Alexandre da Silva Corrêa, *História de Angola* (Lisbon, 1937), a reprint of a late eighteenth-century writing.

[106] David Magno has written a brief history of the native resistance to the Portuguese from 1915 to 1919 in his *Guerras angolanas* (Oporto: Companhia Portuguesa Editôra, 1934?).

tion of a Portuguese presidio by the *soba* Bongo at Caconda in 1684. The Portuguese advance into the highlands was briefly halted about 1660 when the king of Tchiyaka, Kapango I, forced the withdrawal of a Portuguese expedition which was attempting to reach the plateau. In 1698 the *soba* of Huambo failed in an attempt to expel the Portuguese. The kingdoms of the plateau were able to maintain a degree of autonomy and independence, however, and it was not until the early twentieth century that Portuguese domination was assured, but not without a struggle.[107] In 1902 the Bailundo king, Mutu-ya-Kevela, led dissident Africans in rebellion in an attempt to recover land held by the Europeans, and consequently the Bailundo area was swept by a wave of murder, looting, and destruction of trading posts.[108] Although the Portuguese quickly retaliated, and peace was secured, an area northwest of Nova Lisboa continued open hostility until 1904. In the kingdom of Humbe about 1904 the Cuanhama people of the region ambushed a Portuguese force encamped at Cuamato, killing three hundred. Although two thousand Portuguese troops subdued the rebels in 1906, resistance continued until a major campaign in 1915 assured control of the area.[109]

In Portuguese Guiné hundreds of sporadic revolts can be documented over the past few centuries. During the fifteenth and sixteenth centuries, African rulers maintained control over the interior and the coast as well. Portuguese attempts to penetrate the interior and to pacify the rebellious tribes met also with relatively little success during the seventeenth century. In February 1753 the Papéis resisted a Portuguese attempt to rebuild a fortress at Bissau. In May and June of 1792 the Bijagós attacked the English settlement at Bolama. In May 1824 there was a lengthy battle at Cacheu between Papéis and Portuguese, and not until December of the following year was peace secured. In November 1842, in September 1844, and in 1846, there were Papel uprisings in Bissau. In December 1846 *grumetes* (Christianized Africans) allied with Mandingas to attack Farim. Gêba was attacked nine years later. In December 1878 a Portuguese military force

---

[107] General works which unfortunately lack extensive detail on the African resistance are Ralph Delgado, *Ao sul do Cuanza: ocupação e aproveitamento do antigo reino de Benguela* (2 vols.; Lisbon: Edition of the Author, 1944), and also his *A famosa e histórica Benguela: catálogo dos governadores, 1779 a 1940* (Lisbon: Edições Cosmos, 1940?), including a description of each governor and an appendix of forty documents.

[108] On the 1902 campaign, see the account by the then governor-general of the colony, Francisco Cabral de Moncada, *A campanha do Bailundo em 1902* (2d ed.; Lisbon: Livraria Ferin, 1903).

[109] Besides the sources already mentioned, I have found scattered official references in the magazine *Portugal em África* (Lisbon), and in missionary reports in *The Missionary Herald* (Boston); both periodicals published during the late nineteenth and early twentieth centuries. The archives of the West African mission of the United Church Board for World Ministries are in the Houghton Library of Harvard University and contain occasionally useful information.

was massacred by Felupes near the Bolor River. In 1880 there was an attack on Buba by Fulas and their leader, Mamadú Paté of Bolola. In 1886 and the years immediately thereafter, Mussá Moló and his Fula-Pretos waged war against the Portuguese and seized extensive areas around Buba and south of the Gambia River. Hostility and resistance continued well into the twentieth century as the Portuguese launched a series of military campaigns in an attempt to pacify the rebellious tribes. As late as September 1931 a state of siege was declared in Bissau, and in 1936, after a two-month struggle, Portuguese forces finally overcame Bijagós rebels at Canhabaque.[110]

In Moçambique before 1890 Portuguese occupation and influence had been limited to the island of Moçambique while the coast remained in the hands of the powerful Mohammedan chiefs of mixed Arab and Makua blood whose external relations were dependent on trade with Zanzibar. About the time pacification was assured in the Gaza region in 1897, the Portuguese moved against the Namarrães on the mainland opposite Moçambique island; a Portuguese fort was overrun in 1898. Marave, the most important of the rebellious Namarrães chiefs, was not defeated until about 1906. In the north Mataka III Bonomali, an important Ajáua or Yao chief, led the resistance to the Portuguese from about 1890 until his death in 1903, and his successor denied Portugal effective occupation of the territory until a series of campaigns in 1908-1912. In order to quell disorder among Africans, the Portuguese sent four expeditions to the Moçambique district during 1914-1918.[111]

Our second pattern, resistance to Portuguese cultural domination, was evident in the territories. An early example occurred in the Kongo. Mpanzu a Nzinga's revolt in 1506 was partially a struggle of his paganism against Portuguese Catholicism. Although the victor of that struggle, Affonso, was apparently a confirmed Catholic, his relations with Portugal

[110] A pattern of African resistance is traced in João Barreto's *História da Guiné, 1418-1918* (Lisbon: Edition of the Author, 1938), which includes references and extensive quotations from primary sources. Also useful is Christiano José de Senna Barcellos, *Subsídios para a história de Cabo Verde e Guiné* (5 vols.; Lisbon: Acadêmia Real das Sciências, 1899–1911). Among the early Portuguese chronicles and writings are André Alvares d''Almada, *Tratado breve dos rios Guiné do Cabo Verdi desde o rio de Sanagá até aos baixos de Sant'Anna* . . . (Oporto: Typographia Commercial Portuense, 1841); Gomes Eannes de Azurara, *Discovery and Conquest of Guinea*, trans. and ed. by E. Prestage and C. R. Beazley (2 vols.; London: Hakluyt Society, 1896–1899); Francisco de Lemos Coêlho, *Duas descrições seiscentistas da Guiné* (London, 1953), which contains two unedited seventeenth-century manuscripts; and Th. Monod, Avelino Teixeira da Mota, and R. Mauny, *Description de la côte occidentale d'Afrique par Valentim Fernandes (1506–1510)* (Bissau: Centro de Estudos da Guiné Portuguesa [11], 1951).

[111] A general source, somewhat useful in identifying confrontation between Portuguese and African, is José Justino Teixeira Botelho, *História militar e política dos portugueses em Moçambique de 1833 aos nossos dias* (2d ed.; Lisbon: Centro Tipografia Colonial, 1936).

ran into unexpected difficulties. When, for example, São Tomé traders felt themselves about to lose their trade monopoly over the Kongo, they opposed King Manuel's *regimento* of codified instructions to implement a plan of acculturation. Affonso never accepted many of the provisions, including the Portuguese code of law, and he argued for bringing about the proposed changes over a long period of time. At the same time we know that he was under considerable pressure from his countrymen to resist the changes and that his opponents were discrediting him with arguments that he was ignoring traditional custom and practice. Near the end of Affonso's regime, there was an attempt by a group of Portuguese to assassinate the king, resulting in general African agitation against all Europeans.[112]

Revolts against outside political interference (a third pattern of African resistance) were also commonplace. In the Kongo, for instance, during the 1560s the people of Mbanza revolted against Portuguese residents who had murdered the African choice of a successor to the monarchy and attempted to name their own candidate.[113] In Guiné, *grumetes* assassinated the governor of Bissau in 1871. The administrative separation of Guiné from Cape Verde in 1879 was followed by intensive military efforts to subdue the rebellious African elements and to occupy effectively the colony of Guiné. Portuguese policy was directed at encouraging intertribal rivalry and undermining the African resistance to the Portuguese occupation. But when a military outpost was established at Buba in 1879 as a first step in the implementation of the new policies, African resistance intensified, and two decades of military struggle ensued.[114]

Despite these successes there were some negative features that characterized the African response to the Portuguese. First, the succession to the throne frequently allowed for civil strife, thereby weakening the power of the kingdom, and allowing the Portuguese to support one faction or another, interfere with internal politics, and sometimes break up the kingdom altogether. Second, although occasional alliances of African kingdoms were created, they tended to be weak and short-lived, and thus unable to resist the Portuguese advance over long periods. Apparently the major kingdoms considered their outer provinces as tributaries which enjoyed internal autonomy. The result was that the kingdoms not only did not

[112] Vansina, *Kingdoms of the Savanna*, pp. 47–48, 57.

[113] The Portuguese constantly meddled in the political affairs of the Kongo. One of the major nationalist movements during the early 1960s was led by Holden Roberto with a constituency of Bacongos or Bakongos from northern Angola. Roberto's uncle had been nominated by Protestant Angolans in the Congo to be successor to the old Kongo monarchy in 1954, but the candidate of rival Catholics living in Angola, with Portuguese support, was named instead.

[114] A useful chronology of the Portuguese military campaigns in Guiné and the other territories is in Luiz Teixeira, *Heróis da occupação* (Lisbon: Editôra Atica, 1943).

fight each other for long, but they were unable to build a strong network of alliances.[115]

Portuguese interference in African political life, however, resulted occasionally in the aggregation of several tribes or kingdoms into an alliance to ward off the European penetration. Such was an alliance established by the Ngola of Ndongo with Alvaro II of the Kongo and the Jagas of Matamba. In December 1590 the alliance defeated a Portuguese expedition at Angoleme Aquitambo (Ngoleme a Kitambu). For nearly a decade the alliance withstood the Portuguese advance.[116] In the early seventeenth century, Queen Nzinga built a new alliance of African kingdoms, including Ndongo and the states of Matamba, Kongo, Kassanje, Dembos, and Kissama. With this alliance Kassanje and Matamba emerged in the 1630s as powerful kingdoms representing an important shift in the balance of power in Angola.[117] When the Portuguese turned to the distant kingdoms for slaves, they failed to negotiate a peace and then resorted to military conquest. With the Dutch capture of Luanda in 1641, however, the Portuguese found themselves confined on two fronts. An accord with Nzinga was not reached until 1656.[118]

In Benguela, a coalition of kingdoms led by Tchiyaka successfully attacked the fortress at Caconda, forcing a Portuguese withdrawal from the region in 1718. In 1886 Ekuikui II of Bailundo established an alliance with Bié and persuaded King Tchyoka to abandon his Portuguese allies in 1886. This move was an attempt to halt the disintegration of the traditional Ovimbundu order and the region's gradual loss of autonomy (see details below). The Portuguese response was to launch a series of campaigns, and war with the African kingdoms was carried well into the twentieth century.[119]

In Moçambique, the invasion of several Ngoni tribes into the Gaza region constituted a challenge to the Portuguese presence. Led by Soshangane, they swept across the lands of the Tonga, crossed the Limpopo, and settled on the grazing lands beyond. They besieged Lourenço Marques in the 1820s and in 1833. In 1834 they attacked Inhambane and, in 1836, Sofala

[115] Vansina, *Kingdoms of the Savanna*, pp. 246–247.

[116] Birmingham, *Trade and Conflict in Angola*, p. 55.

[117] An attempt to portray Queen Nzinga from an African perspective is Castro Soromenho, "Queen Nzinga of Angola," *Voice of Africa*, IV (March-April 1964), 12–13, 18.

[118] Some of the background on the Portuguese position is in Charles R. Boxer, *Salvador de Sá and the Struggle for Brazil and Angola, 1602–1608* (London: University of London, the Athlone Press, 1952), especially chapter 6. The threat to the Portuguese and the significance of the African challenge are apparent in Birmingham's analysis in his two books, *op. cit.*

[119] See the chronology in Teixeira, *op. cit.*

as well; they overcame the *prazos* ("land concessions") south of the Zambeze and occupied Sena. Soshangane died in 1859, but one of his sons, Umzila or Mzila, continued to raid Portuguese settlements and landholdings while at the same time maintaining official relations with the Portuguese. He was succeeded by his son Gungunyane who at first cooperated with the Portuguese but also looked to the British as a potential ally. When he apparently consented to British protection over his dominions in return for ceding both Beira and the mouth of the Limpopo to the British South Africa Company, he also encouraged African insurgents to move against Lourenço Marques in October 1894. In early February 1895, the Portuguese had subdued the insurgents, defeating them at Marracuene and, a half year later, also had defeated the Gaza force and captured its capital, as well as Gungunyane. Gungunyane's great military leader, Maguiguana, however, was able to carry on with the resistance until his death in August 1897.[120]

A fourth pattern of African resistance evolved with reaction to foreign penetration and domination of the indigenous economies. This reaction related to at least four developments: slavery, trade and control of local markets, forced labor, and the search for minerals in the interior of the territories. Quite naturally the African response to the Portuguese was conditioned by diplomatic relations between the two. Relations in turn depended upon the behavior of the kings who stood at the apex of the political structure and whose personalities and behavior left deep imprint on the African role in history.

In large measure slavery conditioned economic life in the Portuguese

[120] On Gungunyane, see Douglas L. Wheeler, "Gungunyane the Negotiator: A Study in African Diplomacy," *Journal of African History*, IX, no. 4 (1968), 585–602. For the 1833 attack, see Gerhard Liesegang, "Dingane's Attack on Lourenço Marques in 1833, *Journal of African Studies*, X, no. 4 (1969), 565–579.

Among the many important Portuguese writings that reflect the late nineteenth-century African resistance, see: Agência Geral das Colónias, *As campanhas de Moçambique em 1895* (Lisbon: Atica, SARL, 1947); Felipe Gastão de Almeida de Eça, *História das guerras no Zambeze: Chicoa e Massangano (1807–1888)* (2 vols.; Lisbon: Agência Geral do Ultramar, 1953); António Ennes, *A guerra de Africa em 1895* . . . , (2d ed.; Lisbon: Gama, 1945), and *Moçambique* . . . (3rd ed.; Lisbon: Agência Geral das Colónias, 1946); Joaquim Mousinho de Albuquerque, *Mousinho de Albuquerque* (2d ed., 2 vols; Lisbon: Agência Geral das Colónias, 1934–1935), and *A prisão do Gungunhana* . . . (Lourenço Marques: Typografia Nacional de Sampaio e Carvalho, 1896); Ayres d'Ornellas, *Campanha do Gungunhana, 1895* (2d ed.; Lisbon: Escola Typografia de São José, 1930), and *Colectanea das suas principais obras militares e coloniais* (2 vols.; Lisbon: Agência Geral das Colónias, 1934); J. C. Paiva de Andrade, *Campanhas da Zambézia* . . . (Lisbon, 1887); João de Azevedo Coutinho, *Memórias de um velho marinheiro e soldado de Africa* (Lisbon, 1941); and Ernesto Jardim de Vilhena, *Relatório e memória sôbre o território da Companhia do Niassa* (Lisbon, 1905), chap. 9, pp. 237–293.

territories for several centuries. The slave trade with European nations began about 1500 and intensified thereafter. It fostered raids and wars and brought guns and munitions, first to the trader and later to the rulers in the interior, who monopolized the markets. It fomented war among kingdoms, and it provoked an African reaction to the Portuguese trader, administrator, and colonizer alike.

We can briefly identify examples of this African reaction. First, it is clear that the settler of São Tomé antagonized the African kingdoms by monopolizing the slave trade. Affonso, the Kongo king, complained as early as 1514 that the situation was bringing ruin to his nation. By 1526 he had established some control over the trade which reached an annual export figure of four to five thousand slaves, most of whom were shipped to São Tomé. Undoubtedly this trade brought a deterioration in relations between the Kongo and Portugal, ending a "dream of collaboration in equality [which] could hardly have failed more dramatically." [121]

Affonso resorted to a policy that would prevent the capture of slaves among the Kongolese but tolerate the export of other African peoples. Thus the Kongolese often warred and raided the populous Mbundu to the south. However, eventually the wealth and power of the Mbundu kings grew, and they in turn enjoyed prosperity through Luanda from the sale of captive slaves.

One of the essential aspects of the Portuguese militant policy, initiated in Angola in 1575, was the exploitation of the slave trade in order to justify the crown's expenses and effort, and thereafter soldiers joined traders in the attempt to fulfill that objective. Thus, much of the chaos provoked throughout the more than a century of wars between the Portuguese and the Angolan kingdoms can be attributed to the intensification of the slave trade itself. The lure of the profitable trade resulted in the disaffection of many Jagas in the Matamba kingdom who emigrated south to Benguela in search of slaves to be sold to the Portuguese. Their departure was a first sign of disunity in the alliance of the kingdoms of Ngola, Kongo, and Matamba that was able to provide some resistance to the Portuguese between 1590 and 1600. [122]

Although Portugal attempted to monopolize the slave trade, it encountered difficulties in maintaining extensive control over the kingdoms which supplied the slaves. During the last half of the seventeenth century, for example, the Ngola Kanini emerged as a powerful leader in Matamba. At first assisted to power by the Portuguese, he later turned against them and their trading ally, the kingdom of Kasanje, which he plundered and de-

---

[121] Vansina, *Kingdoms of the Savanna*, pp. 52–57, quote on p. 57.

[122] Ronald H. Chilcote, *Portuguese Africa* (Englewood Cliffs, New Jersey: Prentice-Hall, 1967), p. 68.

stroyed. He also defeated a Portuguese military force at Katole. Thereafter the Portuguese attempted unsuccessfully to bypass Kasanje and Matamba to establish direct links with the eastern Lunda and Holo states which had been filtering slaves to the Portuguese markets. Matamba prevailed, however, and continued its trade dominance.[123]

In establishing themselves as the principal slave traders along the Angolan coast, the Portuguese used the African auxiliary units or *guerra preta*, in addition to maintaining their taxation practices and established treaties and oral agreements with the African *sobas*. The tactic was to employ African against African in order to weaken resistance and unity. With the enactment of antislavery legislation elsewhere and ever-increasing attacks by abolitionists, foreign competition lessened, and during the first half of the nineteenth century, Portugal emerged as the principal slave trader. Although slavery later was officially abolished, forced labor (labeled slavery by critics) prevailed well into the twentieth century.[124]

Much of the resistance in Guiné was attributable to the slave trade. In the late seventeenth century, for example, the Papel chief, Incinhate, launched the first of several wars with the Portuguese. His principal concern was that trade restrictions be liberalized and that abuses to the slave trade be ended. In the same year Mandingas attempted to expel the white populace at Farim.

The slave trade and the activities of slave traders were linked closely with the general disruption of local market patterns and the commerce of agricultural and other products. Agricultural production was altered by the introduction of new commodities, maize for example, which probably was first brought to Africa by the Portuguese in order to provide slaves with a cheap staple food.[125] The economic motivation to penetrate and dominate the interior served not only to disrupt the African kingdoms but also to encourage Africans to unite in common resistance. An excellent example of such a phenomenon was the 1886 alliance between Bailundo and Bié, already mentioned above. During much of the nineteenth century,

---

[123] See Birmingham, *Trade and Conflict in Angola*, pp. 123–132, 143, and *The Portuguese Conquest of Angola*, chap. vi.

[124] Among Englishmen who accused the Portuguese of labor malpractices were William A. Cadbury, *Labour in Portuguese West Africa* (2d ed.; London: G. Routledge and Sons, 1910); John H. Harris, *Portuguese Slavery: Britain's Dilemma* (London: Methuen, 1913); and Henry W. Nevinson, *A Modern Slavery* (London and New York: Harper and Brothers, 1906). An excellent general treatment of the Portuguese slave trade, which, however, does not attempt to examine the African reaction to economic conditions of the times, is James Duffy, *A Question of Slavery: Labour Policies in Portuguese Africa and the British Protest, 1850–1920* (Oxford: Clarendon Press, 1967).

[125] See Marvin P. Miracle, "The Introduction and Spread of Maize in Africa," *Journal of African History*, VI, no. 1 (1965), 39–55.

the kingdoms of the plateau experienced anarchy and a general disintegration of traditional trade patterns and indigenous productivity, especially in handicrafts. It was a period in which Bailundo and Bié dominated trade with the Portuguese while the other kingdoms were left competitively disadvantaged. There was also considerable rivalry and warfare between kingdoms. King Ekuikui II of Bailundo brought a temporary halt to the declining Ovimbundu order and attempted to regain the region's gradually slipping autonomy and independence. While prospering from the lucrative rubber trade with the Portuguese, the king also concentrated on the development of agriculture and artisan crafts. His break with the Portuguese was signaled by an alliance with Bié. The alliance resulted in limitations being imposed upon Portuguese labor practices and on commercial relations. Although the Portuguese were able to occupy the kingdoms by 1890, Ekuikui's successor, Numa II, carried on with the struggle, himself dying in battle in 1896; and in 1902 the Bailundo king, Mutu-ya-Kevela, led dissident Africans in rebellion in an attempt to recover land held by Europeans. The Bailundo area was swept by a wave of murder, looting, and destruction of trading posts, and open hostility to the Portuguese continued well into 1904.[126]

Disruption of the general trade provoked revolts in Guiné. Among the many examples are the uprisings of the African chiefs, Mata and Mompataz, who in 1679 unsuccessfully attacked the Portuguese at Cacheu on the pretext of having been discriminated against in trade with foreigners. Seventeen years later, the Portuguese put down the rebellion of a Christian African, Bibiana Vaz, who desired the profitable trade with French and English merchants.[127]

In Moçambique, the imperial design of the Portuguese was to control trade through commercial centers along the coast. In replacing the Arab as the principal trader, it was also necessary to penetrate the interior and establish relations with the African tribes that dominated the hinterland. Attempts to establish permanent stations on the Zambeze in 1513, at Sena in 1531, and at Tete were unsuccessful, partially because of African opposition. About 1613 a Portuguese expedition barely defeated a rebellious chief, Chombe, of the Sena region in the Zambeze Valley. It was their first encounter with an African force supplied with firearms, and it took several months of fighting to defeat the chief and prevent the lower Zambeze

[126] Some of the principal sources on these disturbances have been cited previously. This writer is investigating the 1886–1904 period in some detail in the attempt to develop a case study of the relationship of economic conditions in colonial society and the African response.

[127] These rebellions and others are outlined in Barreto, *op. cit.*, pp. 109–111. See also A. de Teixeira Mota et al., "Efemérides do centenário," *Boletim Cultural da Guiné,* special number (October 1947), pp. 11–105.

from being closed to the munitions, trade goods, and reinforcements that customarily were supplied to Tete and nearby Portuguese centers. In 1693, an African chieftain, Changamire, attacked the Portuguese settlements of the interior, destroying the important settlement of Dambarare. He continued to terrorize the Portuguese until his death two years later.[128]

The search for minerals also upset relations with the African. From the outset of their venture, the Portuguese believed that there were rich mines in the Kongo. Affonso prevented a commission of specialists from looking for the gold, silver, and copper ores believed to be plentiful. A report by a German miner in 1539 affirming that the area was indeed rich in several minerals became the pretext for the ultimate invasion of the Kongo in 1665.[129]

One of the Portuguese objectives in the Angola kingdoms was the discovery and control of mineral wealth, especially silver, believed to exist in the interior. An important phase in the Angolan wars was the drive to reach the silver mines of Cambambe which was accomplished in the years 1602 to 1605, but no silver was found, shattering the Portuguese dream of many years. In Moçambique, the building of a fortress at Sofala was part of the Portuguese plan to gain possession of the gold mines of Manica and the gold trade between the Monomotapa and the Arabs. The Portuguese were able to establish treaties with the Monomotapa who sometimes relinquished his silver and gold mines, but such agreements were often tenuous. For instance, at the beginning of the seventeenth century the Monomotapa was challenged by rival chiefs, and in return for Portuguese military assistance, ceded his mines on the condition that Portugal maintain him in power. He defeated his chief rival, but received no tribute from the Portuguese and thus began to raid their camps, depriving them of silver mines and disrupting the gold trade as well. In 1629 the Portuguese had to defeat the Monomotapa Nyambo Kapararidze and name a successor in order to assure control over the gold mines.[130]

Although the slave trade eventually ended, labor conditions continued to affect relations between Africans and Portuguese. In 1913 and 1914, for example, Alvaro Tulante Buta led a revolt against the deportation of Congolese laborers to São Tomé. In 1953, hundreds of African workers on São Tomé were reportedly massacred by police after they had protested labor conditions.[131] On August 3, 1959, fifty striking dockworkers at Bissau were

[128] These developments are included in Eric Axelson, *Portuguese in South-East Africa, 1600–1700* (Johannesburg: Witwatersrand University Press, 1960), pp. 178–185.

[129] Vansina, *Kingdoms of the Savanna*, p. 54.

[130] Axelson, *op. cit.*, pp. 69–71, 74–75.

[131] See the description of Buanga Fele (pseud. of Mário de Andrade), "Massacres à São Tomé," *Présence Africaine*, new ser., Fr. ed., 1–2 (April-July 1955), 146–152.

killed and many others wounded in an incident which solidified a weakened nationalist movement and resulted in a change in strategy and tactics, culminating three years later in a guerrilla war against the Portuguese.[132]

SECRET SOCIETIES, NATIVISTIC AND MESSIANIC MASS MOVEMENTS

Distinguishable from the sporadic and spontaneous movements of resistance to the Portuguese conquest, occupation, and pacification of the African territories are other types of traditional and transitional movements—movements with organization, principles, and sometimes a doctrine, as well as a program of action. For example, there have been nativistic or messianic mass movements, often of a magicoreligious character, which provide psychological and emotional outlets for the tensions created with alien rule.[133] There have also been separatist religious groups which have broken from the white Protestant or Catholic churches. Then too, there have been tribal associations established to promote sentiment for the formation of or resurrection of political units whose boundaries coincide with the locale and influence of the tribes themselves.

Many such movements were active in Central Africa. An eighteenth-century chronicle reported the impact of Christianity on traditional religious beliefs. A prophetess named Beatrice, claiming to be the reincarnation of Saint Anthony, founded a movement called Antonian which attracted a large following dedicated to the restoration of the African kingdom at São Salvador and to the revival of all customs suppressed by missionaries. For her heresies she was burned at the stake, but a large following continued to pursue the goals of the martyred prophetess.[134]

Through the use of fetishism (worship of inanimate objects which have specific uses and magical powers), secret societies and cults and messianic movements have evolved to express hostility to the white man and protect the African from the effects of black magic. The early movements that emerged in the Belgian, French, and Portuguese Congos apparently repre-

[132] A useful report which explains the change in strategy is Amílcar Cabral, *Rapport général sur la lutte de libération nationale* (Conakry: Partido Africano da Independência de la Guinée "Portugaise" et des Iles du Cap-Vert, July 1961). See also Basil Davidson, *The Liberation of Guiné* (Baltimore: Penguin Books, 1969).

[133] Nativism was defined by Ralph Linton as "any conscious, organized attempt on the part of a society's members to revive or perpetuate selected aspects of its culture." See his "Nativistic Movements," *American Anthropologist*, XLV (April-June 1943), 230.

[134] Vittorio Lanternari, *The Religions of the Oppressed* (London: Macgibbon and Kee, 1963), p. 8. See also L. Jadin, "Le Congo et la secte des Antoniens, restauration du royaume sous le Pedro IV et la 'Saint Antoine' congolaise (1694–1718)," in *Bulletin de l'Institut Historique Belge de Rome*, XXXIII (1961), 205; and Adalberto Postioma, "A heresia do Antonianismo," *Portugal em Africa*, 2d ser. XIX (November-December 1962), 378–381.

sented responses to the arbitrary division of territory by the European powers at the Berlin Conference of 1884–1885. Frequently these movements were more than fetishist and xenophobic. Often members were pledged to resist passively the European rule and to refuse to pay taxes or serve the white man in any capacity. The formation of a movement sometimes was followed by an uprising against imperialism, initiated under the cover of a religious façade. Such sentiment might be aroused, for example, by the African belief that God would assure redemption and a paradise after death, thus justifying the launching of military campaigns or holy wars to prevent the *anjos do mal* ("Europeans") from the future paradise.[135]

One prominent form of a traditional movement is the secret society, which flourished among Africans because economic necessity or opportunity had displaced them from their tribe.[136] In discussing the importance of these societies and other movements, Santos identifies the *homens-leopardos* ("leopard men") of the Belgian Congo in 1920 who refused to pay taxes; the 1930 sect of miners in Katanga, known as Pangaou Muana Okanga; and the Sociedade Imâni of railroad workers in the Congo. These and other societies influenced the formation of groups in Angola. According to Santos and Frazão, the more important societies include the Nevemba, a sort of special school of the Kongo king directed by a witch known as Ndêmbu who was inspired by the siren, Nevemba, an inhabitant of the Congo River.[137] Cavazzi referred to the secret society known as Kimpási (also known as Kimpási Kindêmbu) which today is still influential in Zombo and Damba and has had ties to contemporary messianic movements. The Bassucos founded the Ndêmbu e Nkimba, a society with characteristics similar to Kimpási. The Bahungos have two secret sects known as Mbumba and Nkita, and the Baiacas and Bassucos maintain an organization known as Ngôngi.[138]

135 One of the best syntheses of Angolan messianic movements is Alfredo Margarido, "Movimenti profetici e messianici angolesi," *Rivista Storica Italiana*, LXXX, no. 3 (September 1968), 538–592. Another recent source, biased but useful, is Eduardo dos Santos, *Maza: elementos de etno-história para a interpretação do terrorismo no Noroeste de Angola* (Lisbon: Edition of the Author, 1965), p. 209.

136 Lanternari, *op. cit.*, p. 11.

137 Santos, *op. cit.*, pp. 232–233; and Serra Frazão, *Associações secretas entre os indígenas de Angola* (Lisbon: Editôra Marítimo-Colonial, 1946).

138 Santos, *op. cit.*, pp. 234–242. Additional sources on secret societies are H. Chéry, *L'offensive des sectes* (Paris: Collection Rencontre [44], Les Editions du Cerf, 1959); Ed. de Jonghe, *Les sociétés secrètes au Bas-Congo* (8th ed.; Brussels: Polleunis, 1907); P. E. Joset, *Les sociétés secrètes des hommes-léopards en Afrique noire* (Paris: Payot, 1955); A. le Roy, *La religion des primitifs* (7th ed.; Paris: Collection Etudes sur l'Histoire des Religions [1], Gabriel Beauchesne, 1925); Jules Mees, "Les sociétés secrètes au Bas-Congo," *Boletim da Sociedade de Geographia de Lisboa*, XXV ser.

A second general classification, the nativistic or messianic mass movement, includes both traditional and transitional forms. In contrast to the secret societies, which tend to attract dislocated Africans, these movements with their religious, especially Christian, overtones, gained their following largely among Africans who had remained in their own villages.[139] After the Berlin Conference of 1884–1885 and the division of the Kongo kingdom, four Bakongo prophets emerged: Simon Kibangu or Kimbangu, who was especially active in the former Belgian Congo and whose call for emancipation inspired other followers; Simon Peter Mpadi or M'padi; Simon Lassy; and Andrew Grenard Matswa.[140] Matswa was born near Brazzaville of the Balali people and raised a Roman Catholic. He fought in the French army during World War I and in Paris encountered several black organizations. While there he formed the Amicale Balali (Friendly Balali Society), known later as Amicalism, which proceeded to pressure the French government to find solutions to black problems. When Matswa died he became martyred as "Jesus" Matswa, and by 1939 Mpadi had become Amicalism's new apostle and prophet. These prophets and their movements had varying degrees of impact upon similar movements and messianism in Angola, but all were influential. It was the Kimbangu movement, for example, that submitted in 1956 a memorandum to the United Nations demanding an end to Belgian and Portuguese rule in Africa.[141]

The Congolese movements probably influenced Simão Toko and his movement which is the focus of Alfredo Margarido's essay in this book. Toko, born in Angola near Maquela do Zombo, was apparently influenced by a Baptist mission in Angola and the Salvation Army in Léopoldville. Eventually Portuguese authorities grew suspicious of the movement, and Toko was imprisoned and later exiled to the Azores. Despite this suppression the movement continues today and is especially influential in Maquela do Zombo, Pôrto Alexandre, Caconda, Malange, Benguela, Carmona, and other areas.[142]

LL (1907), 361–366; Herculano de Oliveira, "Religiões acatólicas de Angola," *Portugal em Africa*, 2d ser., XIII, no. 73 (1956), 36–50; Merlos Pinch, "Sectes nouvelles en Angola," in *Devant les sectes non-chretiennes. Rapports et compte rendu de la XXXe Semaine de Missiologie Louvain, 1961* (Brussels: Desclée de Brouwer, 1961), pp. 140–143; A. Rodrigues Pintassilgo, "Seitas secretas no Congo," *Portugal em Africa*, 2d ser. X, no. 60 (1953), 361–371; and J. Van Wing, *Etudes Bakongo, sociologie, religion, et magie* (2d ed.; Brussels: Desclée de Brouwer, 1959).

[139] Lantarnari, *op. cit.*, p. 11.

[140] For these and other messianic movements, see Georges Balandier, *Sociologie actuelle de l'Afrique Noire* (Paris: Presses Universitaires de France, 1955), especially chapter ii, "Le messianisme Ba-Kongo en tant que 'révélateur,'" pp. 417–485.

[141] Lantarnari, *op. cit.*, p. 24.

[142] See for additional information, Alfredo Margarido, "L'Eglise Toko et le mouvement de libération de l'Angola," *Le Mois en Afrique*, 5 (May 1966), 80–97.

Among other movements considered to be offshoots of the above or prenationalist religious movements are the Movimento Tônsi, founded in the former Belgian Congo by a group that had emigrated from northern Angola; the Movimento Maiange or Nlênvu, founded also in the Congo but very influential in the enclave of Cabinda; the Movimento Tonche or N-tonche, founded in the Congo about 1941 and influential in Maquela do Zombo; and the Grupo Saint Esprit or Dibundo Mpeve ia Londo, a derivation of Kimbanguismo.[143]

WRITTEN AND ORGANIZATIONAL PROTEST

This category includes organizational and written protest, as well as revolts that occurred in an urban setting. Generally these activities have been prenational in character, that is, perhaps oriented toward the purpose of advancing the material welfare and improving the socioeconomic status of Africans but not yet oriented toward the creation of a modern independent nation-state.

Written protest is the focus of Douglas Wheeler's essay in this volume, and Michael Samuels, in his essay, has presented one example of organizational protest. Wheeler examines late nineteenth-century protest in Angolan journalism, basing his analysis on four examples over two generations. This tradition of protest was carried on by the rebellious post-1948 generation of *assimilados*, centered in Luanda and led by Viriato da Cruz. Samuels's case study of an educated African who demanded local autonomy from Portugal and greater educational opportunities chronologically precedes the emergence of several legal and semilegal organizations through which some protest and demands were filtered. Often cited in contemporary literature are such organizations as the Partido Pro-Angola, formed in the early twentieth century with a program of administrative autonomy for Angola; the Liga Nacional Africana, established by white settlers in 1921; the Grêmio Africano, founded in 1929 and later known as the Associação Regional dos Naturais de Angola. In Portuguese Guiné, the first and only labor organization, the Sindicato Nacional dos Empregados do Comércio e da Indústria, was established within the Portuguese corporate structure; no protest or strike was tolerated by the government. Apparently dissent was manifested through the Sports and Recreation Association, however, for the government banned that organization in 1954. In Moçambique, sev-

[143] One of the important Portuguese sources on these movements and others discussed above is Silva Cunha, *Aspectos dos movimentos associativos na Africa negra* (2 vols.; Lisbon: Junta de Investigações do Ultramar, Estudos de Ciências Políticas e Sociais [8] and [23], 1958 and 1959), especially the second volume which focuses on Angola.

eral organizations similar in structure to those of Angola were established, including the Grêmio Africano, for "civilized" Africans and later known as the Associação Africana; the Instituto Negrófilo, represented by black Africans and later renamed the Centro Associativo dos Negros de Moçambique; and the Associação dos Naturais de Moçambique, founded by whites born in Moçambique.[144]

Revolts in urban settings seem to have been few; at least we have little documentation with which to judge their significance. Three examples are noteworthy: first, the revolt of Alvaro Tulante Buta in the Portuguese Congo, referred to above; second, the strike at Bissau on August 3, 1959, which today is remembered by nationalists as the "massacre of Pijiguiti"; and third, the uprising of February 4-6, 1961, in Luanda in which Africans attacked a prison, radio station, and military barracks.

III

CONCLUSIONS

The movements examined have emerged and evolved from many conditions and circumstances. My conclusions will attempt to identify these conditions in an effort to demonstrate some comparability between Brazil and Portuguese Africa and also to assess the significance of such movements in the context of the overall experience of those territories. Therefore, let us examine geographical, social, economic, political, and cultural conditions.

First, geography has played a role in the formation and activity of the movements. Oligarchies of landed families ruled the backlands of Northeast Brazil from the seventeenth century onward. Likewise such families controlled large expanses of land in the Portuguese African territories. For example, among the large *prazo* holders of Moçambique were the Lobo and Pereira clans who respectively ruled over the Zumbo and Tete districts in the late nineteenth century. With the large land grants in the hands of wealthy and powerful colonists, the mass of population remained propertyless and dependent on the landowners.[145] Resources, their lack or abund-

---

[144] See Eduardo Mondlane, *The Struggle for Mozambique* (Baltimore: Penguin, 1969).

[145] See M. D. D. Newitt, "The Portuguese on the Zambezi: An Historical Interpretation of the Prazo System," *Journal of African History*, X, no. 1 (1969), 67–85. On *prazeiro* resistance to the Portuguese, see M. D. D. Newitt, "The Massingire Rising of 1884," *Journal of African History*, XI, no. 1 (1970), 87–105; and M. D. D. Newitt and P. S. Garlake, "The 'Aringa' at Massangano," *Journal of African History*, VIII, no. 1 (1967), 133–156. In analyzing the relationship between the large landowners and the mass population in Northeast Brazil, Gonçalves Fernandes focuses on "the communal and associative spirit of the man without land in the backlands and his cooperativist

ance, also contributed to differences between rulers and followers. The anticipated discovery of a mineral, for instance, would often be accompanied by outside capital and foreign influences which, in turn, would affect the daily life of local peoples. Climate and natural catastrophe often have contributed to the formation of movements, especially those messianically oriented which view the catastrophe as a signal of the end of the world.[146] Drought and flood can be correlated to many of the movements identified in Northeast Brazil, an area subject to harsh and recurrent drought. The drought of 1877–1879 often is related to the increase of banditry and also to the formation of Padre Cícero's movement.[147]

The origin of many of the movements and rebellions was frequently rooted in social problems. Classes were stratified by property ownership which divided the wealthy from the mass. Such social relationships may allow for the absence of effective law enforcement, the growth of rivalry among ruling families, and eventual strife. In Northeast Brazil such conditions resulted in instability, insecurity, and nonparticipation and involvement for the landless masses. The general population was forced to choose sides, joining the army of a certain landowner or moving outside the dominant system by adopting banditry as an alternative.

Economic conditions affected the populations also. Frequently, large landowners would convert their land to grazing for cattle, forcing dependent farmers off the land altogether. Such was the case at Galiléia which marked the beginning of Francisco Julião's peasant leagues in Northeast Brazil. Then too, the primitive slash and burn techniques of the subsistence and semisubsistence farmers would leave them sometimes with infertile land and in difficulty. The intrusion into local markets by the colonist, the changing patterns of trade, and the economic advantages to Portugal of exploitation of slaves and minerals affected indigenous life in both Africa and Brazil and stimulated the formation of a variety of movements. General economic crises also have affected the formation and growth of the movements. Andersson has identified the growth of such movements as related to low prices and trading possibilities, and the inability to pay taxes, but concludes that "economic crises may very well contribute to the outbreak of such movements, but not serve as their actual cause." [148]

---

orientation." See Gonçalves Fernandes, *Mobilidade, caráter e região* (Recife: Instituto Joaquim Nabuco de Pesquisas Sociais, 1959), pp. 69–70.

[146] Efraim Andersson, *Messianic Popular Movements in the Lower Congo* (Sweden: Almqvist and Wiksells, 1958), pp. 227–228.

[147] See for additional details, Sue Anderson Gross, "Religious Sectarianism in the *Sertão* of Northeast Brazil, 1815–1966," *Journal of Inter-American Studies*, X (July 1968), 369–383.

[148] Andersson, *op. cit.*, p. 155. Gonçalves Fernandes, *op. cit.*, pp. 73–74, discusses the psychological impact on migrants from the backlands of Northeast Brazil.

Political policies and actions affect the movements as well. The government's land policy favoring the European settler in Angola and Moçambique has sometimes excluded blacks from lands with abundant water, resources, and fertile soils and furthermore prevented them from more qualified and better paid work. The granting of political liberty or the right to form an association has led to political liberation movements in all three African territories. It is also known that antiwhite tendencies are strongest in colonies with direct administration and that "abuses of freedom . . . frequent recourse to prison even for the most trivial offenses, no exception being made even for the chiefs, contributed to the dissatisfaction that may have been one of the causes of the anti-white character gradually assumed by the prophet movements." [149] Then too, the arbitrary administrative division of territory without any consideration for tribal boundaries and national frontiers had its impact on Africans, the Bakongo in particular.

In the cultural sphere, we have noted that the primitive, traditional, and transitional movements identified in this essay have been influenced and affected by the clash of foreign with domestic culture, by attempts to impose language and customs, laws and policies. Alien religious influences, expecially Catholic and Protestant, have stimulated the formation of syncretic and messianic movements in Brazil and Africa. While the movements have some of their roots in folk religion, they have been modified by outside influences, but "they are to be regarded as contact and reaction phenomena arising from the shock constituted by the meeting between two cultures." [150] The result is the fusing of disparate elements into a unity, and this is due generally to the frequency of a remarkable leader—important because "the movement does require as its ideological basis the myth of a culture hero, who, one day, would appear and lead them to a terrestial paradise." [151]

It should be apparent that the conditions just elaborated suggest a relationship between deprivation and crisis, on the one hand, and protest, resistance, and conflict, on the other. Many of these movements have sought supernatural assistance, the result of a sense of futility or loss of confidence in ordinary action. The ensuing deprivation or crisis often is brought about by aspirations and expectations that certain objectives will be achieved, goals fulfilled. Aberle suggests that deprivation relates closely to status, possession, behavior, or work and often stems "from change, actual or an-

---

[149] Andersson, op. cit., p. 235.

[150] Ibid., p. 258. Andersson's generalization applies to syncretic movements everywhere, but seems particularly appropriate to Brazil and Portuguese Africa.

[151] Bernard Barber, "Acculturation and Messianic Movements," American Sociological Review, VI (October 1941), 663–669, quote on p. 663.

ticipated." [152] Thrupp, extracting explanations from a symposium on millenarian movements, identifies those movements as the result of deprivation, disruption of tribal cultures for example; the universal human propensity to suffer from distress and anxiety; the aesthetic attraction in an official cosmic view; and the tensions in social structure stirred by rival leaders.[153] Cohn elaborates additional explanations.[154] Finally, Bastide sees in messianism and in movements of protest and resistance "an attempt to redeem native culture." [155] But he moves a step further and analyzes the correlation between such activity and social and economic development. Messianism, he believes, does not hinder the advancement of peoples, but on the contrary represents an initial awakening, a conscious awareness, and "an early manifestation of a refusal to accept colonialism." He adds that "it also represents a first step in the direction of social change and an acceptance of new economic and social values." Perhaps more important is his observation that "messianism was the first truly effective form of resistance to colonialism and the first conscious manifestion of nationalism, however veiled in appearance." [156]

Bastide thus refutes the common thesis that messianism and traditional forms of protest and resistance are obstacles to progress, a position with which I agree. Rather than viewing resistance as against change, protest as undermining consensus, or crisis as disturbing to stability, we suggest that these phenomena contribute positively to social and economic development, for, to quote Bastide again, the positive elements comprise "the first steps in acquiring a sense of history, the need for a collective effort to create new responses and behavior patterns." [157]

[152] David F. Aberle, "Note on Relative Deprivation Theory as Applied to Millenarian and Other Cult Movements," in Sylvia L. Thrupp, ed., *Millennial Dreams in Action: Essays in Comparative Study* (The Hague: Mouton & Company, 1962), pp. 209–214.

[153] Sylvia Thrupp, *op. cit.*, pp. 25–27.

[154] Norman Cohn, "Medieval Millenarism: Its Bearing on the Comparative Study of Millenarian Movements," in Thrupp, *op. cit.*, pp. 31–43.

[155] Roger Bastide, "Messianism and Social and Economic Development," in Immanuel Wallerstein, *Social Change: the Colonial Situation* (New York: Wiley, 1966), p. 270.

[156] *Ibid.*, pp. 270–273. An interesting discussion which links resistance to nationalism is in T. O. Ranger, "Connections between 'Primary Resistance' Movements and Modern Mass Nationalism in East and Central Africa," *Journal of African History*, Part I in IX, no. 3 (1968), 437–453; Part II in IX, no. 4 (1968), 631–641.

[157] Bastide, *op. cit.*, pp. 274–275.

Index

Index